Holding Fast to
an Image of the Past

Holding Fast to an Image of the Past

✺ Explorations in the Marxist Tradition ✺

NEIL DAVIDSON

Haymarket Books
Chicago, Illinois

This paperback edition
published in 2014 by
Haymarket Books
PO Box 180165
Chicago, IL 60618
773-583-7884
www.haymarketbooks.org
info@haymarketbooks.org

ISBN: 978-1-60846-333-6

Trade distribution:
In the US, Consortium Book Sales and Distribution, www.cbsd.com
In Canada, Publishers Group Canada, www.pgcbooks.ca
In the UK, Turnaround Publisher Services, www.turnaround-uk.com
All other countries, Publishers Group Worldwide, www.pgw.com

Cover design by Eric Kerl. Cover image of New York City long-distance
telephone operators voting to strike in 1945, from the Cleveland Press,
Special Collections, Michael Schwartz Library, Cleveland State University.

This book was published with the generous support of Lannan Foundation
and the Wallace Action Fund.

Printed in Canada by union labor.

Library of Congress Cataloging-in-Publication data is available.

10 9 8 7 6 5 4 3 2 1

For Raymond Morell, and in memory of
Neil Smith (1954–2012): proof that James Connolly
was not the last Marxist to be born in Edinburgh

Contents

Preface

T his book, the first of two collections to be published at Haymarket in 2014–15, consists of essays published between 1999 and
2013, presented in order of appearance.* Although all have different origins, they share a common approach, as each assesses the work
of an important thinker on the political left. Most of these figures are associated with Marxism, a tradition that two (Alasdair MacIntyre and Tom
Nairn) eventually abandoned and to which one (Benedict Anderson) has
always maintained a certain ambivalence. The only complete exceptions
are the writers who lie at opposite ends of the historical period traversed
here. The most chronologically distant is Adam Smith, whose death in
1790 predated the emergence of Marxism by over fifty years, although
he had an important influence upon it as one of the masters of political
economy, a discipline rightly considered one of what Lenin called the
three "sources and component parts" of historical materialism.[1] The most
recent is Naomi Klein, who more than any other participant articulated
the views of the alter-globalization movement that coalesced around the
Battle of Seattle in late 1999, above all in her books *No Logo* (2000) and
The Shock Doctrine (2007), the latter of which is reviewed below. These
two individuals suggest some of the problems involved in the concept of

---

*As its subtitle suggests, the second collection, *We Cannot Escape History: Nations,
States, Revolutions*, will be organized along thematic lines.

the Marxist tradition. In the case of the first, the problem is whether Marxism is simply an extension of the Enlightenment thought represented by Smith, as the late Eric Hobsbawm tended to argue.[2] In the case of the second, it is the relationship to historical materialism of the kind of anticorporate radicalism represented by Klein, which is not necessarily hostile to Marxism, but rejects it—and indeed all alternative doctrines—as a theoretical basis for the movement while displaying deep hostility to Marxist revolutionary organizations.[3]

By chance rather than design I have approached representatives of the classical Marxist tradition discussed here in slightly oblique ways. I trace the development of the concept of progress (and related notions such as "advanced" and "backward") in the thought of Karl Marx and Friedrich Engels through the prism of their changing attitude toward the Scottish Highlands. I explore Leon Trotsky's life and legacy through an examination of the image of him presented in Deutscher's magisterial, but subtly misleading, biography. Antonio Gramsci's work has been contested perhaps even more strongly than Trotsky's, not least because his prison notebooks have provided such a fruitful basis for multiple conflicting interpretations: here I attempt to show how some notable misrepresentations arose by following the process of their reception in Scotland. Finally, I consider the relationship to classical Marxism of Walter Benjamin, a figure who, while sharing many interests with Gramsci, is, unlike him, generally regarded as belonging to the Western Marxist tradition—a categorization that, in part at least, I dispute. The chapters devoted to more recent thinkers are more conventional in form, mainly because the occasions for which they were commissioned or composed—book reviews in all but one case—lent themselves more easily to career overviews.

All of these essays were written in or around the capital of Scotland, the country where I happened to be born but continue to live as a matter of choice. "No one could come away from it without knowing it was written by a Scot," said Alex Callinicos of my book *How Revolutionary Were the Bourgeois Revolutions?*[4] This was certainly my intention, but not one motivated by any nationalist impulses on my part. As will soon become apparent, there are few issues on which I agree with Nairn, but I do identify with one of his statements: "I have never hidden the fact that my own dilemmas and oddities emanate from those of my country, Scotland."[5] I would perhaps put this slightly differently. I have always assumed that a grounding in the local and specific is a necessary precondition for understanding the global and general, and have therefore taken as a starting point for understanding the characteristic features of our epoch the ways in which they have affected Scotland. These features include the consolidation of neoliberalism as the dominant form of capitalist organization, the emergence of secessionist nationalism as a phenomenon of the developed world, and the decline of social democracy as the expression of working-class reformism. It is appropriate, then, that in addition to chapters assessing the impact of the Highlands on the work of Marx and Engels, and the influence of Gramsci's writings over the Caledonian left, this volume should include discussion of three Scottish thinkers. Two of these are from Fife (Nairn himself from the village of Freuchie and Smith from the nearby metropolis of Kirkcaldy), and one from Glasgow (MacIntyre).

The essays reproduced here differ from the originals in five main ways. First, in keeping with my publisher Haymarket's location in Chicago, I have rendered the language into North American. This is a painless process that largely involves changing the letter "s" into the letter "z" in certain words, changing the word "which" into the word "that" in certain sentences, and—as in the case of this sentence—adding a comma before the word "and" prior to the last item in a list. I have retained my Scotticisms (of which "outwith" seems to cause particular bewilderment in copy editors). Second, I have made the layout and endnotes stylistically consistent. Third, I have excised references to the publications in which the essays first appeared (of the "as has been argued previously in *International Socialism* . . ." or "readers of *Historical Materialism* will be familiar with . . ." type). Fourth, I have removed passages that appeared in more than one essay except for the essay in which they first appeared (or in some cases except from the essay in which they seemed most appropriate) and replaced them with a "see chapter x in this volume" reference. Fifth, I have restored some passages that editors originally omitted, either because they disagreed with them on theoretical grounds or—more usually—because the article would otherwise have simply been too long for the publication concerned. Chapter 13, on Adam Smith, has the majority of these restorations. Excisions on grounds of taste, decency, or to prevent the publishers being bankrupted in a libel court have not, however, been reinserted. I have resisted the temptation to revise texts or add new material; anyone sufficiently motivated to check back against the originals would therefore be able to confirm that previously unpublished additions contain no references that post-date their appearance. Neil Rafeek predeceased the publication of his book, but three of the other authors discussed—Hobsbawm, Victor Kiernan, and Neil Smith—have died since I wrote the chapters dealing with their work, the last-named at a tragically early age; nevertheless, here too I have retained the original text in which they appear in the present tense.

Only in the case of chapter 6, on MacIntyre, is the text significantly different from previously published versions. This is a combination of several pieces—or more precisely, a reconstruction of one original piece of research, which I subsequently parceled up into several different chapters and papers. I had been working off and on since 2000 on an edited collection of MacIntyre's Marxist writings for the *Historical Materialism* book series. Around 2003 Paul Blackledge, who had independently discovered these works, joined me in the project at the instigation of the series editors, who for some reason suspected that it might otherwise never be completed. Paul has subsequently written extensively on Mac-Intyre and, while our views are not identical, they are compatible. A few brief passages from our jointly written introduction to *Alasdair MacIntyre's Engagement with Marxism*, reproduced in this chapter, are actually Paul's, but it would have been pointless to rewrite sentences with which I was in basic agreement, even if it were possible to disentangle our respective contributions at this late date. I am grateful to him for permission to reprint such passages here.

Any assessment by a Marxist of other Marxists involves a particular standpoint within the tradition. As chapters 11 and 12, which deal with aspects of Stalinist organization and historiography, make clear, my standpoint is that of Trotskyism; but to self-identify in this way still leaves many questions unanswered, given the notoriously fragmented nature of that movement. Chapters 4 and 6 respectively discuss Deutscher and Mac-Intyre, two figures who, between them, demonstrate how one can arrive at different, not to say diametrically opposed, positions while ostensibly starting from the same body of work. MacIntyre declared that he could no longer consider himself a Trotskyist or indeed a Marxist of any sort by 1968. Deutscher remained faithful to his own conception of Trotskyism until his death the previous year. Yet I would argue that the latter effectively made as decisive a break with Trotsky's thought as the former, all the more misleading for being unacknowledged. In any event, my sympathies here are with MacIntyre-as-a-Trotskyist, since my own political formation was in the International Socialist (IS) tradition to which he adhered between 1960 and 1968, although in a very different period. I first encountered the IS eight years after MacIntyre's departure, at the point when the organization was transforming itself into the Socialist Workers Party, through Rock Against Racism and then the Anti-Nazi League, whose great achievements I discuss in chapter 5.

IS was one of the heterodox varieties of Trotskyism that tried to understand the system that emerged from the Second World War in ways that more orthodox variants refused or were unable to. My own adherence to it indicates that I regard it as superior to the other heterodoxies, although it has more in common with them than is often supposed.[6] Nevertheless, I do not regard it as complete or self-contained. The late Daniel Bensaïd, always the most unorthodox of the orthodox, wrote:

> The alternative to Capital's barbarism will not take shape without a thoroughgoing balance sheet of the terrible century that has just ended. In this sense, at least, a certain type of Trotskyism—or a certain spirit of Trotskyism in all its variants—is not outmoded. Its instruction-deficient legacy is certainly insufficient; but it is nonetheless necessary for those who wish to unravel the association between Stalinism and communism, to free the living from the weight of the dead, and to turn the page on the disillusions of the past.[7]

The notion that Trotskyism, even embracing all of its most positive manifestations, is a necessary but insufficient basis for any kind of renewal of Marxism seems incontestable to me. One of Trotsky's most important achievements, perhaps even more important than his role in the Russian Revolution, was to preserve and pass on the traditions of Bolshevism that made October 1917 possible; but the manner in which revolutionary continuity was maintained engendered its own problems. An understandable interest in the Russian experience as the only socialist revolution in history translated into the assumption that subsequent revolutions would necessarily take the same form, even when many of the conditions that enabled it were becoming increasingly historical in nature. A deserved admiration for the Bolsheviks resulted in the attitude that there was little or nothing to be learned from any other source, even though there were quite fundamental problems—above all the formation and maintenance of reformist consciousness—with which they had not dealt and on which they had little or nothing to say.

I will return to these issues in a forthcoming book; but they have a bearing on the title of this one. It comes from a famous passage in Walter Benjamin's last and greatest essay, "On the Concept of History":

> Historical materialism wishes to hold fast to that image of the past which unexpectedly appears to the historical subject in a moment of danger. The danger threatens both the content of the tradition and those who inherit it. For both, it is one and the same thing: the danger of becoming a tool of the ruling classes. Every age must strive anew to wrest tradition from the conformism that is working to overwhelm it.[8]

One of the key words here is "unexpectedly"—the notion that in a crisis we may learn from aspects of tradition that had been ignored, overlooked, or expunged, but that have now acquired a hitherto unanticipated significance. The point is not that contemporary Marxist revolutionaries are in danger of becoming "tools of the ruling class" in the way Benjamin indicates here. He was most likely thinking of the way in which social democracy first colluded in the face of imperialist war and then, along with Stalinism, capitulated in the face of Fascism. The danger we face is quite different, namely of assuming that the tradition is fixed and immutable, providing a set of "lessons" applicable in any situation, no matter how inappropriate, and in that way handing victory to the ruling class by mistaking what *is* to be done for what *was* done. If we are to prevent this, the task of "wresting tradition from the conformism threatening to overwhelm it" must be urgently undertaken in the knowledge that—to adapt a metaphor deployed by both Engels and Benjamin—we are passengers on a runaway train who are trying to bring it under our control before disaster occurs.[9]

Neil Davidson
Scotland
July 26, 2013

Tom Nairn and the Inevitability of Nationalism[1]

INTRODUCTION

The 1960s saw an upsurge of separatist nationalisms at the core of the capitalist system, with the movements in Catalonia, Eskudai, Occitania, Quebec, Scotland, Wallonia, and Wales all making their first serious impact during that decade. Nationalist demands went on to play a role—although by no means the most important role—in the social upheavals that shook the capitalist system between 1968 and 1976. And although none of them succeeded in establishing new states, several—Catalonia, Quebec, and, more recently, Scotland—gained a significant degree of formal autonomy within the state framework of the dominant nation. These events inspired a number of important studies of nationalism, the majority of which appeared in two clusters. The first appeared between 1977 and 1982 and the second between 1989 and 1992, following a further and, in terms of establishing new states, more successful revival of nationalist aspirations in Eastern Europe. Whatever criticisms might be leveled at these works, the best have nevertheless helped to advance our understanding of the phenomenon in important, if partial, ways.[2]

Only a minority of these studies approached the question from an avowedly Marxist perspective. One of them was by the Scottish writer

Tom Nairn, who is regarded by many as the foremost modern theoretician of the subject. It is ironic, therefore, that his contribution emphasized the supposed inadequacy of the Marxist tradition as a tool for understanding nationalism, persuading many on the left that, in the famous opening sentence of one key essay, "The theory of nationalism is Marxism's greatest historical failure."[3] Most of the essays in which he put forward these arguments were collected in a book first published in 1977 called *The Break-Up of Britain*; but Nairn has recently returned to the subject in a further collection of essays called *Faces of Nationalism*.[4] On the evidence of this work he no longer considers himself to be any sort of Marxist, even one deeply critical of the tradition. Indeed, it is questionable whether he can in any sense still be described as belonging to the left. Nairn has reneged on his previous socialist commitments to quite the same extent as Lucio Colletti, Andre Glucksman, Ernest Laclau, or any of the other writers once feted in the *New Left Review* (*NLR*) while he was a member of the editorial board, and he has done so in the name of nationalism. Nairn is no longer merely a theorist of nationalism—Marxist or otherwise—but a nationalist theorist, advocating nationalism not only for his own nation but as a universal political program for the peoples of any potential nation-states, in much the same way as revolutionary socialists argue for working-class power, regardless of the state in which workers happen to be situated. The extent to which Nairn has abandoned not only Marxism but socialism itself has been missed by both his critics and his supporters.[5] Such misunderstandings should not be allowed to continue. What Nairn advances is nothing less than a theoretical justification for the endless subdivision of the world into competing capitalist nation-states.

With the collapse of Stalinism and reduction of social democracy to the most servile position it has ever held in relation to capital, there is a powerful tendency for nationalism to become the vehicle for local opposition to the effects of the global crisis. This is certainly true in Scotland itself, where disillusion with the Blair government has already led to increased levels of support for the Scottish National Party (SNP). And while it has never been true that working-class support for the SNP necessarily reflected an increased level of nationalism, the danger is that it might.[6] Avoidance of that possibility will depend, at least to some extent, on socialists successfully demonstrating to other workers that nationalism is not a solution to our problems but a manifestation of them. One aspect of that demonstration, although by no means the most important one, is to challenge the type of theory advanced by Nairn, where nationalism is presented not only as desirable but natural and inevitable. The first part of this chapter traces the development of Nairn's theory of nationalism; the second is a critique of his current position.

I. FROM HISTORY TO HUMAN NATURE

Nairn writes that "the motives and background" of any writer have to be taken into account when assessing his or her views, including of course his own: "I have never hidden the fact that my own dilemmas and oddities emanate from those of my country, Scotland."[7] In fact, for the first part of his writing career, between 1962 and 1968, Nairn showed no discernible interest in Scotland whatsoever, but devoted his attentions to constructing a thesis on English development with Perry Anderson, then editor of the *NLR*. This Anderson-Nairn thesis owed far more to Nairn than to Anderson, at least in its original formulation.[8] For the purposes of this article the most important aspect of the thesis, in relation to the direction subsequently taken by Nairn, concerns the supposedly archaic nature of the British state. It was only in this context that Scottish nationalism, and through it nationalism in general, became the focus of Nairn's work.

The British state, the working class, and the Labour Party

Nairn acknowledges that the combined effects of the Civil War and the Glorious Revolution were to establish a fundamentally capitalist economy in England. He argues, however, that because these events occurred at such an early stage in capitalist development, the English bourgeoisie, unlike the French Jacobins a hundred years later, did not require a theoretical under-standing of the revolution it had made. Consequently, the culture of the new ruling class was shaped by the more established and durable values of the landowning aristocracy who exercised hegemony over their immature junior partner, the bourgeoisie proper. Unlike other bourgeoisies that followed it to power, the English bourgeoisie did not become conservative after its economic power was assured, because it had always been conservative. This state, consolidated in England by 1688 and, by extension, in Scotland after the Union of 1707, was therefore premodern in structure:

3

"Although not, of course, an absolutist state, the Anglo-British state remains a product of the general transition from absolutism to modern constitutionalism: it led the way out of the former but never genuinely arrived at the latter."[9] The premodern character of the British state was preserved beyond the term of its natural life by the spoils of empire, which rendered any subsequent "modernization" unnecessary for the ruling class. Ultimately, however, when the British state was overtaken by modernizing rivals and undermined by the retreat from empire, it entered an almost permanent condition of crisis that no government of either left or right has been able to resolve.

Superficially, this analysis bears some resemblance to that advanced by Trotsky in his writings on Britain.[10] But although Trotsky was perfectly aware of what Alex Callinicos calls the "disadvantages of priority," he also situated this in the context of the world system and argued that the resultant crisis could be resolved by the working class.[11] Nairn, however, focuses almost exclusively on the national arena and does not accept the revolutionary potential of English workers. Here too he regards the early formation of English capitalism as decisive. The English working class was formed in the classic period of bourgeois revolution (1789–1848), but because the English bourgeoisie had already achieved its victory, the former fought alone for political rights and social progress, unaided by the petty bourgeois insurgencies characteristic of the rest of Europe. Defeated, the working class was forced into a form of "apartheid": the separateness of a class all too aware of what distinguished it culturally from other classes but unable to identify the opposed interests that this also involved. Marxism, which might have clarified the situation, was available to the English working class only after it had already entered into its caste-like isolation within bourgeois society. According to Nairn these characteristics were inherited by the political party that is usually thought to speak for English workers. Dominated by a bureaucratic gradualist right, besotted by the supposed wonders of the British constitution, and opposed only by a succession of moralistic but impotent "lefts," the Labour Party was a useless instrument for achieving socialism. His rejection of the Labour Party meant that Nairn never shared the same illusions as Anderson did about Harold Wilson in the early 1960s; yet his critique was not based on the premise that Labour had betrayed its supporters but rather that it had all too faithfully reflected their lack of class consciousness.

It is not my intention to subject Nairn's analysis to detailed criticism here, since a massive literature exists that does precisely that.[12] The main theme, however, is clear: the British state is an archaic formation in deep crisis, which nevertheless exercises such a hold over society that no force exists that can destroy or even restructure it.

Tartan waistcoats and the dreams of May

In the beginning Scottish nationalism offered no prospects of playing a modernizing role. Throughout the 1960s the SNP had been gathering electoral support almost unnoticed by political commentators of the left or right. In 1961 their candidate polled a respectable 18.7 percent of the vote at a by-election in Glasgow Bridgeton. The following year SNP chairman William Wolfe came second to Labour candidate Tam Dalyell in West Lothian with 23 percent of the vote more than the Conservatives and Liberals combined. Finally, in November 1967, Winifred Ewing won a by-election in the previously safe Labour seat of Hamilton, beating Labour into second place by 18,397 votes to 16,598.[13] Nairn drew attention to the significance of these developments in 1968 in an article for the *NLR* called "The Three Dreams of Scottish Nationalism," which was resolutely hostile to the nationalism of the SNP.

Nairn argues that the Scots have undergone three successive attempts to define their identity. The first of these was Calvinism. Nairn correctly argues that the "rising bourgeoisie" did not initiate the Reformation of 1559. It was to remain inconsequential for another century and only achieved full dominance after 1746. Instead, the Church of Scotland acted both as a substitute for absent state power and as the unifying factor in a civil society. After the Union with England of 1707, the Kirk was, along with the legal system, one of the institutions specifically preserved from the dissolution of the state. Consequently, it became the main vehicle through which a separate national identity was maintained.

The second attempt was not, as might be expected, the Enlightenment, in which Scotland attained greater eminence than any nation apart from France, but Romanticism. The leading figures in the Enlightenment were not concerned with Scottishness, but identified themselves with the British nation politically and were concerned with discovering universal laws of human development: "While the Enlightenment was only

5

an episode, Romanticism entered her soul."[14] But the way in which it did so was markedly different from that of other European nations. Whereas, in Italy or Germany, Romanticism was part of the formation of national identity, in Scotland, particularly in the work of Sir Walter Scott, it acted as another substitute for it.

The third attempt was—more precisely, is—modern national consciousness of industrial Scotland, which Nairn sees as being positively schizophrenic. One element is the debased romanticism of a popular culture that then still revolved around tartan and bagpipes, whisky and haggis, the Loch Ness Monster and Greyfriars Bobby, Calvinism, and a militarist celebration of the Scottish contribution to the British Empire. The other is the "ethereal tartanry" of the intelligentsia, which begins as a rejection of such images of Scotland but ultimately reproduces them at a more refined level.

Nairn notes that the SNP represents "bourgeois nationalism," a political formation that socialists have seen as historically justified in only two situations: first, during the original bourgeois revolutions that completed the transition from feudalism to capitalism; and second, as the means by which mainly non-European peoples have mobilized to liberate themselves from the imperialism of these original capitalist nation-states. Scotland has long since accomplished the first and consequently has no requirement for the second—indeed, Nairn takes great relish in pointing out that Scotland has never been a colony of any sort.[15] Nevertheless, Nairn argues that there are two reasons why the national aspirations of the Scots must be supported. First, "as a blow against the integrity of British imperialism," and secondly, "because it represents some transfer of power to a smaller arena."[16] The first is certainly a legitimate reason for not opposing Scottish separatism; the second is more problematic, suggesting that a government in Edinburgh might be politically, rather than merely geographically, closer to the people who elected it than one in London. Nevertheless, neither of these reasons requires socialists to have illusions about the "lumpen-provincials" of the SNP. Instead, he argues, Scottish socialists should develop their own form of nationalism with which to oppose bourgeois nationalism: "Is it really impossible that Scotland, which has dwelt so long and so hopelessly on the idea of a nation, should produce a liberated and revolutionary nationalism worthy of the name and the times?"[17]

The events of May 1968 in France, which exploded as the article appeared in print, clearly had an effect on Nairn, as did analogous occurrences closer to home. He wrote a collaborative contribution to the literature of May during a struggle in which he was personally involved: the occupation of Hornsey College of Art in London. On May 28 Nairn and a number of other lecturers joined their students in a semipermanent teach-in until the college closed on July 4, an action for which he was ultimately sacked from his job when the college opened again in November.[18] The proximity of social revolution seems to have both simplified his hitherto torturous writing style and even made it rather poetic: "The social world appears to us every day like a giant leaden globe turning with a crushing and inevitable weight nothing can alter; our ideas and enthusiasms, our visions, appear like flimsy muslin by contrast, a smoke of feeling with no purchase on fact. Then in the revolutionary situation, it is seen and felt that this is utterly, radically untrue."[19] But Nairn was also alert to the utter failure of French Stalinism to understand the aims and desires of the students and young workers in revolt, who he argued would be less frightening to the bureaucrats of the Parti Communiste Français (PCF) if they were "green and had six legs": "But these are real monsters, walking paragraphs from the *Manuscripts of 1844* and the *Grundrisse,* the living accusation of all that Western Communism has become." The point was not that an insurrection was bound to succeed:

> Whether or not success, a seizure of power, was possible (a problem one could debate), there is absolutely no doubt that the Party of the Revolution could have at least recognized its own, in May, could have generously welcomed the beauty of May, and advanced the process of revolution in a thousand ways. It could have reached out to the new workers, instead of shutting them off from old workers. It could have tried to rise to the level of the Italian Communists of fifty years ago, by leading the factory occupations and urging the formation of worker's councils. All that could be asked of these apostles of reasonableness was to exploit the situation in a reasonable, realistic fashion. Instead, they spat phlegm at the revolution until the barricades, and spent the rest of the month building their own barricades against the revolution itself.[20]

His newfound radicalism was displayed in a revised version of "The Three Dreams of Scottish Nationalism," included in the 1970 collection

Memoirs of a Modern Scotland, in which the counterposition of revolutionary socialism to Scottish nationalism is strengthened still further. Nairn notes that the "tartan waistcoated bourgeoisie" had not remained unchallenged in Scottish history: "I do not want to turn aside either from Scotland's native tradition of working-class protest, John Maclean, Clydeside radicalism, or the communist tradition of the miners." The problem was that these alternatives had never come close to dislodging their class enemies. Bourgeois nationalism, however, was a false solution to the problem, proposing as it did a false unity of interest between different classes. Nairn goes on to argue that the Scots have two choices, one of which leads into "the prison of an archaic bourgeois nationality" and the other to a "revolutionary" consummation that would destroy the prison and lead toward a "real, meaningful future existence." Nairn makes it clear that the latter possibility has been inspired by the movements of 1968: "In the same years in which nationalism again became a force in Scotland, the Western world was shaken by the first tremors of a new social revolution, from San Francisco to Prague." The next sentence suggests the Gallic inspiration for the "revolutionary nationalism" he desired:

> I for one am enough of a nationalist, and have enough faith in the students and young workers of Glasgow and Edinburgh, to believe that these forces are also present in them. I will not admit that the great dreams of May 1968 are foreign to us, that the great words on the Sorbonne walls would not be at home on the walls of Aberdeen or St Andrews, or that Linwood and Dundee could not be Flins and Nantes. Nor will I admit that, faced with a choice between the *Mouvement du 22 mars* and Mrs Ewing, we owe it to "Scotland" to choose the latter.[21]

The famous concluding flourish—"Scotland will be reborn the day the last minister is strangled with the last copy of the *Sunday Post*"—is almost an anticlimax, refocusing attention from the main supports of capitalist power to the debased bourgeois culture that surrounds it.[22] Although understandable at one level, this counterposition of a specifically Scottish socialist alternative to the bourgeois nationalism of the SNP constituted Nairn's first concession to the latter. Why did "the great dreams of May 1968" have to be considered in a purely Scottish context in the first place? Nevertheless, the overall tone of the piece is clearly aligned with the revolutionary movement of the time: this was not to last.

European integration and British disintegration

In 1972, at a time when the class struggle in Britain was at the highest
level since 1919, Nairn devoted an article, comprising the whole of *NLR*
75, to a critique of the dominant left positions on British entry to the
Common Market, as the European Union was then known. His central
argument was that although there had indeed been a major upturn in
the industrial class struggle, it had failed to find new organizational forms.
At the same time the Labour Party, the Trades Union Congress (TUC),
the Communist Party of Great Britain (CPGB) and—he claimed—the
revolutionary left were all engaged in channeling the massive levels of
worker discontent into the relatively safe question of opposition to
British entry to the Common Market. According to Nairn, this position
was disastrous as it tied the left to supporting British nationalism and, ultimately, the British state, either consciously (as in the cases of the Labour
Party, the TUC, and the CPGB) or by default (as in the case of the revolutionary groups).[23] Two aspects of this argument should be noted as
foreshadowing his current position. The first is the assertion that when
the British left counterposes socialist internationalism to the capitalist
Common Market, it is "really" using this as a cover for defending the integrity of the British imperialist state. As far as this issue went Nairn
claimed to see no difference in outcome between the arguments of the
Labour right and those of International Socialism, which he uncharac-
teristically subjected to scrutiny. The second is that Nairn now saw the
only possibility of transforming the British state in any direction as coming from forces external to the state itself, in this case the supranational
institutions of Western European capital.

It was in this context that Nairn returned to the subject of Scottish
nationalism, in the aftermath of the second important SNP by-election
victory at Govan in Glasgow during November 1973. The tone was now
very different. The article in question, "Scotland and Europe," which appeared in *NLR* early in 1974, is much more concerned with a historical
analysis of Scottish distinctiveness than the nature of the SNP and, in this
respect, it may be the best thing he has ever written. Nairn begins with
the central problem: the absence of Scottish nationalism during the periods when other national movements dominated European politics.
Why did it only take political form in the 1920s, at the very moment
the modern European state system had taken shape? Only a detour

through a general theory of nationalism gave Nairn the answer. He wrote that "nationalism, unlike nationality or ethnic variety, cannot be considered a 'natural' phenomenon." Instead, it must be defined as "mobilization *against* the unpalatable truth of grossly uneven development."[24] The modern capitalist world emerged from the combined pressures exerted by the British Industrial Revolution and the French Revolution. These forced all other states into copying their achievements in order to compete effectively with or be dominated by their more advanced rivals. But this could not be simply an acceptance of "progress" as defined by the front-runners; it also necessitated a rejection of progress in the terms on which they offered it. This process, which is more or less parallel with that of the bourgeois revolution, spread out from the unifications of Germany and Italy during the 1860s to contemporary national liberation movements in places as different as Ireland and Bangladesh. Where did Scotland fit in to this dualist view of historical development? Did it belong to the "bourgeois-revolutionary lands" or to the "underdeveloped" hinterland? His answer was that it belonged to neither. Uniquely, through the Union of 1707, Scotland "exploited" the achievements of the English bourgeois revolution, thus entering—indeed, helping to define—the advanced world of capitalism. Scottish capitalist development was fully attained before the age of nationalism began, and so, although Scotland had all the ingredients necessary for a nationalist movement—a rising bourgeoisie, an intelligentsia, a popular tradition of hostility to England, a national church—no social class required such a movement.

The political implications of this analysis did not become clear until the following year, when an essay by Nairn called "Old and New Scottish Nationalism" appeared in a collection called *The Red Paper on Scotland,* edited by Gordon Brown in his earlier, more left-wing incarnation. Nairn now argued that, like several other areas in Western Europe, Scotland was experiencing the rise of what he called "neo-nationalism," to distinguish it from the more familiar stateless nationalism associated with Kurdistan or Eritrea. In the Scottish case, the arrival of American-based oil companies in the North Sea had provided a functional equivalent of the imperialist intrusions that had provoked "modernizing," "developmental" nationalisms of which Scotland had previously no need.

Did this require socialists to change their position? Nairn now dismissed the earlier analysis of "The Three Dreams of Scottish Nationalism," which assumed that Scottish self-determination would come as a result of socialism, as based on "two misjudgements": "[to] overestimate . . . socialist potential and underestimate . . . capitalism's ability to mutate further." The first of these misunderstandings apparently had a history dating back to the period between the world wars, when socialism had proved to be weaker than nationalism: "When revolution came to the world of advanced capitalism, it came as fascism, the ultra-nationalist reaction to the threat of socialist and communist advance (a threat which was in fact remote)." According to Nairn, "the left had pinned too much faith on the rationality of working class based struggle (understood as a potentially international force), and far too little upon the non-rational strengths of nationalism." In these circumstances socialists had little option but to accept the continued influence of nationalism: "In my view it has become totally inadmissible to oppose such tendencies in the name of an abstract internationalism, a universal socialist or class struggle which exists only in aspiration."[25]

These words were written in 1975, during which the revolutionary period that opened in 1968 was drawing to a close. Indeed, Nairn seems to have seen Scottish nationalism as a substitute for the inability of the working class to destroy the British state: "More than any other factor, more even than the miners' strikes of 1972 and 1974, it has exposed the senility of the old consensus and its two-party system."[26] These claims are quite astonishing. The British state has only been in actual crisis (as a result of internal social contradictions rather than external geopolitical conflict) on three occasions in the twentieth century: first between 1910 and 1914, then in 1919 and finally between 1969 and 1974. On each occasion the crisis was the result of historically high levels of industrial militancy combined with civil war in part of Ireland: Scottish nationalism trailed some way after class and anti-imperialist struggles in the list of factors causing this crisis. This misjudgment might be explained on the grounds that, having mistaken the overall pattern of British decline as a never-ending "crisis" for so long, Nairn was unable to identify the genuine article when it finally occurred. In fact, there was a deeper reason. In practice (that is, after discarding ritual genuflections regarding its class character), Nairn treats the state in classically liberal fashion, as an autonomous body exercising a constricting power over society. His hatred of this state is undeniable, but it springs less from the fact that it exists to run society in the interest of the bourgeoisie than from its inability to "modernize." From this perspective events at the summit of politics that threaten the coherence of the British state, such as the fracture in the party system caused by the rise of the SNP or the restrictions on sovereignty consequent on entry to the Common Market, take on a special significance for Nairn that workplace struggles do not immediately seem to possess.

In keeping with his instrumental view of nationalism, Nairn does not indulge in the glorification of Scottish history in the manner of more conventional Scottish nationalists. Indeed, if anything, he achieves the almost impossible task of exaggerating both the backwardness of pre-Union Scotland and the mindlessness of tartanry.[27] For this he was denounced by two self-proclaimed nationalist "philosophers," Craig Beveridge and Ronald Turnbull. These authors draw a distinction between those, like Nairn, whom they see as "fighting for a socialist future" within which nationalism is simply a "tactical possibility," and those, like themselves, who are fighting for "a culture, a history, [and] a people as an integral part of a socialist politique."[28] In the mid-1970s this distinction was certainly still relevant. Nairn maintained that Scottish nationalism should be supported because it offered the possibility of an alternative road to socialism besides the hopelessly economistic struggle waged by miners and the like. In 1977 he made explicit the perspective implied by privileging Scottish (and to a lesser extent, Welsh) nationalism over the class struggle:

> The fact is that neo-nationalism has become the gravedigger of the old state in Britain, and as such the principal factor making for a political revolution of some sort in England as well as the small countries. Yet because this process assumes an unexpected form, many on the metropolitan left solemnly write it down as a betrayal of the revolution. The reason is that proletarian socialism is supposed to be the gravedigger, and no-one else will do. So they tell the nationalists to drop their shovels and put up with the pathetic limits of "devolution": the revolution will solve their problems along with the others. Meanwhile they should wait until the time is ripe—i.e. the time for socialism—taking a firm grip on their petty bourgeois, backward looking impulses. The essential unity of the UK must be maintained till the working classes of all Britain are ready.[29]

No revolutionary could object to the forces of neonationalism "unhinging" the British state, but the task of achieving socialism, rather than modernizing any capitalist successor states, would still remain to be accomplished, and for this the "readiness" of the working class will be required—whether they inhabit one state or three, since the "new time" of which Nairn spoke will not arrive with establishment of border posts at Berwick on Tweed.

Nairn originally developed a general theory of nationalism in order to explain the particular Scottish variant. Now he moved back from the particular to the general, taking with him the pessimism about working-class politics that characterized "Old and New Scottish Nationalism." In "The Modern Janus," also written in 1975, he summarized his views as they had evolved over the previous seven years. First, it is important to note that Nairn does not pretend that all nationalisms—or indeed, any nationalisms—are wholly virtuous. While recognizing that judgments have to be made about specific cases based on political criteria, Nairn maintained that this was not decisive. Ultimately, all nationalisms share the same contradictory nature: "nationalism can in this sense be pictured as like the old Roman god, Janus, who stood above gateways with one face looking forward and one backwards. Thus does nationalism stand over the passage to modernity, for human society. As human kind is forced through its strait doorway, it must look desperately back into the past, to gather strength wherever it can be found for the ordeal of 'development.'" Here is the familiar analysis of the spread of nationalism after 1789 as a necessary response on the part of modernizing elites to the uneven development of capitalism. Now it is accompanied with a dismissal of the independent role of the oppressed: "The new middle class intelligentsia of nationalism had to invite the masses into history; and the invitation had to be written in a language they understood." The possibility that "the masses" might have been able to make their own entry into history for purposes other than merely creating new nation-states was not discussed: it has not happened therefore it could not have happened—a conclusion of such empiricist banality that even the supposedly befuddled nineteenth-century English bourgeoisie might have rejected it. Nevertheless, these comments might have been taken to suggest that, even if nationalism was necessary as part of a "modernizing" project, there was at least the possibility that it might be dispensed with once modernization was achieved; but not a bit of it. Later in the same essay Nairn argued that nationalism is inescapable in the core and periphery of the system alike. Refusing to face this fact allegedly constituted the main failure of Marxist thought on the subject: "There was never any chance of the new universal class which figured in the Marxist doctrine emerging as 'proletarians' rather than as 'Germans,' 'Cubans,' 'Irishmen' and so on." Why not?

> Nationalism could only have worked, in this sense, because it actually did provide the masses with something real and important—something that class consciousness postulated in a narrowly intellectualist mode could never have furnished, a culture which however deplorable was larger, more accessible, and more relevant to mass realities than the rationalism of our Enlightenment inheritance. If this is so, then it cannot be true that nationalism is just false consciousness. It must have a functionality in modern development, perhaps one more important than that of class consciousness and formation within the individual nation states of this period.[30]

Nairn attempted to put his theory into practice by joining the Scottish Labour Party (SLP), the organization set up by former Labour MPs Jim Sillars and Alex Neil in January 1976. In retrospect, the brief history of the SLP, whose membership never rose above a thousand, shows that there is little room in Scotland for a reformist party straddling the ground between the Labour Party and the SNP. For Nairn, the attempt by that organization to combine socialism and nationalism in equal measures was its strength: "A new, distinctively left-wing socialism would give meaning to self-government; but, also, a breakthrough in the area of national self-rule would provide a new opportunity for socialism." At this stage his argument was still: "We have to fight coherently on both fronts."[31] What led Nairn to abandon the socialist front? As with the origins of his theory of nationalism, the answer lay in events in Scotland.

By 1978 the Labour government had been reduced to a minority in the House of Commons and was under extreme pressure from socialists opposed to its attacks on trade unions and the welfare state, as well as, more importantly, from a resurgent Conservative Party under Margaret Thatcher, for not attacking trade unions and the welfare state hard enough. The government survived on the basis of three conditional forms of support: financial support from the International Monetary Fund, which kept it in credit; political support from the minority parties (Liberals, Ulster Unionists, and the SNP), which maintained the Labour majority; and—more important than either of these—industrial support from the trade union bureaucracy, which helped impose pay restraint on its own members through the mechanism of the Social Contract. The minority Labour government was therefore partly reliant on SNP votes at Westminster, and therefore needed simultaneously to undermine nationalist support while appearing to meet nationalist demands. The trick was to be performed by offering the Scots a largely powerless Assembly that Labour ministers hoped would nevertheless meet national aspirations sufficiently for Scottish independence to be seen off, at least for the duration of the immediate crisis. The scheme might have worked, but it was sabotaged from inside the Labour Party itself. The Scotland Bill of July 1978 offered administrative devolution, providing the proposal was backed by a majority of the Scottish voters in a referendum. George Cunningham, a Scottish MP who sat for the London constituency of Islington, introduced an amendment to the bill that required 40 percent of the entire registered Scottish electorate to support it in a referendum, rather than a simple majority of those voting. The subsequent campaign saw the Labour Party split down the middle, with one wing supporting the "Labour Vote No" committee and the other the "Labour Movement Yes" campaign.

Outside the Labour Party, the left in Scotland showed far greater unanimity in supporting devolution. The CPGB had already adopted a policy of "national self-determination" for Scotland in 1964. Among the orthodox Trotskyist organizations the International Marxist Group supported devolution (indeed their Scottish members had recently been expelled from the SLP after a botched entrist maneuver) and supporters of Militant, who had originally taken an abstentionist position, switched to one of support during the campaign when it became apparent that a "no" vote would threaten the survival of the Labour government. Only the Socialist Workers Party (SWP) stood aside from this unusual display of left unanimity on what might be called a position of "malign abstentionism," although it should be noted that this was the majority position of the party in Scotland at the time and was opposed by the Central Committee, which unsuccessfully argued for a position of critical support for devolution. However, the point is not that the SWP took a wrong position on the issue—the lesson was subsequently learned—but that, contrary to what Nairn has subsequently claimed, the majority of the left supported devolution.

In the end only 32.9 percent of the electorate voted "yes." Indeed, only 63.8 percent turned out to vote at all. It is possible that the concerns of most Scots, certainly most Scottish workers, were elsewhere. The campaign had been conducted in the aftermath of the last great general wave of industrial struggle in Britain to date, the so-called Winter of Discontent, when the pressure from below against wage restraint finally forced the union leaderships to call action against the Labour government. Unlike the strikes between 1969 and 1975, however, these strikes were not imbued with feelings of optimism and hope but of pessimism and despair. The election of a Tory government was felt by many to be inevitable months before the poll was announced. In the event, the SNP reaction to the inevitable repeal of the Scotland Act was to bring a motion of censure, supported by the Tories, which saw the government defeated, a general election called, and the election of the first Thatcher government. As Andrew Marr has written, "Part of the bitterness and disillusion with which the Scottish political and journalistic world greeted the result [of the referendum] reflected the amazement of Scotland's suburban leftish-leaning establishment that their views were not shared more widely throughout the country."[32] At the time Nairn reflected these feelings of "bitterness" and "disillusion" but did not, however, blame the Scottish people for their lack of enthusiasm for devolution. For Nairn the blame lay elsewhere, with the left.

In a new endnote to an essay called "Internationalism: A Critique," written after the 1979 referendum, Nairn writes of the fiasco: "In very adverse circumstances, a small majority had actually voted in favour of the Labour government's Devolution Act; and yet had been frustrated by a mixture of old imperialism and the 'internationalism' analysed here."[33] There is something in this. "Old imperialism" is straightforward enough. Labour right-wingers like George Cunningham and Tam Dalyell were then, and are now, committed to defending the integrity of the British imperialist state against any form of constitutional reform, no matter how superficial, on the grounds that it will inevitably lead to separatism. "The people of Scotland must be made to realize," wrote Dalyell in 1977, "that there is not, and can never be, a tenable half-way house between remaining an integral part of the United Kingdom and opting for a Scottish State."[34] What about "internationalism"? The same case was essentially made by the Labour left, although with different emphases. As Eric Heffer wrote in his memoirs, "I feared that devolution for Scotland and Wales would weaken Britain as a united economic unit and be detrimental to socialism as a whole."[35] Nairn's error is to assume that every objection to Scottish nationalism must universally be based on "Unionist" support for the British state.

Reviewing the arguments of *The Break-Up of Britain* in October 1981, Nairn wrote of his attempt to steer a course between two "primitive but vigorous opponents" both advancing equal and opposite errors: "On one side a bourgeois nationalism denied region and class altogether; on the other a lumpen socialism denied nationality any progressive significance whatever (unless its frontier ran through the middle of the English Channel)." He nevertheless refuses to see that any of the critics who were alarmed at "the spectacle of a Marxist sympathising with the notoriously bourgeois nationalism of the SNP" might have had a point, dismissing their objections as "bilge, the product of reheated stereotypes and the sermonising impulse so important to a frustrated left." For Nairn the "majority" who did not awaken to national consciousness, which presumably includes most of the working class, were afflicted by "a peculiarly Scottish torpor" comprised of "respectable servility" and a "Jekyllish conformism and a fear of reversion to being 'natives.'"[36]

Nairn allowed that, just possibly, a combination of the revived Labour left, then mobilized around the Alternative Economic Strategy, and the more left-wing nationalism he saw developing in Scotland, might point toward a socialist solution to the crisis of the British state.[37] Such hopes were quickly dashed. The Bennite left had already peaked by the time these cautious hopes were expressed in late 1981 and the left within the SNP, in the shape of the '79 Group, was expelled during the same year. Scottish nationalism, far from recovering from the disaster of 1979, retained a low level of support until the third Conservative electoral victory in 1987 brought a new dimension of support that extended far beyond the ranks of the SNP. Long before then, however, Nairn's fundamental pessimism reasserted itself. A dispute within the editorial board of *NLR* in 1982 resulted in a split, caused partly by personality differences, but also by the question of whether the decline of Stalinism, both as state power in the East and working-class organization in the West, could herald the revival of a genuine revolutionary movement. Anderson and the editor, Robin Blackburn, were at this stage still committed—albeit somewhat abstractly—to a perspective that saw such a development as being possible; Nairn sided with the faction that held that it was not, and after they lost the fight, he resigned in solidarity with them.[38]

The remainder of the decade was largely taken up with writing his book on the British monarchy, *The Enchanted Glass* (1988), whose central thesis concerning the ideological dominance of the Windsors has been so comprehensively refuted by events that further comment is unnecessary. It was at this point, however, that Nairn resumed his engagement with nationalism proper. The majority of the essays contained in *Faces of Nationalism* were written after the Eastern European revolutions of 1989 and—an event of somewhat less earth-shattering importance—the Scottish constitutional referendum of September 11, 1997. It is the former that casts the longest shadow over its contents. Here Nairn raises to new extremes all the positions that he had previously held in earlier writings. Three themes have now emerged full blown that until now had only been hinted at; the identification of Marxism with Stalinism, the introduction of "human nature" as an explanatory framework for the existence of nationalism, and the consequent rejection of internationalism even as a theoretical possibility.

The extent to which even nominally anti-Stalinist socialists like Nairn tended to identify the Stalinist states with socialism was only fully revealed after their collapse. Nairn was never particularly enthusiastic about them, although he evidently accepted their own evaluation as "post-capitalist" in some sense. He now performs the familiar exercise of rejecting Marxism along with the states that described themselves as Marxist. In the following passage—which has to be quoted in full to appreciate its mixture of flippancy, ignorance, and dishonesty—Nairn is discussing the two "garbled or even insane forecasts" that exercised the greatest influence on human affairs during the twentieth century: "Around 1940 . . . Spielberg fans will be intrigued to know that Heinrich Himmler's Ancestral Heritage organization, Ahnenerbe, included people convinced that the Aryans were of extra-terrestrial descent, and had been sent to earth equipped with super-human electrical powers. Expeditions went looking for scientific proof of this hypothesis to the usual location: Tibet. Had the Nazis got away with it, one may be reasonably confident that academic learning of a sort would then have tried to oblige them." Nairn has, however, another example of apparent political dementia to share with us: "Equally, the conviction that 'primitive communism' might be successfully re-created in a super-national and industrialized form out of the ruins of the Romanov and Hapsburg Empires was a prophetic mirage. What it involved was the discovery of an entire electric super-national class equipped with equivalent electrical powers. Geographical Tibet was not on the menu. However, Lenin did think that a virtual-Tibetan elite of superman-monks was required to galvanize the proletariat." So: the attempt to establish "the realm of freedom" in Russia is to be equated with Nazi attempts to discover evidence of extraterrestrial life in the Himalayas. The reader may wonder at this point if these comments constitute the "strikingly original" new work promised on the back cover of *Faces of Nationalism;* but Nairn has more to say on the subject: "Attempts to realize these prophesies (and the struggle between them) have accounted for much of the past century. Fortunately they ran out of steam before annihilating the species. But does even the most fervent optimist think this could not have happened? ... Early in the twentieth century it really mattered to oppose Nietzsche and Lenin, and to do so in terms other than those of die-hard conservatism or philistinism."[39]

It is genuinely difficult to know how to respond to these comments without descending into the same type of vulgar abuse to which Nairn subjects Lenin here. As the dismembered and disemboweled bodies piled up across the battlefields of Europe, victims mobilized by the very nationalism Nairn would have us embrace, it is not entirely obvious to me that the most important task would have been to oppose (in non-philistine terms, of course) one of the few politicians committed to stopping the slaughter—and who, as far as Russia was concerned, actually succeeded in doing so. One would be rather more impressed by this call to arms if Nairn were seriously to criticize the thinker with whom he links Lenin; but to criticize *Nietzsche* now—when fashionable vulgarizations of his thought dominate the academic world with mindless rhetoric about "difference" and the insurmountability of the will to power— would of course involve courting far greater unpopularity than is risked by slandering Lenin.

Humans need nations

It seems likely that the events of 1989–1991 simply gave Nairn an occasion, rather than a reason, for publicly abandoning Marxism and its associated political commitments. Accordingly, he no longer argues for nationalism as an alternative road to socialism. He now argues that it is the fate of humanity because it corresponds to the requirements of human nature. This is extreme, even by Nairn's previous standards. He rightly dismisses the notion, associated with currently fashionable cant about globalization, that the nation-state has run its course. However, his alternative is based on the opposite and equally damaging error. Discussing the new wave of nationalisms that have arisen since 1989, he writes that if "people have not been able to help being like that (inventors of cultural contrasts, antagonistically differentiated, etc) then what is to prevent blood and accursed 'human nature' coming into their own once again?" If true, these remarks would be the occasion for despair. But Nairn is neither despairing nor depressed, for such responses would be the result of misunderstandings. Nationalism, in this account, has been the downfall of empire, from the Dutch revolt against Spanish absolutism in the sixteenth century to the Eastern European revolt against Russian totalitarianism in the twentieth. For this reason, it has to be welcomed, despite its continual splitting up of existing states: "If the role of primordial human nature was greater than [Gellner's theory of modernization] allows, however, then may it not be that what saved us [i.e. from Stalinism–ND] may also be condemning us to an indefinite futurity of differentiation?"[40]

"Primordial human nature?" Surely you're joking, Mr. Nairn? Although he circles evasively around the issue, distancing himself from the "dreadful simplicities of racism and ethnic nationalism," Nairn ultimately opts precisely for this oldest of reactionary creeds: "Any new paradigm depends, in other words, on establishing a more plausible link between biology and kinship on the one hand, and the world of politics, nation states and resurgent nationality on the other."[41] To this end, he expects the Human Genome Project, and other research into the "life sciences" more generally, eventually to prove the link between biology and nationhood. The scientist Steve Jones is brought in for support: "The term 'nature' itself derives from the Latin *natus,* that which is born, 'nation' is from the same root."[42] The same point was made more simply in an article from 1992 not reproduced in *Faces of Nationalism:* "If diversity was never merely a 'given,' in the meaningless accident sense, a different light must be thrown upon its persistence. If internal species-diversity through cultural means has always been 'human nature,' presumably it will go on being so in a way that has nothing to do with ideology of blood or race."[43] The appropriate response to this irrationalism was given by a fellow Scottish nationalist, Pat Kane, who condemned the resort to "biological or species-hereditary determinations":

> The only universally-binding terms which might help us through this international liberation-chaos are not our hominid instincts, but those "circumstances of Modernity" which Nairn foolishly attempts to go behind. Pursuing a progressive-nationalist game with the cards of biological science means that your opponent may defeat you, still playing poker—but with higher, more terrifying stakes, holding infinitely dirtier and dishonest hands. The packet of nationality and biology should be left unopened, in the drawer of the first half of this century.[44]

It should be noted that Nairn does not attempt to excuse what he calls "blots, excrescences or failures" in the record of nationalism since 1989. He merely considers that "the bombardment of Dubrovnik or the political rape of Muslim women" are a price worth paying for the downfall of the Soviet Union and the other oppressor states of the Stalinist bloc: "Insistence that the small battalions are likely to be 'on the whole' better than the large—particularly the multi-ethnic large—does not imply there can be no pathology of the ethnic, or no cases where nationalists are wrong."[45]

In fact, Nairn does attempt to explain the genocidal aspects of nationalism. The problem, he claims, is not nationalism as such, but ethnic nationalism, particularly where it used to mobilize a peasant population whose way of life is under threat from "modernization." On this basis, Nairn not only seeks to explain the Cambodian and Rwandan massacres, but the lack of violence in the history of Scottish and Welsh nationalism compared to that of rural Ireland.[46] In a subsequent article in *NLR* he extended this analysis to include the rise of Nazi Germany, identifying the centrality of rural Bavaria and its capital, Munich, in inculcating Fascism. Indeed, in combination with a range of other factors, Nairn treats the persistence of peasant life and its forced entry into modernity as the prime cause of what he calls "nationalist disasters." Munich was "a town of peasant culture," Cambodia and Rwanda were "virtually 100 percent peasant," Bosnia and Serbia were "less touched by the process of halting industrialization than many outside observers realized," and so on.[47]

In reality, these cases have little in common. The genocide in Rwanda took the form of an inter-peasant conflict about access to land, and was neither a rural revolt against the towns nor a national struggle in any recognizable sense. Cambodian Stalinism certainly embodied a ferocious anti-urban bias, but the victims of Khmer nationalism were not, in the main, killed because of their ethnicity, but because of their supposed opposition to the New Order: most of the bones now preserved in Tual Sleng extermination centre are of "ethnic" Khmers. Indeed, the second greatest example of systematic internal violence in the twentieth century (after Nazi Germany), Stalinist Russia between 1929 and 1956, can scarcely be said to have rested on peasant support, since at one level the industrialization of the Soviet Union can be seen precisely as a civil war waged by the bureaucracy against the peasantry. The reason why Irish nationalism has repeatedly been forced to resort to violence is not the consequence of peasant trauma at modernization (in 1798!) but a response to the institutionalized violence of the British state and its Orange offshoot—and this is a violence that the Scots certainly have been responsible for exercising.

In short, the entire argument is an exercise in apologetics: tragically, these premodern peasants are susceptible to ethnic mobilization that can lead to genocide; happily, we modern urbanites have attained a level of civic nationalism that allows us to engage in democratic state-building without relapses into tribal barbarism. But the distinction between "civic" and "ethnic" nationalism is extremely dubious. "Ethnicity" is as much an invented characteristic as "race" (or indeed "nation"); political conflicts create ethnic divisions, not the other way around, and there is no nationalism that could not begin to adopt "ethnic" distinctions in situations of social crisis. Given the way in which Scotland (and the Scottish national consciousness) has been implicated in the atrocities of the British Empire and the racism that accompanied them, can Nairn be so sure that these elements would not rise to the surface of Scottish nationalism if economic conditions were bad enough? The legacy of Britishness is not escaped so easily.

This is why the question of German Fascism is important to Nairn's argument: Nazi Germany, for Marxists, is an example of a modern, developed capitalist power succumbing to extreme right-wing nationalism in its Fascist form. If it can be shown to be the product of peasant backwardness, rather than modern capitalist society, however, then nationalism emerges without responsibility for the Second World War and the Holocaust. Now, as Zygmunt Bauman has pointed out, the anti-Semitism that formed the core of Nazi ideology was, as Nairn suggests, a form of resistance to modernity.[48] But this only explains the origins of anti-Semitic ideology, not how significant sections of the German nation, including its most "modern" sections, could succumb to it. As Geoff Eley has written, against earlier attempts to blame Nazism on supposed German backwardness, the answer lies "in the immediate circumstances in which the Nazis came to power—namely, the successive conjunctures of the First World War, the post-war crisis of the 1917–23 period, and the world economic crisis after 1929."[49] Twenty years before the Nazis came to power, Germany as a whole had long since left "rural backwardness" behind: "In 1913, Germany was producing two-thirds of all European steel . . . double the British figure and not far short of the American one. She produced almost as much coal as Great Britain, and took many European markets from her." More importantly, the class structure changed as a result. In 1880 German society was one in which the majority of the population worked on the land and industry was confined to small workshops: "In 1914, not much more than one third worked in agriculture (thirty five percent), almost two fifths in industry. But within industry there was a great change over from small firms employing a handful of workmen to middle sized and, most spectacularly of all, very large concentrated firms whose huge ugly factories dominated the Ruhr, Silesia, Saxony."[50] In short, Germany was not a society in transition to modernity but one that had arrived. Bauman's comments on the Holocaust are also appropriate to describe the frenzy of German nationalism that accompanied it: "the Holocaust was born and executed in a modern rational society, at the high stage of our civilization and at the peak of human cultural achievement, and for that reason it is a problem of that society, civilization and culture."[51]

Nairn seems to believe that, against the "big battalions," small is always beautiful. "Regrettably," he writes of Italian and German unification in the nineteenth century, "both these great and exemplary unification projects ended in fascism."[52] The corollary of this is his enthusiasm for "micro-states," a category in which he numbers Andorra, Gibraltar, Hong Kong, Jersey, Liechtenstein, Malta, Monaco, and San Marino.[53] Ulster, he hints, may also belong in this company. Is this the future of the international state system? There are at least three reasons why this is extremely unlikely.

First, the list itself is extremely heterogeneous. Hong Kong was the creation of British imperialism (as are those other non-European "micro-states" that Nairn unaccountably omits—Kuwait and the other Gulf dictatorships); Singapore developed out of the retreat from empire; both economies are primarily geared to the export market that developed out of the postwar boom. The European examples are remnants of the tiny precapitalist principalities that once covered Europe and that have established themselves as offshore tax havens. The circumstances in which these quite different states came into being are unlikely to be repeated.

Second, these are not nations. The discussion of "micro-states" is the one point in the book where Nairn blurs the difference between states and nations—with good reason, for the notion of a Monacoan nationalism is implausible to say the least; but so too, more importantly, is a Hong Kong nationalism. All of the forces that opposed the Chinese takeover, bourgeois and proletarian, did so on class, not nationalist, grounds. The national identities that have developed in "micro-states" tend to be those of the dominant power that guarantees their existence. In Ulster and Gibraltar (and the Falkland Islands) it is British nationalism that holds sway, not that of the territory itself.

Third, there is no reason to suppose that the future direction of nationalism will only involve the disintegration of existing nation states. It is at least as likely that nationalism will find expression in policies of aggressive integration. In this respect the failed Iraqi attempt to absorb Kuwait and the successful Chinese attempt to absorb Hong Kong reveal the shape of things to come as much as or more than the splitting of Czechoslovakia into its component parts.

What this section of the book does reveal, however, is another element that Nairn expects to form an eternal aspect of human existence. At one point he draws a revealing comparison between nationalism and the state, both of which are "very unlikely to wither away."[54] His acceptance of the continued existence of the state is of course a necessary concomitant to his argument concerning the inescapability of nationalism, but Nairn's eternal state is a capitalist state. Nairn lets this slip during a discussion of the components of the Eastern European revolutions: "There was a popular, democratic rebellion against one party autocracy and state terror. There was an economic revulsion against the anticapitalist command economies that for forty years had imposed forced-march development on the East. And thirdly there was the national mould into which these revolts were somehow inevitably flowing—the new salience of the ethnic, or (as in Bosnia) of the ethnic-religious in post-communist society."[55] Bourgeois democracies, capitalist economies, nation-states—these are the components of our future, according to Nairn. He implies that anyone who objects to the disastrous imposition of multinational capitalism in Russia since 1991 is seeking a return to the genocidal certainties of the Cold War, as if these were the only alternatives facing humanity. In fact, the revolt against the market has already begun in Russia. In 1995, workers in 8,856 enterprises took strike action, followed in January 1996 alone by workers in 2,108 enterprises, including half a million miners. In one survey conducted in both 1993 and 1995 workers in St. Petersburg were asked what measures they would take to defend their rights: the number prepared to engage in "armed struggle" rose from zero in 1993 to 7 percent in 1995—20,000 workers in that city alone. What advice would Nairn have for these workers, in the face of the still-greater suffering they have subsequently faced? The authors of the study from which these figures are taken note a "new development" in the class struggle in Russia: "co-ordination of strike activity across international borders," citing how the Russian miners delayed taking strike action in 1996 until it could be coordinated with action by miners in the Ukraine.[56] This is the very type of internationalist action that Nairn thinks is impossible or irrelevant, perhaps even undesirable. Why?

The impossibility of internationalism?

For Nairn, nationalism is so rooted in our nature that attempts to displace it in the name of international working-class solidarity are misguided:"An authentic *Internationale* can only be based upon the liberation of human nature: which means (in the first instance) nationalities, the precondition for democracy and individual emancipation."[57] As with his definition of the state, Nairn's own definition of internationalism is classically liberal: "Internationalism, understood as a systematic outward-looking and inquiring attitude, an imaginative search into the meaning of other experiences, is the most valuable way of counteracting the disadvantages of this truth [that most people live in 'backyards']."[58] Now, even if I accepted the notion that discrete national cultures exist (which I do not), the outcome desired by Nairn would still be serial nationalism, rather than internationalism. This conclusion in fact predates Nairn's final break with Marxism, and is argued most clearly in "Internationalism: A Critique."

He begins by distinguishing between "internationality" and "internationalism." Internationality is the objective result of a capitalist world market in which the same social classes increasingly wear the same clothes, watch the same television programs, and consume the same food and drink, no matter where they are geographically situated. Economic and cultural integration has not, however, led to an identification of political interests between these people, even those that belong to the same social classes. Instead, they have tended to identify with their particular nation, which ultimately involves supporting the state that rules over it. With this much we can agree. The conclusion Nairn draws, however, is that internationalism is therefore an ideology that, in both Marxist and liberal variants, sets out an essentially moral agenda for overcoming the dominance of nationalism: "Internationalism poses a moral alternative to the way in which the world has actually gone since the Franco-Prussian War, the end of the First International and, more emphatically, since 1914."[59]

The reference to 1914 is significant. The collapse of the Second International was a defining moment for Nairn, but not because it demonstrated the betrayal of the international working-class movement: "There was neither betrayal nor regression in this sense."[60] On the contrary, Nairn argues, the socialist parties simply recognized the reality of working-class nationalism. Working classes are, at the moment of their initial formation, spontaneously internationalist and anticapitalist; but this lasts only as long as it takes for them to become integrated into the system, with their own trade unions, cooperatives, and political parties—a stage that had been realized in Europe long before 1914.[61] Unable to accept the reality of the situation, however, Marxists retreated into an essentially religious adherence to the internationalist faith, which prevents them responding to the actual—and invariably national—crisis situations that do arise. "At moments of maximum bitterness," he writes, "I have been tempted to see all of our internationalists in Scotland in this light."[62]

Ultimately, conforming to the doctrine of internationalism led socialists into one of two dead ends, whether they were Stalinists or anti-Stalinists: "The former usurped internationalism into the service of the Soviet Great Russian state, ultimately in still more theocratic terms; the latter responded to this and the other betrayals of the revolution either with distance and pessimism (like some Western Marxists) or with even greater idealization of the international ideal." Internationalism for Nairn has therefore essentially been maintained by socialist intellectuals as compensation for the defeats that have dogged the movement since 1917: "as all-the-samism it is a standing invitation to the notion that 'I' (the subject of international revolution, not the unshaven native of Aberdeen or Neusiedle-an-See) am better engaged supporting the revolution where it happens to be at, rather than where I (unshaven native) happen to be located."[63] But even this is no solution, for these distant revolutions have tended to be driven precisely by the nationalism that the subjects of international revolution oppose: "To put it crudely—what orthodoxy required was a plausible way of supporting and not supporting national movements at the same time." Lenin provided the theoretical solution to this conundrum: "Hence the general principle that all nationalist struggles and movements are bad; however, special and pragmatically identifiable circumstances may make them good—though only for a time, and in a highly qualified fashion." Thus socialists are free to support national movements until they come to power, then denounce them for refusing to conform to the internationalist ideal: "Each new tragedy of Balkanization serves to underlie the ever fresh principle that only the international class struggle can prevent this kind of thing, if only the revisionist and narrow nationalists can be stopped, next time." The alternative to this, Nairn argues, would be the psychologically impossible one of admitting the inevitability of nationalism: "Hence, to concede even the equivalence of ethnic-national factors with social-class ones in the new struggles amounted to a victory of the contingent over the essential. The thought that the former could be more important than the latter, generally, for a prolonged historical era—that was no better than the foundering of [Marxist] philosophy."[64] Marxists are therefore taxed with refusing to recognize the power of nationalism, with adhering to an illusionary theory of internationalism, and with hypocritically supporting national movements (as "exceptions") in the inevitable absence of that internationalism. There is, however, one final indictment to be added to the charge sheet. As Callinicos has written, "It has become part of the common sense beliefs of large sectors of the Western intelligentsia that every universalism is a masked particularism."[65] For Nairn, the universalism of internationalism disguises a particularism of "big battalion" nationalism, such as that displayed by socialists who opposed Scottish self-determination in favor of the British state, or, for that matter, those who opposed self-determination for Azerbaijan in favor of the old Soviet Union.

2. THE REALITIES OF NATIONALISM

I have given Nairn the benefit of an extended presentation of his position, delivered as far as possible in his own words. This is more than he usually grants his opponents: the shadowy and usually nameless "Leninists" or "sectarians" who populate his essays and who are rarely allowed to speak for themselves, but only through his caricatures. The remainder of this chapter is therefore taken up with why he is wrong, from the position of a socialist internationalist who is, as it happens, also "an unshaven native of Aberdeen"; in doing so I will examine the relationship of nationalism respectively to modernity, capitalism, reformism, and internationalism, before returning to engage with Nairn's current position on Scotland.

Nationalism as an aspect of modernity

According to Anthony Smith, there are three basic positions on the place of nations and nationalism in historical development. The first, appropriately enough, is primordialism: "proponents of this view claim that nations and ethnic communities are the natural units of history and integral elements of human experience, [the] basic organising principles and bonds of human association throughout history." The second is perennialism, whose advocates argue that "units and sentiments found in the modern world are simply larger and more effective units and sentiments traceable in much earlier periods of human history."[66] The third and final position is modernism, where "the nation is a purely modern phenomenon, a product of strictly modern developments like capitalism, bureaucracy and secular utilitarianism . . . Nations and nationalism, the argument continues, can be dated with some precision to the latter half of the 18th century . . . anything which appears to resemble it, either in antiquity or the Middle Ages must be understood as purely fortuitous or exceptional."[67] The modernist position (once held by Nairn) refuses all attempts to claim that nationalism is an inescapable part of the human condition. As the late Ernest Gellner wrote, the primordialist theory is the most commonly invoked of the three, but "in one sense it is barely a theory, because it treats the principle as something inherent in human nature, or the very principles of social organization, so obvious as not really to require explanation." If anyone points out that for most of human existence this aspect of our nature has been absent, nationalists have an answer: "Nationalists are in fact aware of the *evidence* which makes some of us contest the universality of nationalist sentiments: they do know, often with anger, that in many societies and many historical periods, nationalism is conspicuous by its absence. They know it, with great bitterness, especially when it relates to the recent past of their own nation. But they explain it in their own way, and their explanation is contained in what is probably the most commonly used word in the nationalist vocabulary: *awakening*."[68]

Nairn is aware of Gellner's critique, not least because the latter has used it several times before and Nairn cites one of these occasions here.[69] Yet the notion of "awakening" is the basis of his explanation for the revival of Scottish nationalism and indeed of all other nationalisms. The reader may have already noted his use of the term in passing—"As far as the 'bourgeois' aspects of the 1970s national movement are concerned, I remain convinced that in our specific conditions only the middle strata could have brought about such an awakening"—but now we learn that "the Treaty of Union came just in time to bury a nascent Scottish nationalism, but could only put it into a shallow grave." And from this grave: "The corpse may simply step out from temporary interment to claim his rights."[70] In a sense this goes one better than Gellner: not only an awakening but a veritable second coming. We will examine the Lazarus of European nationalisms at the conclusion of this article. For the moment, however, let us stick with the question of modernity.

Those who accept that nationalism is a modern phenomenon tend to uphold one of two main theoretical approaches. On the one hand, followers of the German sociologist Max Weber argue that nations are a product of the process they call modernization, particularly during the phase involving industrialization. On the other, Marxists argue that these terms ignore the fact that "modernizing" societies have been subject to a much more specific process: domination by the capitalist mode of production. It was the first of these approaches, embodied in the work of Gellner, which influenced Nairn in his original reflections on the national question, but Nairn avoided the issue by treating modernity and capitalism as equivalent.[71] Since Nairn now treats nationalism as a permanent aspect of the human condition, he has consequently dissociated it from both modernization and the capitalist mode of production, although, as we have seen, he is happy to use the notion of a transition from "traditional" to "modern" societies as an explanation for the actions of nationalisms of which he disapproves.

29

Nationalism and capitalism

Once a nation-state has been established, those who control the state apparatus always seek to consolidate the hold of national consciousness among the people who inhabit the state territory. As Nigel Harris puts it: "Once the boundary is beaten back and troops posted around the perimeter, the state undertakes to colonize all within, to drill all the inhabitants who find themselves trapped behind the fence with an invented common inheritance of loyalty, supposedly to a common culture or way of life, but in practice to a particular state."[72] This certainly happens, although Nairn is largely silent on the issue, but the suggestion that nationalism exists purely as the result of indoctrination is hardly the whole explanation. Why do workers support nationalist movements before states are established? Why do they accept it afterwards? One reason is clearly that bourgeois ideology is at its most convincing when it appears to confirm the inevitability of the world as it is organized under capitalism, which is one consisting of actual or potential nation-states. There is, however, another reason. Nairn is correct to suggest that nationalism provides a framework of identity, a sense of "belonging"; the question is whether it is the only form of consciousness that can play this role.

Benedict Anderson once suggested that the origins of national consciousness lay in the collapse of "three fundamental cultural conceptions" during the rise of capitalism: the identification of "a particular script-language" (such as Latin in Christendom) with access to religious truth; the belief that society was organized in a natural hierarchy, at the summit of which were "monarchs who were persons apart from other human beings"; and a view of the indistinguishability of cosmology and history that rendered "the origins of the world and of men essentially identical." The interconnected decline of these three meant that human beings required "a new way of linking fraternity, power and time meaningfully together."[73] As Chris Harman has noted, this argument makes the connection of nationalism with capitalist development contingent rather than necessary, with the latter simply allowing expression to an "existential yearning," providing an outlet for "the satisfaction of innate psychological needs."[74] It is, however, possible to reformulate the position held by Anderson in a way that relies not on a conception of the eternal human condition—which would be to surrender to the position held by Nairn—but on the human needs that are created by capitalism.[75] As

George Kerevan once wrote, ironically in Nairn's journal, the *Bulletin of Scottish Politics:* "If civil society separates itself from people's social-political designation (as opposed to their party-political designation); if individuals only face one another in the market connected in only one all-embracing unit of civil society—the nation. A mass social allegiance is born; an allegiance to something beyond the class antagonisms of civil society, beyond language, beyond ethnicity, beyond geography: nationalism. For the feudal peasant, whose unfreedom is not masked by the market, no such allegiance is possible." For workers under capitalism, however, such an allegiance is not only possible, it is—from the point of view of the capitalist class in individual nations—absolutely necessary; for without it, the danger is always that workers will identify not with the nation in which they happen to be situated, but with the class to which they are condemned to belong, regardless of the accident of geographical location. Consequently, as Kerevan points out, workers are confronted by "two materially conditioned allegiances." On the one hand, "*Nationalism,* reflecting the social position of the individual caught in the allegiances imposed by civil society and its exterior state." On the other, "*Proletarian internationalism,* reflecting the class position of the worker and the kernel of the socialist mode of production developing within capitalism." The two are quite different in nature: "The former is materially determined by the external appearance of bourgeois society, the latter by its essence."[76]

Nationalism and reformism

Nationalism should not therefore be seen as something that only "happens" during separatist movements on the one hand, or during Fascist and imperialist manifestations on the other. The capitalist system generates nationalism as a necessary, everyday condition of its existence. Consequently, it forms part of the reformist consciousness among the working class. Reformism, long before it becomes embodied in organization, is produced by the tension between accepting the system as an unchanging feature of human life and rejecting the way in which specific aspects of it actually impact our lives. The task for revolutionaries is, as it were, to expand this "rejectionist" side of reformist consciousness until it becomes total, proving through a combination of argument and activity that, for example, the inadequacy of our schools is neither accidental nor incidental, but a direct effect of how the system operates.

The difficulty is that reformist political organizations are constantly pulling in the opposite direction, reinforcing nationalism at the same time as they encourage workers to accept the system. This is for two reasons. The first is the well-known tendency of reformist parties to appeal to the lowest levels of working-class consciousness, rather than attempt to raise them; to pander to the worst forms of working-class prejudice rather than attempt to challenge it. The second is that these reformists hope to take over national government office themselves—despite all the talk of globalization, the assumption is still that the national state is the arena in which "politics" is conducted. Nairn therefore completely underestimates (or rather, willfully disregards) the extent to which the reformist and Stalinist left have been responsible for the continued dominance of nationalist consciousness among the working class under capitalism.[77] Rather than having no alternative but to reflect an overwhelming nationalist feeling among the working class, they consciously attempt to foster these feelings.[78] Within the trade unions this can occur in two ways, both of which can be illustrated from the experience of the labor movement in Scotland.

The first is the argument that particular industries or workplaces belong to "the nation," rather than to capitalist firms or (more rarely these days) the capitalist state. The disastrous effects of this ideology became apparent during the Miners' Strike of 1984–1985.[79] One of the key objectives of the NUM was to stop steel production nationally. Unfortunately the leadership relied on their fellow officials in the steel unions to deliver this rather than organizing picket lines at the steel works. The latter had been badly defeated in the steel strike of 1980 and more than half the workforce had been lost in the ensuing three years. The leadership of the Iron and Steel Trades Confederation opposed shutting down steel production. It was at this point that the Scottish nationalist argument kicked in. In Scotland, the NUM Area officials signed an agreement allowing enough coal to enter the strip mill at Ravenscraig in Motherwell to keep the furnaces operating. The reason given by Area President Mick McGahey was that the deal was "in the interests of Scotland's industrial future." In fact, not only did the amount of coal entering Ravenscraig not drop from its normal levels to that required on a care-and-maintenance basis, it increased. Picketing by the miners and their supporters was unable to close the plant in the absence of practical solidarity from other unions or the STUC. And so the "Scottish national interest" helped play its part in the defeat of the NUM, the destruction of the British mining industry, and the perpetuation of Tory rule for another 12 years. Pursuit of the national interest also left a legacy of division within the Scottish working class that should not be underestimated. Joe Owens, a miner who worked at Polkemmet Colliery in East Lothian before the strike, gave vent to his feelings in an interview several years later:

> And when the miners asked the men at Ravenscraig not to accept imported coal, they just put two fingers up at them, which was another contributing factor to the closure of Polkemmet. Since that event, of course, Ravenscraig has been closed and they're looking for everybody's sympathy after turning down the miners' appeals. I've no sympathy for them, same as I've none for the Nottinghamshire miners [i.e. who formed the scab Union of Democratic Mineworkers during the strike]. I'm actually praying for pits to close in Nottingham so that I can laugh at them.[80]

The second way in which nationalism is fostered by the reformist bureaucracy is in the advocacy of all-class, pan-Scottish alliance as the way to defend jobs. Despite the comments quoted above, delegates at the Scottish NUM conference in June 1990 voted to support the campaign to save Ravenscraig from closure, and union convener Tommy Brennan was even invited to speak at the annual Miners' Gala in Edinburgh. But this was simply the latest in a series of campaigns that had followed the same disastrous course over every threatened closure since the Upper Clyde Shipbuilders' work-in of 1971. The composition of these coalitions, invariably led by the STUC, was summarized by one friendly critic as consisting of "trade unionists, clergymen, artists, politicians of various hue [i.e. they included Tories], thinkers, councillors, professionals, and the rest."[81] They inevitably refused to consider industrial action and focused instead on "mobilizing Scottish public opinion" (unnecessarily, since in most cases it was already in sympathy with the threatened workers) and attempting to "persuade" the government to intervene (pointlessly, since it was usually in complete agreement with the employers). Of these campaigns, only the first at Upper Clyde Shipbuilders achieved any kind of success and that because it was accompanied by a militant occupation that took place in the context of the great upturn in British working class struggle of the early 1970s. The others—Singer at Clydebank, the Carron Iron Works,

British Leyland at Bathgate, the Corpach paper mill, the Invergordon smelter, Linwood, Caterpillar, Ravenscraig—took place in a period of defeat and contributed to extending it by their failure. As Keith Aitken writes: "Retrospection yields the dispiriting, and somehow surprising, realization that almost none of the eighties issue coalitions achieved their primary objectives. They did not save Caterpillar or Ravenscraig. They did not change government policy on health, devolution or the economy."[82] It was not until the Timex workers in Dundee fought back in 1993 that this strategy was effectively challenged and not until the victory of the Glacier RPB workers in Glasgow during 1996 that the cycle of disaster was broken, although there is no sign that the STUC have learned any lessons from the experience. And there can be little doubt that in an independent Scotland there will be increased reformist pressure on workers, both to identify with "their" capitalism against that of other rival nations, and to unite with other social classes in Scotland to solve the local manifestations of the global crisis. The point is that what Nairn identifies as the dominance of nationalism within the working class is to a large extent the dominance of reformism, of which nationalism is a necessary component. But if nationalism in this sense is part of reformist consciousness then it can be challenged in exactly the same way as reformism can in every other sphere of life. Indeed, one might say that workers remain attached to nationalist loyalties to the extent that they remain subject to reformist consciousness.

Nationalism and internationalism

Internationalism is as much a component of revolutionary consciousness and politics as nationalism is of reformist consciousness and politics. It has two aspects. On the one hand, it involves workers in one nation giving solidarity to workers in other nations, even at a cost to themselves: for example, the support given to the Liverpool dockers from as far afield as the United States and Australia. Here the issue is the unity of working-class interests against employers or the state, regardless of national boundaries. On the other hand, internationalism also involves workers in one nation giving solidarity to the national aspirations of the people of another nation, who will by definition include non-workers and are usually led by quite alien class forces: for example, the opposition mounted in both Britain and the US to the bombing of Iraq.

A small but illuminating example of both aspects—solidarity with both a working class and a nation—was once given, appropriately enough, in Nairn's native region of Fife. In 1974, a year after the military coup in Chile, the Chilean submarine *O'Brien* docked in Greenock in order that tailshafts could be repaired, protected, and then sent back to South America as spares. When the tailshafts arrived at the Royal Navy dockyard at Rosyth the TGWU shop stewards in the stores organization refused to release them and wrote to the Ministry of Defence, informing it "that no future Chilean Navy work will be done in Rosyth dockyard until the fascist *junta* is removed and a freely, democratically elected government put in power and human rights restored in Chile." The blacking went on for four years until the MOD eventually agreed that no work would be carried out or supplies provided to the junta by that dockyard. Rosyth was not traditionally a militant workplace; it had participated in the "Hands Off Russia" agitation in 1919, but in that case the driving force had been a group of Portsmouth engineers temporarily based in Fife. In 1974 the catalyst for action was a group of left-wing stewards who were active locally in the Labour Party, demonstrating that where internationalist arguments are consistently put, they can influence the actions of workers.[83]

Internationalism is not simply a moral imperative that workers can respond to or not, according to inclination, but a *practical necessity* given the nature of the capitalist order. The Fife shipyard workers referred to above may not have been immediately threatened by a military dictatorship, but they understood that the ease or difficulty with which the junta was able to go about its business in the world would have a bearing on whether other ruling classes were inclined to go down the road to repression. Furthermore, it is a necessity that the interconnectedness of the system—its "internationality," to use Nairn's phrase—makes possible because it is not simply a question of the clothes people wear or the television programs they watch, but a shared relationship to the reproduction of an international system. At a trade union level, the support shown by the Australian maritime union to the Liverpool dockers—which involved blacking one customer of the Liverpool Docks and collecting over $A600,000 on one occasion alone—was at least partly a recognition that their own employers were planning a similar onslaught, which eventually came within weeks of the dispute coming to an end.[84] The tragedy here was that their own defeat left the Liverpool dockers unable to return the solidarity they had been shown. It is also true that the cultural aspects of "internationality," notably the growth of a global media, have simply made people more aware of the similarity between their struggles and those happening in other parts of the world: the poll-tax demonstrators in Britain watched the Eastern European revolutions on TV at the end of 1989 and drew enough parallels with events in their own nation to shout "Stasi! Stasi!" at the Metropolitan police during the Trafalgar Square riot in 1990; black South Africans in turn watched that riot on TV and drew enough parallels with their nation to chant "No poll tax!" during the township battles with their security forces later that year.

I want, however, to dwell briefly on the second aspect of internationalism, since it is one of the biggest sources of confusion, not least to Nairn, who persistently mistakes the effect of Stalinism (including the effect it has had on orthodox Trotskyism) and the ideological rubbish left in its wake for the genuine Marxist position. It is important to state first of all that there is no metaphysical "right of nations to self-determination" (the unfortunate title of Lenin's otherwise indispensable pamphlet notwithstanding). Nor, contrary to what Nairn asserts, has the Marxist position ever been to support "exceptional" or "good" nationalisms. Socialists never support nationalism but they do support specific national demands under certain conditions. What are these?

This question is often reduced to the attitude taken by Marxists to oppressed peoples struggling against imperialism and its local agents—understandably, since for more than the first half of this century this issue largely was "the national question." The basis of socialist support for these nationalist movements was set out in the debates at the first four Congresses of the Communist International; the rise to full human dignity of peoples who had previously been regarded (and in some cases regarded themselves) as naturally inferior to their colonial masters, the weakening effect that national revolts had on the world system as a whole, the opportunity that they gave for socialists to break workers in the West from racism and support for imperialism and, consequently, to demonstrate to the colonial peoples that Western workers supported them rather than their "own" capitalists or state. None of this meant supporting the politics of the national movements themselves. Not the least distorting effect of Stalinism was to convince the majority of the international left that these national movements were socialist in content (so that when the true nature of, say, the Vietnamese regime was exposed it contributed to disillusion with the very idea of socialism). Since the end of Stalinism this view has nevertheless remained alive, but in the form of arguing that in every situation there must be one national movement that is oppressed and deserves support.

For socialists, however, the question of support for particular national demands (not for particular nationalisms) is determined by their relationship to the struggle for socialism, regardless of whether the nation concerned is oppressed or not. Furthermore, it should openly be undertaken with the purpose of weakening the support of workers for that nationalism. In this context several questions have to be asked. Does support strengthen or weaken the capitalist or imperialist state? Does support strengthen or weaken the class consciousness and organization of the working class? Does support strengthen or weaken the tolerance of people of different nations or "races" for each other? These are not always easy questions to answer, particularly where (as in Scotland) no element of national oppression is involved. Nevertheless, to try and answer them seems preferable to conceding in advance both the legitimacy of every nationalism and our inability to make any value judgments between them.

3. POLITICS AND THE MODERN LAZARUS

The previous paragraph brought us back to Scotland, our starting point. Let us examine Nairn's current views on this subject, then conclude. First, we need to understand his assessment of contemporary Scottish nationalism. According to Nairn, the political nationalism that arose in the 1960s "was not solely a wish for exit from the United Kingdom: it was, in effect, the desire to escape from 'civil society' and resume business as a political society" in his native Scotland, where, we learn, "a 'civil' social order (with the sense of 'decency', privacy, individual and group minority rights, *freedom of initiative and enterprise,* etc.) depends in the long run upon an appropriately civil form of national identity."[85] From this perspective, "civil society" is merely "a fall-back position for middle class internationalists" opposed to Scottish nationalism.[86] It should not be thought, however, that Nairn is opposed to the middle class as such; on the contrary, it must be at the heart of the Scottish nationalist project.

In fact, at one level, Nairn is far more honest about the class basis of Scottish nationalism than the SNP could ever be: "Though led in the name of a indeterminate 'people,' national liberation struggle can only be led by certain people with more determinate and vested interests in the process; nor could it conceivably be otherwise." And who is this class in Scotland? According to Nairn, it is the one that "runs Scotland: the institutional middle class," with which he identifies himself as a "recalcitrant member": "No collective presumption is intended here, for the important term is 'runs': the Scottish institutional middle class has never ruled this country, it merely manages it."[87] Actually, no middle class—institutional or not—has ever ruled any country; the bourgeoisie does that. For Nairn, however, failure to win the support of the former group was at the root of the SNP's inability to make an electoral breakthrough: "In this sense, perhaps, the SNP version of national identity has never been half 'bourgeois' enough—it was a twopenny solution aimed at a bit of everyone and no one in particular." However, the Scottish middle class was now beginning to take its national identity seriously under "the lash of Thatcherism."[88]

Now, there is a sense in which this is absolutely correct. The original class basis for the SNP during the 1960s and 1970s was the old petty bourgeoisie, "the small man, the frustrated Scottish businessman smelling profit in oil yet unable to cash in, only to spectate, and the lower middle class and professional elements watching their hard non-status and security disappear in the furnace of inflation."[89] There is no doubt that elements of the new middle class are now dominant within the SNP, their presence symbolized by the leadership of former Bank of Scotland economist Alex Salmond. The important fact here, however, is that the working class has not been won over to political nationalism, a fact of which Nairn is no doubt aware, but that has no great significance for him precisely because he now regards working-class politics as irrelevant. For revolutionaries, however, it is crucial. Yet the failure of Scottish nationalism in this respect is often unappreciated both inside and outside Scotland, largely as a result of misinterpreting two kinds of opinion poll.

The first are those that show a growing tendency for respondents to claim that they feel more Scottish than British (33 percent in June 1998 compared to 29 percent in September 1991).[90] Yet this indicates an increase in national consciousness, not nationalism as such, although the former is a necessary precondition of the latter. This consciousness has been shared, since the latter half of the eighteenth century, with a sense of Britishness, but assertion of the Scottish "side" of this dual identity has no necessary political implications. As Joyce McMillan once noted, "Scottish identity requires constant assertion, whereas . . . British identity is something taken for granted by every institution with which [the Scots] have to deal, and inclined to assert itself in the half conscious assumption that politics is something that happens at Westminster."[91] The point here is not that there is anything desirable about feeling British rather than Scottish or any other nationality but rather that, precisely because political and economic issues have tended to be resolved at a British level, that side of the national identity is where class unity is usually expressed. Britishness tends to be assumed at some level by all classes in Scotland (the same poll cited above shows that only 28 percent of Scots do not feel British to any degree). A genuine hardening of Scottish consciousness into a political nationalism would necessarily be accompanied by an emphasis on the unity of all Scots against that of British workers, precisely because its goal would be to establish a new state.

The second set of polls show a growing tendency for Scots to say that they would vote for independence in a referendum about the constitutional future and vote for the SNP in the Scottish Parliament: the most recent shows 56 percent opting for the former and 40 percent for latter—the the same percentage as those saying they would vote for Labour.[92] What these results both demonstrate is not some asocial upsurge of primeval nationalism but a response to the actions of the Blair government. The SNP made few advances in working-class areas during the general election of 1997. Despite posturing as the inheritor of Labour's social democratic past it gained only two Tory seats in predominantly rural areas. Yet after the hopes of 1 May 1997 were dashed, the SNP provides an electorally credible and seemingly left-wing alternative for Scottish voters of a type that is not (and cannot be) available in England. The SNP is not a reformist party like Labour, but we are dealing here with perception, not reality.[93]

Two other points of interest arising from these polls deserve to be mentioned. First, the numbers claiming to favor independence for Scotland exceed by 16 percent those claiming they would vote for the SNP, which suggests that independence as means of achieving certain political objectives and Scottish nationalism as a set of political beliefs are not necessarily seen as linked. Second, these are voting intentions for the Scottish

Parliament, not Westminster, where the SNP has consistently failed to achieve levels of Labour support, which suggests that voting for the SNP might be seen as a luxury that can be indulged without the threat of doing too much damage—which in turn suggests that not everyone shares the rather exalted opinion of the Scottish Parliament held by Nairn and others for whom the constitutional question is all-important.

The establishment of a Scottish Parliament was, after the election of a Labour government, the solution most commonly offered by reformists to problems of the working class in Scotland (or rather, "the Scottish people") during the years of Tory rule. Given the nature of the current Labour government, it comes as no surprise that those who are anxious to take the path of least resistance have focused still more on what the Parliament will deliver. Does Nairn share these illusions? Here we return full circle to the question of the British state. Nairn so loathes the aged beast that his reaction to the Labour victory on May 1, 1997, was restrained to the point of realism: "Democracy won a remarkable victory on May 1, but so (inevitably) did archaism."[94] Nairn correctly saw that Blair would do nothing to disturb the existing setup, unless forced to, but completely misunderstood what lay behind the vote for a Parliament with "tax varying" powers on September 13, 1997: "The most important thing for a recalled Parliament to decide, I need hardly point out, is not raising or lowering income tax by a few percent. It will be whether to alter the conditions of UK affiliation."[95] Nairn now seems confident that this will happen. In a speech to the annual conference of the Centre of Research into Elections and Social Trends during November 1997 he foresaw that: "Within the crumbling clam-shell of British sovereignty, serious home rule will find it hard to avoid *de facto* sovereignty."[96] There are two issues here.

First, what is sovereignty for, exactly? This obsession with sovereignty for its own sake (taking into account Nairn's concern to protect "enterprise") is about the most right-wing position available within the pan-nationalist camp. Compare this with the views of the Scottish historian, William Ferguson, who has never to my knowledge claimed to be a socialist of any sort: "And, to put the matter in its wider setting, sane nationalism the world over is perhaps all that stands between the earth and the ruthless pillaging by global gangs of Mammonites that would cheerfully ruin the planet for profit."[97] Socialists would disagree with his solution, but at least Ferguson identifies the enemy and sees the purpose of sovereignty as being to fight it.

Secondly, are the "conditions of UK affiliation" the central issue for most Scots? The 1997 Scottish Election Survey found that 54 percent of respondents expected the economy to be better after the establishment of a Scottish Parliament (13 percent by "a lot," 41 percent by "a little"), 38 percent expected unemployment to be better (6 percent and 32 percent), 62 percent expected education to be better (17 percent and 45 percent) and 60 percent expected the NHS to be better (16 percent and 44 percent).[98] These findings tend to suggest two conclusions. One is that the main reasons why people want a Scottish Parliament are immediate social issues, not abstractions about sovereignty. The other is that, even so, they do not expect it to make more than marginal improvements to the quality of their lives. This is a realistic assumption, and may even be too optimistic. Nairn, on the other hand, believes that a Scottish polity will somehow be innately beneficent. Writing of the anti–poll tax campaign he notes that: "Everyone there knew perfectly well that no Scottish legislation would ever conceivably have imposed such a tax to begin with."[99] This, on the other hand, is not a realistic assumption, and it involves some fairly heroic assumptions about the powers and likely composition of the Parliament. As is well known, the powers enjoyed by the Parliament will be extremely limited, although opportunities will exist for agitation and propaganda around issues like education where it does have some control. The voting system for the elections of May 1999 has been deliberately devised to prevent, as far as possible, any individuals or organizations from outside the established parties getting elected. Furthermore, it is likely to produce a coalition politics in which both Labour and the SNP will be able to claim that they are unable to carry out radical policies because of the need to placate their coalition partners, whoever they are. Finally, the process by which the Labour candidates have been selected has eliminated all but a few token left-wingers in favor of faithful Blairites. On the whole, the prospects of the Scottish Parliament producing something as offensive as the poll tax are probably rather high.

Nairn is obviously aware of all this, but probably thinks that an increase in power for the parliament is inevitable, its very existence leading a heightened desire for more "sovereignty." But this in turn is predicated on the false belief that "sovereignty" is a matter of importance to the majority of Scots. What most working-class Scots want is the control over their lives and conditions that no bourgeois parliament in Westminster or Holyrood can give them—the control that bourgeois parliaments are in fact specifically designed to prevent working-class people achieving. When it becomes apparent that the Scottish Parliament will not live up to even the minimum expectations invested in it, then a number of responses are possible. One might be the outcome desired by Nairn (and in a more directly electoral way by the SNP), where parliamentary failure is seen as stemming from the absence of Scottish sovereignty and leads to the demand for independent nationhood becoming irresistible. Another might be that failure condemns it to irrelevance, and instead of provoking high levels of public interest it becomes the object of the same sort of bemused contempt with which local authorities are currently viewed. Still another might be that its failures are seen, not as the result of a lack of independence, but as a result of its being a reformist institution incapable of challenging capitalism in Scotland or anywhere else. The latter perception is, of course, correct and the one that revolutionaries will seek to make hegemonic among the working class. If we fail, it will be for political reasons, not because our audience was genetically predisposed to embrace nationalism.

One final point is worth considering. Nairn always tended to treat the British state as if it had a life of its own, apart from the class interests that it represents. His argument nevertheless assumed that "the break-up of Britain" would represent a defeat for the British ruling class, and that it would oppose the departure of Scotland—indeed, this was one of the very reasons why the idea of Scottish independence had such a resonance on the left. It is by no means certain, however, that the British ruling class will necessarily remain committed to the preservation of the British state in its current form, if it can be demonstrated that other constitutional arrangements will equally serve their interests. As early as 1990, the *Economist*, playing its usual role as outrider for the most extreme doctrines of free market ideology, suggested in a lead article that there might be advantages in Scotland achieving independence: "unable to rely on handouts from the British exchequer, Scotland's political classes would take unpopular closure decisions for themselves, or leave managers free to do so." The editorial looked forward to "the replacement of today's half angry, half embarrassed dependency status by a grown up political culture," capable of closing down plants like Ravenscraig without concession to "industrial romanticism."[100]

This was a lone voice at the time, but there are signs that the bourgeoisie itself—and not just its ideologists—might now be prepared to contemplate full independence, not on free-market doctrinal grounds, but as part of the search for stability. The *Financial Times* reported recently that "what worries business is the prospect of endless uncertainty and altercation over Scotland's status, rather than the nature of the eventual settlement."[101] The declining Scottish economy is unlikely to reproduce the relative success of Catalonian devolution. The prospect of the national question becoming a permanent feature of Scottish politics, as it has become in Quebec, would therefore make independence attractive simply because it would decide the issue once and for all. This is a view that may gather strength once the parliament is established. At the moment, much more typical is Andrew Neil's talk of creating a "new Unionism" within a much more devolved, even federalist, United Kingdom, but Neil—once accurately described by Nairn as an "archetypal Scotch crawler"—will ultimately be less important in deciding the path of the British state than the capitalists he admires so much.[102] If Scottish independence does become something that the British capitalist class can live with, then one of the key arguments on the left for supporting it—that it is against the interests of the bourgeoisie—will have effectively dissolved. One of the tragedies of Nairn's trajectory toward the acceptance of "enterprise" is that this is no longer even an issue for him.

CONCLUSION

In one of the essays in *Faces of Nationalism,* Nairn reviews *The Race Gallery,* by Marek Kohn, from which he extracts two morals. The first is that "human biological diversity needs to be explored not denied." And the second is that "diversity needs some new defences in order to survive." The reader will have no difficulty in guessing what the nature of these new defenses is likely to be. Nairn is thinking here in particular of the Roma population of East Central Europe, who have suffered renewed levels of racism since the fall of Stalinism. Needless to say, as far as Nairn is concerned there is no possibility that this can be resisted; Roma people must simply establish their own nationalism in opposition that will "inevitably" be "ethno-linguistic" or "racial."[103] The tragedy of Nairn's long retreat from Marxism is that for one brief moment he did recognize, in all its grandeur, the possibilities for socialist revolution, not as a myth, but as an actuality that provided the solution to racial and national oppression:

> When de Gaulle spoke with condescension of "the new blood of France," to be "given a voice" after May, he revealed only his own ignorance of a generation that had spewed out that "France" along with the priests, professors and policemen, and adopted "Nous sommes tous des Juifs–Allemands" as its motto, doing more for the cause of internationalism and European unity in one day than the governments and labor bureaucracies of Western Europe had achieved in twenty years.[104]

"Nous sommes tous des Juifs–Allemands"—"We are all German Jews"—was the slogan of the French students and workers who demonstrated in May 1968 after attacks on Daniel Cohn–Bendit as a "German Jew" in the bourgeois press had led to his attempted assassination. Nairn could once use the very same slogan against the paltry vision offered to Scotland by nationalism: "to acquiesce in the SNP's version of our future, in the year where a new generation cried 'Nous sommes tous des Juifs– Allemands' before the Palais Bourbon and ground the nationalism of the past to dust at the Saarbrucken bridge, is merely an uninteresting form of suicide."[105] It seems likely that when another new generation arises to proclaim themselves German Jews (or perhaps Punjabi Scots), Nairn will now be one of those pressing the hemlock into our hands. "A false political theory bears within itself its own punishment," wrote Trotsky in 1933.[106] There is no need for the working class in Scotland or anywhere else to suffer that punishment, but one prerequisite for escaping it is precisely to see ourselves primarily as workers, and to reject all theories that would have us believe that the accidental fact of Scottish nationhood, or any other, is what will determine our fate.

Marx and Engels
on the Scottish Highlands[1]

INTRODUCTION

Marx and Engels wrote little about North Britain. A compilation called *Marx and Engels on Scotland,* of the kind once regularly produced by Progress Publishers in Moscow, would be short, the contents mainly extracted from incidental comments and the quality highly uneven. If this imaginary publication ever did appear in print, however, the Highlands would feature more often than any other topic in the index, and the majority of these references would be to the destruction of Highland society after 1746.[2] Two different and opposed responses to the fate of the Highlands—which I will henceforth refer to as Interpretations 1 and 2—have been ascribed to Marx and Engels on the basis of these fragments.

According to Interpretation 1 Marx and Engels treated the Highlands as part of the underdeveloped world, one geographically closer than most to the metropolitan centres of capitalist power, but still requiring "development" in the same way as far-off India, and with as little consideration for the wishes of the native inhabitants. Engels is particularly identified with this position. James Young, for example, writes that "Engels, who lived out his life under the shadow of [Walter] Scott's understanding of Enlightenment thought, was thoroughly racist in his attitude to the Scottish Highlanders and the extermination of primal peoples."[3] Evidence to support this claim is usually found in an article from 1849 called "The Magyar Struggle," in which Engels dismisses the Highlanders as "a people without history," doomed to be the foot soldiers of counter-revolution until deservedly crushed at the Battle of Culloden by the forces of progress. Yet shortly afterwards, in 1853, Marx wrote several newspaper articles, some of which were later incorporated into *Capital,* attacking the treatment of the Highlanders during the Clearances. Is this an example of a different attitude on his part? Young asserts that "Unlike Scott and Engels, Marx did not approve of the capitalists' 'improvements' in the Highlands resulting in mass expulsion and expropriation of countless peasants and land workers."[4] For more consistent adherents of Interpretation 1, however, these differences are more apparent than real, and Marx is simply guilty of hypocrisy—or more charitably, inconsistency—in failing to face up to the logical consequences of his own theory. Harvie concludes that: "Marx violently attacked the Sutherland clearances in *Capital* vol. II, but the Duke only seemed to be carrying out his own prescription."[5]

According to Interpretation 2, Marx and Engels originally held the position represented by Interpretation 1, but later rejected it for a position that saw the communism of the Highland clan system (and comparable social organizations elsewhere), not as a fetter on capitalist development, but as a model for and means of entering into the realm of socialist freedom. Alan Armstrong argues that:

> Only recently has it become clear that Marx did not believe that all ancient communal property must first dissolve into individual property, before further social advance was possible.... Marx saw that where communal property still existed, it might be possible to move directly to higher stages of social organization, without passing through the capitalist stage. It increasingly depended on an alliance with the new popular forces, which also had an interest in opposing private property relations.

Eventually this change was registered even by Engels, who "looked back sympathetically on 'primitive communism,' or the 'liberty, equality and fraternity of the ancient gens,' based on 'communal property.'"[6]

Marx and Engels are therefore either blamed for an economic determinism that retrospectively makes them complicit in the suffering of the Highlanders during the Clearances, or praised for adopting a political voluntarism in which Highland clan society could have been the basis for the transition to socialism, regardless of its low level of socioeconomic development. However, these interpretations merely apply to the Scottish Highlands more general claims concerning the attitude of Marx and Engels to "primitive" societies faced with capitalist development. Interpretation 1 has clear affinities with the position represented in the following passage by John Strawson:

> For Marx the Indian uprising of 1857 was no more progressive than the resistance of the first nation Americans against the European settlers. In the triumph of European colonialism—including its genocide—Marx saw the progress of Capital and with it the creation of a working class that would put an end to it. To the victim of colonialism there was not much to choose between Marx's progress and the Imperialist conquest. Both represented Europe's power to destroy cultures and languages, introduce forms of slavery, and in the Americas and Australia, genocide. For these peoples there is little in Marx's talk of creating the material conditions for human liberation that contained much attraction. Human liberation appears more as European power built on their graves.[7]

Or, as Robert Young writes, "the dominant force of opposition to capitalism, Marxism, as a body of knowledge remains complicit with, and even extends, the system to which it is opposed."[8]

Interpretation 2 has equally strong affinities with a more general position that, in this case, asserts that Marx and Engels later abandoned their earlier endorsement of capitalist progress, however qualified this may have been. Hobsbawm was perhaps the first writer to make this claim: "It seems probable that Marx, who had earlier welcomed the impact of Western capitalism as an inhuman but historically progressive force on the stagnant pre-capitalist economies, found himself increasingly appalled by this inhumanity."[9] Later writers ascribed this shift to a more complex set of determinations. Teodor Shanin argues that four developments of the 1860s and 1870s helped produce what he calls the thought of the "Late Marx." First, the occurrence of the Paris Commune of 1871 suggested not only the actuality of the socialist revolution but the form that it might take. Second, the increasing availability of scientific knowledge about prehistoric communities by the middle decades of the century suggested that primitive communism had held sway over human society for a much longer period than had previously been accepted: it could therefore be argued that primitive communism, rather than relatively short-lived forms of class society, was the "natural" condition of human beings. Third, the growing awareness of contemporary noncapitalist communities suggested an existing link with primitive communism. Fourth, and finally, his interest in the revolutionary potentialities of Russian society brought together all three other developments, in "the theory and practice of Russian revolutionary populism" and the "rural communes," whose existence seemed to stretch from the primitive communist past to the present-day peasant mir. Shanin particularly stresses not only the negative impact of capitalism on tribal societies but also the positive example that these societies offered as a model for contemporary socialists. "The Iroquois 'red skin hunter' was, in some ways, more essentially human and liberated than a clerk in the City and in that sense nearer to the man of the socialist future."[10] Similar views have been expressed by Franklin Rosemont, who claims that, after reading of the Iroquois described by Lewis Morgan, Marx's "entire conception of historical development, and particularly of precapitalist societies, now gained immeasurably in strength and precision," and that this new knowledge of tribal societies "sharpened his sense of the living presence of indigenous peoples in the world, and of their possible role in future revolutions."[11]

Both interpretations present difficulties for those who stand in the Marxist tradition. Interpretation 1 undermines the moral authority of Marxism to speak on behalf of the oppressed and exploited, for it appears to imply that their needs must be sacrificed to those of capitalist development. Interpretation 2 restores our image of Marx and Engels as defenders of the oppressed and exploited, but brings into question the explanatory power of Marxism to interpret human history, for it suggests that socialism is possible at any stage of development—indeed, perhaps the more backward the better, because nearer to the original state of primitive communism. We are not, however, required to choose between these interpretations (which generally involve isolating individual fragments of their work and treating them as representative), for either the Highlands in particular or the noncapitalist world in general.

In the argument that follows, I want to reconstruct the views of Marx and Engels on the Scottish Highlands, stripping away later misrepresentations—introduced by supporters and opponents alike—to show their views to be not only more complex than the two existing interpretations, but also morally and politically defensible in ways that these interpretations are not. The subject is not only one of interest in its own right, but acts as a barometer for their changing positions on "progress" and "development," since their discussions of the Highlands present these issues in a remarkably clear form, despite—or perhaps because of—the fact that the region was not territorially situated in the colonial world but in that of the most developed capitalism of that time: the British state where they lived out their exile after 1849. Despite the physical distance of the Highlands from the rest of the noncapitalist world, Marx and Engels's views on the former are not separable from their views on the latter. It will therefore be necessary to refer, at various points in the argument, to what Marx and Engels wrote about three other areas in particular: Ireland, India, and Russia.

INTERPRETATION I: THE ONWARD MARCH OF THE PRODUCTIVE FORCES

What evidence is there that Marx and Engels held the views ascribed to them by Interpretation 1? Take Engels first. He spent twenty-one months in Britain between 1842 and 1844, ostensibly working in the Manchester thread-making factory of his family firm, but in fact spending much of his time researching his first major work, *The Condition of the Working Class in England,* which was published in Germany the year after his return. Engels was not a "Marxist" when he wrote this book since the theory did not yet exist. (Indeed the two men only renewed their friendship—and began their partnership—in Paris while Engels was on the return journey to Germany.) It is unsurprising, therefore, that it leaves a contradictory impression. Engels was among the first commentators to see beyond the existential misery of the British working class—a subject that had already exercised such notably nonrevolutionary figures as Thomas Carlyle—to the potential power it possessed, and in this he was in advance of Marx himself. Nevertheless, in those sections of the book where his focus shifts away from the working class to a more general discussion of the industrialization process, Engels frequently repeats the ideological preconceptions of those bourgeois commentators whose analysis he had otherwise surpassed. In such passages we first encounter him on the subject of the Scottish Highlands:

In Scotland the Department of Public Works built since 1803 nearly 900 miles of roadway and more than 1,000 miles of bridges, by which the population of the Highlands was placed within reach of civilization. The Highlanders had hitherto been chiefly poachers and smugglers, now they became farmers and hand-workers. And although Gaelic schools were organized for the purpose of maintaining the Gaelic language, yet Gaelic-Celtic customs and speech are rapidly vanishing before the approach of English civilization.[12]

Such uncritical advocacy of "English civilization," which in this context can only mean capitalist civilization, seems to align Engels closely with his bourgeois contemporaries, an impression strengthened by reading his comments on non-European peoples written shortly afterward. In an article of 1847, Engels considered the suppression by the French of a prolonged rising of Algerian Bedouins: "The struggle of the Bedouins was a hopeless one, and although the manner in which brutal soldiers . . . have carried on the war is highly blameable, the conquest of Algeria is an important and fortunate fact for the fate of civilization." Engels goes on to remind his readers that the Bedouins survived through robbing and enslaving more settled communities: "And after all, the modern *bourgeois*, with civilization, industry, order and at least relative enlightenment following him, is preferable to the feudal lord or to the marauding robber, with the barbarian state of society to which they belong."[13] A similar attitude, but concerning Europeans rather than Africans, permeates a more famous article, to which I have already referred, "The Magyar Struggle," written for and published in the *Neue Rheinische Zeitung* in January 1849.

As the Europe-wide revolutionary movement of 1848 began to recede, Engels tried to identify the social basis of the emergent reaction, and thought he had done so in the particular characteristics of certain national groups. Engels was particularly concerned with whether or not support for any particular national movement would help prepare the way for capitalism and ultimately the working class itself. From this perspective the Slav nationalism that Engels targets in his article is an obstacle to both. Indeed, for him it cannot even be described as a genuine national movement, since it ultimately relies on the Russian absolutist state—then the main bastion of reaction in Europe—for its continued existence:

There is no country in Europe that does not possess, in some remote corner, at least one remnant-people, left over from an earlier population, forced back and subjugated by the nation which later became the repository of historical development. These remnants of a nation, mercilessly crushed, as Hegel said, by the course of history, this *national refuse,* is always the fanatical representative of the counter-revolution and remains so until it is completely exterminated or de-nationalized, as its whole existence is in itself a protest against a great historical revolution.

There were, however, earlier examples of such "human refuse" than those that concerned Engels in 1848, and the reader will no doubt have guessed their identity:"In Scotland, for example, the Gaels, supporters of the Stuarts from 1640 to 1745." Engels concludes by expressing his hopes for a revival of the revolutionary movement of the French proletariat and the German and Magyar peoples:

The general war which will then break out will scatter this Slav Sonderbund [that is, "special path"], and annihilate all these small pig-headed peoples even to their very names. The next world war will not only cause reactionary classes and dynasties to disappear from the face of the earth, but also entire reactionary peoples. And that too is an advance.[14]

This makes uncomfortable reading for contemporary socialists, since we associate calls for "extermination" or "annihilation" of whole peoples—understandable if not forgivable even given the counterrevolutionary danger of time—with another political tradition altogether. The "pig-headed peoples" of the Scottish Highlands had of course already seen their society destroyed, although their names and (in most cases) their persons survived. Engels returned to the theme in later years, again within the context of a comparison with Eastern Europe. In an article of 1866 for *Commonwealth* discussing the Polish question, he noted, more restrainedly but no less decisively:"The Highland Gaels and the Welsh are undoubtedly of different nationalities to what the English are [sic], although nobody will give these remnants of peoples long gone by the title of nations, any more than to the Celtic inhabitants of Brittany in France."[15]

These remarks can be usefully compared with those of John Stuart Mill in *Representative Government* on the advantages to "the Celtic inhabitants of Brittany" of adopting French nationality, thus gaining access "to all the privileges of French citizenship, sharing the advantages of French protection, and the dignity and *prestige* of French power." The alternative being "to sulk on his own rocks, the half-savage relic of past times, revolving in his own little mental orbit, without participation or interest in the general movement of the world." The relevance for Scotland is pressed home at the conclusion of this observation: "The same remark applies to the Welshman or the Scottish Highlander, as members of the British nation."[16] Eric Hobsbawm (who quotes this passage) has suggested that Engels's views can therefore be assimilated to those of "every impartial mid-nineteenth century observer," all of whom would apparently have agreed that "non-civilized" peoples should be incorporated into more advanced national bodies for their own benefit.[17] As is so often the case, however, Hobsbawm is too eager to discern an identity of interest between Marxism and the more advanced forms of Liberal thought. For these views were not only shared by commentators like Mill, which for the period after 1848 were compatible with certain kinds of reformist socialism. Matthew Arnold was none of these things; yet in a very similar program advanced in 1866 with regard to the Welsh he calls for "the fusion of all the inhabitants of these islands into one homogeneous, English-speaking whole," as a "necessity of what is called modern civilization." Elsewhere Arnold makes it clear that these remarks are also applicable to the other "Celtic" areas of Britain: "But at any rate, let us consider that of the shrunken and diminished remains of this great primitive race, all with one insignificant exception, belongs to the English Empire; only Brittany is not ours; we have Ireland, the Scotch Highlands, Wales, the Isle of Man, Cornwall."[18]

The last example from Engels that appears to support Interpretation 1 is a letter to Eduard Bernstein of 1882, on the national question in the Balkans:

[The] independence [of the Croats and Montenegrins] consists in demonstrating their hatred of the oppressor by stealing cattle and other valuable chattels from their own oppressed Serb compatriots as they have done for the last 1,000 years, and any attack on their right of rapine is regarded as an attack on their independence. I am enough of an authoritarian to regard the existence of such aborigines in the heart of Europe as an anachronism. And even if these little folk had a standing as high as Sir Walter Scott's vaunted Highlanders, who were also really shocking cattle thieves, the most we could do is condemn the *manner* in which they were treated by present day society. If we were at the helm, *we too* should have to put an end to the Renaldo Renaldini-Shindehannes business which, by long tradition, these laddies indulge in.[19]

Let us summarize the case for the prosecution on the basis of the evidence presented so far, leaving aside questions of interpretation for the moment. Pre-1848, Engels did indeed occasionally display an uncritical attitude toward capitalist development. Post-1848, he expressed the view (which—on one interpretation of the material cited above—he appears to have held until the end of his life) that certain peoples, including the Scottish Highlanders, were congenitally incapable of either forming nations or—as a consequence—of achieving capitalist development. Were these perspectives peculiar to Engels alone? Did Marx, perhaps as a result of his knowledge of the Highland Clearances, take a different attitude?

There is some evidence to support this contention. In 1845, the same year as *The Condition of the Working Class in England* was published in Germany, Marx and Engels began joint work on what was to become *The German Ideology.* The finished text was to remain unpublished in their lifetimes but nevertheless is of key importance in clarifying the theoretical basis of Historical Materialism. For our purposes, it is important because it features the first reference to the Clearances in their writings, albeit as the punchline of a Hegelian joke ("for example, if one says that the real 'task' which the institution of landed property 'originally set itself' was to replace people by sheep—a consequence which has recently become manifest in Scotland").[20] Authorship of this can safely be ascribed to Marx, if only because the following year the same example is used for a similar purpose, although more elaborately, in the individually written *The Poverty of Philosophy:* "It is a fact that in Scotland landed property acquired a new value through the development of English industry.... by successive transformation, landed property in Scotland has resulted in men being driven off by sheep. Now say that the providential aim of the institution of landed property in Scotland was to have men driven out by sheep, and you will have made providential history."[21] In both quotations Marx uses the example of how the Highlands were depopulated to make way for capitalist sheep grazing to satirize the philosophical views of two political opponents (respectively, Max Stirner and Pierre-Joseph Proudhon). Between January 1853 and May 1854 Marx returned to the question no less than four times in a series of articles written between 1853 and 1854, published in the *New York Daily Tribune*.[22] In these articles, however, the impact of the Clearances is not used as a stick to beat the philosophical pretensions of Stirner and Proudhon, but to express outrage at events that clearly haunted his imagination, for he returned to them again in the first and only volume of *Capital* to be published in his lifetime (1867). In the most famous of the articles, written a mere four years after Engels wrote "The Magyar Struggle," we find Marx launching a morally outraged defense of the very same Highland society. Here he attacks the hypocrisy of Highland landowners who verbally opposed North American slavery while forcing ("clearing") their own tenants off the land: "As for the large number of human beings expelled to make room for the game of the Duke of Atholl, and the sheep of the Countess of Sutherland, where did they fly to, where did they find a home? *In the United States of North America*. The enemy of British Wages-Slavery has a right to condemn Negro-Slavery; a Duchess of Sutherland, a Duke of Atholl, a Manchester Cotton Lord—never!"[23] Material from these articles was subsequently incorporated into *Capital* Volume 1, in the famous lines describing the process whose origin Marx traces back to the civil war of 1745–6:

> What "clearing of estates" really and properly signifies, we only learn in the promised land of modern romance, the Highlands of Scotland. There the process is distinguished by its systematic character, by the magnitude of the scale on which it is carried out at one blow (in Ireland landlords have gone to the length of sweeping away several villages at once; in Scotland areas as large as German principalities are dealt with) . . . [24]

We can therefore reject the claim by James Young that "most of the evidence touching on the middle Marx's attitude to the Scottish Highlanders is mostly anecdotal," although it is certainly true that "he was more sympathetic towards them than Engels had ever been."[25] Did this sympathy however also extend to other indigenous peoples?

The original article attacking the Duchess of Sutherland was dated January 21, 1853, and published on February 8 in the *New York Daily Tribune*. Yet in the concluding passage of his equally famous article "The British Rule in India," dated June 10 and published on June 25 in the same paper, his comments are quite different in tone from those on the Highlands, but strikingly similar to those written by Engels on Algeria. Both condemn colonial *methods*, rather than objectives, and endorse the civilizing role of colonialism, rather than supporting the colonized, and England is described as "an unconscious tool of history" in causing a "social revolution" in Asia.[26] This disparity is all the more striking since Marx and Engels believed that social relations in both India and the Highlands were essentially the same. Such comparisons were not original to Marx. James Mill had noted that "some curious strokes of resemblance appear in the following particulars of the Celtic manners, in the highlands and islands of Scotland." He then proceeds to quote from a description, by Samuel Johnston, of a cow being divided into specific parts between various members of Clan Donald according to their function. Later in the same book, we learn that "the domestic community of women among the Celtic inhabitants of Britain was a diversity, to which something very similar is said to exist among some of the castes on the coast of Malabar."[27] We know that Marx had read Mill on India and presumably absorbed these comparisons.[28]

In his critique of the article "The British Rule in India," Edward Said accuses Marx of succumbing to an "orientalist" discourse that overtakes his human sympathy for the sufferings of Indians subject to British colonialism.[29] For other commentators their work can be dismissed more generally as merely another Eurocentric defense of capitalism, no more concerned with the resulting impact on indigenous peoples and their civilizations than apologists for the World Trade Organization. Indeed, according to critics, treating the extension of the capitalist mode of production as a necessary precondition for socialism necessarily led them to support the destruction of all obstacles to capitalist dominance, both retrospectively in their historical judgments and contemporaneously in their political interventions. And if those obstacles were people—Indians, Native Americans, or Scottish Highlanders—this was merely the unfortunate but unavoidable cost of human progress.

Given his belief in the similarity of Indian and Highland social forms, it could be argued that Marx was being inconsistent or hypocritical in not showing the same degree of support for the "social revolution" imposed by the British in the Highlands as he did for that imposed on India. If so, then Engels was speaking the "truth" of Marxism in his attack on the Highlanders. It is certainly true that the positions associated with Interpretation

1 were prevalent, for example, among many—perhaps a majority—of early Scottish Marxists. John Carstairs Matheson, for example, was a leading member of the Social Democratic Federation (SDF) and subsequently of the mainly Scottish "impossiblist" secession of 1903, the Socialist Labour Party (SLP). Although himself a Gaelic speaker of Highland descent, he declared in 1910 that, prior to 1746, "The Highlander in tartan dared not, unless in time of war, venture on the south side of the River Forth if he wished to avoid being hanged on sight, and if he had, he would have created as big a sensation as a Red Indian Chief, who took a promenade along the Broadway, equipped with a blanket, moccasins, and a scalping knife."[30] What is of interest here is not the historical inaccuracies concerning the Highlanders, or the racist references to Native Americans, but the *comparison* between the two peoples, on which Matheson was quite explicit, writing that "the Highlands are no more part of the Scottish nation than the Sioux are part of the American nation." How faithful is Matheson to his mentors in these passages?

AGAINST INTERPRETATION I

Interpretation 1 combines, in relation to the Scottish Highlands, two general beliefs that Marx and Engels are supposed to have held throughout their careers: the existence of "non-historic" nations on the one hand, and the essentially progressive role of capitalism in relation to the non-capitalist world (which "historic nations" inhabited) on the other. Ephraim Nimni, for example, alleges that, for Marx and Engels, "historic nations" "are national communities capable of being agents of historical transformation, that will further the formation of a strong capitalist economy." Consequently: "The theory of 'non-historic nations' is not a curiosity, a slip of the tongue, an ad hoc argument, or a regrettable mishap. It is rather the result of the rigid and dogmatic universal laws of social evolution that define the precise historical location of the 'modern nation' and by default render obsolete national communities that cannot fulfil this rigid Eurocentric political criterion."[31] In fact, opposition to the "non-historic nations" and unqualified support for capitalist progress are not necessarily linked. Furthermore, Marx and Engels not only abandoned their belief in the former but never subscribed to the latter.

The belief in the existence of "non-historic" peoples was closely linked in the thought of Marx and Engels with that of "races," including a distinctly "Celtic" race that included the Highlanders and native Irish, as opposed to the "Anglo-Saxon" Lowlanders and English. "Nearly four-fifths of the whole emigration are, accordingly," wrote Marx in 1853, "to be regarded as belonging to the Celtic population of Ireland and of the Highlands and islands of Scotland."[32] This notion was familiar in the work of contemporary bourgeois writers. Macaulay wrote that the difference between Scotland and Ireland in the nineteenth century was that: "The Anglosaxon and the Celt have been reconciled in Scotland, and have never been reconciled in Ireland."[33] In *The Condition of the Working Class in England,* Engels's references to the civilizing role of "Anglo-Saxon" capitalism in the Highlands are matched by similar effusions regarding its impact across the Irish Sea: "so, too, in Ireland; between the counties of Cork, Limerick and Kerry, lay hitherto a wilderness wholly without passable roads, and serving, by reason of its inaccessibility, as the refuge of criminals and the chief protection of the Celtic Irish nationality in the South of Ireland. It has now been cut through by public roads, and civilization has thus gained admission even to this savage region." Not only was the region characterized by savagery, but the inhabitants: "The southern facile character of the Irishman, his crudity, which places him little above the savage, his contempt for human enjoyments, in which his very crudity makes him incapable of sharing, all favour drunkenness."[34] It is clear that Engels does not place the blame for the misery of the native Irish entirely at the door of the British: "That poverty manifests itself in Ireland thus and not otherwise, is owing to the character of the people, *and* to their historical development."[35] That national character might itself be the product of historical development does not seem to have occurred to Engels at this stage. These notions are important in our context because they make clear that, contrary to what is claimed by Nimni, Engels began his literary career by *including* the native Irish alongside the Highlanders in the "non-historic" category, which is clearly linked to the notion of racial groups ("peoples") discussed above.[36] There are two issues here, one general and the other specific to the Highlands.

The general issue, as the Ukrainian Bolshevik and Left Oppositionist Roman Rosdolsky wrote in his classic critique, is that nonhistoricity "represents a relic of the idealist interpretation of history and so has no place in Marxism."[37] To argue that particular national groups display inherent and, moreover, eternal characteristics seems particularly idealist and, unsurprisingly, led Engels into wrong predictions. Many of the peoples that he attacks as incapable of forming nations, such as the Czechs, subsequently went on to do precisely that, while those that failed to do so, such as the Basques, were prevented then, and continue to be prevented now, by repression, not some congenital incapacity bred in the bone. In other words, the content of national movements changes over time. Whatever the role of the Basques in 1848, would any socialist argue that their struggle for independence was reactionary during the period of the Franco regime in Spain?

The specific issue is that to talk about nationality in the context of the Highland clans is in any case anachronistic. One of the chief characteristics of the clan rank and file was the fact that they considered themselves to be neither a separate nation—their level of development would scarcely have allowed them to do so—nor part of the Scottish nation before 1707. This was explicit even in their vocabulary: the word *sassenach* (in Gaelic, *sasunnach*) means "saxon," and was used to describe both the English and Lowland Scots.[38] Far from wishing to form a nation, but being incapable of doing so because of their socioeconomic backwardness, their condition ensured that the Highlanders hardly knew what the word meant. The possibility that a separate Gaelic nation could have formed beyond the Highland Line is not a theoretical absurdity, but was rendered practically impossible by the destruction of Highland society during and after 1746. As Nairn writes: "It started from too far back (having been left relatively untouched by the weak authority of the Scottish monarchy, during the period of Absolutism) and was then exposed too abruptly, and too brutally, to the very dynamic capitalist societies in proximity to it."[39] In other words, the Highlanders, unlike the Irish, did not have the structural capacity or material resources to form a nation of their own during the period in which national formation occurred in Europe.[40]

But Engels abandoned the notion of "non-historicity" toward the end of his life. Why? One answer might be that his views had been influenced by current events in the Highlands to which Marx had drawn his attention. There is no suggestion in his writings, however, that Engels was ever hostile to the contemporary inhabitants of the Highlands, nor does it seem credible that he would have needed Marx to stimulate his outrage at the Highland landlords. What is puzzling is his changed attitude toward historical clanship. Two factors seem to have been involved.

One was a refinement of his concept of the nation. In an unpublished manuscript written as late as 1882 Engels still treats nations as "primordial" constructs, the German nation apparently having existed as early
as the first century BC.[41] Two years later he situates their formation at a
specific historical juncture—the emergence of the absolutist states out
of the feudal estates-monarchies during the fifteenth century.[42] Whatever
one thinks of this later assessment—and I believe that Engels still places
the process far too early in the development of capitalism—it clearly
constitutes a break with racial conceptions of the nation.[43]

The other, connected, factor was the realization that supposedly
"non-historic" nations could become "historic" through the process of
struggle. The particular nation to illustrate this type of transformation
was one that acquired ever-greater significance for both men during their
exile in Britain: Ireland. Engels fails to mention Ireland in "The Magyar
Struggle," yet as we have seen, both he and Marx originally regarded its
native inhabitants as equally "non-historic" as the Highland Gaels. And
as Rosdolsky correctly points out, the native Irish played as reactionary
a role in the British Revolution as the Highlanders, and one of much
greater political significance. Far from remaining so until the socialist
millennium, however, they had, within a century, ceased to be the main
basis of support for absolutist reaction in the British Isles and moved to
the forefront of revolutionary republicanism in Europe, where their role
was celebrated by, among other revolutionaries . . . Karl Marx and Frederick Engels.

By 1855, Marx was already expressing a more positive view of the
Irish in the *People's Paper:* "It is a . . . very remarkable phenomenon that in
the same measure as Irish influence in the *political* sphere grows in England,
the Celtic influence on the *social* sphere decreases in Ireland." His explanation for the latter aspect contained elements of the same belief in English
civilization that had characterised Engels's first comments on the question:
"Irish society is being radically transformed by an Anglo-Saxon revolution."[44] By the occasion of his visit to Ireland in 1856, Engels too was emphasizing the effects of colonial rule on shaping the Irish character:
"through systematic oppression, they have come to be a completely
wretched nation and now as everybody knows, they have the job of providing England, America, Australia, etc with whores, day labourers, maque-
reaux [that is, pimps], pickpockets, swindlers, beggars and other wretches.[45]

By the time Engels came to prepare notes for his uncompleted *History of Ireland,* after a second visit to Ireland in September 1868, his attitude has undergone a further shift. Now the stress is less on the oppressions the Irish people have endured at the hands of the British, with the consequent degeneration of their national character, and more on their resistance to that oppression. More importantly for our purposes, he also notes that although "the English have been able to reconcile people of the most diverse races to their rule," including the Scottish Highlanders, there is difference between the latter and the Irish, who alone "have proved too much for the English to cope with."[46] Ireland in this sense had national "advantages" that the Highlands lacked, and their assertion by the Fenians led Marx and Engels to reassess the source of Irish liberation and consequently to change their attitude to the Irish people. From being a consequence, almost an offshoot, of the revolutionary movement in Britain, Marx and Engels came to regard the revolution in Ireland not only as being brought about by the Irish themselves but as preceding that of Britain. Contrary to what is sometimes said, however, they did not believe that the former would cause the latter; rather they believed that it would weaken the British ruling class by removing from its control the land that was one of its main sources of wealth ("one *prerequisite* for the proletarian revolution in England"), ending the supply of cheap immigrant labor to British industry and ("most important of all!") resolving the hostility between the working classes of both countries caused by racism on the British side.[47] The most important thing about the shift is that it involves the tacit abandonment of the theory of "historic nations" as a determining factor in deciding which national movement to support—for Ireland was originally not one of these—and an assertion instead of the centrality of politics.

By mid-1870 Engels could draw definite conclusions from the failure of the Lowland Scots and the English to assimilate Ireland to Britain: "If . . . assimilation has failed after seven hundred years of struggle; if instead all the intruders who swept in over Ireland in waves, one after the other, were assimilated by *Ireland;* if, even at present, the Irish are no more English or "West Britons," as they are called, than the Poles are "West Russians" after a mere century of oppression, if the struggle is still not yet at an end and there is *no* prospect of any end at all except through the extermination of the oppressed race—if all this is so, then all the geographical excuses in the world will not suffice to prove that England's calling is to conquer Ireland."[48] As Engels wrote to Kautsky in February 1882, "I am of the opinion that *two* nations in Europe are not only entitled but duty bound to be national before they are international—Ireland and Poland."[49] To have attained parity with Poland—one of the nations described in "The Magyar Struggle" as having "actively intervened in history" and being "still capable of independent life"—can only mean that Engels had by this point completely, if implicitly, abandoned the notion of "non-historicity," which he used in relation to the Highlands as late as his *Commonwealth* article of 1866.[50]

How then can we explain the letter to Bernstein, also written in February 1882, in which Engels comes out in retrospective support for "put[ting] an end" to the activity of the "cattle thieves"? Surely this indicates that his attitude toward the historical clans had not changed? James Young is in the habit of quoting from this letter—in his habitual tone of injured sanctimony—to prove that Engels remained unregenerate over this issue to the end of his life.[51] It will be worthwhile, however, to consider what Engels is actually saying. He is discussing the necessity, under socialism, of "putting an end," not to peasant communities, but to banditry, to the ability of parasitic elements (such as existed in the Balkans during the 1880s and had existed in the Highlands before 1746) to live by stealing from the peasant community. This seems an eminently reasonable position, unless Young actually believes that one of the characteristics of socialism will be the conscious maintenance of antisocial gangs to prey on the citizenry.

Both Marx and Engels were acutely aware of the contradictory nature of "progress" in relation to capitalism. In a remarkable speech to celebrate the fourth anniversary of the Chartist periodical *The People's Paper* in 1856, Marx devoted the majority of his comments to this theme: "On the one hand, there have started into life industrial and scientific forces, which no epoch of former human history ever suspected. On the other hand, there exist symptoms of decay, far surpassing horrors recorded of the latter days of the Roman Empire."[52] His understanding of how "everything seems pregnant with its contrary" was also present in his concrete analysis of particular societies. Let us return to his writings on India, which as we saw earlier have been held to demonstrate his inconsistency or hypocrisy over the Highlands.

As Ahmad has written:"For buttressing the proposition that Marxism is not much more than a 'modes-of-production narrative' and that its opposition to colonialism is submerged in its positivistic 'myth of progress,' it is always very convenient to quote one or two journalistic flourishes from . . . 'The British Rule in India' and 'The Future Results of British Rule in India.'"[53] Said is an example of a writer availing himself of just such a convenience. Although he nowhere suggests that the first article is representative of Marx's views, his highlighting of particular passages from it implies that it can be treated as such. It is not the case that the article is beyond criticism. As Callinicos notes, it suffers from at least three major defects: a teleological attitude to history implied by the notion of England acting as "an unconscious tool"; a reliance on the concept of an unchanging "Asiaticism" that—whatever its relevance for earlier periods in history—cannot be justified in relation to nineteenth-century India; and—most relevantly for this discussion—an unqualified acceptance of the progressive impact of capitalism in areas where it had not previously existed.[54] Ahmad argues however that these weaknesses were in part the result of shortage of accurate information on Marx's part, particularly with regard to the nature of the dominant mode of production, Marx's "sustained oppositional practice" leading his materialism "in a direction where it is impelled to assert universal laws of its own, different from those it opposes, but without sufficient evidence of its own." But this is not all that there is to the article. As Ahmad writes, the best reference point for the argument it contains is not the notion of "Orientalism" but his own writings on the development of Western capitalism, "where the destruction of the European peasantry in the course of the primitive accumulation of capital is described in analogous tones, which I read as an enraged language of *tragedy*—a sense of colossal disruption and irretrievable loss, a moral dilemma wherein neither the old nor the new can be wholly affirmed, the recognition that the sufferer was at once decent and flawed, the recognition also that the history of victories and losses is really a history of material production, and the glimmer of hope, in the end, that something good might yet come out of this merciless history."[55] This is very well said, yet it still does not come to terms with the full complexity of Marx's views; for these, we must turn to the second article to which Ahmad refers, which Said ignores: "The Future Results of the British Rule in India."

Written on July 22 and published in the *New York Daily Tribune* on August 8, this second article clearly belongs to the same set of considerations as the first ("I propose . . . to conclude my observations about India"). That is to say, it is not a subsequent rethinking at a later date. Here the tragic dimensions of the Indian colonization are fully articulated: "All that the English bourgeoisie may be forced to do will neither emancipate nor materially mend the social condition of the mass of the people, *depending not only on the development of the productive powers, but on their appropriation by the people.*" Marx holds out two possible ways by which British rule can be ended—proletarian revolution in Britain itself or a colonial rebellion by the native population in India—before ending ("I cannot part with the subject of India without some concluding remarks") with a passage that dwells on the "profound hypocrisy and inherent barbarism of bourgeois civilization" in the colonies. The best that can be said for bourgeois society is that it has "laid the material basis of a new world" in "the mutual dependency of mankind" and "the development of the productive powers of man and the transformation of material production." As a result: "When a great social revolution shall have mastered the results of the bourgeois epoch, the market of the world and the modern powers of production, and subjected them to the common control of the most advanced peoples, then only will human progress cease to resemble that hideous pagan idol, who would not drink the nectar but from the skulls of the slain."[56] Even this magnificent passage is not without its ambiguities ("domination of natural agencies," "the most advanced peoples"), but as Callinicos writes, it can scarcely be accused of evading the consequences of British rule for the Indians.[57] More positively, the concept of progress that Marx employs here is not merely the development of the productive forces as such, but in so far as this "represents an expansion of human capacities," the potential for which can only be realized by a revolution, a revolution that, it will be noted, Marx does not suggest will necessarily be achieved for the Indians from outside. In the drafts of his letter to Zasulich during 1881 the change of perspective is made explicit: "As for the East Indies, for example, everybody except Sir Henry Maine and others of his ilk realizes that the suppression of communal landownership out there was nothing but an act of English vandalism, pushing the native peoples not forward but back."[58] It is clear from these comments that Marx not only refused to share the views of those who colonized India but also that his hostility to what they did there increased throughout his life.

The final position of both Marx and Engels is perhaps best expressed by the latter in a response of 1882 to one of Kautsky's endless requests for clarification:

> As I see it, the actual colonies, i.e. the countries occupied by European settlers, such as Canada, the Cape [i.e. South Africa], Australia, will all become independent; on the other hand, countries that are merely ruled and inhabited by natives, such as India, Algeria and the Dutch, Portuguese and Spanish possessions, will have to be temporarily taken over by the proletariat and guided as rapidly as possible towards independence. How this process will develop is very difficult to say. India may, indeed very probably will, start a revolution and, since the proletariat that is effecting its own emancipation cannot wage a colonial war, it would have to be given its head, which would obviously entail a great deal of destruction, but after all that is inseparable from any revolution. . . . Once Europe has reorganized, and North America, the resulting power would be so colossal and the example set will be such that the semi-civilized countries will follow suit quite of their own accord, their economic needs alone will see to that.

Engels closes his letter by stating the impossibility of saying how long it would take for the ex-colonies to reach socialism, only that it cannot be imposed upon them by a victorious proletariat in the metropolitan centers: "Only one thing is certain, namely that a victorious proletariat cannot forcibly confer any blessing whatever on another country without undermining its own activity in the process."[59] It could still be argued, however, that his opposition to the Highland Clearances was inconsistent with this theoretical position, and that he should have welcomed them with at least the same ambivalence as he did the modernizing role of the British in India. Such an argument would, however, be based on a misunderstanding of their nature.

Many socialists take their view of the Clearances from a misinterpretation of the discussion in chapter 27 of *Capital* Volume 1, "The Expropriation of the Agricultural Population from the Land."[60] Here Marx demonstrates how the expulsion of the rural population from their holdings, the enclosing of common land, and the turning over of arable land to pasture were crucial components of the "primitive accumulation of capital." These characteristics of the origins of capitalism can be traced in England back to the period after the Tudor accession in 1485. Reading about the Clearances in this context, many socialists have tended to assume that the Clearances were equally necessary for the establishment of capitalism in Britain and, indeed, were the last episode in the process. Grigor, for example, writes that "Marx and Engels, albeit very briefly, explained, or at least began to explain, the Clearances in terms of primitive accumulation of capital."[61] These claims are wrong, and quite unnecessarily provide Scottish nationalists like James Young or Harvie with a license to accuse Marxists of retrospectively endorsing the Clearances in the name of historical progress. Even if the Clearances had been necessary for capitalist development, the solidarity of socialists would still retrospectively be with the dispossessed peasants rather than with their oppressors, but the fact is that the Highland Clearances had nothing whatsoever to do with the primitive accumulation of capital.

The introduction of capitalist agriculture was so long delayed in the Highlands that the process was concentrated into a much shorter timescale than the original English pattern of enclosure and eviction. Consequently, as Marx noted, "the clearing of the land proceeded more ruthlessly."[62] Not only did the Highland Clearances have a different duration from that of, say, East Anglia, they also took place at a different time in the historical development of capitalism. The Highland Clearances are conventionally dated between 1760 and 1860, but the vast bulk of the enforced migrations fell within the latter half of this period and the outrages that accompanied them were being closely reported, particularly as the process reached its climax in the 1850s.[63] The newspapers during the period in which *Capital* was written seemed to show Marx what he had previously only observed in the writings of Sir Thomas More or Sir James Steuart. But by the time the Clearances were taking place—and certainly by the second phase—capitalism was already dominant throughout Britain and the working-class movement had begun to organize against it. While soldiers were helping expel tenants from their homes in Ross-shire during 1848, considerably greater numbers of them were mustering in Edinburgh to repel the Chartist challenge. If there is a parallel to the English "primitive accumulation" in Scotland it is not to be found in the Highlands, but in the transformation of the *Lowlands* between 1750 and 1780. The Highlands, far from being crucial to the development of British capitalism in any economic sense, were peripheral to it, which is where they remain to this day.[64]

What Marx was actually doing in *Capital*, apart from expressing his own moral revulsion at the Clearances, was drawing an *analogy* between the events then taking place in the Highlands and the original process of primitive accumulation, as if to say to his readers: "If you want to see what the process was like, this is the nearest parallel in the contemporary world." But clearing the land of people in the first half of the nineteenth century had different implications from doing so in the sixteenth, seventeenth, or eighteenth centuries. The Highland Clearances were carried out by an existing, and thoroughly rapacious, capitalist landowning class seeking to increase its income as efficiently as possible. Far from being "necessary" to the development of capitalism, the Highland Clearances were an example of the activities of an already triumphant capitalist class whose disregard for human life (and, indeed, "development") marked it as having long passed the stage of contributing to social progress. The difference between the Highlands and India, which accounts for the more ambivalent tone taken by Marx in relation to the former country, is therefore that the Highlands were already part of the capitalist world; India (and similar territories) were not, and would not succeed in becoming so without the external intervention of the existing capitalist states. The issue here is not that Marx was right about the supposed "immobility" of sections of Asian society—there is now a significant body of work that suggests he was in fact wrong—but that his views were an expression of this theoretical assessment, not a racist or "Eurocentric" disregard for the fate of Asian people.

INTERPRETATION 2: BACK TO COMMUNISM AND FORWARD TO COMMUNISM

The textual evidence to support Interpretation 2 can be presented more briefly, as it largely consists of two letters by Marx to Russian revolutionaries (one of which exists in several drafts) and of Engels's *The Origin of the Family*.[65] Let us look at these sources in turn.

In 1877 Marx wrote a letter to the Russian journal *Otechesivenniye Zapiski* criticising the interpretation of *Capital* made in its pages by the populist N. K. Mikhailovsky. Marx makes two points in this epistle.[66] The first is that the Russian peasant commune *may* provide the launching pad for the advance to Communism in Russia, but the possibility of that happening is *already* being undermined by the advance of capitalism. The second is that even if the latter development does come to fruition, it will not replicate exactly the earlier process in Western Europe, contrary to what is asserted by Mikhailovsky, who wants to turn a "historical sketch of the genesis of capitalism in Western Europe into a historic-philosophical theory of general development, imposed by fate on all peoples, whatever the historical circumstances in which they are placed, in order to eventually attain the economic formation which, with a tremendous leap of the productive forces of social labour, assures the most integral development of every individual producer." Marx was to repeat the first point in a letter to Vera Zasulich of March 8, 1881. He reaffirms his conviction that "the commune is the fulcrum of social regeneration in Russia," but then adds the same rider as in his earlier critique of Mikhailovsky: "in order that it may function as such, it would first be necessary to eliminate the deleterious influences which are assailing it from all sides, and then ensure for it the normal conditions of spontaneous development."[67] Under what conditions might the peasant commune play the role that Marx has suggested for it? These were outlined the following year in a preface, published under the names of both men, for the second Russian edition of the *Manifesto:* "The only possible answer today is this: if the Russian Revolution becomes the signal for a proletarian revolution in the West, so that the two complement each other, the present Russian common ownership of land may serve as the starting point for communist development."[68] That the victory of a revolutionary movement in the West could establish a socialist context for Russian development and thus avoid the fate of capitalism was in their view a possibility, but by no means a certainty.

In 1884, three years after Marx had given his assessment of the Russian situation (and only two years after Engels wrote to Bernstein retrospectively supporting the suppression of Highland cattle thieves), Engels wrote in *The Origin of the Family, Private Property and the State* that "the oldest Celtic laws" characteristic of primitive communism were "still in full bloom in Scotland in the middle of the last century" before clan organization "succumbed only to the arms, law and courts of the English" after 1746: "The precise function of the Scottish clan in this organization still awaits investigation; but that the clan is a gentile body is beyond doubt."[69] These remarks certainly indicate a more sympathetic attitude toward Highland society as it existed before 1746. Nevertheless, does the shift evident in Engels's position justify the positions associated with Interpretation 2? The very paucity of material to support Interpretation 2 means that later Marxists are drafted in to strengthen the case, notably John Maclean, who along with James Connolly is the greatest of all Scottish revolutionaries.[70]

Like Matheson, Maclean began political life as a member of the SDF. Unlike him, MacLean remained a member until the Russian Revolution convinced him of the political and organizational inadequacies of the Second International.[71] The clan societies of the Scottish Highlands (and Ireland) were treated positively by Maclean in a review of Thomas Johnston's *History of the Working Classes in Scotland* during 1920, in which he upbraided the author for failing to recognize the difference between the feudal and clan systems, namely "that in feudalized Scotland the abominations of serfdom obtained because of feudalism, whereas in those parts of the country that escaped feudalism and remained under the Celtic or communistic system these abominations were non-existent."[72] Earlier in the same year Maclean drew explicit parallels between the historical Scottish and contemporary Russian examples:

> The communism of the clans must be re-established on a modern basis. (Bolshevism, to put it roughly, is but the modern expression of the communism of the *mir.*) Scotland must therefore work itself into a communism embracing the whole country as a unit. The country must have but one clan, as it were—a united people working in co-operation and co-operatively, using the wealth that is created. We can safely say, then: back to communism and forward to communism.[73]

The political implications of this were spelled out in another article of 1920: "The old communal traditions of the clans must be revived and adapted to modern conceptions and conditions. If the Bolshevik notion of world communism through national communism is scientifically correct, then we are justified in utilising our latent Highland and Scottish sentiments and traditions in the mighty task confronting us of transforming capitalism into socialism."[74] Maclean had doubtless read *The Origin of the Family,* but could not have been aware of Marx's letter to Zasulich, since (although both the letter and the drafts were discovered by David Ryazanov in 1911) they were only published for the first time (in German and Russian) in 1924, the year after Maclean died.[75] By 1920 Maclean was committed to the demand for a Scottish Socialist Republic and is clearly using the supposed communist nature of the historical clans for two purposes: first, to reassure his readers that Communism was not an alien form of society in Scotland, but was already present in Scottish history; second, to make the Russian Communist experience more comprehensible by comparing Scottish clan society to the Russian mir. The merits or otherwise of Maclean's strategy during this period is not our concern here. (Although it is worth noting that the last quotation misrepresents the entire attitude to the mir, not merely of the Bolsheviks, but of the entire Russian Marxist movement from the Emancipation of Labour group onward.) The case is different from that of Matheson in relation to Interpretation 1, for Maclean is clearly following Engels's (if not Marx's) view of clan society. The issue is rather: was this view correct?

AGAINST INTERPRETATION 2

Interpretation 2 also combines in relation to the Scottish Highlands two general beliefs held by Marx and Engels, only in this case they are supposed to have arrived at them later on in their careers: the continued existence of communal property amidst a world capitalist economy and the possibility of societies based on this form of property becoming the basis of future Communist society. Again, these claims cannot be sustained. First, Marx and Engels were aware of the existence of what they took to be communal property in Scotland and in the contemporary colonial world from no later than 1853, over two decades before their encounter with Lewis Morgan and the Iroquois, but this assessment was in fact wrong, at least as far as Scotland was concerned. Second, they never believed that communal property could be the basis of modern Communism.

The first expression of the theory of patriarchal society in Marx's own work actually appears in the same article in which he attacks the Duchess of Sutherland, where we learn that "the *clan* system belonged to a form of social existence which, in the scale of historical development, stands a full degree below the feudal state; viz., the *patriarchal* state of society." He was also aware of the comparisons between this society in Scotland and in Asia: "The *clan* is nothing but a family organized in a military manner, quite as little defined by laws, just as closely hemmed in by traditions, as any family. But the land is the *property of the family*, in the midst of which differences of rank, in spite of consanguinity, do prevail as well as in all the ancient Asiatic family communities."[76] Marx means by "patriarchal," not primitive communism, but what is usually referred to as the Asiatic mode of production, the first form of class society to emerge, but one that nevertheless still maintained many features of that earlier state of equality. Marx believed that the land was still collectively owned by the clan, but was divided up amongst clan members according to their military function by the chief for nominal tributes: "These imposts were insignificant, more a tribute by which the supremacy of the *'great man'* and of his officers was acknowledged than a rent of land in the modern sense, or as a source of revenue." Engels only expressed this view in print much later, with the publication of *The Origin of the Family*, but took it further, identifying clan society with primitive communism itself. Engels drew the comparison again on the eve of his death in 1894: "It [i.e. common ownership] prevailed among the Germans, Celts, Indians—in short, all of the Indo-European peoples in primeval times; it was only recently suppressed by force in Ireland and Scotland, and although it is dying out, still occurs here and there in Germany today."[77] Where did these views come from?

The theory of social development ("modes of subsistence") bequeathed by the Scottish Enlightenment to Marx and Engels was one of the great intellectual achievements of the modern epoch and is particularly evident in the early sections of *The German Ideology*. Unfortunately, it also erroneously identified the inhabitants of the Scottish Highlands as examples of the first and most primitive stage of that development. The specific insertion of Highland society into the reworked Marxist theory ("modes of production") was carried on the basis of the writings of Sir Walter Scott, who was in many ways the climactic figure of the Scottish Enlightenment, but not, alas, a reliable guide to the nature of the Scottish Highlands.[78] Scott was as capable of comparing Highlanders to Native Americans or similar peoples as Macaulay. He wrote of the historical Rob Roy, subject of his novel of the same title, that: "Thus a character like his, blending the wild virtues, the subtle policy, and unrestrained licence of an American Indian, was flourishing in the Augustan age of Queen Anne and George I."[79] He was also capable of more sophisticated analysis. In a letter to Lord Dalkeith in 1806 he noted of clan organization: "The patriarchal right or dominion of a Chieftain of a Clan over those of the same name and who were presumed to be of the same family with himself—a right of dominion the most ancient in the world—was acknowledged in both countries, while the authority exercised by the lowland Scottish nobles and barons depended upon the feudal principle of Superior and vassal, or upon that of Landlord and tenant."[80] It was this concept of "patriarchal" society that was carried into the novels that were so admired by Marx. Eleanor Marx wrote of her father: "I should say that Scott was an author to whom Marx again and again returned, whom he admired and knew as well as he did Balzac and Fielding."[81] According to Paul Lafargue, Scott was among the "modern novelists whom he found the most interesting" and he considered *Old Mortality* "a masterpiece."[82] It is Engels, however, who makes the connection most clearly: "In Walter Scott's novels the Highland clan lives before our eyes."[83] The concept of "patriarchal" society was also carried into the work of Lewis Morgan, from where it was absorbed by the revolutionary duo again, reinforcing their original beliefs:

> The Celtic branch of the Aryan family retained, in the Scottish clan and Irish sept, the organization into gentes to a later period of time than any other branch of the family, unless the Aryans of India are an exception. The Scottish clan in particular was existing in remarkable vitality in the Highlands of Scotland in the middle of the last century. It is an excellent type of the gens in organization and spirit, and an extraordinary illustration of the power of the gentile life over its members. The illustrious author of *Waverley* has perpetuated a number of striking characters developed under clan life, and stamped with its peculiarities.[84]

Morgan had a significant influence on both men in that his book appeared to demonstrate, using the existing example of the Iroquois, the reality of "primitive communism."[85] Ironically, Morgan may have been more alert to the realities of Scottish history than Engels, writing at one point: "The same clans [as written about by Sir Walter Scot], a few centuries earlier, *when clan life was stronger and external influences were weaker,* would probably have verified the picture." In other words, the original clan organization had begun to dissolve before 1746.[86] But even this does not go far enough. In fact, Marx, Engels, Morgan, and Maclean all misunderstood the nature of Highland society, which was not dominated by the primitive communist or even Asiatic mode, but by one much more familiar in the West: feudalism.[87]

Clannic organization was typical of all human societies before the origin of classes. By the time the kingdom of the Scots was established in 1057, however, none of the original kinship groups survived anywhere in Europe, even in Scotland, where feudalism in the socioeconomic sense was dominant across the entire territory. The transition to feudalism involved the disintegration of the original clan lineages, and the substitution of notional familial identities in which clan membership signified little more than a political allegiance. This took place in several ways. One was "artificial kinship," where warriors swore to act as if they were kin of the chief. Another was the submission of one kin group to another, where the now subordinate leaders take on the role of headmen. Still another was where captives were brought up as warriors. The most important of all was where "companions" handpicked by the chief agreed to fight, in return for land, against their actual kin if necessary. The last was of course the very model of the vassal relationship at the core of military feudalism, and its existence undermines the view that clans were examples of primitive communist organization that had survived through geographical isolation into the early modern period. Indeed, even the type of military tenure supposedly introduced by David I, and allegedly so alien to the clan ethos, could be found in the Highlands well before the opening of his reign, albeit in a less systematic form than the Anglo-Norman model.

No clans are listed as fighting at the Battle of Bannockburn in 1314. Their appearance, or rather their reappearance, was a response by the Highland lords to events after the death of Robert I in 1329. The extent to which the power of the central state collapsed after this date was unparalleled in Western Europe. No monarch ascended the throne as an adult between 1390 and 1625, and between 1406 and 1587 alone there were nearly one hundred years of minority and regency rule. "Feudalism collapsed as a vehicle for unity," writes Christopher Smout, "and became instead the vehicle of faction."[88] The collapse was general throughout Scotland, but in the Highlands the process of fragmentation continued even after relative stabilization had been achieved in the Lowlands. The second coming of the clan system was therefore a product of the general chaos of these centuries.[89] There were three options for a local lord who wished to hold onto power with any degree of legitimacy in the eyes of his followers, rival lords, and the crown—although, given the weakness of the monarchy for much of this period, the crown was often the least important: first, the straightforward imposition of the feudal military relationship on those lesser landowners who had previously held land directly from the Crown, but now agreed to hold it as a subvassal of the lord; second, by "banding" or "bonding," whereby men formed alliances, either as equals or where the lesser man bound himself and his followers to obey the greater in return for protection; and third, by claiming authority as the senior in a real or (more usually) imagined kin group. These methods were common to both Lowland and Highland Scotland, but only in the latter did they lead to the formation of clanships.

The physical qualities of the Highland region had a bearing on this outcome in two ways. On the one hand, the expanses of moor and mountain that comprises much of the Highlands presented natural obstacles to permanent human settlements and acted as physical barriers between those that did exist. The true distinctiveness of the Highland region lies, however, at a still deeper geological level. The amount of rock that breaks down into soil is as low as one percent in many areas, resulting in a land supremely inhospitable to arable farming. Agriculture in much of the Highlands was therefore mainly pastoral by necessity. On the other hand, communities already widely scattered by the nature of the terrain, and whose main produce took the mobile form of cattle (and to a lesser extent sheep and goats), were more susceptible to attack and theft than even their Lowland counterparts. The threat of a subsistence crisis, too, was ever-present. In such circumstances the defensive political structures developed by the local lords, usually formed out of the "bonding" and "kinship" options, gave them some level of security. In return for joining his host and taking his name, the lord-cum-chief would promise military protection and a guaranteed food supply in times of need.

The political groupings typical of the transition from tribal to feudal society had therefore returned to the Highlands (and, for a shorter period, the Borders) of Scotland: the core minority of gentry with real blood ties to the chief; the septs or kin groups with their own chiefs who accepted his authority as the more powerful; and the conquered groups and "broken men" who would otherwise have been outside any defensive structure. Had the quasi-egalitarianism of the original clan societies returned with them? Three supposedly distinct aspects of clan life in particular are cited to support the view that they represented a permanent bonding of "kin" whose loyalties and activities lay outwith the structure of feudal society.

The first was the practice of collective agriculture. The form of tenure known as runrig is often thought to have involved communal farming, with the strips of land being reallocated by lot on an annual or at least regular basis, so that the best land was never permanently in the possession of any one tenant family. In fact, runrig was practiced in parts of Scotland other than the Highlands and involved a type of shareholding tenancy. Tenancy granted on these terms gave each shareholder a separate title to a specific *quantity* of land, but not to a specific *location,* which might vary at different times in the history of the lease. The allocation of the actual land would happen either at the start of a lease or upon its renewal, which—given the short-term nature of most leases—would often be on an annual basis, but this would be a condition of the individual lease, not a collective decision by the tenants.[90] In short, far from representing what Weber called a "diluted village communism," it is hard to see runrig as anything other than a form of private property in land.[91]

The second supposedly distinctive aspect of clan life was less the material situation of the Highland peasant than the beliefs they held about their place in society. The peasants who took the name of Fraser or MacDonald or Campbell were aware that this was a symbolic act.[92] But whereas Lowland peasants knew how dependent their continued occupancy of the land was on the will of the lord, Highland clan members believed that they had rights as kinsmen of the chief—artificial or not—to heritable possession of the land. The chiefs were prepared to encourage this belief as long as they needed the presence of fighting men on their territory, but, as was to become all too apparent after 1746, a right that subsists on the sufferance of the powerful is no right at all.

The third and final distinctive aspect of clan society was the fact that clan territories tended to cut across those of the heritable jurisdictions. If peasants had all been tenants of the chief whose name they adopted, then clanship would appear little more than an elaboration of existing feudal relationships, but their conditions of life drove many to seek the protection of the nearest lord capable of delivering it, even though he was not their own feudal superior and indeed might even be in dispute with their feudal superior, as the Camerons of Locheil and MacLeans of Duart were with the House of Argyll. At one level, therefore, clanship appears to be both different and perhaps opposed to feudalism. At a deeper level, however, the differences and oppositions assume a lesser significance. A feudal superior might indeed act as chief to a clan whose members only partially corresponded to his own tenants, but if some clan members were not his tenants they would certainly be those of some other lord. None of the peasantry was free from the necessity of handing over the product of their labor to one lord or another, and it was this labor that provided the wealth enjoyed by the Highland nobles, whether they were considered lords, or chiefs, or both. Indeed, those who entered a clan led by a man who was not their feudal superior might also have to pay a tribute to him *in addition* to paying feudal rent to their lord. Clan organization was therefore not only *compatible with* but also *dependent upon* the feudal exploitation of the peasantry and must therefore be understood as part of the political superstructure of Scottish feudalism; it corresponded to no other mode of production. There is a certain irony in the fact that, contrary to the myths of Highland exceptionalism, by 1688 the majority of the clans had organized themselves on the classic military-feudal system of vassalage supposedly so alien to their nature. Indeed, Scotland may well have been one of the last areas in Europe, outside of Poland, where such organization still flourished at the end of the seventeenth century. The differences between Highland and Lowland society were therefore matters of degree rather than of kind. If anything, the clans, far from being *opposed* to feudalism, were *representative* of its most extreme form.

Where does this leave the argument that Marx and Engels believed primitive communism, where it still existed, could act as the basis for that overthrow? It will be recalled that this was an open question for them in relation to Russia. By January 1894 it had become clear which direction events had taken. In the "Afterword" to "On Social Relations in Russia"— his last intervention on this subject—Engels attempts to compile a balance sheet that is clearly loaded against those who still expected the peasant commune to act as the social basis of the Russian Revolution. The Russian commune, he notes, "has already forgotten how to till its land for the common good"; its ultimate salvation must await "the industrial proletarians of the West." Engels explicitly links the Russian experience to that of Scotland:

"The Russian commune has existed for hundreds of years without ever providing the impetus for the development of a higher form of common ownership out of itself; no more than in the case of the German Mark system, the Celtic Clans, the Indian and other communes with primitive, communistic institutions." In response to the capitalist impositions all "lost more and more of their communistic character and dissolved into communities of mutually independent landowners." Engels notes that the few thousand Russians who are aware of the problems that capitalism will bring to their nation are as isolated from and as irrelevant to the 50 million who live in the commune as Robert Owen was to the Scottish working class who filled his factories: "And, of the working men Owen employed in his factory in New Lanark, the majority likewise consisted of people who had been raised on the institutions and customs of a decaying communistic gentile society, the Celtic-Scottish clan; but nowhere does he so much as hint that they showed a greater appreciation of his ideas." Why? Primitive communism is incapable of producing out of itself "the future socialist society, this final and most intrinsic product of capitalism": "Any given economic formation has its own problems to solve, problems arising out of itself; to seek to solve those of another, utterly alien formation would be utterly absurd. *And this applies to the Russian commune no less than to the South Slav Zadruga, the Indian Gentile community or any other savage or barbaric form of society characterised by the common ownership of production.*" With typical generosity of spirit toward Russian revolutionaries of the time, Engels adds that "we do not blame them for regarding their Russian compatriots as the chosen people of the social revolution. But this does not mean that we need to share their illusions." There seems no good reason to revive these illusions today.[93]

If the "peasant commune" was not to be the basis of socialism in backward Russia at the end of the nineteenth century it was clearly of no relevance whatsoever in Scotland, which had been at the forefront of capitalist development since the latter half of the eighteenth century. Contrary to what is sometimes asserted, this was understood by Maclean. For all that he shared the mistaken views of Marx and Engels concerning the historical nature of clan society, he also shared their correct assessment, expressed by Engels in the 1894 "Afterword," of how little this mattered in the contemporary struggle for socialism. Maclean's evocations of the clan system talk of "re-establishing" and "reviving" the communism of the clans, which suggests—quite rightly—that it no longer exists and must be created anew for the whole of Scotland, as a result of the proletarian revolution.

CONCLUSION

Marx and Engels made two theoretically compatible claims about the nature of Highland society and advanced two apparently incompatible political positions (one of them retrospective) based on those claims. I want to argue in conclusion that although neither claim can be upheld in the light of modern research, both political positions were in fact correct, in relation to the different historical periods for which they were formulated.

The theoretical claims involved defining Highland society in two ways: on the one hand, politically, as a "non-historic" nation unable to attain statehood and consequently condemned to rely on the forces of counter-revolution—in this case the Stuart dynasty and the French absolutist state—for national preservation (Engels); on the other, socioeconomically, as a formation transitional between primitive communism and class society of the type that would later be described as being based on the Asiatic mode of production (Marx). The category of "non-historic" nations is an idealist one whose lack of explanatory or predictive power in relation to Ireland led Engels eventually to abandon it, but even had the category possessed greater validity, it would still have been irrelevant in the context of the Highlands since the Highlanders did not think of themselves as constituting a nation, nor were they the only or (the '45 apart) even the main supporters of Jacobite counter-revolution between 1688 and 1746. Equally, had Highland society been as Scott described, then Marx would have been correct to assimilate it to the Asiatic mode of production, but it was not, and the classification on these terms fails on simple empirical grounds. In fact, the Highlands were dominated by the feudal mode of production, albeit in the "classical" military variant that had by 1746 been superseded across the rest of Western Europe.

The political positions involve the alleged discrepancy between the respective positions of Marx and Engels. The first was that the defeat of the Jacobite rising of 1745–46 was necessary for the development of British capitalism. The second is that the clearing of the estates between 1780 and 1860 was a crime against the Highland population. James Young asks: "How can Marxists argue that the extermination of the Scottish Highlanders was necessary for the growth of capitalism, and yet

77

morally criticize the historical actors who brought this about?"[94] The first position is that of Engels in "The Magyar Struggle"; the second, that of Marx in *Capital*. Is there a way of resolving this apparent contradiction? The term "extermination" (which is in any case hyperbolic) conflates the repression directly after Culloden, in which hundreds were killed, with the Clearances themselves, in which thousands were forced to leave their homes. Yet although these processes are clearly linked, they also fall into distinct historical times. The general point is well made by Vogel, who notes of Marx (and I take this to include Engels) that

> until the contingent fact of the advent of the working class, there was no satisfactory resolution for, or conduct-guiding political answers available to, the question of what we should do as historical or political agents. Before the development of the working class our choice was either to support the suppression and misery of the masses or to oppose economic and cultural development and the potential for human liberation. Neither of these is minimally acceptable.... Now we have a political choice other than choosing either to suppress the masses or to stop human progress. The development of the working class is the basis for Marx's political recommendations, which allows him to act on the basis both of action of human dignity and human progress.[95]

It is in this context that we must look for an explanation of the apparent difference between Marx and Engels over the fate of the Highlanders.

The Jacobite rebellions whose suppression Engels retrospectively supported took place in a period when the survival of capitalism was still precarious ("our choice was either to support the suppression and misery of the masses or to oppose economic and cultural development"). The fact that both he and Marx overestimated the importance of the Highlands as the basis of Jacobite support and misunderstood the precise nature of Highland society does not infirm this judgment: inside Scotland the Jacobite movement was based on a precapitalist social class (the lesser feudal gentry—some of whom were also clan chiefs); outside Scotland it was allied to precapitalist states (principally France). The alternative to the Hanoverian victory in 1746 was the dismemberment of the United Kingdom and the effective reduction of the British Isles to dependencies of absolutist France. Nor would this outcome have saved the Highlands, since the Stuarts, no longer dependent on Highland support, would no doubt have resumed the absolutist onslaught against the clans that they had pursued (except at times of crisis) since 1455, but would now have done so with the support of the most powerful state in Europe. No social force existed that could have offered a positive outcome for the Highlanders. Not even Armstrong, who has argued that an alliance between the English Levellers and Scottish and Irish "clan democracy" in the mid-seventeenth century could have bypassed "Western capitalist development," believes that a similar alliance was possible by 1746. It is therefore with this period in Highland history, rather than that of the Clearances, that Marx's comments on India have the greatest relevance.

The Clearances themselves, however, although separated from the aftermath of Culloden by mere decades, belong to a different period of historical time, one in which capitalism was already triumphant and, in Marx's view, on the verge of being overthrown. ("Now we have a political choice other than choosing either to suppress the masses or to stop human progress.") For Marx the "clearing of estates" was, not a tragic but unavoidable aspect of capitalist development, but one of the brutal and avoidable aspects of capitalism as the dominant mode of production. The tragedy that the Highlanders experienced was not, as it was after the '45, that no social force existed that could have come to their aid, but that the social force that did exist failed to do so. The landlords were not predestined to *succeed* in driving their tenants off the land, since the Clearances took place against the development of the labor movement in Scotland, from the Friends of the People through the United Scotsmen, the Radicals of 1820, and finally to the Chartists. What we are registering here is the failure of that movement to intervene or to intervene sufficiently to prevent the tragedy of the Highlanders.[96]

In the 1880s, Highland crofting communities were to rise in the first successful struggles for tenurial rights that we know as the Highland Land War. James Hunter has noted, in the second edition of his great work on the crofting communities of the Western Highlands, that a Marxist theoretical framework was essential for him to tell the story of that struggle and those that followed it.[97] If the framework had simply been one that either uncritically welcomed the development of the productive forces under capitalism, or unthinkingly expected socialism to circumvent capitalist development altogether through the agency of "clan democracy," it is unlikely that it would have been of much use to Hunter, or indeed anybody else. But Marx and Engels were involved in neither apologetics nor utopianism. They understood that the expansion of the productive forces brought about by capitalism was a necessary condition for the ultimate goal of human emancipation, because without it there will be neither a working class to seize power from the capitalists nor a sufficient level of material resources with which to feed, clothe, house, or educate the world's population. It was also an insufficient condition, because unless the working class was conscious and organized it would not succeed in achieving its revolutionary potential. But the objective situation (the existence of capitalism) precedes the subjective (the conscious mobilization of the social classes that capitalism has brought into being).

The possession of this general theory enabled them to correctly evaluate the political meaning of historical and contemporary events in the Scottish Highlands, despite the errors and misconceptions that they inherited about clan society. Their writings on this subject are entirely compatible with the overall attitude to capitalism that they maintained from *The German Ideology* to the end of their lives. Shorn of the misinterpretations that this article has tried to correct, they offer no reason why Marxists should either abandon their tradition or believe that Marx and Engels themselves did so.

ᴥ Chapter 3 ᴥ

The Prophet, His Biographer, and the Watchtower
Isaac Deutscher's Biography of Leon Trotsky[1]

Introduction

The materialist conception of history was once described by a notable practitioner, the late Edward Thompson, as "perhaps the strongest discipline deriving from the Marxist tradition."[2] Of all the different modes available to that discipline, biography is the least commonly employed. Why? One reason is that, while Marxism does not deny the role of individuals in the historical process, the balance required by Marxist biographers in relation to their subjects is extraordinarily difficult to achieve. Focus too narrowly on their lives, and run the risk of treating the social context in which they played their role as a mere historic backdrop. Place too much emphasis on their times, and stand in danger of reducing them to the sum of the social forces that shaped their personalities. It is not entirely surprising, therefore, that there are very few biographies among the classics of Marxist historiography.[3] The exceptions, such as Thompson's own *William Morris* (1955 and 1977), tend to be excursions into

81

the genre by writers whose reputations rest on works of broader scope than any one individual.

There are two main Marxist responses to the difficulties that biography presents. One, long established, but relevant only when dealing with conventionally important historical figures, is the "political" biography. Here, attention is mainly restricted to the public world of theoretical controversy and organizational affiliation, without the complications inherent in dealing with the inner life. The other, more recent response has become known as "microhistory." Here, the focus is on otherwise anonymous individuals whose experiences can be taken as either characteristic of a distinct way of life or emblematic of a particular historical moment. Both approaches have resulted in important work.[4] Both approaches also involve serious problems. In the first, the subject rarely emerges in the round and, indeed, often simply becomes the embodiment of a series of political positions. In the second, the full human personality is more likely to be represented, but often at the expense of revealing anything of significance about the wider society it inhabited.

Given these difficulties, the achievements of Isaac Deutscher (1907–1967) are all the more remarkable. Of all the great Marxist historians, he was unusual, perhaps unique, in making biography his primary mode of expression. With the exception of a handful of substantial essays, most of which were posthumously collected in *Marxism, Wars and Revolutions* (1984), Deutscher's biographies, *Stalin* (1949 and 1966) and *Trotsky* (1954–1963), are his central and most enduring legacy. It is fair to say that not everyone shares this opinion, including many of his erstwhile admirers. David Horowitz, former US student radical, author of *From Yalta to Vietnam* (1965), and subsequent convert to neoconservatism, wrote in the course of a dispute with Christopher Hitchens: "When all is said and done the Trotsky biography must be seen as an incomparably sad waste of a remarkable individual talent."[5] Horowitz has, at any rate, read it. Others have suggested that even this effort is unnecessary. Martin Amis informs us, in the course of yet another dispute with Hitchens, that he has fairly definite views about Trotsky, whom he describes as "a murdering bastard and a fucking liar. And he did it with gusto. He was a nun-killer—they [i.e., the Bolsheviks] all were. The only thing that can be entered in the other side of the ledger is that he paid a price that was very nearly commensurate. Death was visited on him and all his clan." It therefore

comes as no surprise to learn on the previous page from this outburst
that: "No, I haven't read Isaac Deutscher's *The Prophet Armed* and *The
Prophet Unarmed* and *The Prophet Outcast,* but I have read Volkogonov's
Trotsky: The Eternal Revolutionary."[6] Martin, we had guessed as much.
Horowitz, Amis, and Hitchens are a trio of political corpses in search of
a decent burial; we can safely leave them to their literary dance of death.
What can those who still want to oppose the new rulers of the world
rather than grovel at their feet learn from these books? Whatever the problems with Deutscher's political judgments—and as we shall see these are
considerable—any criticism of them must start from the simple recognition that they represent not only a model of Marxist biography but also
two of the essential histories of the Russian Revolution written in any
historical mode. The history of the Russian Revolution is refracted
through the lives of two of the three great protagonists, but the revolution
is never relegated to the background, nor are the protagonists ever detached from the process.[7] Verso is therefore to be congratulated for re-
publishing the Trotsky trilogy and making one of the classic works of
socialist literature available to a new generation of activists.

THE QUALIFICATIONS OF A BIOGRAPHER

A general level of imaginative sympathy is, of course, necessary for any
biographer to engage with his or her subject. In Deutscher's case, this
faculty seems to have been heightened in relation to Trotsky because
of four specific personal characteristics or experiences that the two men
had in common.[8]

First, they shared a political commitment. Deutscher joined the Communist Party of Poland in 1926 or 1927 when the factional struggle within
Russia was reaching its climax. He was quickly elevated to the leadership
and remained there until his expulsion in 1932 for opposing, in the party
press, the disastrous Stalinist policy in Germany. He was, in other words,
one of the very few Communists who both accepted and was prepared to
act on Trotsky's analysis. Deutscher helped form the Polish Trotskyist organization and led it throughout the 1930s. Furthermore, unlike most of
the Trotskyist leaders of the time, he was capable of independent thought:
the Polish delegates to the founding conference of the Fourth International
in September 1938 carried his—essentially correct—arguments against
proclaiming the new organization at that time.[9]

Second, they shared the experience of exile. While in London seeking work as a journalist in 1939 Deutscher was stranded by the outbreak of the Second World War and the partition of his country between the Third Reich and Stalinist Russia. He joined the Polish Home Army in Scotland, but spent much of the war in a detention camp for political undesirables as a result of his opposition to the anti-Semitism he found in its ranks. His political opposition to the regime imposed by Stalin after 1945 meant that he was never able to return to Poland. Deutscher once wrote of Trotsky that "like Thucydides, Dante, Machiavelli, Heine, Marx, Herzen, and other thinkers and poets, Trotsky attained his full eminence as a writer only in exile."[10] These sentiments equally apply to their author.

Third, they shared exclusion from academic life. Trotsky had not the slightest desire to be included, of course, and the very idea of the great revolutionary ensconced in the groves of academe is grotesquely comic. In Deutscher's case, however, it would have saved him from relying on journalism for a living, since his writing in this capacity is by far the weakest part of his output. After the Second World War, Deutscher supported himself by working for bourgeois publications like the *Economist* and the *Observer*. When the Cold War closed off even these options, he was forced to promote himself as an expert on Russia and the Stalinist bloc. There is no doubt that his ensuing work as a Sovietologist was often highly speculative and his predictions mostly wrong. Nevertheless, as Peter Sedgwick wrote in an obituary in *International Socialism*, it is misguided to criticize Deutscher on the basis of what he wrote while carrying out what was, in effect, his day job: "It is as if Marx's theoretical standing was to be criticised on the basis of the rubbish he wrote against Palmerston in the Tory press."[11] Deutscher was not, of course, alone in the Trotskyist tradition in standing outside academia. Perry Anderson has identified three of Trotsky's "heirs" who "filled no chairs in universities": Deutscher himself, Roman Rosdolsky, and Ernest Mandel.[12] The parallels between the first two are fairly exact, in that Rosdolsky was also a Left Oppositionist exiled to the United States from his native Ukraine after the Second World War, where he abandoned direct political activity in order to write his classic *The Making of Marx's "Capital"* (1968). Mandel's situation was somewhat different in that he—a party man his entire life—had the resources, however meager, of the Fourth International behind him. At least all three of these men were able to write in relative tranquillity. Victor Serge, another exiled Left Oppositionist and the only one to equal Deutscher in literary terms, was denied even this. When Deutscher could have benefited from a university position in Britain, to enable him the time and a regular income to complete his *Life of Lenin,* he was denied one on political grounds. The circumstances of this episode are interesting for what they reveal about the cowardice and hypocrisy of Cold War liberalism. In 1963 the University of Sussex offered Deutscher a professorship as Head of Soviet Studies. The offer was first suspended then withdrawn as the direct result of an intervention by Isaiah Berlin, then a member of the University Board. Berlin wrote to the vice-chancellor of Deutscher that he was "the only man whose presence in the same academic community as myself I should find morally intolerable." (Obviously this had nothing whatsoever to do with Deutscher's Marxism, or his anti-Zionism, or the fact that he had earlier launched a devastating attack on Berlin's ignorant claim that Marx believed in historical inevitability.) Berlin even made the—highly implausible—claim that he would have supported other radicals like C. Wright Mills or Eric Hobsbawm who, unlike Deutscher, "did not subordinate scholarship to ideology." Shamefully, but typically, Michael Ignatieff defends his hero in these terms: "The difficulty lay in supposing that Deutscher could be trusted to teach non-Marxist concepts with the fairness requisite in a university teacher." Berlin's sabotaging of Deutscher's chance for an academic career is therefore "a fair enough application of the standards of liberal tolerance in a university."[13] This probably tells us all we need to know about "liberal tolerance." Actually, Deutscher's scholarship, at least in his serious historical work, was usually impeccable. Unlike, one might add, that of the sainted Sir Isaiah: his *Karl Marx* (1939 and 1960), particularly the first edition, is a byword for factual inaccuracy and elementary theoretical misunderstandings (even Ignatieff has to concede that "its defects are obvious enough").[14] Indeed, so bad is this book that it might almost tempt one into making ludicrously sweeping statements like: "The difficulty lay in supposing that Berlin could be trusted to teach Marxist concepts with the fairness requisite in a university teacher."

Fourth, Deutscher and Trotsky shared a command of literary expression.[15] Like another Pole from an earlier generation of exiles, Joseph Conrad, Deutscher mastered the English language rather better than many a native. In his major works, socialist commitment and firsthand knowledge of the labor movement are combined with a technical skill in handling primary source materials. Indeed, his abilities in this sphere put to shame many of those academics who spent their professional lives doing little more than warming the professorial chairs that he was denied. One advantage he retained from being denied access to university employment, however, was the freedom to write for a general audience, unconstrained by the bloodless conventions of British academic propriety. Two examples, out of the many that could be chosen, convey not only his descriptive powers but also how irony—now mainly used as a self-congratulatory sign of one's postmodern sensibility—can be part of the historian's repertoire. Here, we are shown the Red Army as it attempts to retake the naval fortress at Kronstadt during the sailors' and soldiers' rebellion:

> White sheets over their uniforms, the Bolshevik troops, under Tukhachevsky's command, advanced across the Bay. They were met by hurricane fire from Kronstadt's bastions. The ice broke under their feet; and wave after wave of white-shrouded attackers collapsed into the glacial Valhalla. The death march went on. From three directions fresh columns stumped and fumbled and slipped and crawled over the glassy surface until they too vanished in fire, ice, and water. As the successive swarms and lines of attackers drowned, it seemed to the men of Kronstadt that the perverted Bolshevik revolution drowned with them and that the triumph of their own pure, unadulterated revolution was approaching. Such was the lot of these rebels, who had denounced the Bolsheviks for their harshness and whose only aim it was to allow the revolution to imbibe the milk of human kindness, that for their survival they fought a battle which in cruelty was unequalled throughout the civil war.[16]

And here we follow the Russian peasants—the so-called kulaks—as they slaughter and eat their own animals rather than see them collectivized:

> So began the strange carnival over which despair presided and for which fury filled the fleshpots. An epidemic of orgiastic gluttony spread from village to village, from *volost* to *volost,* and from *gubernia* to *gubernia*. Men, women and children gorged themselves, vomited, and went back to the fleshpots. Never before had so much vodka been brewed in the country—almost every hut had become a distillery—and the drinking was, in the old Slav fashion, hard and deep. As they guzzled and gulped, the kulaks illuminated the villages with bonfires they made of their own barns and

stables. People suffocated with the stench of rotting meat, with the vapours of vodka, with the smoke of their blazing possessions, and with their own despair. Such was the scene upon which a brigade of collectivizers descended to interrupt the grim carouse with the rattle of machine-guns. The smallholder perished as he had lived, in pathetic helplessness and barbarism; and his final defeat was moral as well as economic and social.[17]

It is—to use a Marxist cliché that Deutscher generally avoids—no accident that the first quotation concerns the impasse that the revolution had reached by 1921 and the second the consequences of its final destruction in 1928. There are very few passages of comparable power describing the victorious days of worker insurgency in 1905 or—especially—1917. I will return to this point below as it reveals a problem with Deutscher's attitude to the working class. And, despite all that he had in common with Trotsky, it also suggests a fundamental political divide between the biographer and his subject. But there will be time to criticize Deutscher in due course; I want first to complete our overview of his achievement.

Although the politics of the Russian Revolution are at the heart of these books, they never display the tendency toward depersonalization that, as I suggested above, is often a feature of "political" biography. Deutscher does not avoid this trap simply by filling the book with trivial personal detail; instead he situates the personality of Trotsky as a factor in political developments. At the beginning of *The Prophet Armed* we are introduced to the proud and impetuous youth who is prepared to follow any idea of which he is convinced to its logical conclusion; we still recognize him at the end of that volume in the leader determined to impose militarization of the trade unions if that is what it takes to preserve the revolutionary state. Equally, Deutscher can suggest analogies between the fate of individuals and societies, and the connection between the two, without extending these into absurdity. A chapter in *The Prophet Outcast* called "Reason and Unreason" deals, among other things, with the rise of Fascism in Germany. Here, Deutscher gently draws a parallel between the psychological collapse and suicide in Berlin of Trotsky's eldest daughter, Zina, and the descent into madness of the German society in which she vainly sought refuge.[18]

Let us explore one example of his approach in more detail. Trotsky was universally recognized as one of the great orators of the socialist movement—as great as Jean Jaurès, it is said. Throughout the trilogy,

Deutscher takes the relationship of Trotsky as a public speaker to his audience as both a barometer of the health of the Revolution and an index
of his personal fate. To begin with, between February and October 1917,
we see Trotsky addressing the thronging crowds at the Cirque Moderne
in Petrograd as an agitator and member of a Bolshevik Party still con-
testing for leadership of the working class:

> He spoke on the topics of the day and the aims of the revolution with
> his usual piercing logic; but he also absorbed the spirit of the crowd, its
> harsh sense of justice, its desire to see things in sharp and clear outline,
> its suspense, and its great expectations. Later he recollected how at the
> mere sight of the multitude words and arguments he had prepared well
> in advance receded and dispersed in his mind and other words and ar-
> guments, unexpected by himself but meeting a need in his listeners,
> rushed up as if from his subconscious. He then listened to his own voice
> as to that of a stranger, trying to keep pace with the tumultuous rush of
> his own ideas and phrases and afraid lest like a sleepwalker he might sud-
> denly awake and break down. Here his politics ceased to be the distilla-
> tion of individual reflection or of debates in small circles of professional
> politicians. He merged emotionally with the warm dark human mass in
> front of him, and became its medium.[19]

Later, in 1921, after the Civil War, the suppression of the Kronstadt rebellion,
and the introduction of New Economic Policy, we find Trotsky addressing
the crowds in an official capacity, as a senior member of the ruling party:

> Trotsky's appearance and speech still thrilled the crowds. But he no
> longer seemed to find the intimate contact with his audiences which he
> found unerringly during the civil war . . . Trotsky on the platform ap-
> peared more than life-size; and his speech resounded with all its old
> heroic tones. Yet the country was tired of heroism, of great vistas, high
> hopes, and sweeping gestures; and Trotsky still suffered from the slump
> in his popularity caused by his recent attempts to militarize Labor. His
> oratorical genius still cast its spell on any assembly. But the spell was al-
> ready shot through with doubt and even suspicion. His greatness and
> revolutionary merits were not doubted; but was he not too spectacular,
> too flamboyant, and perhaps too ambitious?[20]

Later still, in 1926, as Stalin and his faction consolidate their grip on
power, Trotsky and the other leaders of the Opposition are depicted at-

tempting to take their case to the rank and file in party cells and work-place meetings:

> Trotsky made surprise appearances at large meetings held in Moscow's motor–car factory and railway workshops. But . . . for the first time in nearly thirty years, for the first time since he had begun his career as a revolutionary orator, Trotsky found himself facing himself helplessly. Against the scornful uproar with which he was met and the obsessive hissings and hootings, his most cogent arguments, his genius for persuasion, and his powerful and sonorous voice were of no avail.[21]

Finally, we observe the circumstances of Trotsky's last public meeting, late in 1932. Now three years into his last exile, he speaks at the invitation of Danish social democratic students whose politics were distant from his own (he describes them as "opponents" in the speech), and under the threat of attack from Stalinists or Fascists or both:

> The lecture passed without obstruction or disturbance. For two hours, speaking in German, he addressed an audience of about 2,000 people. His theme was the Russian Revolution. As the authorities had allowed the lecture on the condition that he would avoid controversy, he spoke in a somewhat professorial manner, giving his listeners the quintessence of the three volumes of his just concluded History [of the Russian Revolution]. His restraint did not conceal the depth and force of his conviction; the address was a vindication of the October Revolution, all the more effective be-cause free from apologies and frankly acknowledging partial failures and mistakes. Nearly twenty-five years later members of the audience still re-called the lecture with vivid appreciation as an oratorical feat.[22]

In each of these successive incarnations, from agitator to statesman to oppositionist to exile, Trotsky's oratorical powers remain the same, but their effect is conditioned by the circumstances in which he is called upon to use them. Thus Deutscher, while unraveling the specifics of Trot-sky's life, illustrates the truth of the general Marxist proposition that human beings not only make history under conditions unchosen by themselves, but that these conditions also determine whether it is possible to make history at all.

THE REVOLUTIONARY AS TRAGIC HERO

For nearly a decade the only work that stood comparison in scale with Deutscher's was E. H. Carr's *History of the Bolshevik Revolution*. But Carr wrote like the senior civil servant that, for at least part of his life, he was; Deutscher wrote, in Peter Sedgwick's phrase, as a "tragedian."[23] What does tragedy mean in this context? The distance between human aspirations and the material conditions that might allow them to be realized is necessary, but insufficient. Also required is the attempt to overcome that distance, "to beat against history with one's fists," no matter how unyielding the stuff of history might be. Trotsky himself offered the example of the French revolutionary, Gracchus Babeuf: "Babeuf's struggle for Communism in a society which was not yet ready for it was a struggle of a classical hero with his fate. Babeuf's destiny had all the characteristics of true tragedy, just as the fate of the Gracchi had whose name Babeuf used."[24] Trotsky rejected the notion of tragedy as illegitimate with respect to his own life. In 1929, at the end of the first year of his third and final exile from Russia, he wrote in his autobiography that he had "more than once read musings in the newspapers on the subject of the 'tragedy' that has befallen me." Against these musings he declared that: "I know no *personal* tragedy."[25] At the time when he wrote this passage, the point seemed doubly justified. On the one hand, the fate of the Russian Revolution was the collective experience of the Russian people. Trotsky had no wish to elevate his own share of that experience to a special category simply because of his fall from political preeminence. On the other, it was by no means clear to Trotsky at this time that the Russian Revolution had been lost. He still believed that, degenerated though it was, the state that had exiled him could still be reformed through working-class pressure. Consequently, he thought that there was no need in either case to invoke the notion of tragedy. In the first it was self-aggrandizing and in the second premature. These judgments reflect both his personal modesty as a historical figure and—in his refusal to abandon established positions until they had been conclusively proved redundant—his sobriety as a theorist. Nevertheless both judgments were to be proved wrong.

Russia had been ready for Communism in 1917 in a way that France had not in 1796. But Russia had been ready only as part of an international movement, not isolated and devastated in the way that it emerged from the Civil War in 1921. The bureaucratic degeneration that these conditions engendered culminated, by 1928, in a counterrevolution that was as complete as it was unacknowledged by the perpetrators—perhaps even to themselves. Trotsky never accepted that the counterrevolution had triumphed in Russia. Indeed, he was only prepared to contemplate it, even as a theoretical possibility, at the very end of his life. No matter. Whatever the weaknesses in his analysis—and it is only our position on Trotsky's shoulders that allows us to see what he could not—it is from the struggle that Trotsky conducted against Stalinism, particularly during his last exile, that his status as tragic hero derives. Deutscher was therefore right to speak of "the truly classical tragedy of Trotsky's life, or rather a reproduction of classical tragedy in secular terms of modern politics."[26] No other biography or work of art has ever captured the nature of that tragedy so well. One only has to think of the dire representations of Trotsky in books such as Bertrand D. Wolfe's *The Great Prince Died* (rightly dismissed by Deutscher) or a series of films from Joseph Losey's *The Assassination of Trotsky* (1969) to Julie Taymor's *Frida* (2003).[27] There are two great exceptions, both appropriately Modernist in conception: Meaghan Delahunt's novel, *In the Blue House* (London, 2001), which reconstructs Trotsky's life during his Mexican exile, and Ken McMullen's film *Zina* (1985), which focuses on the fate of Zinaida Lvovna. *Zina* may well be the only film in cinema history to feature an exposition of Trotsky's views on the United Front in relation to fighting Fascism in Germany.

New facts have obviously come to light since Deutscher wrote, and in some cases they mean that some of his specific conclusions must be revised. Deutscher argues, for example, that prior to the twelfth party congress in 1923, Trotsky failed to argue in the Politburo for the publication of Lenin's Testament attacking Stalin and abstained during the vote. According to Deutscher this was because he felt secure in his own position, was contemptuous of Stalin, and was unwilling to jeopardize the compromise that he thought had been reached with his rivals.[28] We now know that Trotsky voted for publication in the Politburo: his refusal to carry the argument into the Central Committee was not the result of complacency, but out of his respect for the decision-making process of the party and unwillingness to take any action that might have given the impression that he was acting from personal motives.[29] Similarly, Deutscher tends to downplay the level of Left Opposition support and to portray it as essentially passive, at least beyond the core membership. There is at least some evidence, from contemporary participants and witnesses like Victor Serge, that it was more significant than Deutscher allows, and his failure to take account of their testimony (of which he must have been aware) is another indication of a certain fatalism in his attitude to the opposition to Stalin. We now know that the Left Opposition had far higher and more active levels of support in both the Bolshevik Party and the working class more generally than was conceded by Deutscher or—to be fair—most other writers at the time.[30] However, neither of these examples, nor any of the others that could be cited, fundamentally alter our view of Trotsky. Nor do the materials that have become available in the Russian archives since the fall of Stalinism in 1989–91. Trotsky's most recent Russian biographer, the late, Martin Amis–approved General Dmitri Volkogonov, lists "the former Central party Archives, the Central State Archives of the October Revolution, those of the Soviet Army, the ministry of Defence, the Committee for State Security" as new sources.[31] But these have not led even to the type of marginal modifications discussed above. As Daniel Singer wrote of Volkogonov's own book: "What is important is not new and what is new is relatively unimportant."[32] Deutscher's books therefore remain indispensable for an understanding of the period they discuss and unsurpassed in bringing their hero alive. An honest assessment of these three volumes cannot, however, restrict itself to highlighting their many positive qualities.

PROBLEMS OF DEUTSCHERISM

Deutscher had been a leading figure in both Polish Communism and Polish Trotskyism. He was not opposed to the founding of the Fourth International on principle but because of a strategic disagreement over the possibilities for revolutionary progress at that time. I reemphasize these facts because there is a type of argument, all too common in certain varieties of Trotskyism, which explains away any personal retreat from revolutionary socialism by uncovering some flaw (a theoretical deviation here, a personality susceptible to "alien class influences" there), the ominous significance of which can only now be revealed. Any doctrine in which the renegade must be shown to have always been a heretic has more in common with Protestant fundamentalism than Marxism, not least because of the implication that experience of the world has no bearing on how opinions change in the course of a life. Rather than argue from a secularized version of Original Sin, it might be more productive to view Deutscher as suffering from the same pessimism about the revolutionary potential of the Western working class that affected most socialists after the Second World War and drove them, with varying degrees of enthusiasm, into the arms of either Washington or Moscow. Deutscher was severely critical of *Nineteen Eighty-Four,* but his own position was in many respects the mirror image of Orwell's reluctant embrace of the Western side of the Cold War.[33] I suggested above that there were four reasons why Deutscher might have been particularly empathetic toward Trotsky as an individual. Against them, however, it also seems that his pessimism led to two major political differences with Trotsky. These both distorted Deutscher's account of Trotsky's life—particularly in the final volume—and gave many of the thousands of radicals who read his books a basic orientation toward Stalinism that, in some cases at least, was to prove deeply disabling for their politics.

The first difference was in relation to revolutionary socialist organization and activity. After the outbreak of the Second World War—or rather, after Russia's entry into the Second World War—Deutscher never again seems to have considered active participation in a political organization. In 1951 Deutscher reviewed *The God That Failed,* a collective confessional by ex–Communist Party writers justifying their abandonment of revolution for various forms of social democracy. His alternative was revealing:

> [The ex-Communist] cannot join the Stalinist camp or the anti-Stalinist Holy Alliance without doing violence to his better self. So let him stay outside any camp. Let him try to regain critical sense and intellectual detachment. . . . This is not to say that the ex-communist man of letters, or intellectual at large, should retire into the ivory tower. (His contempt for the ivory tower lingers in him from his past.) But he may withdraw into a watchtower instead. To watch with detachment and alertness this heaving chaos of a world, to be on sharp lookout for what is going to emerge from it, and to interpret it *sine ira et studio*—this is now the only honourable service the ex-communist intellectual can render to a generation in which scrupulous observation and honest interpretation have become so sadly rare.[34]

Tony Cliff argued that Deutscher was effectively describing his own situation, but that in practical terms his position in the watchtower was no different from one in the ivory tower that he ostensibly rejected.[35] As we shall see, there is evidence that Deutscher had descended from the watchtower toward the end of his life, but during the period in which his biographies were written there is no doubt that Cliff's criticism was substantially correct. Deutscher joined neither the Fourth International nor of any of the dissident organizations that split from it after Trotsky's death. Indeed, his attitude to Trotskyism was deeply dismissive and Trotskyists paid him back in the same coin, with virtually every one of the 57 different varieties taking turns to attack his work, often while simultaneously plagiarizing his scholarship.[36]

Deutscher had firsthand personal experience of the weaknesses of Trotskyism. The endless arguments that preoccupied many of the small groups were usually unproductive. The activities that they undertook in the breaks between arguing were often unrewarding. Yet Trotsky regarded it as essential to establish, with whatever human material was available, organizational and theoretical continuities with the early years of the Third International and the traditions of classical Marxism that it embodied. During 1935 he wrote in his diary that "my work is now 'indispensable' in the full sense of the word." He rightly noted that there was "no arrogance" in this statement: "The vicissitudes of my personal fate have confronted me with this problem and armed me with important experience in dealing with it. There is now no one except me to carry out the mission of arming a new generation with the revolutionary method over the heads of the leaders of the Second and Third International."[37] Very little of this emerges in Deutscher, creating, at the very least, a severe imbalance in *The Prophet Outcast*. We learn that, for Trotsky, "neither his character nor his circumstances permitted him to resign from formal political activity. He would not and could not contract out of the day-to-day struggle."[38] Yet the impression is given that all of the energy that Trotsky expended during the 1930s attempting to resolve the internal disputes of his followers, all of the effort that he spent trying to guide them toward more productive activity in the labor movement, really involved so much wasted time. The only dispute discussed in any detail is the one that split the US Socialist Workers Party at the end of decade and, even here, Deutscher focuses almost solely on the aspect that turned on the class nature of the Soviet Union, rather than the debate over the political direction of the organization within which this issue arose. Why is Deutscher so uninterested in the issue that preoccupied his hero for virtually the entire period between his exile and his murder? The answer seems to be that he considered organization unnecessary because another mechanism existed that could bring about socialism. This brings us to the second difference between the two men: their attitude to Stalinism.

What was Trotsky's position? This changed at least four times between 1923 and 1940, but always in increasingly radical directions.[39] His initial approach to reversing the bureaucratic degeneration of the Russian Revolution, before Stalin had consolidated his power, envisaged workers reforming the apparatus through the medium of the existing Soviets. His final position, recognizing that Soviet democracy had long been completely suppressed, advocated working-class political revolution to overthrow the bureaucracy. Why only a political as opposed to a social revolution? Because, according to Trotsky, the continued existence of nationalized property meant that Russia remained a worker's state; the bureaucracy represented a caste that was parasitic on these property relations rather than a new ruling class. Now, as Cliff noted in 1948, this definition of a workers' state is not the one Trotsky originally held. On the contrary, in the immediate aftermath of the Russian Revolution, he had believed, along with Lenin and the entire Bolshevik party, that a workers' state was defined by the political rule of the working class through its representative institutions, regardless of whether property initially remained in private hands or not—and between 1917 and 1928 most of it did remain in private hands, particularly in the countryside. It is possible, of course, to debate the extent to which the working class exercised political rule between these dates, but the basis of the definition itself is unambiguous.[40] On this basis of his revised definition, Stalin's "second Revolution" after 1928 could be deemed far more revolutionary than October 1917 because it introduced the nationalized property relations upon which the "worker's state" was supposed to depend. Furthermore, if the decisive criterion was nationalized property, then why did it matter which class or social force introduced it? What need was there for the revolutionary party, the working class, or indeed any of the tenets of classical Marxism? The Red Army would be sufficient.

The anti-Marxist implications of shifting from working-class power to nationalized property relations were largely held in check in Trotsky's own work. He was careful to emphasize in his last writings that nationalized property was a remnant, a last remaining vestige of the workers' state, and that the progressive content of nationalization would only be realized after the overthrow of the bureaucracy. Moreover, he did not expect the Stalinist regime to survive the Second World War. He regarded it as a deeply unstable formation that would either be overthrown by working-class revolution or bourgeois restoration—and imminently, not in fifty years' time. If it survived, let alone expanded, the territory under its control, then the Stalinist bureaucracy would have demonstrated that it was indeed a class.[41]

The war ended. Russian Stalinism survived. Russian Stalinism expanded. Worse, indigenous Stalinist movements founded new states based, in all essentials, on the Russian Stalinist model. Yet the vast majority of orthodox Trotskyists continued to hold fast to a position that had been proved inadequate by events, and even extended it to Eastern Europe and China. Like them, Deutscher accepted that Russia, its satellites, and its imitators were all "workers' states" because they were based on nationalized property. Yet his description of how *The Revolution Betrayed* (1937) became "the Bible of latter-day Trotskyist sects and chapels whose members piously mumbled its verses long after Trotsky's death" conveys his impatience with the religious veneration they accorded Trotsky's last writings. Why? Not because they clung to its definition of a "workers' state," but because they refused to abandon their formal commitment to political revolution.[42] Deutscher described himself as "free from loyalties to any cult," by which he meant Trotskyism as much as Stalinism.[43] From 1948 the dominant tendency within the Fourth International, associated with Michael Pablo, had successfully argued that the Stalinist states in Eastern Europe and China were "workers' states." But even Pablo had assumed that it would be Stalinist parties that would—under "exceptional circumstances," "pressure from the masses," and the like—carry out revolutions. Deutscher was able go much further than orthodox Trotskyists could without rendering their existence completely redundant and claim that Stalinist Russia was not only capable of internal self-reform, but that, even unreformed, it was the major force for world revolution. At one level this is, of course, merely the logic of orthodox Trotskyism taken to its conclusion. For many Trotskyists, therefore, their rage at Deutscher was that of Caliban at seeing his face in the mirror.

Deutscher's position does at least have the benefit of consistency. Unfortunately it is consistently wrong. "We need not doubt," he wrote, "that . . . the logic of [Trotsky's] attitude would have compelled him to accept the reality of the revolution in Eastern Europe, and despite all distaste for the Stalinist methods, to recognise the "People's Democracies" as workers' states."[44] I do doubt this, for the simple reason that it is entirely incompatible with Trotsky's view of Stalinism. Deutscher undoubtedly thought it would be desirable for these property relations to be supplemented by democracy, but that was not decisive. "No one can foresee with certainty whether the conflict will take violent and explosive forms and lead to the new 'political revolution' which Trotsky once advocated, or whether the conflict will be resolved peacefully through bargaining, compromise, and the gradual enlargement of freedom."[45] This leaves the question open, but effectively concedes that the bureaucracy is capable of self-transformation, of bringing the degenerate political superstructure into line with the socialist economic base, so to speak. At no point, even before his exile, did Trotsky ever believe that the bureaucracy could reform itself. Even more damaging, Deutscher believed that the working class refrained from any activities that threatened this self-reformation or opened the door to the return of capitalism: "Eastern Europe (Hungary, Poland and eastern Germany) . . . found itself almost on the brink of bourgeois restoration at the end of the Stalin era; and only Soviet armed power (or its threat) stopped it there."[46]

The theoretical roots of these attitudes are suggested by Deutscher's inability to distinguish between different types of revolution. In *The Unfinished Revolution* (1967) Deutscher actually makes several sensible observations on the nature of bourgeois revolutions. In particular, he notes that their class nature does not depend on the presence of the bourgeoisie in the revolutionary process, but rather on whether the outcome of the revolution "was to sweep away the social and political institutions that had hindered the growth of bourgeois property and of the social relationships that went with it." In this respect, as he rightly remarks: "Bourgeois revolution creates the conditions in which bourgeois property can flourish."[47] These remarks are perfectly compatible with the views of several of his critics, including those of the present writer. The problem arises when Deutscher extends his model from bourgeois to proletarian revolutions, whose structures are necessarily quite different.[48]

In several places Deutscher argues that all of the "great revolutions" (English, French, Russian) follow the same pattern. First comes the rising against the old regime that unites the majority of the oppressed. Then follows the civil war that exhausts the new society and leads to the supposedly temporary suppression of many of the freedoms for which the revolution was made. Finally, the new ruling class entrenches itself and decisively abandons the egalitarian dreams of the popular masses, leading the most radical elements to cry "the revolution betrayed" before their ultimate suppression.[49] The only real difference he sees in the case of Russia is that, unlike the Independents and Jacobins, the Bolshevik Party was formed prior to the outbreak of revolutionary crisis: "This enabled it to assume leadership in the revolution and, after the ebb of the tide, to play for many decades the part the army had played in revolutionary England and France, to secure stable government and to work towards the integration and remodelling of national life."[50] In all other respects, Deutscher finds the parallels exact, even down to role of the leader who eventually emerges. "What appears to be established is that Stalin belongs to the breed of the great revolutionary despots, to which Cromwell, Robespierre, and Napoleon belonged."[51] If Hegel saw Napoleon as the World Spirit mounted on horseback, then, reading this passage, one has the impression that Deutscher saw Stalin as the World Spirit mounted on a tank. We are therefore lucky that Trotsky set down his own thoughts on Stalin's despotic lineage, for they are very different from Deutscher's: "In attempting to find an historical parallel to Stalin, we have to reject not only Cromwell, Robespierre, Napoleon, and Lenin, but even Mussolini and Hitler." His own preferred comparisons are with Kemal and Díaz, the Turkish and Mexican modernizing dictators.[52] Deutscher was evidently disturbed by the fact that Trotsky did not support his view of Stalin: "Here the lack of historical scale and perspective is striking and disturbing."[53] Deutscher's views are here influenced by those of Christian Rakovsky in his "Letter to Valentinov" published in the Opposition press in 1928. In effect, Rakovsky described the Opposition as being "between a demoralised, treacherous bureaucracy on the one side, and a hopelessly apathetic and passive working class on the other": "It followed (although Rakovsky did not say it) that the bureaucracy, such as it was, would remain, perhaps for decades, the only force capable of initiative and action in the reshaping of Russian society."[54] In fact, Trotsky was far nearer the truth, and it is a matter of regret that he did not live to pursue these comparisons further; for a parallel with the bourgeois revolutions is relevant, but not the one

Deutscher imagined. Stalin's historical role was in fact unique. The "second Revolution" from 1928 was both a counterrevolution in terms of socialism and the functional equivalent of the bourgeois revolution in terms of (state) capitalism, the class triumph of the bureaucracy. Any serious parallel for Stalin would have to embrace, not the political leaders of the bourgeois revolutions, but the individual landowners, capitalists, and imperialists who carried out the original process of primitive accumulation, a process that took nearly 250 years to accomplish in the case of Britain but only twenty-five in the case of Russia—with all that implies in terms of compressed suffering. Deutscher's confusions between bourgeois and proletarian revolutions lead him to make two central distortions in relation to the Russian experience.

One concerns the role of the working class. Discussing the *History,* he notes of Trotsky that: "He does not . . . overstate the role of the masses."[55] At first, this seems an odd sentence: Trotsky allocates to the masses their rightful—that is, preeminent—place in the revolutionary process. When one understands, however, that Deutscher has very little confidence in the masses, then it becomes far more comprehensible: "By 1921 the Russian working class had proved itself incapable of exercising its own dictatorship. It could not even exercise control over those who ruled in its name. Having exhausted itself in the revolution and the civil war, it had almost ceased to exist as a political factor."[56] There is a difference between "exhaustion" and "incapacity." A class can recover from exhaustion, but to be described as incapable suggests a permanent condition. Deutscher occasionally tries to enlist Trotsky in support of the latter contention, but only by massive distortion.

> Contrary to a myth of "vulgar Trotskyism," he did not advocate any "direct workers' control over industry," that is, management by factory committee or workers' councils. . . . He conceived proletarian democracy as the workers' right and freedom to criticise and oppose the government and thereby to shape its policies, but not necessarily as their "right" to exercise direct control over production.[57]

Deutscher is basing himself here on the temporary solutions to which Trotsky and the other Bolsheviks were driven as a result of economic collapse and civil war. Now it is true that Trotsky wrote some dire stuff—mostly in *Terrorism and Communism* (1920)—about the necessity for centralized authority of the one-party state under all circumstances. The way in which he, to put it mildly, made a virtue out of necessity during this period may well be the least glorious episode in his political life. But it was not his final position. In his writings on Germany from the 1930s, for example, Trotsky writes of the period of dual power, before the victory of the working class, that "the worker's control begins with the individual workshop. The organ of control is the factory committee." After the conquest of power: "The organs of management are not factory committees but centralized Soviets."[58] "Management" is a higher form of activity than "control," indicating that the Soviets will be making the decisions, not merely checking decisions made elsewhere. Deutscher's attitude toward the Russian working class is of a piece with his attitude towards the European working class as a whole after the First World War: "The majority exerted themselves to wrest reforms from their governments and propertied classes. But even when they exhibited sympathy for the Russian Revolution, they were in no mood to embark upon the road of revolution and civil war at home and to sacrifice in the process the standards of living, the personal security, the reforms they had already attained, and those which they hoped to attain."[59] Again, this was not Trotsky's view. His position—admittedly often exaggerated to the point of absurdity by some of his followers—was that working-class failure to consistently take the revolutionary road was in part due to a crisis of leadership that it was the task of Communists to overcome. Deutscher underestimates the role of revolutionary leadership to an even greater extent than he underestimates the revolutionary capacity of the working class. His treatment of Lenin during 1917 is instructive here.

In *The History of the Russian Revolution* Trotsky argues that the arrival of Lenin in Russia in April 1917 was decisive in pushing the Bolshevik Party toward the socialist revolution and the seizure of power: "Without Lenin the crisis, which the opportunistic leadership was inevitably bound to produce, would have assumed an extraordinarily sharp and protracted character. The conditions of war and revolution, however, would not allow the party a long period for fulfilling its mission. Thus it is by no means excluded that a disorientated and split party might have let slip the revolutionary opportunity for many years." Trotsky is not saying that the Bolsheviks would never have arrived at the correct strategy without Lenin, or that the revolutionary opportunity would never have come again, simply that in revolutionary situations time is of the essence and that, without Lenin, it would have been allowed to pass. "Lenin was not an accidental element in the historic development, but a product of the whole past of Russian history."[60] Deutscher finds this intolerable and devotes several pages (far more than Trotsky's original discussion) in an attempt to refute it. "If it were true that the greatest revolution of all time could not have occurred without one particular leader, then the leader cult at large would by no means be preposterous; and its denunciation by historical materialists, from Marx to Trotsky, and the revulsion of all progressive thought against it would be pointless." For Deutscher, such a lapse from "the Marxist intellectual tradition" can only be explained by Trotsky's psychological response to his own isolation: "He needed to feel that the leader, whether Lenin in 1917 or he himself in the nineteen-thirties, was irreplaceable—from his belief he drew the strength for his solitary and heroic exertions."[61] These are among the very worst passages in the entire trilogy and they are rather more revealing of Deutscher's "needs" than they are of Trotsky's.

If both the masses and the individual leaders are irrelevant to the accomplishment of socialism then what remains? What great impersonal historic forces can take their place? Deutscher often claimed to uphold what he called "Classical Marxism" against the "Vulgar Marxism" practised by Stalin, Mao, and their epigones, and the virtues of his works confirm that this was no idle boast. Yet within the category of "Classical Marxism" he included many of the thinkers of the Second International, like Kautsky and Plekhanov, whose work was characterized—to different degrees—by an extreme determinism. For them, socialism was inevitable, given a certain level of development of the productive forces. "Classical Marxism" was therefore divided between the determinists and those (like Lenin, Trotsky, Luxemburg, Lukács, or Gramsci) who understood the relationship between material circumstances and human activity. Reading Deutscher's trilogy it is difficult to avoid the conclusion that the experience of the defeat of the Russian Revolution led him to revive the determinism of the Second International. If defeat is too overwhelming, if the prospect of starting again is too difficult, then the temptation can be to present it, through the application of pseudo-dialectical voodoo, as a victory—or at least in the process of being transformed into a victory. Hence the title of the postscript to *The Prophet Outcast*, "Victory in Defeat": "The Soviet Union emerged as the world's second industrial power, its social structure radically transformed, its large industrial working class striving for a modern way of life, and its standards of living and mass education rising rapidly, if unevenly. The very preconditions of socialism which classical Marxism had seen as existing only in the highly industrialised countries of the West were being created and assembled within Soviet society."[62] There is a name for the social system that produces "the preconditions of socialism": it is capitalism. Yet this was the conclusion that Deutscher wished so much to avoid, that he dedicated his considerable powers to persuading his readers of the opposite.

DEUTSCHER'S INFLUENCE

The trilogy exerted a great influence over the New Left when it emerged after 1956, an influence that was as contradictory as the books themselves. To understand it, we need to envisage the context in which they were first read and discussed.

When Trotsky was murdered in 1940 Stalinist rule was restricted to Russia itself and its immediate western border regions. By 1954, when the first volume of the trilogy appeared, Stalinism had encompassed the whole of Eastern Europe, China, North Korea, and North Vietnam. It also held the allegiance of the most militant sections of the world working class. Some threats to the stability of the Stalinist ruling class had, of course, already appeared: the first internal split came with the expulsion of Yugoslavia from the Cominform in 1948 and the first serious opposition from below came with the rising of East German workers in 1953. It was only retrospectively, however, that these events were generally seen as exposing the inherent problems of state capitalism. For all practical purposes, in the early 1950s Stalinism appeared to offer the only real alternative to Western capitalism and imperialism. Against the seemingly unstoppable rise of the system established by his archenemy, Trotsky seemed irrelevant, a figure from another time or another world—perhaps "the lost world of Atlantis" that Deutscher invokes on more than one occasion. As he notes in the Preface to *The Prophet Armed:* "For nearly 30 years the powerful propaganda machine of Stalinism worked furiously to expunge Trotsky's name from the annals of the revolution, or to leave it there only as the synonym for archtraitor."[63] There was little effective defense against this onslaught.

Few of Trotsky's own works were in print at this time, except for a handful of pamphlets produced by the nominally Trotskyist organizations that, during this period at least, had few members and little influence. The three biggest groups in the West—the US, French, and British— had maybe three thousand members between them. Even if we apply the label of "Trotskyist" beyond adherents of the Fourth International to such dissident groups as the Workers Party in the United States and the *Socialist Review* Group in the United Kingdom, their total memberships would have been less than that of, for example, the relatively small Communist Party of Great Britain (CPGB). The CPGB reached its numerical peak with 56,000 members in 1942, although membership had declined to 35,000 by 1951. In other words, the CPGB probably lost considerably more members in these years than the total of number people across the globe who became Trotskyists during the same period.[64] Asked whether he was aware of Trotsky's writings during and immediately after the Second World War, Raymond Williams—perhaps the leading academic socialist thinker of his generation and one who organizationally broke with Stalinism during the late 1940s—replied: "No. That was a crucial lack. It wasn't until much later that I really learnt of the existence of a socialist opposition in Russia." This is somewhat disingenuous, since Williams would of course have learned something from his days in the CPGB about "the socialist opposition in Russia," namely that it was composed of class traitors in the pay of MI6 and the Gestapo. But Williams is correct to describe the existence of a "generational block."[65] The point is confirmed by John Saville, a Marxist historian and member of the CPGB until 1956, who writes that "before the war or after I personally never met a Trotskyist, or was confronted with one at any meeting I addressed; and the same was true, with only a very few exceptions, of members of the ILP."[66] And even if Williams or Saville had chanced to meet a Trotskyist, he would have found that his or her relationship to Trotsky's own theory and practice was increasingly distant. For all the brilliance of many of the individuals associated with Trotskyism, Alasdair MacIntyre was right to say in his review of *The Prophet Outcast* that

> so-called Trotskyism has been among the most trivial of movements. It transformed into abstract dogma what Trotsky thought in concrete terms at one moment in his life and canonised this. It is inexplicable in purely political dimensions, but the history of the more eccentric religious sects provides revealing parallels. The genuine Trotskyism of [Albert] Rosmer

and Natalya [Sedova] must have at most a few hundred adherents in the entire world.[67]

Nor did Trotsky's non-revolutionary admirers keep his memory alive. It was possible to support Trotsky without supporting his politics. John Dewey, for example, opened the Preliminary Commission of Inquiry into the accusations against Trotsky by saying: "In the United States, it has long been customary for public-spirited citizens to organize committees for the purpose of securing fair trials in cases where there was suspicion concerning the partiality of the courts." But as he later added: "Membership on such a committee does not, of course, imply anything more than the belief that the accused is entitled to a fair trial."[68] During the 1930s several centrist groups and individuals had independently arrived at interpretations of Stalinism, particularly its international role, which were compatible with that of Trotsky—George Orwell's *Homage to Catalonia* (1938) is perhaps the best example—but it soon became apparent that, for the majority, the political conclusions that they drew were quite different and, in most cases, quite unrevolutionary. Orwell himself wrote: "Trotsky, in exile, denounces the Russian dictatorship, but he is probably as much responsible for it as any man living, and there is no certainty that as a dictator he would be preferable to Stalin, although undoubtedly he has a much more interesting mind. The essential act is the rejection of democracy."[69] Emrys Hughes, the editor of *Forward* and subsequently a Labour MP, published articles by Trotsky despite the great hostility of the CPGB and conducted a sympathetic correspondence with him between 1937 and his death. Yet after the assassination he wrote: "There has been no greater irony in modern history than the fate of Leon Trotsky, the advocate of the dictatorship of the proletariat in Russia, the apologist for revolutionary ruthlessness and violence—the leader of the Red Army—being destroyed by the methods of political terrorism which he had defended in the belief that they would preserve revolutionary socialism."[70]

More generally, many intellectuals, particularly in the United States, were attracted to Trotsky, not only by his anti-Stalinism, but because of his literary and theoretical abilities, and what they saw as the romance of the revolutionary exile—the superficial aura of tragic heroism that Trotsky himself rejected. It was this admiration that led, for example, the students of Edinburgh University to invite Trotsky to accept their nomination as

Rector, a proposal that he of course declined on the grounds that it was an entirely apolitical post.[71] Some went so far as to join Trotskyist organizations, but most were unwilling to adopt the life of political commitment that membership entailed. Deutscher vividly describes their gradual retreat: "They balked; and their exalted reverence for him gave place first to uneasiness and doubt, or to a weariness which was still mingled with awe, then to opposition, and finally to a covert or frank hostility. One by one the intellectual *Trotskyisants* came to abjure first timidly then angrily their erstwhile enthusiasms and to dwell on Trotsky's faults."[72] Nor were his ideas sustained by academics, since as Deutscher rightly points out, the Stalinist version of history "strongly affected the views of even independent Western historians and scholars."[73] As late as 1967, *New Left Review*—later to be the vehicle for the super-Deutscherism of its editorial board—could publish, as its first serious consideration of Trotsky's work, an article by Nicolas Krasso that concluded: "In practical political struggle, before and after the Revolution, his under-estimation of the specific efficacy of political institutions led him into error after error."[74]

It was onto this scene, where Trotsky was regarded, at best, as a harmless icon of non-specific anti-Stalinism or, at worst, as a counterrevolutionary renegade from the socialist cause, that the first volume of Deutscher's biography exploded in 1954. Not the least of our debts to Deutscher is that, in spite of his own disagreements with Trotsky, he played a major role in transmitting the legacy of his hero to subsequent generations. Deutscher was not the first person to refer to Trotsky or his role in the Russian Revolution. Orwell had done so through the characters of Snowball in *Animal Farm* (1945) and Emmanuel Goldstein in *Nineteen Eighty-Four* (1949), whose book, *The Theory and Practice of Oligarchic Collectivism*, is—as Deutscher himself acknowledged—clearly derived from *The Revolution Betrayed*.[75] Nor was his the first biography: Bertram D. Wolfe had published his triple biography of Lenin, Trotsky, and Stalin, *Three Who Made a Revolution*, in 1948.

Nevertheless, the impact of Deutscher's trilogy was qualitatively different. His timing was fortuitous. Two years after his first volume appeared the revelations in Khrushchev's Secret Speech and upheavals in Eastern Europe, culminating in the suppression of the Hungarian Revolution, blew apart the Stalinist myth. For virtually the first time, revolutionary socialists had in their hands a substantial, documented history that broadly supported their arguments about the respective roles of Trotsky and Stalin in the Russian Revolutions. More importantly, open-minded socialists who had no contact with Trotskyists—which at this time would have meant most of them—had an independent source of information from which to construct an alternative to the disintegrating orthodoxies of Stalinism. As David Widgery once noted: "Even [in 1968], the range of readable socialist literature didn't overtax a table top."[76] From 1956 to 1968 Deutscher's three volumes would have accounted for quite a large part of the table's surface. The Scottish miners' leader, Lawrence Daly, who broke with the CPGB in 1956, wrote of Deutscher that "his books on Stalin and Trotsky certainly enlightened thousands of active trade unionists, people who were not only trade union conscious but politically conscious, and they undoubtedly played a very important role in rescuing some thousands of people in this country, dedicated workers in the Labour Movement, from a kind of mummified Marxism, within the narrow and stultifying confines of which they had been ideologically asphyxiated."[77] Tariq Ali, for example, wrote that: "My own political formation has been greatly influenced by Isaac Deutscher, Leon Trotsky and Ernest Mandel (in that order)."[78] Now, the fact that Ali places Deutscher before Trotsky may indicate nothing more than the order in which he read these authors, but in many cases newly radicalized workers and students read Trotsky through Deutscher's interpretation. From Widgery's account, Deutscher's Trotsky anthology, *The Age of Permanent Revolution,* was one of three main sellers on bookstalls at the London School of Economics during the student rebellions of the late 1960s.[79] And for some radicals at least, it was possible to be a Deutscherist without becoming a Trotskyist. In 1989, David Horowitz, whom we have already encountered, confessed to a Polish audience: "I was inspired to join the new Left by a Polish Marxist called Isaac Deutscher, who was my teacher. It was Deutscher who devised the theory out of which we hoped to revive the socialist dream."[80]

In his autobiography Tony Cliff recalled his concern over the dominance that Deutscher began to exert over audiences during the 1960s: "I remember going to lectures by Deutscher at which there were 1,000 or more present. Twice I spoke from the floor in the discussion criticising Deutscher's position, but I hardly cut any ice with the audience. . . . Our puny group, offering a tough approach to Stalinism, could not overcome

Deutscher's soft soap."[81] Cliff thought that, because Deutscher's position did not involve a complete break from Stalinism, it was easier for people from that tradition to accept than one based on a harder Trotskyist analysis, let alone that associated with *International Socialism*. The claim has some validity for the period in which the books first appeared—it clearly explains Lawrence Daly's enthusiasm, for example. But it cannot explain why people with no previous history of Stalinism, who were becoming socialists for the first time, found Deutscher's arguments so compelling. Nor can it explain why they continued to do so long after the nature of Stalinism was accepted even by the majority of Communist parties. The answer is that, as I have already suggested, Deutscherism was a theory of consolation. It was—and here the cliché really is inescapable—no accident that Deutscherism reached its maximum influence between the onset of the downturn in international class struggle in 1975 and the fall of Stalinism in Eastern Europe in 1989. No matter how difficult the current situation may have been in Western Europe or the United States, no matter how few papers were sold on the high street of a rainy Saturday morning, socialism—or societies "transitional" to socialism—already existed in the world and their number was being added to year-on-year: Guinea-Bissau, Mozambique, Angola, Ethiopia, South Vietnam, Laos, Cambodia (where the phenomenon of a genocidal "workers' state" was shortly to be discovered), and Afghanistan.

The main vehicle for spreading these views was a journal in which Deutscher's work had regularly appeared: *New Left Review.* The apotheosis of "theoretical Deutscherism" was attained in an essay of 1983 by Perry Anderson, somewhat misleadingly called "Trotsky on Stalinism." After a brilliant summary of Trotsky's changing analysis of the Soviet Union, Anderson discusses the limitations of Trotsky's analysis, which supposedly led to failures in prediction. All are derived from Deutscher.[82] The key example of what might be called "applied Deutscherism" is Fred Halliday's *The Making of the Second Cold War* (1983 and 1986), about which Anderson wrote "it is fitting that the best work confronting the current Cold War should have been produced out of direct inspiration of [Deutscher's] example."[83] Deutscherism was perhaps best summed up by Mike Davis as the proposition that "the Cold War between the USSR and the United States is ultimately the lightning-rod conductor of all the historic tensions between opposing international class forces."[84]

The fall of the Soviet bloc destroyed all the assumptions upon which Deutscherism was based. Some of his acolytes had already changed sides before the debacle of 1989–91, but after it became apparent that that the Soviet Union would neither economically compete with the United States nor politically reform itself in a socialist direction. Horowitz explained to a Polish audience in 1989 how he "waited in vain" for the self-reform of the Stalinist states before concluding that "Deutscher was wrong. There would never be a socialist political democracy erected on a socialist economic base."[85] For those, like Fred Halliday, who had essentially seen the Soviet bloc as the bearer of socialist progress, the debacle "means nothing less than the defeat of the communist project as it had been known in the twentieth century and the triumph of the capitalist."[86] Incredibly, some writers who had previously accepted the argument expressed here latterly began to endorse a Deutscherist position *after* the Soviet Union had collapsed. Christopher Hitchens wrote of "the dismantling of the Soviet Empire" (an event, incidentally, that he attributes solely to the activities of Mikhail Gorbachev) that "if that momentous process vindicated anyone, it was perhaps Isaac Deutscher (who had believed in a version of 'reform communism')."[87] Horowitz has no difficulty disposing of these claims: "In particular, the failure of Gorbachev's reforms in the Soviet Union and the collapse of what proved to be the hollow shell of the Soviet Empire brutally contradict and refute the essence of all that Deutscher wrote about them."[88] It would be going too far to say that every Deutscherist has now switched sides to support the United States, capitalist globalization, "liberal values," and the invasion of awkward third-world states. For every Halliday or Hitchens there is a Davis or an Ali. Nevertheless, Deutscherism made it easy, for those who had no countervailing belief in the ability of the working class to sustain them, to transfer their allegiance from Moscow to Washington.

CONCLUSION

Toward the end of his life Deutscher began, in response to the Vietnam War, to engage in political activity for the first time in decades. In 1965 he was invited to speak at the National Teach-In about the War in Washington, and then at the far more political event of the same name in Berkeley. He said of the latter event: "This is the most exciting speaking engagement I have had since I spoke to the Polish workers thirty years ago." More important, perhaps, was his address to the Socialist Scholars Conference the following year ("On Socialist Man"), when he criticized the assembled ranks of the left academy (much smaller in those days, of course) for their failure to connect with the US working class:

> Can't you approach the young worker and tell him that the way to live is to work for life and not for death? Is it beneath American scholars to try to do that? . . . Your only salvation is in carrying the idea of socialism to the working class and coming back to storm—to storm, yes, to storm—the bastions of capitalism.[89]

These remarks, and his involvement in the Bertrand Russell International War Crimes Tribunal, do not suggest the attitude of a man contemplating the world from a watchtower. And why should that come as a surprise? The crisis over the invasion and occupation of Iraq in 2003 not only had the effect of smoking out of the closet supporters of US imperialism, but of revitalizing socialists who had previously appeared lost to activity. Deutscher, a product of the finest traditions of European socialism before Stalin and Hitler had done their worst, was scarcely likely to be unaffected by the revival of struggle that surrounded him.

Changed circumstances enabled Deutscher to reengage in political activity, but it was the circumstances that prevailed for decades beforehand that shaped both the strengths and weaknesses of the trilogy. The Deutscher who resisted Stalinism gave us what is most valuable in it; the Deutscher who capitulated gave us those aspects most redolent of that epoch of defeat. Now that the false alternative of Stalinism is itself history, the latter will diminish in significance, but the virtues of Deutscher's great work are likely to endure for as long as we still need to discuss the rise and fall of the Russian Revolution. And of how many other books of the period can that be said?

Chapter 4

There's No Place
Like the United States Today
Victor Kiernan and Neil Smith
on US Imperialism[1]

INTRODUCTION

These two very different books are notable contributions to the debate over the nature and role of contemporary US imperialism. Both authors are Marxists, albeit from different generations, left-wing organizations, and academic disciplines. Both examine their subject from a longer historical perspective than is usual.

Of all his contemporaries in the Communist Party of Great Britain (CPGB) Historians Group Victor Kiernan has the most eclectic range of interests. As Hobsbawm notes in an informative preface (that itself contains some acute remarks on the continuities of US foreign policy): "Who else has written with comparable expert knowledge about the ancient Roman poet Horace, twentieth-century Urdu poets (whom he translated) and Wordsworth, on early modern Europe and England in the era of the French Revolution, together with books about Shakespeare, duelling, tobacco and the Spanish Revolution of 1854?."[2] Indeed, it may be

that the very widespread nature of Kiernan's subject matter has contributed to his relative obscurity compared with—to take the most obvious example—Christopher Hill, whose reputation was based on work
almost entirely about seventeenth-century England. Even Hobsbawm,
who has a comparable range of interests to Kiernan, is most identified
with his great quartet on the history of capitalism since 1789. From 1948
until his retirement Kiernan taught at Edinburgh University, and it is perhaps for this reason that he was virtually alone among the British Marxist
historians in showing any serious interest in Scottish history.[3] More important for our purposes, however, is the fact that he was also exceptional
among them in paying sustained attention to imperialism, in a series of
articles and books across three decades.[4] The book under review here,
America: The New Imperialism, first appeared in 1978, in the aftermath of
the catastrophic defeat for the United States in Vietnam.

Neil Smith's *The Endgame of Globalization* is a different type of book.
Smith comes from a much later generational cohort and stands in a different political tradition from Kiernan. A Scot currently based at City University of New York, he became active around the time *America: The New
Imperialism* was originally written and was for several years a member of
the International Socialist Organization in the United States. Like his former supervisor and current colleague David Harvey, Smith is part of the
radical geography tradition that emerged in the 1980s. It is interesting that
both men, in their recent works, have increasingly moved beyond the
boundaries of their discipline to classical Marxist political economy in order
to deal with issues that confront them. *The Endgame of Globalization* is an
angrier, more polemical work than those with which Smith first drew attention.[5] Composed in the aftermath of the assertion of US power in the
Middle East, rather than its defeat in Indochina, *The Endgame of Globalization* is both a demonstration of how the Marxist theory of imperialism can
be used to shed light on current events and an implicit rejoinder to those
sections of the left that see the United States as virtually invulnerable.[6]

US EXCEPTIONALISM?

Kiernan writes in a style quite unlike most modern academic historians,
for which we can only be grateful. We gather an impression of how US
imperialism developed through an accumulation of characteristic details,
often derived from letters, diaries, novels, and other examples of what

are sometimes dismissed as "literary sources" by those who believe that only quantifiable methods are valid. But Kiernan is not interested in painting miniatures. Instead, his canvas contains the whole of US history as such, which he treats as virtually coextensive with that of US imperialism. On this basis he begins his account with the puritan settlers "building in the wilderness the better society that the Levelers tried in vain to build in England."[7]

The implication is that the process by which territory was acquired, by colonization, conquest, or (that quintessentially US method) cash, constituted the construction of an "internal" empire. There are interesting parallels here with the Russian internal empire in the Baltic states, Georgia, and so on. And in this, as in so many other areas of history, US state expansion has not been so much different from that of Russia as simply more lastingly successful. So successful, indeed, that an external empire was initially unnecessary. In the aftermath of the Civil War: "The great fact was that industrial capitalism, now firmly installed as arbiter of the national destinies, had a rapidly growing market and a spacious field of enterprise at home, without needing to look for colonies outside."[8] But neither was it necessary in the twentieth century. It is this absence of a formal empire, in contrast to those that preceded it, that constitutes the "newness" of the US Empire.

Kiernan comments with pungent irony on the crimes and follies that fill these pages, but without adopting the persona of the detached observer, judging from outside history. Instead, he holds his subjects to account for transgressing their own self-proclaimed codes and values: "In Washington's eyes, since the ultimate goal, preservation of democracy, was righteous, all means toward it were warrantable, including suppression of democracy."[9] At the same time, we always know where Kiernan stands in relation to the peoples and classes whose fate he recounts. He treats the question of the Native Americans seriously, at a time when this was far from conventional even in left-wing histories of the United States, and devotes a substantial part of the book to recounting how they were killed or driven from what were once their lands, but he never romanticizes them.[10] From these sections could be derived a textbook example of the relationship between ideology and material interest, as we see the same policy toward the Native Americans being justified by a succession of different beliefs, from Protestant fundamentalism to social Darwinism.

The book is recommended then, but two cautions are in order. First, Kiernan's style, attractive though it is, can also be an obstacle to clarity.[11] It works well in relation to broad themes in social and cultural history, as he demonstrated in his masterpiece, *The Lords of Human Kind,* a sweeping survey of how the Western merchants, soldiers, and colonists regarded the non-European peoples with which they came into contact.[12] But because it is primarily illustrative of the ideological expressions of imperialism, it is less effective in dealing with its central political and economic aspects. Second, his refusal to privilege one historical moment over another has the effect of obscuring decisive turning points: the long view tends to present a flat landscape. This is particularly noticeable in relation to Vietnam. Writing in the immediate aftermath of the fall of Saigon, the book certainly avoids the misguided triumphalism that was briefly common on the Maoist and orthodox Trotskyist left of the time. But Kiernan goes to the opposite extreme and underplays both the seriousness of the resistance to the war within the United States and the implications of the defeat for US power: "Yet as soon as the risk of having to serve at the front was removed, agitation and concern over Vietnamese sufferings died down abruptly; a year or two more, and Vietnam was forgotten."[13] This judgment would certainly surprise US strategists, since they have spent the last thirty years trying to overcome the "syndrome" to which Vietnam gave rise. Nor is this simply a retrospective assessment: it was clear from the refusal of the US military to sanction intervention in Angola during 1975 that the defeat had instantly curtailed the ability of the United States to act at will.[14]

If these were the only difficulties then one would simply say that this is not a book for beginners, and that it should be used to supplement more straightforward narrative accounts. But there is a greater difficulty here, which springs not from style or method, but from the underlying theory of imperialism with which Kiernan undertakes his survey: "Very broadly, and whatever the relation between economic and other forces among the causes at work, imperialism today may be said to display itself in coercion exerted abroad, by one means or another, to extort profits above what simple commercial exchange can produce. In this light it may be seen as a continuation or recrudesce within the capitalist era of the 'extra-economic compulsion' which is the hallmark of any feudal dominion."[15] There is nothing specifically Marxist about this definition of imperialism, nor does it apply only to capitalism, since "coercion exerted abroad . . . to extort profits above what simple commercial exchange can produce" was taking place during the days of the Roman Republic, to go no further back in history.[16] The classical Marxist definition of imperialism envisages it as a particular stage in the development of capitalism with two key characteristics: on the one hand, the fusion of financial and industrial capital with the state; on the other, the expansion of capital beyond the territorial boundaries of individual states. In this conception, although we can still refer to "American (or whichever) imperialism" as shorthand for the activities of particular state capitals, it is the system as a whole that is imperialist, and that compels these states to act in certain ways. Consequently, imperialism in this sense is not necessarily concerned with the relationship between oppressor and oppressed states, as Kiernan believes, but on the rivalry between the oppressor states themselves. In this respect, Smith has a surer grasp of what the Marxist theory of imperialism involves:

> Where Lenin did turn out to be extraordinarily prescient is in his distinction between imperialism and colonialism. Imperialism, for Lenin, was not simply a land grab of the colonial sort but a logical result of capitalist competition working through a system of national states. Hence his focus on finance capital: colonialism was at best a means of imperialism, but there were others. Where many on the left have still not yet embraced this insight, and still treat colonialism and imperialism as the same phenomenon, the neocons who have embraced empire are in this respect at least the truer Leninists.[17]

LIBERAL IMPERIALISM?

Given the theoretical differences between Kiernan and Smith, it is interesting to compare their respective accounts of that main episode in US history where the logic of imperialist rivalry manifests itself most clearly: the ultimately abortive colonial adventures in Cuba and the Philippines in 1898. For Kiernan:

> There was going to be a surplus of manufactures . . . all the more formidable because of its novelty, and because it was being hastened by the depression at home. Bigger markets abroad came quickly to seem, not merely desirable, but vital for survival. There was of course no *rational*

need of mountainous exports; hence an irrationality tingeing all the epoch of expansionism now starting. . . . Here was both the curious logic of capitalism and the American obsession with destiny; a latter-day example also of how, as in the 17th century, Calvinist determinism could be fused with superabundant energy.[18]

Smith, on the other hand, is equally mindful of the ideological aspects of imperialism, but grounds them far more in the needs of an expanding capitalist economy, rather than in a cultural metaphysics: "The spurt of manly colonialism culminating in 1898 surely expressed a certain cultural impulse, a 'surplus energy' inherent in the twinned projects of nation building and empire building . . . but it just as surely provided the prospect of outlets for an overflowing economy that began powering itself out of crisis." Moreover, Smith suggests that, initially at any rate, the brief excursion into formal empire-building was contingent, rather than springing from any essential difference between US and European imperialism:

> It was a short-lived colonialism, however, not because of some liberal American antipathy to Empire—quite the opposite—nor because it solved the questions of economic and liberal expansion. It was short-lived because it didn't solve these problems. A successful colonialism would have been pursued. But by 1898, where else was there to go? Mexico, Canada, Japan, Russia, Venezuela, or Brazil? . . . The geographical reality was that, with a few minor interstitial exceptions, the entire surface of the earth was already carved out by republics, states, and colonizing powers. Most of the colonies of 1898 had to be wrested away from a declining Spanish power, and few (if any) significant opportunities of this sort remained. Would the US really stand up to Britain militarily? Invade Brazil? Take on China? For all the pundits who pointed in this direction, others were more sober.[19]

Smith's core thesis is that the current period is the third attempt by the United States to establish a world order based on liberal capitalism. The periodization he uses here was first unveiled in his 2003 biography of Isaiah Bowman, "Roosevelt's geographer."[20]

In 1919 and 1920, the nationalist rejection of Woodrow Wilson and the Versailles Treaty in the Senate was central to the defeat of the first thrust at US global dominance. In the 1940s, the Americanism that presented itself as the bulwark against communism, and therefore as an active participant of the cold war, may also have drawn borders around a supposedly "free world," but it also drove a stake through the "new world order" and the second moment of US globalism. Today, for a large sector of America's rulers, the war on terrorism is the new war on communism, and the hardening of national borders—geographical, political, symbolic, economic—raises to an acute level the contradiction between global aspirations and elite, national self-interest.[21]

It is within this overall framework that Smith discusses the specific reasons for the invasion and occupation of Iraq, in which he takes due account of the defeat in Vietnam: "The rationale for the Iraq war emerged from the amalgam of . . . three elements: the geopolitics of oil, the dramatic loss of US political power after the 1970s, and the partial fragmentation of the delicate system of power interdependencies that had let the region's petro-capitalism flourish."[22]

Powerful though the main lines of Smith's argument are, the book is not entirely convincing at every level. It bears some signs of having been written in haste although, unlike Kiernan, Smith is of course trying to deal with these crucial issues while events are still unfolding. Nevertheless, some of his judgments are questionable. Two examples stand out.

One is his treatment of Israel. Where Kiernan simply expresses puzzlement at US support for Israel ("no nation in history has had a more expensive and more disobliging ally"[23]) Smith explains its origins in terms of domestic politics: "It was in no way a principled response to the horrors of the Holocaust, but a cynical attempt to win Jewish votes at home, in a tight upcoming election, and it had global consequences." In discussing the subsequent history, he broadens this out to include "the need for oil" as well as "a domestically inspired support for the Israeli."[24] Now Smith is absolutely correct to connect the internal politics of the United States to its external relationships with other states; the question here is the extent to which the pro-Israeli lobby in decisive in determining policy. If it had not existed, would successive US governments have taken a different attitude to Israel? It seems scarcely conceivable that they would have behaved any differently. From 1967 in particular, the US ruling class has regarded Israel as the only stable force representing the interests of US capitalism in the region, and everything that has happened since, from the fall of the Shah in 1979 onward, has confirmed it in this view.

A more general issue is the distinction Smith draws between "global aspiration" and "national self interest" in determining US imperial policy. Running through his book is the argument that America's imperial ambitions have previously run aground on the shoals of nationalist isolationism. This is a real division within the US ruling class, but surely the advocates of global intervention were also motivated by "national self interest"? This may simply be a question of Smith's presentation, but there seems to be a problem in elevating opposing strategies for advancing those interests into a fundamental political difference.

Any criticisms that might be made of either book, however, must be set alongside the fundamental service to truth that, in their different ways, they perform. Members of the pro-war left are fond of explaining America's tendency to support murderous military dictatorships by claiming that this was an unfortunate by-product of the Cold War, and not an intrinsic part of the operation of US foreign policy. These days are supposedly over and—whatever their previous record—the United States is now free to roll into Bosnia, Afghanistan, and Iraq, overthrowing dictators and establishing capitalist democracy with the loyal support of its faithful British deputy. (Against this kind of self-deluding cant, openly right-wing arguments for a new imperial order can be—at least momentarily—refreshing in their honesty and cynical recognition of the needs of capitalist power.[25]) However, the historical record set out by Kiernan and Smith makes it quite clear that US imperialism preceded the Cold War by a long way, and that current interventions have to be considered and understood in this context rather than as a new form of humanitarian militarism. Writing now, Smith has been granted that opportunity to engage directly with the B-52 liberals, and he makes the most of it in demolition of Michael Ignatieff's "lesser evil" argument for bombing and invading other countries: "By its very logic, the adoption of the Bush doctrine by any power automatically presents a threat to all other powers and would, under that doctrine itself, have been seen as sufficient cause to warrant pre-emptive war." "The result," Smith notes, "should this 'democratic' defence of democracy become generalised, is almost too hellish to contemplate in a nuclear world, and the biggest nuclear power of all would bear primary responsibility."[26]

What then of the future? Kiernan concluded his 1978 study by saying that the "question argued during the First World War between Lenin and

Kautsky, whether capitalism was doomed by its nature to perpetual aggression abroad, or could be brought under restraint, is still an open one."[27] Smith also considers this question:

> Where Lenin thought that inter-imperialist rivalries led inevitably to war, as indeed they did in 1914, Kautsky thought that a coalition of imperialist states might fashion a relatively stable global rule among themselves in pursuit of global economic plunder. That has not happened, but present-day US unilateralism does raise the possibility that Kautsky may have been half-right, anticipating the prospect of US "superimperialism."[28]

Yet, unlike many writers on the left today, Smith does not think that the current situation is one where the United States can proceed, untrammeled, throughout the globe. The resort to a geopolitical strategy and war after 2001 represents a sign of weakness, not strength, for United States power. But it will not collapse of its own accord. His conclusion is apt: "Historical experience tells us that such a nationalism, especially when it is located within the borders of a global hegemon, is just as likely to enhance rather than diminish the violence of the denouncement. That leaves organized opposition as the most realistic alternative to the clash of terrorisms."[29]

ᴋᴄ Chapter 5 ᴏᴊ

Carnival, March, Riot
David Renton on the Anti-Nazi League[1]

INTRODUCTION

Over three years one organization distributed 9 million leaflets, sold 750,000 badges, had 250 branches with 50,000 members, held a conference attracting 800 delegates, and received affiliations from—among other bodies—50 constituency Labour parties, 30 AUEW branches, 25 trades councils, and 13 shop steward committees. These are some of the materials produced, activities undertaken, and supporters enlisted, not by the Stop the War Coalition since 2002, but by the Anti-Nazi League (ANL) between 1977 and 1980.[2]

The goal of the ANL was to stop and reverse the growth of the fascist National Front (NF), and it may be worth reminding ourselves of the extent of the Nazi threat during the later half of the 1970s, since today this is often downplayed. One estimate, by the journal *Searchlight,* has 64,000 people passing through the ranks of the NF between 1967 and 1979, with its highest membership level in any one year reaching 17,500 in 1976–7. In the General Election of October 1974 the NF stood 90 candidates who received 113,844 votes. Three years later, in the local and Greater London Council elections, NF candidates received an average of 5.7 percent of the vote, pushing the Liberals into fourth place in a quarter of seats. And for many black and Asian people the threat was immediate and direct, in the shape of violent and sometimes fatal racist attacks, such as those that took the lives of Gurdip Singh Chaggar or Altab Ali. Yet by the time the ANL was effectively disbanded toward the end of 1981, the NF was unable to demonstrate without challenge, had seen all its candidates in the 1979 General Election lose their deposits, and had suffered disabling internal leadership battles provoked by their failure. By the end of 1984, the NF had lost nine-tenths of its membership.[3]

The marginalization of the NF was, by any standards, a remarkable success for a movement initiated by the revolutionary left, particularly in a period otherwise marked by the beginning of a generalized retreat by the labor movement. It was the formative political experience of an entire cohort of activists, many of whom ended up far from revolutionary politics. "Leon Trotsky has not made a big impact on my life, except for the circles and the arrows," wrote *The Guardian* journalist Jackie Ashley recently: "Everyone on the left in my generation probably remembers them: the symbols of the Anti-Nazi League. It may have been kicked off by the Socialist Workers Party (SWP), but thousands of labor activists, trade unionists and students carried the circles and arrows, back in the 1970s as we marched against the National Front."[4] It is not an achievement, however, that has hitherto been studied in any detail. Until now, the major book dealing with this period had been David Widgery's *Beating Time,* a work of literary and visual fusion that displays all the characteristic panache of its author, but—mainly because of his role as a leading participant—also one that lacks the necessary historical distance from the material.[5] More to the point, it is focused mainly on the role of Rock Against Racism (RAR), rather than the ANL. RAR was launched in September 1976, over a year before the ANL, and was a more specifically cultural intervention with a wider remit, indicated by the opposition to racism rather than Fascism in its name, although the two organizations did of course work closely together.[6] As David Renton points out in the preface to *When We Touched the Sky,* it is therefore "the first book-length study of the Anti-Nazi League" as such.[7]

THE COMPONENTS OF A SUCCESSFUL
ANTI-FASCIST MOVEMENT

Renton begins with two brief chapters setting out the crisis-ridden situation of Britain by the mid-1970s and the history of racism down to that time. The book then moves, more or less chronologically, from 1976 and the formation of RAR in response to racist comments by Eric Clapton (a process that fortuitously coincided with the emergence of Punk; Renton has some interesting comments about the relationship of specific forms of music to RAR); to 1977 and the great counter-demonstration against the NF in Lewisham that led directly to the formation of the ANL; to 1978 and the Carnivals in Victoria Park and Manchester (subject of a particularly exhilarating chapter); to 1979 and the Southall demonstration in which the police murdered Blair Peach; then through to 1980–81 and the collapse of the NF.

It is clear from this account that the ANL strategy had three main components: mobilization of the largest numbers of people possible solely on the basis of their opposition to the NF; physical confrontation to stop the NF from marching or assembling; and political identification of the NF as Fascists whose ideology was the same as those responsible for the Holocaust. These elements were dependent on their mass character for success. There is, for example, a difference between the defensive force of tens of thousands of people, many of whom belong to the threatened community, blocking the path of the NF and their police protectors, and the violence of small gangs of young anti-Fascist men fighting with other small gangs of young Fascist men: the first is a political act, the second is not, and indeed, it obliterates political difference. These elements were also interlinked. The Carnivals were important cultural events, but would have merely left the audiences as consumers affirming their collective anti-Fascism if they had not also been involved in the great demonstrations.

Renton is a prolific author, perhaps too prolific. At least some of his previous books—which include three studies of Fascism and anti-Fascism—give the impression of being over-hastily compiled from research, with all the attendant problems of avoidable errors and incautious judgments, many of which might have been avoided by a longer gestation period.[8] None of this is true of *When We Touched the Sky*, perhaps because (on his own account) it took seven years to complete and therefore involved a greater deal of consideration. At any rate, Renton's strengths are on display here. In addition to archival research, he employs the techniques of oral history and has interviewed both the organizers of the ANL and a wide range of other activists, including members of other antiracist groups. As has been his practice for previous books, Renton refuses to interview

Fascists, but he has used their publications as a source. And, disgusting though the experience of reading the likes of *Bulldog* and *Spearhead* no doubt was, it has been useful in confirming that the NF did indeed see the ANL as a threat to their activities.

The point is important, since it is sometimes claimed that the Nazi vote did not collapse because of ANL activity but because NF voters switched to supporting the Tories in the general election of 1979. If this is true then the future of anti-Fascist activity is bleak, because apparently the only way to demobilize the Fascist right is for conventional right-wing politicians to take their place. Renton rightly rejects this position on two grounds. One is that it rests on the highly implausible assumption that all the ANL activity had precisely no effect, in either demoralizing the NF activists who were for years unable to appear publicly unopposed, or in separating out hard-core supporters from the soft racists through emphasizing the Fascist nature of the former. The second is that we have the counterexamples from those countries where opposition to the Fascist right did not take a similar form to that of the ANL. France, where Le Pen and the Front National were able to establish themselves, at least until 1995, without serious political opposition, is the key example in this respect.[9] (Indeed, partly as a result of the failure of the French left, voters ended up in the final round of the Presidential Elections of 2002 precisely with a choice between the conservative Chirac and the Fascist Le Pen.)

When We Touched the Sky is therefore an invaluable guide to one of the most important movements in recent British left-wing history, perhaps the most important prior to the Stop the War Coalition. My criticisms mainly concern areas that Renton has omitted from consideration. "Social movement history," of which this is a fine example, does seem to have inherited from labor movement history a certain narrowness of focus, particularly in relation to wider issues of the state and economy. The introductory chapters apart, the protagonists here are the ANL/RAR, the NF, and the people they were trying to mobilize or influence. The state enters in the form of the police, usually defending the NF, sometimes remaining neutral, very occasionally siding with anti-Fascists. From the sidelines we hear the babble of a press typically more concerned with denouncing anti-Fascist responses than the Fascist activities that provoked them. But the broader social context in which all this took place, the economic crisis and the origins of neo-liberalism, the rightward turn in British society as a whole, the downturn in industrial struggle (the very existence of which was contested within the SWP at the time)—all these things are certainly mentioned, but they are never integrated into Renton's account, with the result that the conflicts he describes often appear self-contained. The most obvious question that the book implicitly raises—how it was possible for a political victory on this scale to be achieved at a time when the industrial class struggle was stalling or going down to defeat—remains unanswered, although in the absence of a revival of generalized trade union militancy it is one that remains relevant to us today.

THE ANL AS A UNITED FRONT

In other respects, however, the book does provide material of major importance to contemporary debates. I have already referred to the Stop the War Coalition, which is linked to the ANL, not just by the presence of the SWP, but by the common approach both took to building alliances with people who were not revolutionaries. The models of the united front and the popular front are less than useful here if we expect them to take the form that they did between the First and Second World Wars of the last century. The strategy of the united front, as it was codified at the Second Congress of the Communist International in 1920, involves revolutionary working-class organizations offering to work alongside reformist working-class organizations in pursuit of specific goals. It is not about reaching agreement on an entire political program, otherwise there would be no need for two organizations—or, consequently, joint activity—in the first place. Nor does it aim for the immediate overthrow of capitalism: it is a genuine attempt to achieve the specific goals as stated (although revolutionaries obviously try to demonstrate to reformist workers the superiority of their ideas and strategy through the experience of joint work). On the other hand, the popular front, first launched in France in 1935 but a key component of Stalinist politics ever since, involves alliances between revolutionaries and bourgeois political parties solely for electoral purposes.

Several critics have seen the ANL as having most affinity with the popular front. One of the most serious of these, the black cultural theorist Paul Gilroy, wrote: "Rock Against Racism had allowed space for youth to rant against the perceived iniquities of 'Labour Party Capitalist Britain.' The popular front tactics introduced by the ANL closed it down. Being 'Anti-Nazi' located the political problem posed by the growth of racism exclusively in the activities of a small and eccentric, though violent, band of neo-fascists."[10] These remarks involve a fundamental misunderstanding of what both "united" and "popular" strategies involve. Fairly obviously, the ANL was not an electoral alliance between revolutionaries and bourgeois political parties, but was it then a united front? In fact, united fronts in the "classic" Comintern or Trotskyist sense are actually very rare in working-class history, although the essential principle is used every day by Respect or Solidarity activists who convince Labour Party members to jointly take a petition or a collection round their workplace. And it is the principle that is important. Renton quotes one ANL activist: "The Anti-Nazi League wasn't a united front, but it was a united front–type organisation. It wasn't a pact between mass organisations, but there was an alliance between reformists and revolutionaries, unity around specific organisation demands which left the organisations free." The SWP was not in a position to offer "unity" in action with the Labour Party—an organization that then had a membership around one hundred times larger—but it could approach individual members and constituencies in the *spirit* of the united front in order to conduct joint activity. As Renton writes, with commendable restraint: "Perhaps one lesson of the Anti-Nazi League is that unity can be too narrowly conceived."[11]

Gilroy's main point lies elsewhere though. It is that ANL, unlike RAR, wrongly focused on Fascism at the expense of the far greater racist threat posed by the British state and what we, post–Lawrence inquiry, would now call institutional racism: this was what gave the NF the ideological basis for their appeals to the white population. Essentially this means that, unless you are prepared to challenge *every* aspect of a threat, it is wrong to challenge *any* aspect of it; even if the aspect in question poses the most immediate threat. Similar arguments to those of Gilroy were made at the time by groups on the sectarian left, for whom the very idea of the united front itself was counterrevolutionary. According to one typical example of the genre: "The standpoint of the ANL is that of the Labour racists. They are loyal to British imperialism, loyal to the British state, support immigration control and all the actions of the racist Labor government. Thus the ANL has not been for one moment concerned to defend black people. Its sole and single purpose is to prevent the growth of the influence of the National Front. . . . The ANL attempts to mobilise working class patriotism (to British imperialism) against the National Front's threat to British bourgeois democracy."[12] The usual "proof" offered by critics of this sort is that the ANL leadership refused to support calls for the abolition of all immigration controls. In fact the ANL did adopt a policy of opposition to all immigration controls at its first Conference in 1978 (and the SWP carried placards saying:"Stop the Nazis; No Immigration Controls" at the Victoria Park Carnival); what it did not do was make this position either a condition for membership or the basis of its activity. Why not? As Renton asks, "what was the point of the League, to represent internally all the considered positions of the left or to challenge fascism? . . . The League was not a political party."[13] If people already agreed with opposition to all immigration controls, they would be revolutionary socialists and there would be no need for alliances; if not, then making their participation in an organization dependent on their adopting this position is unlikely to result in a mass of recruits. It is important to challenge the views of people who support immigration controls, but you are far more likely to convince someone of the need to oppose them while working together against the Nazis than as a result of demanding that they adopt all of your politics before you condescend to speak to them. Anyone who has been active in both the anti-Nazi movement of the 1970s and the antiwar movement of the 2000s will experience a sense of *déjà vu* in relation to these arguments. Instead of criticism for allying with a supposedly entirely racist and imperialist Labour Party, the left has been criticized for allying with a supposedly entirely homophobic, sexist Muslim Association of Britain.[14] In both cases whole groups of people are written off in advance as incapable of engaging in dialogue or ever changing their views.

CONCLUSION

Toward the end of the book, Renton quotes the speech by Darcus Howe at a memorial meeting for David Widgery: "Howe said that he had fathered five children in Britain. The first four had grown up angry, fighting forever against the racism all around them. The fifth child, he said, had grown up 'black and at ease.' Darcus attributed her 'space' to the Anti-Nazi League in general and to Dave Widgery in particular."[15] Not for the first time, Howe is exaggerating, but there is something in this nevertheless. Perhaps the longer-term achievement of the ANL was to help forge a black and white unity deeper than one required by the immediate needs of anti-Fascist mobilization. As Renton suggests, perhaps it "had been a necessary precondition for the recent alliance between Muslims and non-Muslims in the movement against the Iraq war.... In that sense, the 1970s provide a stock of experiences on which present-day activists can draw."[16]

Alasdair MacIntyre
as a Marxist[1]

INTRODUCTION

Fifty years on from the events of 1956, one might have expected all the important Marxist thinkers who emerged in and around that year to have long since been identified, their works discussed, their contributions assessed, their biographies written. Alasdair MacIntyre has certainly also been afforded the same scrutiny granted to, for example, Ralph Miliband or Edward Thompson, two writers from different generations who came to prominence after 1956; but critical attention has not been focused on the writings by MacIntyre that were contemporary with *Parliamentary Socialism* (1961) or *The Making of the English Working Class* (1963). Instead, it has been directed toward a series of books that only began publication in the 1980s, long after he had abandoned his earlier Marxist positions. The books in question—*After Virtue* (1981, 1984, and 2007), *Whose Justice? Which Rationality?* (1988), *Three Rival Versions of Moral Inquiry* (1990), and *Dependent Rational Animals* (1999)—have elevated his reputation from being that of another philosopher, albeit one highly regarded within his profession, to perhaps the most discussed intellectual in the West. In these works and the numerous articles and interviews in which he has elaborated or commented on their themes, MacIntyre has attempted to articulate what Kelvin Knight has labeled a theory of "revolutionary Aristotelianism."[2] One, relatively trivial, indication of his newfound celebrity was his preeminence in a poll of professional philosophers for the *Observer*, taken immediately after the publication of *Whose Justice? Which Rationality?*[3] The concomitant neglect of his Marxist work can easily be demonstrated by a brief survey of the book-length collections and studies of his work.

The selection of MacIntyre's work by Kelvin Knight in *The MacIntyre Reader* (1998) includes only the 1959 essay "Notes From the Moral Wilderness" from his Marxist work, although the bibliography also lists one article from *Universities and Left Review* ("On Not Misrepresenting Philosophy") and one from *Labour Review* ("The 'New Left'").[4] The two collections that have been published on his ideas, *After MacIntyre* (1994) and *Alasdair MacIntyre* (2003), list only "Notes from the Moral Wilderness" in their bibliographies.[5] Peter McMylor's book, *Alasdair MacIntyre: Critic of Modernity* (1994), is a far more serious engagement with MacIntyre as a Marxist, but one restricted to a very limited number of works, principally *Marxism: An Interpretation* and the inevitable "Notes from the Moral Wilderness" (although there is reference to "Breaking the Chains of Reason" in a footnote and it is included in the bibliography).[6] The overall effect is to present MacIntyre as a commentator on, rather than a practitioner of, Marxism. None of these three books consider the articles or pamphlets published in or by *Universities and Left Review, The Newsletter, Labour Review, New Left Review, Socialist Review, International Socialism*, or even the *Listener;* the places, in other words, where MacIntyre attempted to use his Marxism as a tool for analyzing the world in order to change it. Indeed, McMylor and other commentators seem either to be unaware of the bulk of his early writings, or to consider them unworthy of comment. Why should this be? There seem to be four main reasons why MacIntyre's early work has been ignored, and for the relative obscurity into which it has fallen.

The first is that MacIntyre not only wrote from a Marxist perspective, he belonged to a number of Marxist organizations that, to differing degrees, made political demands on their members, demands from which intellectuals were not excluded. Even the most insightful of MacIntyre's admirers tend to treat the subject of these political affiliations as an occasion for mild amusement. Knight, for example, writes that after leaving the Communist Party, "MacIntyre first joined a dogmatically Trotskyist group. Then . . . he joined another, less dogmatic one." Fortunately, as Knight sees it, MacIntyre's resignation as an editor of the "less dogmatic" *International Socialism* in 1968 came "just in time to avoid association with the posturing of the second and final wave of the New Left."[7] In fact, during the period from 1953 to 1968, he seems to have treated membership of some party or group as a necessary expression of his political beliefs, no matter how inadequate the organizations in question may ultimately have been. In other words, his was not the type of academic Marxism that became depressingly familiar after 1968, in which theoretical postures were adopted according to the dictates of intellectual fashion, by scholastics without the means or often even the desire to intervene in the world. On the contrary, at some level MacIntyre embraced what a classic Marxist cliché calls "the unity of theory and practice," particularly in the Socialist Labour League (SLL) and International Socialists (IS). Membership of revolutionary parties has always been a minority position in British and—especially—North American academic life, even in the sixties, and MacIntyre's ascent to global fame from the early eighties coincided not with the rise of an insurgent left but that of a resurgent right. Nothing could have been less fashionable at this time than a Marxist past, particularly one associated with organized activity rather than passive contemplation. Consequently, MacIntyre's newfound admirers were able to treat his early commitments as either an aberration or a detour that had led to a dead end.

The second reason, consequent on the first, was the sheer unavailability of the work in question. Even if there had been any level of interest in MacIntyre's early work, the relevant pieces were published in the publications mentioned in the preceding paragraph, many of which are the now-forgotten organs of parties, movements, and organizations to which MacIntyre belonged between 1956 and 1968. It is rare to find the *New Reasoner* or *Labour Review* in a university library, and only slightly more common to find *International Socialism,* at least in the case of the first series to which MacIntyre contributed. In short, much of his work was unobtainable for practical purposes and the organizations that originally published it are either long defunct or, if still in existence, unwilling or unable to republish it. This would be less of a problem if MacIntyre himself had shown any interest in reproducing these early writings, but until recently he has not, selecting for reprint in *Against the Self-Images of the Age* only those that appeared in what he describes as "professional philosophical journals" or "journals of general intellectual culture."[8] In skirting over his more explicitly political writings, the essays brought together by MacIntyre in *Against the Self-Images of the Age* acted to distort the image of their author. One side of his persona in the 1950s and 1960s, the high-flying academic, was allowed to eclipse another, the revolutionary socialist. In the most recent "official" selection of his essays to be published, the earliest to be included dates from 1972.[9]

The third reason is their perceived irrelevance. For many commentators on MacIntyre, the main characteristic of his work is the consistency with which it returns to certain key themes. McMylor sees the shifts from Anglican Christianity through Marxism to his current Thomist affiliations as part of the same attempt to find a secure basis for the critique of liberal individualism: "Anyone looking at MacIntyre's work must not only be struck by the remarkable consistency of his intellectual preoccupations but that in many respects he has turned full circle and in his later work returned to the theological issues and concerns that he began with."[10] Knight describes "Notes from the Moral Wilderness" as the paper that "establish[ed] the project," its importance lying in the fact that it "prefigures aspects of *After Virtue*."[11] And these two writers are actually more sympathetic to Marxism than most of MacIntyre's critics. For the others, Marxism is simply an obsolescent doctrine that MacIntyre unaccountably took seriously during the earlier part of his career—a period that should now be decently passed over in silence.

The fourth and final reason is the critical hostility with which MacIntyre's Marxist work was received by other Marxists, notably by those associated with the *New Left Review*. While a dismissive attitude toward MacIntyre's early Marxism is to be expected from those conservative thinkers who have praised his more recent critique of liberalism, it is more perplexing that many on the political left share this condescending outlook. One reason for the disdain shown to his work in these quarters can be traced to an understandable reaction on the part of many of his contemporaries in the New Left to MacIntyre's decision to publish some of his most important political essays of the 1960s in journals such as *Encounter* and *Survey*, whose relationship to the CIA through the Congress for Cultural Freedom was then something of an open secret.[12] For

instance, when the Socialist Society at the London School of Economics
attempted to organize a series of Marxist lectures in 1965–66, problems
arose when Isaac Deutscher did not want to appear on the same list as
MacIntyre because the latter had criticized him on the pages of *Encounter*.[13] While this was embarrassing to MacIntyre's closest contemporary comrades in the IS, the issue was neither raised within the
organization nor with MacIntyre individually. To the editors of the *New
Left Review* (*NLR*), by contrast, MacIntyre's decision to publish in *Encounter* was perceived as an act of renegacy that mirrored more general
problems with his politics. When Robin Blackburn reviewed MacIntyre's book *Marcuse* in the journal *Black Dwarf* during 1970, his polemic
expressed a resentment that extended far beyond that particular work:
"MacIntyre has for a long time specialised in doing hatchet jobs on such
figures as Isaac Deutscher, C. Wright Mills, Georg Lukács and Herbert
Marcuse, as well as purveying slanders on the Cuban, Chinese and Vietnamese revolutions." It was not only the "miserable charlatan" MacIntyre
who was at fault, however, but the organizations that had harbored him:
"Perhaps older groups on the Left have indulged MacIntyre's political
delinquency and intellectual bankruptcy in the past, but that was part
of the traditional philistinism of the Left in this country."[14] In 1972 a
comrade of Blackburn's in the International Marxist Group, Tariq Ali,
advised his readers: "A look at the back copies of the *New Reasoner* provides an interesting insight into the workings of the *New Left* Mind."
He went on: "In particular, readers are recommended to read (for pure
amusement) . . . an article by Alasdair MacIntyre entitled, 'Notes from
the Moral Wilderness.'"[15] During an overview of the work of Edward
Thompson from 1980, Perry Anderson summarized the conventional
view of MacIntyre's trajectory, and the reason behind some of the bitterness expressed toward him, in some passing comments, severely dismissive in tone, on one of "the two philosophers Thompson cites most
frequently and warmly in *The Poverty of Theory*." MacIntyre, we were
told, had entered the socialist movement "fresh from providing books
on Marxism for the Student Christian Movement" and subsequently
"ended up in the pages of *Encounter* and *Survey*." Clearly Anderson
thought there was little more to be said for someone who had been an
unwelcome presence in the socialist camp and latterly become a renegade from it, other than that his work displayed "a remarkable demon-

stration of ideological continuity" at both points in his career.[16] Before the decade had closed, however, Anderson had occasion to refer to Mac-Intyre again, while surveying the transformation of English intellectual life during the Thatcher years. Now the tone, though still critical, held considerably more respect, as MacIntyre was compared to the other theoreticians of morality: Taylor, Griffin, and Honderich.[17] Here again it is *After Virtue* and its successors that confer intellectual respectability and make MacIntyre a fitting subject for Andersonian pronouncement.

It is true, of course, MacIntyre did not engage in the uncritical adoration of the fashionable idols of the New Left, but he was at least as open to the world of European Marxism as contributors to the *NLR*, arguing that one of the main incentives for socialists to support European integration was that it would make more accessible theoretical traditions of which they were shamefully ignorant: "I can see nothing but good in an enforced dialogue with the exciting movements on the Italian Left," he wrote in 1963. "We should have to take seriously brands of European Marxists and brands of European anti-Marxists of whom we had scarcely heard."[18] His discussions of Sartre, Goldmann, Lukács, Deutscher, and C. Wright Mills displayed varying degree of sympathy with their subjects, but in no case were they simply the "hatchet jobs" of which Blackburn was later to complain. More generally, the political culture in which he operated, unlike that of the *NLR* and the writers it promoted, was not one that imitated the writing style of the bourgeois academy. MacIntyre's writing is clear and comprehensible even to readers without philosophical training, never displaying the kind of obscurantism typical of academics whose audience consists solely of their fellow-initiates. MacIntyre's former comrade Peter Sedgwick once wrote of him operating "as an intellectual rather than solely as an academic." This was partly because his range of reference encompassed areas beyond his professional specialism, and partly because of "his enviable capacity to take selected themes from the technical, professionalised debates among philosophers and social scientists and re-fashion them as material for the urgent attention of a non-specialised public, often using dramatic, poetic and prophetic devices in the casting of his arguments."[19]

There were of course socialists who found MacIntyre's Marxist work worth discussing. As noted above, Anderson's first comments on MacIntyre were written in the context of a discussion of Thompson's work, specifically in relation to the latter's reliance on MacIntyre's early ethical thought for his 1973 open letter to Leszek Kolakowski.[20] Unfortunately, Thompson's deployment of MacIntyre's arguments is submerged in the self-dramatization and nationalist bombast for which this essay is notorious. Most of his other admirers, like Sedgwick, were members of the IS, the last organization to which MacIntyre belonged before abandoning organized political activity. Martin Shaw's bibliographical guide to Marxist thought for students, also from 1973, refers to several works by MacIntyre.[21] David Widgery introduced his 1976 collection of British left-wing writings between 1956 and 1968 with the hope that it might convey "what the modern socialist movement feels like from within— its humour and music and oratory and colours and the intellectual sensations of its mentors and inventors," among which he specifically included "the whiskey and ice of Alasdair MacIntyre."[22] During the 1980s Chris Harman identified MacIntyre as a writer who had "produced some useful work" based on the ideas of Lukács's *History and Class Consciousness*, "but then slid back . . . towards liberal reformism."[23] And in the same decade Alex Callinicos thought that MacIntyre might have played a more specific role, writing of how exceptional it was for English-speaking Marxists to directly challenge the analytic tradition in philosophy: "Alasdair MacIntyre might have been another exception, had he not long since bid Marxism farewell."[24]

The second and most easily remedied condition responsible for the ignorance and lack of discussion of MacIntyre's Marxism has been removed, with the republication of the many of the relevant texts in *Alasdair MacIntyre's Engagement with Marxism*. The renewed availability of these writings will in turn remove the third, making it clear that MacIntyre's Marxist affiliation was no mere flirtation, but a passionate encounter that gave birth some of his greatest insights. The arguments presented in this chapter and in various contributions by Paul Blackledge are an attempt to remove the fourth by demonstrating that what MacIntyre had to say was important at the time and remains so for a new generation of activists against capitalist globalization and imperialist war.[25] What cannot be created by publication, reading, and argument is the first condition: the reemergence of a revolutionary movement in which MacIntyre's Marxism once again makes sense. Whether that culture can be re-created is still undecided, but it would be in keeping with the subject of this chapter to conclude that we must actively contribute to its re-creation rather than passively wait upon the outcome.

MARX AND SAINT PAUL: 1953-1958

Alasdair MacIntyre was born in Glasgow in 1929 of Irish descent. He took a degree in classics at the University of London during the late 1940s and subsequently a postgraduate degree in philosophy at Manchester University, where he stayed on as a lecturer between 1951 and 1957.[26] This was a period when the political bipolarity of Cold War international relations was refracted in British working-class politics through the Communist and Labour parties. While the Labour Party, then as now, was hegemonic on the British left, this position was not unchallenged; the Communist Party of Great Britain (CPGB) positioned itself as the left opposition to Labour, most successfully in the trade unions. Unsurprisingly, the Communist Party had long since proved its willingness to perform any number of elaborate political contortions at the behest of its mentors in Moscow; while the Labour Party, though more pluralistic, had developed a parallel relationship to Washington. This situation was not conducive to the development of an independent left capable of articulating a political program that went beyond the dualism of the Cold War.

During his period in London MacIntyre was both a member of the CPGB and a communicant with the Church of England.[27] MacIntyre himself has stated that one of his reasons for joining the CPGB was the influence on him of Executive Committee member George Thompson: "He played a part, I believe, in my joining the Communist Party for a short time. In 1941 he published *Aeschylus and Athens*, which came after a history of Greek philosophy up to Plato written in Irish, entitled *Tosnu na Feallsunachta*, as well as the translation of some Platonic dialogues into Irish."[28] Being a member of the CPGB at that time did not necessarily involve abandoning the Christian faith. From the onset of the Popular Front period in 1935 the CPGB had been involved in what it termed a "dialogue" with various Christians, a process that climaxed when Hewlett Johnson, the Dean of Canterbury, joined the editorial board of the *Weekly Worker* in 1943. Most contributions to this dialogue consisted of vague invocations of the supposedly shared humanist values of Communism and Christianity. MacIntyre entered the debate with his book

Marxism: An Interpretation, which instead made a serious attempt to discern intellectual links between Christian theology and Marxist theory. It was the most significant Marxist theoretical work to appear in Britain since Maurice Dobb's *Studies in the Development of Capitalism* in 1946 and, despite its religious perspective, it gives a far clearer introduction to Marx's views than anything being produced by the official Communist movement at that time.

Drawing heavily on the "Economic and Philosophical Manuscripts" (at that time available only in a German edition), MacIntyre hails Marx for the prophetic quality of his work; in other words, he regards Marx, contrary to the latter's own claims, as an essentially religious writer. Nevertheless, MacIntyre highlights several themes in Marx's early writings that were to be decisive for his own Marxism:

> First, such truth as we possess is the record not of passive observation of the world, but of active discovery. Secondly, Marx is attacking the problem as to whether in changing the world we should start with transforming ourselves and mankind . . . or rather should begin with transforming circumstances. Marx's answer is that you cannot do one without doing the other. To acquire a true philosophy is, of course, part of the transformation of oneself: this truth is only to be acquired in practice.

MacIntyre draws here on the "Theses on Feuerbach" that—in an interesting anticipation of Louis Althusser's notion of an "epistemological break" around 1845—he sees as being prescientific, while ascribing an entirely opposite value to the works on either side of it. For Althusser, the "epistemological break" marks the passage from mere ideology to science.[29] For MacIntyre, *The German Ideology* is the turning point where Marx has "abandon[ed] prophesy for theory," but in doing so he also "abandons himself to all the hazards of empirical confirmation": "Consequently, the claims of Marxist materialism are vindicated, if, and only if, the predictions of Marxist theory are verified." What differences are there between prophesy and prediction? For MacIntyre there are four:

> [First], both prophecy and theory point to a pattern in events: but the pattern to which prophecy points is always one in terms of purpose, in personal terms. [Second], for prediction to be of any value, for it to be a real prediction at all, it must specify accurately what is to happen and

when. Prophecy, by contrast, presents us with a general pattern of events in personal terms which may occur once or several times . . . Thirdly, a prediction should tell us what to expect: a prophecy may come true in quite unexpected ways. Fourthly, a prophecy is guaranteed not by verification but by trust in the prophet: it presupposes a commitment to someone who exemplifies in his or her life the purposeful pattern which enables history to be interpreted in personal terms.

For MacIntyre then, Marx is a prophet posing as a theorist: "Thus, in Marx's later thinking, and in Marxism, economic theory is treated prophetically; and that theory cannot be treated prophetically without becoming bad theory is something that Marxism can teach us at the point where it passes from prophecy to science." In economic terms Marxism is "bad theory" because its empirical claims cannot be sustained. MacIntyre gives two reasons for this. First, "the labour theory of value does not work outside a state of perfect competition." Since perfect competition does not exist in modern conditions of monopoly and oligopoly, MacIntyre claims the theory of marginal utility is superior because of its general applicability. Second, and more important, MacIntyre claims that the increasing immiseration of the working class that Marx predicted has not taken place. Nevertheless, MacIntyre claims that capitalist civilization has failed, even if capitalist economy has not. How so? "The essential failure of capitalism is not that the pursuit of profit is incompatible with the pursuit of social welfare: the essential failure is that the kind of society which capitalism creates is one that can never fully employ the skills of hand and brain and eye, the exercise of which is part of man's true being."[30] These were to be persistent themes in his work over the next fifteen years.

For five years after the publication of *Marxism: An Interpretation* MacIntyre was prepared to praise Marx as an individual thinker: "Marxism is an attempt to provide the conceptual key to both nature and history. The attempt to present Marx as a scientific sociologist in the modern sense is like presenting *Hamlet* as a play about Rosencrantz and Guildenstern."[31] But as late as 1956 he was still dismissing all contemporary Marxist theory as largely "fossilised."[32] What did MacIntyre consider to be "Marxism" at this point? Although he was clearly aware of several key debates within the Marxist tradition—the debates between Bernstein and Kautsky on socialist morality and between Plekhanov and Lenin on the nature of the revolutionary party are both mentioned in *Marxism: An Interpretation*—he did not distinguish between any tendencies or traditions, still less argue that one of these might be more authentically Marxist than another. In drawing examples from outside Marx's own writings to illustrate specific arguments, MacIntyre is entertainingly but also indiscriminately eclectic: a novel by Silone on Fascist Italy, a memoir by Koestler on the Spanish Civil War, a handbook by Liu for Chinese Communists.[33] Crucially, there was no specific discussion of Stalinism. Indeed, one characteristic of *Marxism: An Interpretation* is the way in which it accepts the dominant view of the Marxist tradition in which there is an unbroken succession from Marx and Engels to Lenin and from Lenin to Stalin. This was almost universally accepted, not only by both sides of the Cold War (although they ascribed different and opposing values to the lineage), but also by any surviving anarchists who took neither side. Only Trotskyists continued to insist on the existence of what Trotsky himself had called "a whole river of blood" separating Lenin and the Bolsheviks from Stalinism.[34]

Insofar as there was a commonly held alternative to the continuity thesis on the left, it was concerned to place a break after Marx, so that Lenin and the Bolsheviks bore sole responsibility for initiating the descent into totalitarianism. Ironically, Trotsky's earlier writings, together with those of Rosa Luxemburg, were frequently quoted, in a decontextualized manner, as prophetic warnings about the likely outcome of Lenin's organizational innovations.[35] In this tradition, the former is seen as having succumbed to the Leninist virus and the latter to have heroically, if tragically, maintained her faith in the democratic role of the working class until the end.[36] And sure enough, the only reference to Trotsky in *Marxism: An Interpretation* invokes the passage from *Our Political Tasks* in which he allegedly foresees the emergent dictatorship of the party over the class.[37] There was nothing unusual in his lack of engagement with Trotsky. The fact that Trotskyism later became the dominant tendency on the British far-left has tended to obscure the fact that, before 1956, most people in the labor movement had never read anything by Trotsky or personally encountered any of his followers.[38] Indeed, even today it is not unknown for well-known left intellectuals to admit to ignorance of his work.[39] Only a few years later MacIntyre himself was to acidly suggest in an open letter to a Gaitskellite that "you are perhaps slightly disappointed to find that those who denounced Trotskyism among your friends had never actually read Trotsky."[40]

The Asia-Africa Conference at Bandung in 1955 provided the first sign of an alternative to the bipolar world of the Cold War. At this event, what was coming to be called the "Third World" declared itself for the first time as a major player in international affairs. If this episode opened a crack in the world order, the events of 1956—Khrushchev's Secret Speech, the Russian invasion of Hungary, the thwarting of reforms in Poland, and the Anglo-French invasion of Egypt—together created a much wider space for widespread criticism of the world order as a totality. In striking deep at the heart of the international system these actions opened a space from which independent political forces could grow in Britain, where a "New Left" emerged seeking a third way between both Eastern Stalinism and Western capitalism, and their local left-wing political allies, Stalinism and social democracy. The first New Left, as Peter Sedgwick pointed out in the wake of its collapse in the early 1960s, was less a coherent movement than a milieu within which many diverse political perspectives were aired.[41] It was formed of fragments from both the Labour and Communist parties, alongside members of the revolutionary left, students, and other non-aligned elements radicalized by the events of 1956. However, while the events of 1956 marked the point at which an independent left first emerged in postwar Britain, it was a further eighteen months or so before a movement erupted that offered this milieu the opportunity to test its politics against those of the Labour and Communist parties. The force that brought a new generation of activists onto the streets, and then into the New Left meeting rooms, was the Campaign for Nuclear Disarmament (CND), whose marches from early 1958 saw thousands of the dissatisfied youth come into conflict not only with the government but also with the leaderships of the Labour and Communist parties—both of whom initially opposed the demand for unilateral nuclear disarmament. Indeed, it was through activity within CND that the New Left was able to break out of the political ghetto. However, the promise of radical change, which had nourished both the New Left and CND, was quickly stifled when the right wing of the Labour Party succeeded in overturning the previous year's call for unilateral nuclear disarmament at the 1961 Labour Party conference. Subsequently, both the New Left and CND became casualties of shared overly optimistic hopes for the radicalization of the Labour Party.[42]

MacIntyre did not respond immediately to the emergence of the New Left. He seems to have left the CPGB by 1956—at any rate he was not involved in the debates within it sparked by the events of that year. Indications that he had begun to rethink his position only came two years later, by which time the New Left had become firmly established. What was MacIntyre's attitude to Christianity by this point? In June 1958 he wrote in the BBC journal the *Listener,* bemoaning the social irrelevance of his own community of faith: "As a member of the Church of England, I am concerned that in this situation [i.e. 'of deep moral sickness'] the Church should be effective in its mission, and to that end should not cherish the illusion of a moral integrity which is just not there."[43] As late as 1959 he wrote in a discussion of Hume for *Philosophical Review* that he "would agree with Marxists" about the change for the worse in ethical theory involved in the shift from substantive to formal moral judgments.[44] The reference to "Marxists" as a separate group with which he was in agreement over this issue might be taken to indicate a certain distance; but by the time this article appeared in print he had already identified himself with them. Why he came to do so is suggested by another passage in the same article. Human nature endows us with certain common desires, he points out, which in turn suggests that we should therefore share a common morality; but in class-divided societies this is impossible:

> We have moral rules because we have common interests. Should someone succeed in showing us that the facts are different from what we conceive them to be so that we have no common interests, then our moral rules would lose their justification. Indeed, the initial move of Marx's moral theory can perhaps be best understood as a denial of the facts which Hume holds to constitute the justification for social morality. Marx's denial that that there are common interests shared by the whole of society in respect of, for instance, the distribution of property, meets Hume on his own ground.[45]

The point is of wider application, suggesting that in the entire aspect of social life, the central question is whether Marx was right about the existence of social classes and, perhaps even more importantly, right about the relationships of exploitation and conflict that existed between the main classes in capitalist society.

TROTSKY, NOT KEYNES: 1958-1964

By the time "Hume on Is and Ought" appeared in October 1959 MacIntyre has apparently decided that Marx was in fact correct. His first two Marxist articles appeared in *Universities and Left Review* in 1958.[46] A third, published over two issues of the other main New Left journal, the *New Reasoner*, returned to the question of morality, but now in the context of a discussion of Stalinism rather than class society in general. Edward Thompson had opened a debate on the nature of socialist humanism in the first issue of the *New Reasoner*. His contribution combined powerful criticisms of the inhumanity of Stalinism with a tacit acceptance of the consequentialist frame of reference through which the Stalinists had attempted to justify their actions. Thus, he commented that although the means employed by Stalin could not be defended, he had gone some way toward realizing at least aspects of socialism in Russia.[47] Harry Hanson's reply denounced the Stalinist experiment *tout court* as a strategy of forced industrialization carried out through an assault on the basic human rights of the mass of Russians.[48] MacIntyre's contribution to this debate, "Notes from the Moral Wilderness," argued that both positions were inadequate.

MacIntyre opened this essay with a critique of the implied Kantianism of Hanson's morality: "The ex-Communist turned moral critic of Communism is often a figure of genuine pathos . . . They repudiate Stalinist crimes in the name of moral principle; but the fragility of their appeal to moral principles lies in the apparently arbitrary nature of that appeal." Despite the direction of this criticism, MacIntyre was equally as critical of those apologists for Stalinism for whom socialism's moral core was lost amidst a mechanical theory of historical progress. MacIntyre suggested that the Stalinists, through the medium of a teleological vision of historical progress, came to identify "what is morally right with what is actually going to be the outcome of historical development, such that the 'ought' of principle is swallowed up in the 'is' of history." It was thus not enough to add something like Kant's ethics to this existing Stalinist theory of historical development if one wished to reinsert moral principle into Marxism, for this theory of history negated moral choice. Conversely, neither was it adequate to reject, as immoral, any historical event from some supposed higher standpoint, for "there is no set of common, public standards to which [one] can appeal." Indeed, any such maneuver would tend to gravitate to an existing tradition of morality that, because these had generally evolved to serve some particular dominant class interests, would "play into the hands of the defenders of the status quo." Therefore, MacIntyre insisted, apologists for both the East and the West in the Cold War based their arguments upon inadequate theoretical frameworks. In contrast to these perspectives, MacIntyre argued that we should look for a "theory which treats what emerges in history as providing us with a basis for our standards, without making the historical process morally sovereign or its progress automatic." In his search for a basis from which to reconstruct a Marxist ethics, MacIntyre argued, contrary to "the liberal belief in the autonomy of morality," that it was the purposive character of human action that could both distinguish human history from natural history and provide a historical and materialist basis for moral judgments. MacIntyre suggested that Marxists should follow the Greeks in general and Aristotle in particular and insist on a link between ethics and human desires: "We make both individual deeds and social practices intelligible as human actions by showing how they connect with characteristically human desires, needs and the like." He thus proposed to relate morality to desire in a way that was radically at odds with Kant; for where Kant's "'ought' of morality is utterly divorced from the 'is' of desire," MacIntyre pointed out that to divorce ethics from activities that aim to satisfy needs and desires in this way "is to make it unintelligible as a form of human action." In contrast to the Kantian categorical imperative, MacIntyre therefore argued that we need a morality that relates to our desires. However, while human desires are related to human needs, MacIntyre refused to reify the concept of human nature. Instead, he followed Marx in radically historicizing human nature, without losing sight of its biological basis. Indeed, Marx's greatness, or so MacIntyre argued, was rooted in his historicization of Man: for Marx refused to follow either Hobbes into a melancholic model of human needs and desires, or Diderot into a utopian counterposition of the state of nature against contemporary social structures. Instead, Marx comprehended the limited historical truth of Hobbes's insight, but counterposed to it, not a utopia, but the real movement of workers in struggle through which they are capable of realizing that solidarity is a fundamental human desire. Specifically, under advanced capitalism in MacIntyre's reading of Marx, "the growth of production makes it possible [for man] to reappropriate his own nature." This is true in two ways: first, the increasing productivity of labor produces the potential for us all to lead much richer lives, both morally and materially; and, second, capitalism creates an agency—the proletariat—that embodies, through its struggles for freedom, a new collectivist spirit, through which individuals come to understand both that their needs and desires can best be satisfied through collective channels, and that they do in fact need and desire solidarity. Indeed, he claimed that the proletariat, in its struggles against capital, was beginning to create the conditions for the solution of the contemporary problems of morality: it embodies the practice that could overcome the "rift between our conception of morality and our conception of desire." MacIntyre concluded that once the political left had rid itself both of the myth of the inevitable triumph of socialism, and of the reification of socialism as some indefinite end that could be used to justify any action taken in its name, then socialists would truly comprehend the interpenetration of means and ends through the history of class struggle. Consequently, they would understand Marxist morality to be, "as against the Stalinists," "an assertion of moral absolutes," and, "as against the liberal critic of Stalinism," "an assertion of desire and history."[49]

MacIntyre would quickly have become aware that Trotskyism offered an explanation for the realities of Stalinism that did not simply rely on moral categories—the key problem with which he had wrestled in the pages of the *New Reasoner*. MacIntyre made his first reference to Trotsky or Trotskyism in 1958, in one of his first articles for the socialist press. It was not complimentary. In a review of Raya Dunyevskaya's *Marxism and Freedom* for *Universities and Left Review*, he wrote of the author: "She has been repelled by the arid, seminary text-book Marxism of the Stalinists and the Trotskyists (who share all the dogmatism of the Stalinists without any of their achievements)." Three aspects of MacIntyre's thought emerge from this review. First, he regarded the USSR and the other Stalinist states as socialist, or at least in the process of transition to socialism. He criticized Dunayevskaya for her belief that society had entered "the age of state capitalism, a form of economy common to both U.S.A. and U.S.S.R.," because it involved "a fantastic under-valuation of socialist achievement in the Soviet Union": "she writes of the Soviet state as though the Moscow trials, Vorkuta, and Hungary were its supreme and authentic expressions." Second, he rejected what he regarded as Dunyevskaya's idealized conceptions of the working class: "And of course those who have to idealise the workers are precisely those who have lost their faith in the real flesh-and-blood working class." Third, he did not see any immediate prospect of the actual working class moving into revolutionary action. For this reason it was necessary, like Marx and Lenin in their time, "to be prepared to live without signs of hope": "It is from Lenin's stance of hope in a situation which to the ordinary eye would be one of hopelessness that we have to learn." The source of hope was in fact the opposite of those usually cited by orthodox Marxists, not the supposed law-given predictability of the development of the productive forces, but the potential for working-class creativity suppressed by class divisions and awaiting release:

> We are so used to having Marxism interpreted for us as the science which lays bare the laws of society that we tend to take it for granted that Marxism presents us with a picture of man as a being whose behaviour is essentially predictable. But in fact it is truer to say that Marxism shows us how in class-divided society human possibility is never fully revealed. There is always more potentiality in human beings than we are accustomed to allow for. And because of this, human development often takes place in quite unpredictable leaps. We never perhaps know how near we are to the next step forward.[50]

Here we can still see his opposition to notions of Marxist science and the predictions that it was supposed to enable. MacIntyre was rapidly to change his views on the Stalinist states, but his conviction at this time that they represented societies transitional to socialism might have suggested that he was growing closer to Trotskyism, had his views not been decidedly hostile ("all the dogmatism of the Stalinists without any of their achievements"). Yet by June 1959, less than a year later, MacIntyre had joined one group of Trotskyist "dogmatists," the newly formed SLL. And, as one member recalls: "He was at first full of enthusiasm; he spoke at meetings, sold papers, wrote articles and pamphlets."[51] Why had he taken this apparently unexpected step? There seem to be two reasons why MacIntyre made this particular organizational affiliation. One was that, while avoiding the orthodox Trotskyist terminology of "degenerated workers' states," he had effectively arrived at a similar understanding of Russia as an imperfect society but one transitional to socialism: his first published work after joining the SLL was a review of Herbert Marcuse in which he praised the author for rejecting alternative interpretations, such as state capitalism.[52] The second reason was that the practical bent of MacIntyre's Marxism in this period lent itself to a reengagement with Lenin's political thought at the very moment when the bulk of the New Left was theorizing a break with the ideas of the leader of the Russian Revolution. In contrast with this perspective, MacIntyre's activist interpretation of Marx informed his reading of Lenin as offering a means of escaping from the limitations of mechanical Marxism: he came to view revolutionary organizations as necessary media through which proletarian unity might be won. This perspective sharply differentiated MacIntyre from many leading figures within the New Left, whilst simultaneously drawing him toward those whose break with Stalinism had brought them into the orbit of the Trotskyist left

There were, however, also what might be called nondoctrinal reasons for the SLL to be attractive to a young militant seeking an organizational framework. The SLL was the largest of the British Trotskyist groups and had attracted many of the best ex-members of the CPGB after the events of 1956. Given the sectarian dementia for which the organization became infamous on the British left, especially in its later incarnation as the Workers Revolutionary Party, it is important to understand that it initially presented itself as an open body, keen to encourage debate and facilitate exchanges of views in SLL publications like the weekly *Newsletter* and the monthly *Labour Review*, both of which first appeared in 1957.[53] This stance obviously held attractions for those who had found the regime in the CPGB intolerable. Furthermore, the SLL was able to provide an explanation for the degeneration of the CPGB that—unlike the explanations on offer from the New Left—did not see the problem as lying with the Original Sin of democratic centralism.

Its theoretical approach was however burdened by a dogmatic allegiance to some of Trotsky's later writings that prevented certain subjects, like the nature of the Soviet Union, from being seriously discussed. Furthermore, although it was not immediately apparent to new recruits, the SLL had a deeply undemocratic structure, centred on the leader Gerry

Healy and his immediate coterie. These constraints prevented the SLL from growing or developing, despite several promising initiatives. MacIntyre is captured at one of these, the "National Assembly of Labour" on November 15, 1959, which drew a claimed seven hundred delegates to St. Pancras Hall in London.[54] Described in the report in the SLL paper, the *Newsletter,* as a "lecturer in philosophy at Leeds University and a delegate from the Leeds Branch of the Socialist Labour League," MacIntyre welcomed the fact that the conference included teachers and lecturers as well as traditional members of the working class, but he warned his fellow-intellectuals that they "have got to learn that they are not sent from heaven or the Fabian Society in order to guide the labour movement from above with their theorising, and on the other hand, intellectuals might as well not be in the labour movement if they are simply going to be the office boys of the trade union bureaucrats."[55]

Much of what MacIntyre wrote for the SLL was focused on the question of revolutionary organization. He produced his fullest discussion of the Communist Party experience in a talk delivered—incredible as it now seems—on the BBC Third Programme and later reproduced in the eminently respectable pages of the BBC magazine, the *Listener,* provoking a debate that ran for three months, including contributions from ex-Communists like Thompson and Hanson, and from Peter Cadogan who had recently been expelled from the SLL. In the *Listener,* he identified the key factors behind the decline of the CPGB as the "rise of Stalinism in the Soviet Union" and "the defeat of the British working-class in the General Strike."[56] This is possibly the most "orthodox" statement of his career and there is little in it with which members of any other Trotskyist grouping would disagree. But moving from historical analysis to the contemporary scene, it is clear that MacIntyre was conscious of the need to balance the ability to reach out to the actually exiting audience for socialist politics—whether or not they possessed the correct proletarian credentials—with the need for a revolutionary organization. This democratic approach to political leadership is similarly evident in MacIntyre's critique of the sectarian attitude shown by some leading members of the SLL to the New Left.

Thus, in 1959, he engaged in a debate with Cliff Slaughter on the pages of *Labour Review,* the SLL's monthly theoretical magazine, over the issue of the SLL's relationship to the broader New Left milieu. Slaughter had argued that it was incumbent upon the SLL to "state sharply where we differ on basic questions of theory and method" from the New Left. Consequently, he traced and criticized arguments regarding the nature of social class in the modern world as articulated by a number of important New Left thinkers: principally, Dorothy Thompson, Charles Taylor, and Stuart Hall.[57] In opposition to Slaughter's almost wholly negative indictment of New Left theory, MacIntyre pointed out that the New Left was a more complex phenomenon than Slaughter's essay implied, and that many of Slaughter's own criticisms had been articulated within the New Left itself—most prominently by Edward Thompson. Therefore, while MacIntyre agreed with much of the substance of Slaughter's arguments, he felt that Slaughter's "polemical and sectarian style" was mistaken, for it acted to create a barrier between the SLL and all that was positive within the New Left. "The most important thing about the New Left," he argued, "is that it exists." Therefore, "for a Marxist the question must be: What does the existence of this grouping point to in the changing character of our political life?" On the basis of a generally positive answer to this question, MacIntyre concluded his internal critique of the SLL leadership with the argument that "the relationship of Marxists to the New Left ought not to be one merely negative and critical but one which is continually looking for those points of growth in its theory that can lead on to common political action." More generally, he argued that, as it was at the "point of production" that people in "our society . . . begin to act and think for themselves," then it was the duty of the SLL to argue, fraternally, within the New Left that that they should orientate themselves toward the industrial struggles of the working class. Socialists, he wrote, "can only carry through an effective educational effort as part of the industrial and political struggle." Conversely, despite the good intentions of the New Left, its lack of focus on such struggles tended to "dissipate socialist energy and lead nowhere." His objection to the dismissive tone adopted by Slaughter was because it acted as an obstacle to winning activists in the New Left to a more fully revolutionary politics and party commitment, not because he wanted to perpetuate its amorphous approach to organization.[58]

The internal SLL debate over the nature of revolutionary organization reached its highest level in an article by MacIntyre, "Freedom and Revolution," published the following year. In part, this seems to have been an attempt to defend the theory of the revolutionary party embodied in the SLL against those who—in response to its increasingly undemocratic practice—had either left or been expelled from it. But it was also an attempt to think through his own perspective, which was beginning markedly to diverge from that of his comrades. MacIntyre argues from first principles, starting with the position of people in capitalist society, not with quotations from Lenin and Trotsky (although Lenin's discussion of ideology in "What is to be done?" forms a ghostly backdrop throughout). Indeed, the only thinkers he mentions are Hegel and Marx. He begins his case for the revolutionary party with the apparently paradoxical notion that it is essential for the realization of human freedom—not the usual starting point in Leninist or Trotskyist discussions: "To assert oneself at the expense of the organisation in order to be free is to miss the fact that only within some organisational form can human freedom be embodied." But the role of the vanguard party is not itself to achieve freedom, "but to moving the working class to build it." In order to "withstand all the pressures of other classes and to act effectively against the ruling class," it has to have two characteristics. The first, the need for constant self-education, is relatively uncontentious. But the second, which returns to the paradox of vanguardism and freedom, is more interesting. MacIntyre begins conventionally enough, noting that "one can only preserve oneself from alien class pressures in a vanguard party by maintaining discipline. Those who do not act closely together, who have no overall strategy for changing society, will have neither need for nor understanding of discipline." Appeals for "discipline" by themselves were unlikely to win over members of the New Left, who were only too conscious of how this had been used by Stalinist parties to suppress discussion, but their alternative tended to emphasize personal choice. MacIntyre was able to show that there was an organizational alternative to both bureaucratic centralism and liberal individualism:

> Those who do not act closely together, who have no overall strategy for changing society, will have neither need for nor understanding of discipline. Party discipline is essentially not something negative, but something positive. It frees party members for activity by ensuring that they have specific tasks, duties and rights. This is why all the constitutional apparatus is necessary. Nonetheless there are many socialists who feel that any form of party discipline is an alien and constraining force which

they ought to resist in the name of freedom. The error here arises from
the illusion that one can as an isolated individual escape from the mould-
ing and the subtle enslavements of the status quo. Behind this there lies
the illusion that one can be an isolated individual. Whether we like it or
not every one of us inescapably plays a social role, and a social role which
is determined for us by the workings of bourgeois society. Or rather this
is inescapable so long as we remain unaware of what is happening to us.
As our awareness and understanding increase we become able to change
the part we play. But here yet another trap awaits us. The saying that
freedom is the knowledge of necessity does not mean that a merely passive and theoretical knowledge can liberate us. The knowledge which
liberates is that which enables us to change our social relations. And this
knowledge, knowledge which Marxism puts at our disposal, is not a private possession, something which the individual can get out of books
and then keep for himself; it is rather a continually growing consciousness, which can only be the work of a group bound together by a common political and educational discipline.[59]

Whether the SLL was the type of party that MacIntyre advocated was
less clear. The leadership responded obliquely with an article by Cliff
Slaughter, "What is Revolutionary Leadership?," not criticizing MacIntyre
by name, but identifying what Slaughter evidently saw as an inadequate
conception of the revolutionary party. Slaughter's response was also a serious contribution and one that brought into the debate not only arguments from Lenin, but from the early Lukács and Gramsci, both of whom
were virtually unknown in the English-speaking world at this time.
Lukács in particular was to be important in MacIntyre's development, although there is no evidence that he had read him before this point. Nevertheless, Slaughter's piece also contained warning signs of how the SLL
was going to develop, notably in his insistence on the need to raise "discipline and centralised authority . . . to an unprecedented degree."[60]
    In the course of the debate in the *Listener* MacIntyre had written
that "whether the SLL is or is not democratic or Marxist will be very
clearly manifested as time goes on. I myself have faced no limitation on
intellectual activity of any kind in the SLL."[61] Ironically, within months
of writing these lines MacIntyre was expelled from the SLL alongside a
number of other prominent activists who refused to act as mere puppets
of the leadership, sent on his way with usual denunciations of petty-
bourgeois revisionism and so on.[62] In a letter to Gerry Healy, MacIntyre

observed that it was clearly impossible for a minority to exist within the organization because of his personal dominance and the fact that he effectively owned it as private property, since the assets were in his name. His conclusion, however, was not that these problems stemmed solely from Healy's personal malevolence—real though that undoubtedly was—but because of the small size of the Trotskyist organizations that allowed individuals to play this role.[63]

Around the time MacIntyre left the SLL, he wrote perhaps the single greatest essay to emerge from the first period of the New Left, "Breaking the Chains of Reason," which appeared in Edward Thompson's collection *Out of Apathy*. In a sweeping survey of the contemporary intellectual scene, MacIntyre makes the case for Marxism as a method by defending it against the criticisms of Karl Popper. Popper had claimed that Marxism was deficient on three main grounds, all of which supposedly tended toward totalitarianism on the Russian model. First, it was historicist, meaning that it claimed to have discovered the underlying trends of historical development and could therefore predict future patterns of events. Second, it ascribed views and actions to collective social actors, particularly classes, whereas in reality only individuals could be said to possess these qualities. Third, it was partisan, seeking not to discover partial scientific understanding but to justify positions to which it was already committed because of its historicism. MacIntyre briefly dismantles these positions, which were at the time treated as incontestable, not least on the right of the Labour Party.

First, Marx did not believe that he had discovered the inevitable course of human history, but a potential outcome made possible by developments within capitalism: "Knowledge of the trends that are dominant is for Marx an instrument for changing them. So his belief that he has uncovered "the economic law of motion of capitalist society" is not a belief in an absolute trend, but a trend whose continuance is contingent on a variety of factors including our activity." Second, as an alternative to dealing with collectives, "methodological individualism" was incoherent:

> You cannot characterise an army by referring to the soldiers who belong to it. For to do that you have to identify them as soldiers; and to do that is already to bring in the concept of an army. For a soldier just is an individual who belongs to an army. Thus we see that the characterisation of individuals and of classes has to go together. Essentially these are not two separate tasks.

Third, Popper is wrong in his demand for objectivity, or as he puts it, a concern for means rather than ends. On the one hand, means and ends cannot be separated in this way. On the other, his claim is "self-refuting":

> For to assert that our concern can only be with the means and to add that the result of that concern can only be limited and particular statements of social correlation is already to be partisan. An example of what Popper takes to be a genuine discovery of the social sciences is that "You cannot have full employment without inflation" (the rider "in our type of economy" is not added). If such limited discoveries are all that we can hope for from the social sciences, it follows that we cannot hope to transform society as such; all that we can hope to change are particular features of social life. To adopt this view of the means available for social change is to commit oneself to the view that the only feasible ends of social policy are limited reformist ones, and that revolutionary ends are never feasible. To be committed to this is to be partisan in the most radical way.[64]

MacIntyre now had two organizational choices if he wanted to remain an active revolutionary. One was IS (formerly the Socialist Review Group), which had been formed out of a much earlier split—in fact a series of expulsions—from the last unified British Trotskyist organization, the Revolutionary Communist Party, in 1950. The central position of the IS, elaborated by the group's founder Tony Cliff in 1948 on the basis of his reading of the Marxist classics, was the very view of Stalinist states that MacIntyre had earlier rejected, namely that they represented forms of bureaucratic state capitalism. The other was the post-Leninist, post-Trotskyist, and ultimately post-Marxist organization established by other former SLL members, initially called Socialism Reaffirmed, then (from 1961) Solidarity. This group also rejected the view that the Stalinist regimes were in any sense socialist but was far less specific than the IS in giving them a positive characterization, referring to them instead as examples of "bureaucratic society." There was another difference that was to be important for MacIntyre's later theoretical and political development. Where the IS saw the postwar boom as underpinned by the arms economy, Cliff and its other major theoretician, Mike Kidron, did not see this as a permanent stabilization, but one that would ultimately produce its own contradictions. Solidarity, on the other hand, drew on the work of the one-time Greek Trotskyist Cornelius Castoriadis (known at

the time as Paul Cardan) to argue that capitalism had definitively overcome its tendency to economic crisis.[65] In terms of how these organizations saw their relationship to the working class, however, there
appeared to be far fewer differences, as can be seen by comparing the
statements of their respective leading thinkers.[66] Cliff continued to talk
about leadership, a notion that Maurice Brinton consciously avoids, but
both groups had clearly distanced themselves from the kind of bureaucratic machine-Leninism practiced by orthodox Trotskyist organizations
like the SLL. Solidarity and IS coexisted in a relatively fraternal manner
and the early issues of *International Socialism* contained material by prominent Solidarity members, including Brinton (under the name of Martin
Grainger) and Bob Pennington. It also published material by both Cardan
and other members of his group, Socialism or Barbarism, including the
later prophet of postmodernism, Jean-François Lyotard.[67]

What was the relationship of IS to Trotskyism at this time? In 1965
the US author George Thayer reported an interview with Kidron: "He
claims that his group is not Trotskyist but Trotskyist-derived, pointing
out that Socialism is his first concern and that his conclusions may only
incidentally incorporate the thoughts and conclusions of Trotsky. He adds
that he welcomes all Socialist thought—from Marx, Lenin, E.V. Debs, or
anyone else—if it can be of assistance to him."[68] As a former member of
the Fourth International Cliff identified more closely with Trotsky and
the classical Marxist tradition he had done so much to preserve. There is
no reason, however, to think that Cliff was not being perfectly honest in
his 1959 assessment of the best model for a revolutionary party: "For
Marxists in advanced industrial countries, Lenin's original position can
serve much less as a guide than Rosa Luxemburg's, notwithstanding her
over-statements on the question of spontaneity."[69] MacIntyre would
therefore have regarded himself as having joined a group that had developed out of Trotskyism while rejecting some of Trotsky's specific theoretical and organizational conclusions.

Kidron had greeted MacIntyre's chapter in *Out of Apathy* as "a brilliant
contribution."[70] By the time this appreciation appeared MacIntyre had
joined both the organization and the editorial board of its newly
launched eponymous journal, his first contribution appearing in the third
issue.[71] He was finally introduced to readers in issue six: "Alasdair Mac-
Intyre," the note revealed, "teaches philosophy and has experience of the

Communist Party, the Socialist Labour League, the New Left and the Labour Party; believes that if none of these can disillusion one with socialism, then nothing can."[72] MacIntyre had by this point abandoned his religious beliefs, telling *Twentieth Century:* "Was a Christian. Am not. It is less misleading when asked if I am a Marxist to say 'yes' rather than 'no.' But other Marxists have been known to say 'no.'"[73]

MacIntyre had rejected Trotskyist orthodoxy, but there was no ambiguity in his attitude to Trotsky himself. MacIntyre concluded "Breaking the Chains of Reason" with an incandescent passage establishing his admiration for Trotsky as a model for radical intellectuals:

> Two images have been with me throughout the writing of this essay. Between them they seem to show the alternative paths for the intellectual. The one is of J. M. Keynes, the other of Leon Trotsky. Both were obviously men of attractive personality and great natural gifts. The one the intellectual guardian of the established order, providing new policies and theories of manipulation to keep society in what he took to be economic trim, and making a personal fortune in the process. The other, outcast as a revolutionary from Russia both under the Tsar and under Stalin, providing throughout his life a defence of human activity, of the powers of conscious and rational human effort. I think of them at the end, Keynes with his peerage, Trotsky with an icepick in his skull. These are the twin lives between which intellectual choice in our society lies.[74]

The fullest statement of MacIntyre's attitude toward Trotsky and Trotskyism during this period was given in his review of the final volume of Isaac Deutscher's biography, *The Prophet Outcast* (1963). His first point was that Trotsky himself never succumbed to the theoretical conservatism that later overtook most of his followers: "Throughout his life Trotsky was prepared to reformulate Marxism. The theory of permanent revolution bears striking witness to this."[75] Consequently, it was entirely in keeping with Trotsky's own theoretical boldness to seek to understand the limitations of his positions, where necessary, and to move beyond them. MacIntyre now accepted Cliff's version of the theory of state capitalism as an attempt to do this and raised the possibility that Trotsky himself might have come to share this view, had he been faced with the evidence that private capitalism and socialism were not the only available alternatives; there was also "the collective class rule of the bureaucracy."

For the Trotsky of the 1930s, as for Marx, socialism can be made only by the workers and not for them. It is in part because of this that Trotsky, had he lived, would have had to treat his predictions about the aftermath of the Second World War as falsified. He could not but have concluded from his own premises that Russia was in no sense a workers' state, but rather a grave of socialism. . . . He could never have accepted Deutscher's analysis, which has only one thing in common with his own: the use of nationalized property as a criterion for socialism.

The failure of more orthodox Trotskyists to make comparable theoretical reconsiderations condemned them to sterility. Consequently, his attitude toward these parties in some senses reverted to an earlier dismissiveness:

> So-called Trotskyism has always been among the most trivial of move-ments. It transformed into abstract dogma what Trotsky thought in con-crete terms at one moment in his life, and canonised this. It is inexplicable in purely political dimensions, but the history of the more eccentric re-ligious sects provides revealing parallels. The genuine Trotskyism of [Al-fred] Rosmer or Natalya [Sedova] must have at most a few hundred adherents in the entire world.[76]

It is perhaps worth noting that, since MacIntyre was still active in IS at this time, he presumably did not regard himself as belonging to the po-litical equivalent of a "religious sect."

But, when all due recognition is granted to Trotsky's political, intel-lectual, and moral achievements, was there some connection between the chronic irrelevance of Trotskyist organizations and his own thought? MacIntyre hinted at an answer in a review of *Literature and Revolution*, in which he wrote that Trotsky's literary criticism revealed the "unity of greatness and weakness" in his thought: "The greatness lies in the grasp of actual social connections. . . . The weakness comes out in the substi-tution of an *a priori* scheme of things for the actual complex reality when-ever he comes to a point made difficult by his own theory."[77] In another context MacIntyre gave a specific example of this weakness:

> When, in the early 1930s, Trotsky was confronted with the facts of this growth [in working-class standards of living] by the Marxist economist Fritz Sternberg he remarked that he had no time recently to study the statistics; that on the truth or falsity of the statements involved much else

that he was committed to depended he does not seem to have noticed. Nor was this attitude restricted to Trotsky, whom I select here as the most honest, perceptive and intelligent of post-1939 Marxists.[78]

This is less than fair to Trotsky, who wrote (in a series of notes not intended for publication): "The dialectic does not liberate the investigator from painstaking study of the facts, quite the contrary; it requires it."[79] And this scrupulousness with "the facts" is attested to by, for example, his handling of source material in *The History of the Russian Revolution*. What is of interest here is less the accuracy of MacIntyre's judgment than the source he identifies of Trotsky's theoretical weakness: "Trotsky is as helpless as anyone else imprisoned in the categories of Leninism."[80] As this suggests, MacIntyre takes a far more ambivalent position toward Lenin than toward Trotsky. What then were the characteristics of his Marxism during the period?

First, it was revolutionary: "For the question of *how* socialism could come about cannot be derived from the question of *what* it is to be. And the revolutionary case is in part that nothing worth calling socialism *could* come into being by reformist methods."[81] Indeed, MacIntyre went so far as to claim that the conditions for reformism no longer existed. These, he argued, were a relatively homogenous working class, a state that was believed to be relatively independent of the capitalist class (and consequently had sometimes to behave as if it was), and a ruling class prepared to compromise in order to achieve its broader objectives. None of these remained: "The working-class is far less homogeneous . . . the state . . . is now so well integrated with the key institutions of the capitalist economy that it cannot any longer be conceived of as a neutral, independent source of power that could be used against that economy. . . . the ruling class . . . do not need to accommodate themselves to the working-class now by means of parliamentary institutions." But there was no reason to despair. The very fact of capitalist expansion would produce needs that the system could not fulfill: "Revolutions do not take place in fact against backgrounds of pauperisation and slump. They take place when in a period of rising expectations the established order cannot satisfy the expectations which it has been forced to bring into being. The new capitalism cannot avoid calling into being a new working-class with large horizons so far as not merely wages but also education and welfare are concerned."[82]

Second, as this suggests, MacIntyre saw the working class as the agent of change, not any of the other forces—reformist politicians, Stalinist bureaucrats, peasant guerrillas, or students—that were increasingly being offered as substitutes by sections of the New Left. One of his criticisms of those sections of the New Left that retained a focus on working-class life was that it was fixated on culture: "What one hopes is that opening up these questions will lead one to see the basic antagonism in our society *at the point of production.*" Richard Hoggart's *The Uses of Literacy,* one of the founding texts of the New Left, "pictures the worker entirely at leisure and not at all at work. And this is to miss both the point at which people are formed in their social activities most effectively, the only point at which one can begin to understand the relation of the capitalist system to people who live within it.[83] The key absences, as MacIntyre was later to write in a similar critique of Raymond Williams, were "work, class, power."[84]

Third, his Marxism stressed the importance of human self-activity in transforming society:

> The Stalinists believe that the inner mechanism of capitalism is such that in the long run it must automatically break down. The Social Democrats believe that the devices used by modern capitalists ensure that the machine will keep going. Both speak from the standpoint of passive observers outside the system who ask: "Will it keep going or not?" The Marxist standpoint starts from the view that this question is not a question about a system outside us, but about a system of which we are a part. What happens to it is not a matter of natural growth or mechanical change which we cannot affect. We do not have to sit and wait for the right objective conditions for revolutionary action. Unless we act now such conditions will never arise.[85]

This is not a voluntarist doctrine in which the exercise of human will overcomes all material obstacles, which would simply be the obverse of social-democratic and Stalinist determinism. Rather, it recognizes what many subsequent distinctions between agency and structure do not, namely that our activities (or their absence) change the conditions under which future action takes place, but are indeterminate and consequently unpredictable:

> The fall of capitalism is in no way inevitable; but nor is its survival. The condition of its fall is a long-term mass change in consciousness; and

there are no conditions which can make such a change either inevitable or impossible. It depends on us, but not upon us, because we are borne along by the wheel or tides of history; nor upon us, because we are leaders exempt from the workings of social systems. But upon us because with our working-class allies we may yet learn both what now makes us behave as we do, and what may transform our action until we become capable of making the transition to socialism.[86]

Fourth, the working class required a party; but what kind of party? It was in relation to this issue that his views underwent the greatest change between leaving the SLL and joining the IS. In an obituary for C. Wright Mills, MacIntyre reminds his readers that Mills had described himself as being a Leninist without being a Marxist.[87] And it is clear that he regarded this as a common failing on the supposedly revolutionary left: "Certainly the idea of the impoverished proletariat led by the elitist party cannot be introduced upon this stage without a comic opera effect. Those who identify Leninism with this do terrible injustice to Lenin's keen sense of the politically ridiculous."[88] What would a non-Marxist Leninism, of the sort upheld by Mills, involve? In a discussion during which he accused Sartre of effectively holding this position, he accused him of lacking Lenin's "practical realism."[89] But is that all Leninism is? The core of Marxism is summed up in the phrase Marx wrote into the Provisional Rules of the International Working Men's Association: "That the emancipation of the working-class must be conquered by the working-class themselves."[90] From this perspective the problem with Sartre (and Mills) is more that the working class has no independent role to play in the revolution and consequently will simply exchange one set of masters for another. Non-Marxist Leninism would therefore be the elitist, conspiratorial affair that liberals and anarchists always accused actually existing Leninism of being.

This highlights the ambiguity in MacIntyre's position. In certain places he implies that the charge of elitism falsely identifies Lenin's politics with those of Stalin, and he instead links Trotsky and Lenin together as proponents of socialism from below: "Trotsky's emphasis that socialism can only be built consciously and Lenin's that it cannot be built by a minority, a party, together entail that a pre-condition of socialism is a mass socialist consciousness."[91] In other places, however, he suggests that Lenin's politics were genuinely elitist, in other words, non-Marxist, and he invokes other

Marxists to remedy this apparent defect in Lenin's thought. In particular, he claims that James Connolly had been truer to Marx's notion of political movement of the working class arising in the "transition . . . from the trade union movement concerned with purely isolated economic issues to the trade union movement concerned with the political issue of class power."[92] Here MacIntyre retreats from his own earlier insights in "Freedom and Revolution." The party cannot be an expression of the class because the class itself is uneven in terms of consciousness; instead, it is a political selection of individuals to develop and maintain class consciousness.[93] A trade union cannot fulfill the function of a party precisely because it has to include all eligible workers regardless of their politics. Consequently, unions can be more or less militant in their behavior, more or less progressive in their policies, but inevitably they must embody rather than overcome unevenness. Since MacIntyre does not accuse Trotsky himself of elitism, this reading suggests that the one problem of Trotskyism was the attempt to maintain organizational forms that perpetuated bureaucratic elitism. Whatever there is to be said for this, it is quite clear that, from the point at which Trotsky became convinced of Bolshevism in 1917, he never wavered in his insistence that a revolutionary party was required for the success of the socialist revolution.[94] There may be circumstances in which building the party may not be immediately feasible, which seems to be the conclusion Cliff and his comrades drew in the aftermath of the Second World War; there may be attempts to build the party that in practice reproduce Stalinist rather than Leninist norms, which was ultimately the case with the SLL; but it would be difficult for anyone claiming fidelity to Trotsky's thought to rule out building a vanguard party as a matter of principle, which was one of the reasons why the members of Solidarity no longer considered themselves Trotskyists. Paraphrasing his own judgment on Mills and Sartre, we might therefore say that MacIntyre regarded himself as a highly idiosyncratic Trotskyist without being a Leninist—a position that Trotsky himself would have regarded as an highly improbable, to say the least.

The problem that he thought Lenin and Trotsky had in common lay in what he came to think of as their voluntarism. This was explicable, he acknowledged, as a response to the Mensheviks' "mechanical view of social development," but did not provide a coherent alternative since it did not take account of "the objective limitations of possibility." So Menshevik automatism led to Bolshevik voluntarism; Stalinism's mechanistic philosophy to Trotskyism's voluntaristic talk of crises of leadership; even the orthodoxy of the British CP to the voluntarism of the New Left.[95] In some circumstances it is of course correct to say that the "possible alternatives" are limited: "We may become conscious of the laws which govern our behaviour and yet be unable to change it; for there may be no alternative to behaving in the way that we do. Or again there may be alternatives, but not ones that enough of us would prefer to the present social system."[96] And later he was to point to a specific example from the degeneration of the Russian Revolution: "The key lies in the nexus between Stalin's economic policies—which were directed toward problems for which, as Trotsky never fully understood, there were no *socialist* solutions—and the political need for purges created by the failure to acknowledge that socialist theory had perforce been left behind when these policies were adopted."[97] By contrast, in his earlier writings MacIntyre had emphasized precisely how the subjective intervention of revolutionaries helped shape what would, in due course, become a new set of objective conditions.

Reading MacIntyre's work during the period of his IS membership can produce a dizzying effect as one follows the author moving back and forth between one assessment and another, often in quick succession, suggesting at the very least uncertainty on his part as to his own conclusions. What is interesting about MacIntyre's positive reading of an "activist" reading of history is how closely it echoes some of the positions taken by Georg Lukács in his works of the early 1920s, *History and Class Consciousness* and *Lenin: A Study in the Unity of His Thought*. MacIntyre was soon to revisit the theme, decisively, in the terms set out by Lukács and his pupil, Lucien Goldmann.[98] In his outstanding study of Pascal and Racine, *The Hidden God* (1964), Goldmann wrote:

> Marxist faith is faith in the future which men make for themselves in and through history. Or more accurately, in the future that we must make for ourselves by what we do, so that this faith becomes a "wager" which we make that our actions will, in fact, be successful. The transcendental element present in this faith is not supernatural and does not take us outside or beyond history; it merely takes us beyond the individual.[99]

MacIntyre now expanded on the parallel that Goldmann drew between "Pascal's wager" and the Marxist understanding of the relationship between theoretical understanding and action in the world:

If tragic thought and dialectical thought differ in ... crucial respects, they also resemble each other at key points. Both know that one cannot first understand the world and only then act in it. How one understands the world will depend in part on the decision implicit in one's already taken actions. The wager of action is unavoidable.... Not eternity but the future provides a context which gives meaning to individual parts in the present. The future which does this is as yet unmade; we wager on it not as spectators, but as actors pledged to bring it into being.[100]

Other Marxists, unknown to MacIntyre, had framed the issue in similar terms, notably Gramsci and Benjamin.[101] But it is important to understand that when MacIntyre invokes the notion of tragedy in this context he means this quite literally, for what seems to be entering his work at this point is a view that the basis of the Marxist wager—the revolutionary capacity of the working class—might have been mistaken. Consequently, Marxists tended to invest the actual working class with the characteristics it does not possess, at least to the extent that would allow the revolutionary project to be realized. He sees this as a major theoretical reason for Lukács's collapse into Stalinism.[102] But why was the working class—whose self-activity MacIntyre had hailed only a few years before—now deemed to be incapable of successful revolution?

DISENGAGEMENT: 1964-1968

MacIntyre was not to state his views on the incapacity of the working class and consequently the validity of Marxism until 1968, but his position began to shift from several years beforehand. 1964 seems to have been a turning point, since that year saw his last contributions to any IS publication. The emergent differences between him and his comrades only surfaced, however, in a public meeting in London on June 5, 1965, organized by Solidarity, which had asked MacIntyre to represent the IS position in a debate with Cardan without however formally approaching the other organization. As we have seen, Solidarity and IS had coexisted in a relatively fraternal manner since their respective organizations emerged in 1960. Both had rejected not only Stalinism but the orthodox Trotskyism of the SLL, from the ranks of which many members of Solidarity had emerged. But Solidarity increasingly rejected Trotskyism as such, Leninism, and, as the sixties wore on, Marxism in any form. In this, they broadly took their theoretical lead from Castoriadis, whose positions were outlined at length in his then newly translated book, *Modern Capitalism and Revolution*. On the one hand, he stressed the importance of the formation of revolutionary consciousness rather than the material development of the forces of production; on the other, he claimed that the nature of the crisis was the inability of the society to function rather than economic breakdown.[103]

The outcome of the debate seems to have surprised everyone, although MacIntyre's recent writings had contained similar themes. In 1963 he had noted that, post-war: "Capitalism was transformed by conscious, intelligent innovation, while working-class consciousness suffered diminution after diminution." There were three components to this transformation: "The first—which perhaps came last in time—is growth in economic expertise. . . . Secondly . . . the role of technological innovation. . . . It was this and not the permanent war economy alone which stabilized post-1945 capitalism. . . . Thirdly—and this came earliest in time—the rise of the trade union movement was accompanied by a realization by capitalists that to maximize the rate of exploitation was to create labour trouble in future." His conclusion was that "there are no longer slumps for the same reason that the pig-cycle is no longer with us: the changed self-consciousness of the participants."[104] MacIntyre had previously argued that there were three components of a revolutionary perspective: "The first is the deep and incurable dissatisfaction with social life which capitalism breeds. The second is the recurrent state of objective crises in capitalist social order. The third is socialist theory. Without the third the first does not necessarily come into relation with the second at all, or only in the most fortuitous way. With the third, dissatisfaction can become creative in that it is presented with a radical alternative to the present social order."[105] But as he argued in the "debate" with Cardan, the capitalist class was now in a position to effectively regulate the economy and thus prevent the recurrence of crisis. If that was the case, then revolution depends solely on the possibility of working-class dissatisfaction and socialist theory. This explains the emphasis he began to place on the activist elements of Marx's career, at the expense of his theoretical writings:

> [Marx] cannot allow for the possibility of the capitalist coming to understand the system and taking steps to prevent the system collapsing in the way that Marx predicts. . . . What prefigured socialism to him in later

years was much more the activity of workers in the Paris Commune and the rise of German social democracy than any pure reliance on a theory which was to prove highly vulnerable to Keynes and to others.[106]

In some senses then, it was not surprising that, as the account of the meeting in Solidarity's own journal stated: "The two main speakers, although approaching the problem from different angles, did not disagree on fundamentals. The similarity of many of their views led one comrade, who had come 'expecting a debate,' to deplore the presence of 'two Cardans.'"[107] The comrade was Kidron, whose contribution was one of the more measured from IS contributors. In his response to the discussion MacIntyre detected "a very bad tone in what Kidron and Cliff had said . . . because it was translated from the Russian, about the year 1905":

> The crucial difference between those who managed capitalism in the 19th century and those who manage it today was that the latter had achieved a degree of consciousness as to what they were doing. . . . this doesn't mean—and Cardan never alleged that it meant—that there weren't innumerable obstacles, limitations, etc., to the functioning of the bureaucracy . . . Understanding the movements of the bureaucracy was a question of understanding partly the economic setting in which it operated, partly the history of the bureaucracy which has made it what it was, and partly the fact that it has a dynamic of its own. To define it as simply a reflection of need to control the anarchy of the national or international markets was to ignore the important self-moving aspects of bureaucracy. . . . there is a problem posed here between the bureaucratic political forms and the economic transactions of our society which isn't in traditional Marxism and which Cardan's book poses very sharply.[108]

Ian Birchall, who had known MacIntyre as a member of the Oxford branch of IS, writes of the aftermath of this episode: "I don't think I ever saw MacIntyre again after that day. I'm fairly certain he didn't contribute to the group press or attend any further meetings. However, there was never any suggestion of disciplinary measures against him."[109]

It was clear from the debate that MacIntyre's own position was far closer to that of Solidarity and Socialism or Barbarism than it was to the organization to which he ostensibly belonged, but with one crucial difference: whereas Brinton and Cardan still maintained that the working class was a revolutionary force, this position was precisely what MacIntyre was increasingly coming to reject. MacIntyre's rejection of Marx's crisis theory, alongside his argument that the modern capitalist division of labor increased the fragmentation of the working class, implied that the workers' cries for freedom would remain atomized and therefore that the tasks facing socialists were much more daunting, indeed overwhelming, than more orthodox Marxists allowed. This is the conclusion implied in his works of the later 1960s, which, while written when he was still formally an editor of *International Socialism,* universally suggested little or no hope for revolution. Thus, in his introduction to Marx's ideas for an academic audience, while he argued that "the most crucial later activity of Marx" was not to write *Capital,* but was rather through his actions in "helping to found and guiding the International Working Men's Association," he concluded that Marx "still leaves the question of working-class political growth obscure."[110] Whether or not this observation was correct of Marx, it certainly appeared to be true of MacIntyre, who was unable to conceptualize any contemporary conditions under which a mass movement might realize his vision of socialism. In fact, MacIntyre now extended his political pessimism back into the nineteenth century. In a series of lectures originally given in 1964, but published some three years later as *Secularisation and Moral Change,* he argued that Engels had been mistaken in his overly optimistic perspective for the future secularization of British society, and that this was a corollary of his overly optimistic perspectives for socialism. MacIntyre went on to suggest that "the inability of men to discard Christianity is part of their inability to provide any post-Christian means of understanding their situation in the world." Moreover, while he suggested that this failure was by no means "ultimate," he noted no inherent tendencies with which socialists might engage that could, belatedly, help them to prove Engels correct.[111]

Another reason why MacIntyre was drawn to such a pessimistic conclusion was that by the mid-1960s he moved to reject not only Marx's but also all other competing theories of human nature that might act as a humanist basis for revolutionary politics. This position was made explicit in his classic *A Short History of Ethics* (1966), where, despite some tangential remarks as to the relationship between morality and desire, his own moral standpoint seemed disjoined from any either historical or materialist premises to which he had earlier been committed.[112] Consequently, he rejected the idea of human nature as a benchmark from which to adjudicate moral claims and reduced individual morality to an existential choice.[113] While he still chose Marxism in 1966, he refused any criteria by which this choice could be rationally defended. Therefore, without a theory of human nature with which to underpin it, his theory of revolution, at least as he had outlined it in "Freedom and Revolution," remained baseless. MacIntyre's socialist morality, in this context, could boast no more compelling foundation than any competing moral claim. Indeed, by the late 1960s it appeared that he had ceased to view Marxism either as a science or as a guide to action, but rather saw it as just one competing worldview among many others. One memoir of his academic performances at the time contains the following description:

> In 1965–66 MacIntyre delivered a lecture course at Oxford University entitled "What was Morality?" to a packed room in the Examinations Schools. My image is of a short, jowelled figure in a corduroy suit, the latest in radical chic. The style was at once magisterial and provocative, deadpan but destructive. . . . Like Nietzsche and Sartre, MacIntyre saw "the death of God" as a cataclysmic event in the history of moral systems which had, since the Enlightenment, become a series of failed attempts to attain the objectivity of theism without the embarrassment of theistic doctrines, an objective moral code without God as the author. In the heady 1960s MacIntyre was content to leave us with this deconstructed ruin of history. He viewed the situation with a cheerful irony and ended his lectures with a nod towards the Marxism then propounded by Sartre, which allowed us to seek the ephemeral community of the "group in fusion," while keeping our distance from the supposed errors of historical materialism. If this was "frivolous," said MacIntyre, perhaps that was not a vice. In any case, it was all that we could hope for.[114]

MacIntyre sees two moral issues with Marx's work. First, Marx gives no reasons for why a class formed under capitalism will find the resources to reject it in favor of socialism: "Hence we remain uncertain as to how Marx conceives it possible that a society prey to the errors of moral individualism may come to recognise and transcend them." The second is that he does not explain how the morality of Communist society will function. The only alternatives that have been offered are Bernstein's retreat to Kantian moral imperatives or Kautsky's return to utilitarianism.[115] MacIntyre had a long hatred of utilitarianism.[116] What problem did he see with it? There were two. One is that we can never assess what the good is because there are always alternative conceptions of the good and it is necessary to be able to choose between them, but this cannot be done as if they were rival sets of commodities. The other is that goods can be divided between those that are beneficial in themselves and those that are so because they point toward the future; but in Marxist terms, all goods fall into the latter category. Marxism is forever postponing the attainment of the good until the future.[117] In 1967 he had conceded two points to critics of Lenin. The first was that he was always prepared to make tactical retreats from socialist principle. "The second was that it was certainly true that underlying such Leninist retreats was a crude utilitarianism: the end of socialism justifies any necessary means." MacIntyre is not accusing Lenin here of personal cruelty, but: "It remains true that such utilitarianism corrupts and corrupted, that it formed the moral link between Lenin and Stalin."[118] This became a recurrent theme in the late sixties and early 1970s and suggested that MacIntyre had retreated to before the positions set out in "Notes from the Moral Wilderness," in that the solutions he had proposed there were no longer adequate.[119]

1968 AND AFTER

MacIntyre has referred many times to the change that occurred in his work as a philosopher after moving to the US in 1971.[120] In some respects however, a more significant shift in his position had already taken place three years before his relocation across the Atlantic. Nineteen sixty-eight was as important a year in the development of his thought as 1956, although for the opposite reason: if the earlier date opened the period in which he considered himself to be a Marxist, the latter brought it to a close—a renunciation that naturally had political implications. In a revised version of *Marxism: An Interpretation,* published in 1968 as *Marxism and Christianity,* MacIntyre wrote: "Clearly someone who has been a Marxist may alter his beliefs on some point in such a way that common action with his former comrades becomes impossible."[121] He had recent experience of precisely this situation. The summer 1968 issue of *International Socialism,* the first since the May Events in France, contained a rather bemused editorial note on a departure from both the journal and its parent organization: "Alasdair MacIntyre has resigned from the Editorial Board of IS. He offers no extended account of why he is resigning now, rather than earlier or later, nor has he accepted our invitations to lay out his criticisms of the journal in our columns. But resign he has."[122] What had happened?

MacIntyre's rejection of Marxism as a theory of revolutionary social-ism as a practice had coincided with the greatest upsurge of interest in historical materialism for half a century, an intellectual reorientation in-spired by great struggles that began in or around that year, and of which the combined French student revolt and general strike was one of the first and most spectacular examples. These events filled many Marxists with enormous hope that there might be a future for genuine socialism, distinct from that of both the social or liberal democratic societies of the West and the Stalinist societies of the East, as can be seen from the re-sponse of one of MacIntyre's younger comrades, David Widgery, to the events of 1968. Widgery was born in 1947, nearly twenty years after MacIntyre; but in other respects the men had comparable backgrounds. Both men were born into religious families; MacIntyre's parents were Episcopalians, Widgery's were Quakers. More importantly, perhaps, both men gained their education in left politics as members of the same or-ganizations: the Communist Party of Great Britain, the ultra-orthodox Trotskyist Socialist Labour League, and finally, the International Socialists, which Widgery joined at the very point MacIntyre left.[123] Widgery re-called the atmosphere of the time ten years later: "It was as if an interna-tional pageant was being acted out—the ideas we had treasured in pamphlets and argued about in tiny pub back rooms were now roaming, alive, three dimensional. Marxism had come out of the cold."[124] How could the same experience impact so differently on people who, nomi-nally at least, had the same politics?

History is full of radicals who abandon their opposition to the existing order during periods of political defeat. In the United States, members of an earlier generation of socialists, usually referred to collectively as the New York intellectuals, had been part of the anti-Stalinist left in the 1930s and early 1940s, and in many cases they put their beliefs into practice by joining Trotskyist organizations. From the late 1940s onward, as the trade union movement was beaten and depoliticized, and the political left bro-ken by McCarthyism for two decades, most began to move right, albeit to different points in the spectrum—there was obviously a difference between the social democracy of an Irving Howe and the neoconser-vatism of an Irving Kristol.[125] A similar trajectory was followed in France from the mid-1970s, after the revolutionary period had passed. Here too a group of militants, opposed as much to Stalinism as Western capitalism (usually on idiosyncratic Maoist rather than Trotskyist grounds) shifted rightwards, although in far more consistent fashion than their US predecessors, with many forming the nucleus of the so-called New Philosophers.[126] In both cases, the groups involved claimed to be maintaining consistent anti-Stalinist positions while eliding the fact that these were now on the right rather than the left, with the most right-wing claiming to have discovered that Stalinism was a—in fact *the* only—genuine expression of Marxism, rather than a betrayal of it.

This type of adjustment to an apparently unyielding system is only to be expected in periods during which the left is in retreat; but MacIntyre rejected Marxism in a period when left-wing and working-class movements were in the ascendant. The only other serious Marxist to abandon political activity at this time was the American Hal Draper, a figure with positions close to MacIntyre's own, who left the US International Socialists and active politics in January 1971.[127] But he did not abandon his Marxism; indeed, Draper went on to write one of the great studies of Marx's own thought in *Karl Marx's Theory of Revolution*. MacIntyre's position was therefore *sui generis* at the time. What led him to adopt it? Of course, several "Western Marxists" behaved ambivalently toward the new forces that emerged in 1968, which left their reputations greatly diminished among activists, but most did not entirely renege on their Marxist views. Those who were members of the Communist parties, such as Althusser in France, tended to defer, albeit with greater or lesser reservations, to the deeply conservative positions taken by these organizations.[128] Those who were politically unattached, like the members of the Frankfurt School in Germany—above all, Adorno—actively opposed the activities of the students.[129] In this respect Marxist academics were simply experiencing the same discomfort as others in their profession. One starting point for explaining MacIntyre's course in 1968 might therefore be his reaction to the student rebellion.

Eight years earlier MacIntyre had discussed the situation of students in "Breaking the Chains of Reason." After reviewing the different generations of students that had passed through the universities since the war, he then set out alternative trajectories for the cohort of 1960:

> All that tremendous adolescent energy, which the very rawness of the emotion makes so impressive, is still looking for intellectual satisfaction

at the political level. If no coherent answers are found, then as the student generations pass on they will become all the more frustrated and disillusioned for having been so hopeful in the past. And this is what reactionaries hope for. "I was a socialist when I was young too." The unspoken completion of this—"How good to grow middle-aged, conservative and self-satisfied like me"—points to the danger of silting up the poetry of adolescence into the prose of bourgeois middle age. All the pressures are there: the need to get a job, to succeed in it, to bring up a family, to pay for a house. Not to succumb to these feelings and the questioning must find a theory and a way of life which will transmute the poetry of adolescence into continuous life-long activity.[130]

Now Macintyre appeared to be hostile even to the poetry of adolescence. When the convulsive events of 1968 began to unfold MacIntyre was employed as a Professor of Sociology at the University of Essex at Colchester, where he also acted as Dean of Students. Essex was one of the postwar new universities. It had opened in 1964 and was now experiencing a period of rapid growth. Essex did not escape the general mood of insurgency—indeed, given that it was constructed and run precisely as one of the "knowledge-factories" whose conditions had helped produce the student revolt, it would have been surprising if it had. A body calling itself the Union Reform Committee had been active at least since January, and some of its members produced a pamphlet that month criticizing both the undemocratic nature of the university and the way in which the local Students' Union was integrated into its structures. At least one member of the committee (Mike Gonzalez) was also in the IS.[131] Student unrest grew from February onward, but open revolt was precipitated by the announcement of a campus meeting to be addressed by Dr. T. A. Lynch . on May 7. Lynch was a scientist employed at Porton Down, the experimental laboratory at which research was carried out into chemical and biological warfare (or "defense," in the Orwellian terminology of the British state). One hundred and fifty students broke up the meeting, an act to which the vice chancellor responded by calling in the police and their dogs, and suspending three ringleaders without a hearing. The subsequent campaign to reinstate the three, galvanized by the return of visitors to the Paris events, was finally triumphant on May 17 following a student strike supported by a large minority of the lecturers. The strike was, however, opposed by MacIntyre, who commented shortly afterward:

"Ironically, our mistake was to be so liberal . . . They [the students] have no real practical injustices to fight against; so they had to rebel on ideological grounds like germ warfare and Vietnam—and these we were powerless to alter."[132] Leaving aside that the university was not powerless in the matter of inviting Lynch to speak, these comments are striking, from a Marxist perspective, for two reasons.

One is the idea that it was inappropriate for students to protest against the involvement of universities in arms production and imperialist war, simply because this did not directly impact on their conditions, particularly since only months later MacIntyre was to defend student opposition to the Vietnam War: " . . . when [George Kennan] condemns civil disobedience outright and when he supposes that what the student Left dislike about the Vietnam War is that they might be killed in it, he exhibits an ignorance of the contemporary student scene which is disgraceful in a member of a university. . . . what he does not begin to grasp—and what his dreadful paternalistic style must obscure from him—is that in Vietnam war crimes are being committed and that resistance to the Vietnam War by acts of civil disobedience is therefore not a right, but a duty."[133] But this was in relation to Berkeley, not Essex.

Second, and even more bizarre from someone with MacIntyre's intellectual history, was his implication that both what is taught and the way it is taught are separable from the society in which they take place. MacIntyre was contemptuous of what he described as "Marcuse's idealised students who have produced the first parent-financed revolts in what is more like a new version of the children's crusade than a revolutionary movement."[134] Marcuse was in fact far less influential on the British student movement than is often assumed.[135] It is clear, however, that for MacIntyre the name "Marcuse" only partly refers to that individual, but also acts as a collective label for those who would undermine or overthrow the autonomy of the university: "The defence of the authority to teach and research as it will is in more danger immediately from Marcuse's student allies than from any other quarter—even though Marcuse himself has on occasion exempted the university from his critique."[136] MacIntyre writes of the need for awareness of "the influence of false sociological theorizing and of misinformation": "This is most obvious on a large scale in the Marcusean belief of SDS theorists that they are confronted by a total well-integrated social order in which higher education serves the purposes of the system as a whole."[137] His retreat from the concept of totality now even extended to the Vietnam War:

> The myth of American imperialism in Vietnam is the product of a coalition between the sternest critics of the war and its sternest supporters. In actual fact American involvement in South Vietnam came about through a series of improvisations and ad hoc measures in which Kennedy and Johnson continuously produced larger and larger unforeseen effects; then they identified themselves with what they had produced and ended by producing a war which has been destructive for every party engaged in it and from which no good can result.

Both supporters and opponents of the war "work within frameworks which demand of social life that it have a coherence which it in fact no longer possesses."[138] But one does not have to believe that capitalist society in the age of imperialism possesses coherence, only that, in geopolitics as much as in markets, it follows the logic of competitive accumulation.

At one level, MacIntyre's hostility to Marcuse and those influenced by him is entirely justified, as a rejection of the implied—indeed, often completely explicit—elitism of their position in relation to the working class. In this respect, his polemics from this period show some of the last flashes of his earlier politics, particularly in this entirely realistic dissection of the various movements and groups that were often thoughtlessly lumped together in the 1968 period:

> There are the genuinely aspiring poor of America and peasants in Vietnam and elsewhere who must not be confused with their self-appointed spokesmen; there are the middle-class whites of SDS and their counterparts in Britain, Germany and France who in their combination of insurrectionism and anarchism exemplify what Lenin diagnosed as left-wing communism, an infantile disease; and there are the representatives of the communist bureaucracies in China, Cuba and Vietnam who represent right-wing Communism, an oligarchical disease. These forces have only one thing in common: they are all in conflict with the governments of the advanced industrial societies. But, as both Marx and Lenin knew, to be in conflict with the established order is not necessarily to be an agent of liberation.[139]

But perhaps MacIntyre's rage at Marcuse is also partly symptomatic of the fact that he too had decided that the working class was incapable of liberating itself. Shortly after the events at Essex, on June 20, 1968, MacIntyre gave a broadcast talk on the BBC Third Programme, as he had many times before. Here MacIntyre announced "the death of social democratic England," a judgment that, in retrospect, seems not so much wrong as premature:

> And working-class people will gradually learn that they are still to be excluded, and that in streamed comprehensive schools and expanded universities, it will still be the case that all the advantages lie with the children of middle-class parents. If they learn also that no conventional political remedy can help them, then they will have the choice between a kind of non-political subservience that has been alien to them even at their most apathetic and a new politics of conflict. For my part, I hope that they learn both lessons fast, and if it is said that I've been presenting something akin not so much to a personal view as to a partisan political broadcast, let me point out that I am talking for and of a group that has no party, the British working class.[140]

MacIntyre makes the assumption that, although the class struggle goes on and the working class is right to defend its interests (for example by unofficial strike action), there are limits to it that are set by the structural incapacity of the proletariat to overthrow capital. As he was shortly to write (in an important passage to which I will return): "one might write the history of the age which Marxism illuminated so much more clearly that any other doctrine did, the period from 1848 to 1929, as one in which Marx's view of progress of capitalism was substantially correct, but at the end of which, when the Marxist script for the world drama required the the emergence of the European working-class as the agent of historical change, the working class turned out to be quiescent and help-less."[141] In other words, far from reformism as strategy no longer being possible, as he had once argued, it was now the only option for the working class. He still retained the view that the Labour Party, which at one level had once represented the working class, no longer did so, but this meant that other forces had to play that role. Indeed this might be the real role for revolutionaries. As he wrote later in 1968, in a review of a book by his former comrade, Paul Foot:

> One of the true lessons to be learnt from his narrative is the law of di-minishing socialist returns, a little-known law which states that in the

normal conditions of capitalist society everyone's actions tend to be to the right of their principles. From liberals one gets mildly conservative actions, from Right social democrats liberal actions, from Left social democrats right-wing social democrat actions, and so on. From this law it follows that only those with a revolutionary perspective are likely to promote genuine left-wing reforms. If revolutionary critics of society neglect their responsibility here, no one else is likely to assume it.[142]

The closest MacIntyre came to a contemporary articulation of his differences with IS is to be found in *Marxism and Christianity*. MacIntyre's expert analysis of the lineages of Marx's ideas through Feuerbach and German Idealism and into Christian theology remained from the original 1953 text; expunged, however, was any suggestion of the practical, Christian-socialist purpose of the original. Reviewing the book for *International Socialism* Richard Kuper bemoaned the rewrite, arguing that while the second edition, as a work of theory, was formally closer to classical Marxism than the first edition, the activist core of the first edition had made that much the better of the two books.[143] A similar point was later made by MacIntyre himself in his 1995 introduction to the book: "In the first version of this book there was a chapter on philosophy and practice that was omitted when I revised it in 1968. That chapter was originally included because it attempted to pose what I had rightly recognized as the fundamental problem. It was later omitted because I had by then learnt that I did not know how to pose that problem adequately, let alone how to resolve it. So in 1968 I mistakenly attempted to bypass it."[144]

In 1968, while MacIntyre had reached the negative conclusion that Marxists had not adequately theorized the problem of revolutionary practice, he failed to formulate a viable alternative. He concluded *Marxism and Christianity* with the suggestion that the desires of workers were irredeemably constrained by their fragmented practices, and that, in such a context, Lukács's defense of Lenin's politics amounted to a "deification of the party" that was merely the flip side to Kautsky's earlier "deification of history."[145] The failure of Marxism was that it had accepted the division of the economic, political, and social characteristics of capitalism and the way these divisions were reproduced in the categories of liberal theory. This failure led most Marxists to misunderstand how a class could arise in Russia that had apparently abolished capitalist property relations and used Marxist vocabulary to cover their continued exploitation of the working class.[146]

MacIntyre's version of the Pascalian "wager" depended on the possibility of the working class performing a revolutionary role, but he now no longer believed that this was possible. Ironically, given his earlier critique of Popper, he seems to have treated this failure in Popperian terms as an empirical refutation of the theory of proletarian revolution. MacIntyre argued that hitherto Marxists had explained away the failure of Marx's predictions either by claiming that the time scale was simply longer than had hitherto been supposed or by a series of "supplementary hypotheses," including those of the labor aristocracy and "doctrinal corruption," but these were ways of avoiding two painful facts: "The first of these was that the working class—not just its leadership—was either reformist or unpolitical except in the most exceptional of circumstances, not so much because of the inadequacies of its trade union and political leadership as because of its whole habit of life."[147] Lukács had written in *History and Class Consciousness* that "historical materialism both can and must be applied to itself. . . . Above all we must investigate the social premises of the substance of historical materialism just as Marx himself scrutinised the social and economic preconditions of the truths of classical economics."[148] Cardan subsequently made similar claims in a series of articles first published between 1961 and 1964, which were gradually translated by Solidarity throughout the 1960s and 1970s.[149] But for Cardan, the self-investigation called for by Lukács would reveal that Marxism had to be abandoned, not least because of the ways in which it treats as permanent aspects of human society features that are particular to capitalism. MacIntyre adopted this version of the argument as the sixties drew to a close: "It would be inconsistent with Marxism itself to view Marxism in any other way: in particular, what we cannot do is judge and understand Marxist theory as it has really existed with all its vicissitudes in the light of some ideal version of Marxism. It follows that by the present time to be faithful to Marxism we have to cease to be Marxists; and whoever now remains a Marxist has thereby discarded Marxism."[150] The point therefore, was not that Marxism had never been true, but that it no longer was:

> [Marx] envisages the concentration of workers in large factory units and the limits set upon the growth of wages as necessary conditions for the growth of [political] consciousness; but he says nothing about how or why the workers will learn and assimilate the truths which Marxism seeks to bring to them. . . . Indeed, one might write the history of the

age which Marxism illuminated so much more clearly than any other doctrine did, the period from 1848 to 1929, as one in which Marx's view of the progress of capitalism was substantially correct, but at the end of which, when the Marxist script for the world drama required the emergence of the European working class as the agent of historical change, the working class turned out to be quiescent and helpless.[151]

The second painful fact that had contributed to the "quiescence" was that living standards had generally improved, if unevenly and inconsistently, especially after 1945, when "the ability of capitalism to innovate in order to maintain its equilibrium and its expansion was of a radically new kind. Consequently, not only has the future crisis of capitalism had—for those who wished to retain the substance of the classical Marxist view—to be delayed, there had to be additional explanations why, in the new situation, capitalism is still liable to crisis in the same sense as before." The resulting degeneration can take two main forms. On the one hand, those who "flee from the realities of that society into the private cloud-cuckoo lands of Marxist sectarianism where they tilt at capitalist windmills with Marxist texts in their hands, the Don Quixotes of the contemporary left." On the other, those who "embrace what Lenin called the worship of what is . . . allowing Marx's notion of revolutionary working class power to be confused with that of the administrative manoeuvres of the Soviet bureaucrats."[152]

As a result of these changed conditions, those who continue to describe themselves as "revolutionaries" are, according to MacIntyre, likely to have five main characteristics. First, an "all-or-nothing existence," whose activities allow them, second, to "sustain a plausible social existence." Third, they must believe that their activities have "world-historical significance," justification for their revolutionary beliefs, despite their apparent lack of significance in the world: "In this way miniscule Trotskyist groups can represent their faction fights as a repetition of the great quarrels of the Bolshevik party." Fourth, the tension between activity and aspiration gives their lives an inevitable precariousness: "Joseph Conrad understood this; so did Henry James; so, in his own way, did Trotsky." Fifth, and finally, revolutionaries must feel their activities are justified by both history and their own activity, but since both are refutable by counterexamples: "This requirement is in obvious tension, however, with the revolutionary's commitment to make the predictions derived from his theory come true."

MacIntyre claims that a comparable elitism links the revolutionary with the industrial manager and the professional social scientist: "The ideology of expertise embodies a claim to privilege with respect to power." Consequently, the "contemporary revolutionary" is "antidemocratic."[153]

Examples of "antidemocratic" revolutionaries abounded in the late sixties, of course, not least in the Third World. Yet even at this stage, MacIntyre still counterposes Trotsky the revolutionary democrat against them and their sympathizers in the developed world: "One can well understand why Trotsky's ghost haunts Sartre and Debray. For both Sartre and Debray have a peculiar conception—far more élitist than that of Leninism—of an inert mass of be it workers, be it peasants, who need a leadership of particular gifts to rouse them to revolutionary activity." This does not see Trotskyism as an alternative strategy for revolutionaries in the Third World but an analysis that identifies why they are bound to fail:

> Che himself could not avoid facing dilemmas which in other contexts were responsible for creating Trotskyism, and he could not avoid making choices which were incompatible with Trotskyism. This is because Trotsky himself had had to face at successive points in his career all the dilemmas of those who wish to make a Marxist revolution in an underdeveloped country and because, too, the failure of Trotskyism to provide a recipe for successful revolutionary practice in the face of those dilemmas is an inescapable fact.

A consequence of that failure is an endless repetition of the experience of Socialism in One Country:

> One paradox of post-Stalin Stalinism is that it may be those who are most repelled by the surviving Stalinist features of the Soviet Union who therefore try to build a socialist revolution in isolation from the Soviet camp or at least in the minimum of contact with it. But in so doing they revive the very thesis of "socialism in one country" on which Stalinism was founded and in this way reject Trotskyism.[154]

His description, "Marxism of the Will," indicates that MacIntyre sees the Marxists he is criticizing as succumbing to the illusions of voluntarism. Yet it is Trotsky—whom he had in some contexts accused of the same failing—that he now invokes against them. MacIntyre is not, of course, arguing that Trotsky was a secret gradualist, but rather the supreme realist in the Marxist tradition. In effect, MacIntyre is arguing that Trotsky has demonstrated that there can be nothing beyond capitalism. This general conclusion is brought out with the greatest clarity in the closing pages of *After Virtue:*

> If the moral impoverishment of advanced capitalism is what so many Marxists agree that it is, whence are these resources for the future to be derived? It is not surprising that at this point Marxism tends to produce its own version of the *Übermensch:* Lukács's ideal proletarian, Lenin's ideal revolutionary. When Marxism does not become Weberian social democracy or crude tyranny, it tends to become Nietzschean fantasy. One of the most admirable aspects of Trotsky's cold resolution was his refusal of all such fantasies. A Marxist who took Trotsky's last writings with great seriousness would be forced into a pessimism quite alien to the Marxist tradition, and in becoming a pessimist he would in an important way have ceased to be a Marxist. For he would now see no tolerable alternative set of political and economic structures which could be brought into place to replace the structures of advanced capitalism. This conclusion agrees of course with my own.[155]

But is it legitimate to infer this conclusion from Trotsky's last writings? A passage that seems to have had particular importance for MacIntyre occurs in Trotsky's last sustained discussion of the nature of the Soviet Union before his assassination: "The historic alternative, carried to the end, is as follows: either the Stalin regime is an abhorrent relapse in the process of transforming bourgeois society into a socialist society, or the Stalin regime is the first stage of a new exploiting society. If the second prognosis proves to be correct, then, of course, the bureaucracy will become a new ruling class."[156] This is how MacIntyre interpreted these words in "Trotsky in Exile":

> Although Trotsky continued to defend the view that in some sense the Soviet Union was a workers' state, he had committed himself to predictions about the results of the Second World War, the outcome of which would for him settle the matter. If his view were correct, the Soviet bureaucracy after a victorious war would be overthrown as a result of proletarian revolution in the advanced countries of the West. If the view of those Trotskyists who held that a kind of bureaucratic state capitalism existed in Russia were correct, they would be vindicated by the failure to occur of such a revolution and such an overthrow. It was with this question still before him that Trotsky died.[157]

And here is how he interprets it a superficially similar passage from *After Virtue:*

> Trotsky, in the very last years of his life, facing the question of whether the Soviet Union was in any sense a socialist country, also faced implicitly the question of whether the categories of Marxism could illuminate the future. He himself made everything turn on the outcome of a set of hypothetical predictions about possible future events in the Soviet Union, predications which were tested only after Trotsky's death. The answer they returned was clear: Trotsky's own premises entailed that the Soviet Union was not socialist and that the theory which was to have illuminated the path to human liberation had in fact led to darkness.[158]

Between these two texts the position MacIntyre derives from Trotsky has shifted from the outcome of the war deciding whether or not the Soviet Union was a form of bureaucratic state capitalism to deciding whether socialism is possible. The first vindicates Marxism because it is capable of explaining this outcome; the second condemns Marxism as being responsible for it. Given that MacIntyre dismissed in "Trotsky in Exile" those Trotskyists who transformed "into abstract dogma what Trotsky thought in concrete terms at one moment in his life," there is a certain irony in that this is precisely what he does in *After Virtue*. The position that Trotsky took toward the Soviet Union in the last years of his life is clearly bound up with his "now or never" attitude to the entire world situation on the eve of the Second World War—a perspective that also included the irreversible decline of the capitalist economy, the collapse of social democracy, the impossibility of Third World development, and many other predictions that turned out to be false. The source of MacIntyre's error actually occurs in the first quoted passage, for Trotskyists who identified the Soviet Union as state capitalist did not argue that revolution was impossible in Russia, simply that the state was not an unstable, temporary formation that would shatter under the impact of war, as Trotsky and his orthodox epigones claimed. Indeed, Cliff ended his initial statement of the state capitalist case by predicting "gigantic spontaneous upsurges of millions" in a forthcoming revolution.[159]

At the end of World War II orthodox Trotskyists found that reality did not correspond to what their theory had predicted. Their initial response was to deny reality, then to revise their theory to such an extent that it lost contact with the notion of working-class self-emancipation that had been at heart of both Trotskyism and the classical Marxist tradition it sought to continue. MacIntyre, in effect, did the opposite. He too understood that the world had changed, but was too intellectually honest to produce endless "auxiliary hypotheses" to protect the theory. If MacIntyre had simply overestimated the extent to which these changes signaled permanent shifts in the nature of capitalism, reality would soon have provided a check with the onset of crisis from the mid-seventies. Yet this was not the only or even the main reason why MacIntyre abandoned Trotskyism and, with it, Marxism as a tradition, rather the source of individual insights. He has restated that second reason, working-class incapacity, on several occasions since, most recently in "The Theses on Feuerbach: A Road Not Taken." Here MacIntyre contrasts the world of the handloom weavers documented by Edward Thompson in *The Making of the English Working Class* and the Silesian weavers whose struggle Marx himself noted in 1844, contrasting both of these with the situation of the contemporary working class: "But [Marx] seems not to have understood the form of life from which that militancy arose, and so later failed to understand that while proletarianisation makes it necessary for workers to resist, it also tends to deprive workers of those forms of practice through which they can discover conceptions of a good and of virtues adequate to the moral needs of resistance."[160]

CONCLUSION

MacIntyre began his literary career in 1953 with *Marxism: An Interpretation*. According to his own account, he attempted in that book to be faithful to both his Christian and, in so far as he regarded it as a Christian heresy, his Marxist beliefs.[161] By 1968, he had abandoned both, although in the case of Christianity he seems to have done so as early as 1961. At any rate, by 1971 he was able to introduce a collection of his essays by rejecting these and, indeed, all other attempts to illuminate the human condition.[162] Since then, MacIntyre has of course reembraced Christianity, although that of the Catholic Church rather than the Anglicanism to which he originally adhered. It seems unlikely, at this stage, that he will undertake a similar reconciliation with Marxism. Nevertheless, his insights into the historical origins of moral concepts in specific forms of social life would be unthinkable without it.[163] As late as 1991 he said:

Even if Marxist characterizations of advanced capitalism are inadequate, the Marxist understanding of liberalism as ideological, as a self-deceiving mask for certain social interests, remains compelling. . . . it was Marxism which convinced me that every morality including that of modern liberalism, however universal its aims, is the morality of some particular social group, embodied and lived out in the life and history of that group. Indeed, a morality has no existence except in its actual and possible social embodiments, and what it amounts to is what it does or what it can amount to in its socially embodied forms.

Yet moments later in the same interview, when invited to describe himself as a Marxist, MacIntyre refused, on the grounds that "if I had gone on being a Marxist this lesson would not have been much good to me. For Marxism is not just an inadequate, but a largely inept, instrument for social analysis."[164] Nevertheless, as MacIntyre has frequently reminded his readers, most recently in the prologue to the third edition of *After Virtue* (2007), his rejection of Marxism as a whole does not mean that he rejects every insight that it has to offer: "although *After Virtue* was written in part out of a recognition of those moral inadequacies of Marxism which its twentieth-century history had disclosed, I was and remain deeply indebted to Marx's critique of the economic, social, and cultural order of capitalism and to the development of that critique by later Marxists."[165]

As MacIntyre's response to the debates over *After Virtue,* and his subsequent writings, have shown, his pessimism has not moderated his hostility to either capitalism or its liberal ideologues, which remains as intense as ever. According to MacIntyre's current Aristotelian position "the costs of economic development are generally paid by those least able to afford them," but politics offers no alternative:

Attempts to reform the political systems of modernity from within are always transformed into coalitions with them. Attempts to overthrow them always degenerate into terrorism or quasi terrorism. What is not barren is the politics involved in constructing and sustaining small-scale local communities, at the level of the family, the neighbourhood, the workplace, the parish, the school, or clinic, communities within which the needs of the hungry and the homeless can be met. I am not a communitarian. I do not believe in ideals or forms of community as a nostrum for contemporary social ills.[166]

For MacIntyre, "there are no remedies" for contemporary capitalism: "The problem is not to reform the dominant order, but to find ways for local communities to survive by sustaining a life of the common good against the disintegrating forces of the nation-state and the market."[167] But if reform is impossible, so too is revolution: "I do not see any prospects of overthrowing the dominant social order. But perhaps it can be outlived; and even if it cannot be overthrown, it ought to be rejected."[168]

The difficulty is that it looks increasingly likely that the dominant social order may not allow us the luxury of outliving it. If we do not succeed in overthrowing it, then things will not simply continue in the old oppressive way, perhaps getting a bit better, perhaps a bit worse. Socialism is necessary simply to remove the threats to existence for millions from starvation, epidemic, and war, and for everyone, including the capitalists themselves, of environmental catastrophe. It may be that one of the other Marxists who understood revolution as a form of "wager" was belatedly right in his assessment. "Marx says that revolutions are the locomotive of world history," wrote Walter Benjamin in 1940. "But perhaps it is quite otherwise. Perhaps revolutions are an attempt by the passengers on this train—namely, the human race—to activate the emergency brake."[169] In these circumstances, revolution appears not as a sectarian indulgence but as the only serious option, so we had better find a way to make it work without reproducing the very forms of oppression that make it necessary. In periods of crisis and social upheaval Marxism—or rather, Marxisms—always experience a revival in interest. The variants that attain the greatest popularity are not always those that embody the emancipatory heart of the tradition. And if MacIntyre's critique, of which his engagement with Trotsky was such a central part, cannot be accepted as a whole, it may still alert us to potential dangers and indicate the roads not to take.

۞ Chapter 7 ۞

Reimagined Communities
Benedict Anderson's Theory of Nationalism[1]

INTRODUCTION

"Proverbially," writes Benedict Anderson in a new afterword to *Imagined Communities*, "a writer loses his/her book at the moment that it is published and enters the public sphere."[2] Anderson is thinking specifically about the difficulties experienced by authors when their work is translated into languages they do not understand. Given that his book has been translated into twenty-seven since it first appeared in 1983, these are difficulties with which even the multi-lingual Anderson is now overly familiar. Yet the point is of more general application. For if there is one book on nationalism that every student is expected to read, one book that is certain to be included in any survey of the competing theories, it is *Imagined Communities*. It is, as Josep Llobera has written of the core conception, "as if people had been waiting for such an expression to be coined."[3] That expression can now be encountered in quite unexpected places. The following passage, chosen virtually at random, is from a discussion by Alasdair MacIntyre of the possibility that poetry might also embody a political philosophy:

> One cannot be a monk or a member of café society without being able to imagine oneself as such; living the role of either is a form of imaginative acting out. And so too with the community of a nation: to be

Irish or English, I must be able to imagine myself as Irish or English, something achievable in part by participating in the shared poetic utterance of the nation. Take away shared songs and poetry, shared monuments and architecture, shared imaginative conceptions of what is for this nation sacred ground and you at the very least weaken the bonds of nationality. So nations to be real must first be imagined.[4]

MacIntyre does not refer to Anderson here, but this is not inadequate scholarship: he does not need to. The concept of imagined community has become so much a part of contemporary intellectual common sense that citation is virtually superfluous. And MacIntyre at least understands one of the points Anderson was trying to make. All too often the title has been quoted with such little comprehension that Anderson himself can now describe it as "a pair of words from which the vampires of banality have by now sucked almost all the blood."[5]

The appearance of the third edition therefore gives us an opportunity to reassess this original and influential work, but also to identify some of the problems to which it gives rise, problems that are, in part, the very reason for its popularity. These are not all simply the result of the inevitable misunderstandings that occur when a complex concept is seized upon to fill an explanatory gap; when, as Philip Spencer and Howard Wollman put it, "invocation" becomes "a substitute for analysis."[6] Some are the result of Benedict Anderson's underlying theoretical assumptions. As he himself notes, "the book attempted to combine a kind of historical materialism with what later on came to be called discourse analysis. Marxist modernism married to post-modernism *avant la lettre*."[7] It is the postmodern aspects of the work that have proved the most influential, all too often at the expense of Anderson's Marxism. Nevertheless, it would be ungenerous not to begin by recognizing his achievement. To understand why this book had such an impact, it is necessary first to review how nationalism had previously been dealt with in the Marxist tradition.

STRATEGIES, DEFINITIONS, EXPLANATIONS

Marx and Engels engaged with the issue of nationalism in the middle decades of the nineteenth century—in other words, during the period in which the bourgeois revolution was being completed across Western Europe, North America, and Japan. They argued that the working class (and "the democracy" more generally) should support national movements and the formation of new nation-states where they would hasten the development of capitalism and consequently the emergence of a working class, and where they would weaken the great reactionary powers of Europe, the most powerful of which was absolutist Russia.[8]

Self-determination was not necessarily the absolute priority. Marx and Engels rejected the view that every national group had the right to establish a state, the so-called principle of nationality, as it was then known.[9] On the contrary, for them it entirely depended on whether the success of the movement was likely to lead to a progressive outcome or not. Nor was their attitude to a particular movement determined by the class nature or political attitudes of its leadership. The Hungarian rising of 1848 was dominated by the nobility, the aristocracy led the Polish insurrection of 1863, and even the Irish Fenians—in many respects one of the more politically advanced nonsocialist groups of the time—were heavily influenced by the Catholic Church. None of these negative characteristics was decisive, however, compared with the positive objective consequences of opening up the possibilities for capitalist development or closing down the influence of the absolutist states. By contrast, Marx and Engels refused support to the Czechs and southern Slavs during the revolutions of 1848–49 because they were backed by Russian absolutism—the "*gendarme* of Europe"—for its own purposes.[10]

The specific situations with which these socialist strategies toward nationalism were intended to deal are now largely historical, but the method employed remains of enduring value. It was, however, arrived at without any real explanation of the emergence or nature of nations, whose existence Marx and Engels essentially took for granted. They left the movement a correct strategic orientation on national movements together with an undeveloped theoretical position on the nature of nations, national consciousness, and so on.

The next generation of Marxists quite understandably concentrated, as a matter of practical necessity, on refining the approach of revolutionary socialists to national movements and national demands under the changed conditions of the imperialist era. These discussions, which extended from the mid-1890s to the debates on "the national and colonial question" during the first four congresses of the Communist International (1919–1922), represent one of Marxism's greatest contributions to the question of socialist strategy.[11] But although some participants, notably Kautsky and Lenin, made attempts to explain how nations emerged, these were rarely central to the argument and usually went no further than emphasizing the need for capitalism to dominate a territorial home market and the role of language in unifying the inhabitants of that territory.[12]

The Austro-Marxist tendency, represented by Karl Renner and Otto Bauer, did focus on the question of national formation, above all in Bauer's monumental *The National Question and Social Democracy* (1906). But the definition of a nation offered by Bauer was resolutely nonmaterialist: "The nation is the totality of human beings bound together by a community of fate into a community of character."[13] Bauer did see capitalism as playing a role in the development of national consciousness, but only in the sense that such consciousness can only be complete when it is aware of other nations and the difference between them, which occurs most fully under capitalist development. Bauer's work has been hailed as the only serious Marxist attempt to deal with the national question, but mainly by people who welcome it precisely because of its distance from Marxism. (Indeed, even Bauer is too marked by "economism" and "class reductionism" for some of his present day admirers.[14])

Lenin claimed that Bauer's theory was "basically psychological" and endorsed instead the "historico-economic" explanation associated with Kautsky and in his own writings, but failed to propose a comparably detailed alternative explanation for the emergence of nations or the nature of national consciousness.[15] What was offered in direct opposition to Bauer was not a counterexplanation but a counterdefinition that is unfortunately still widely accepted by many on the left today. In 1913 Joseph Stalin wrote, under Lenin's guidance: "A nation is a historically constituted, stable community of people, formed on the basis of a common language, territory, economic life, and psychological makeup manifested in a common culture."[16] Typically, he also informs us that if a single one of these factors is missing, no nation exists. The trouble with definitions of this sort is that they give a false aura of scientific objectivity, which collapses as soon as you start to think of all the nations it would exclude—the United States of America, for one. And although Stalin dismissed the demand for cultural autonomy associated with Austro-Marxism, his definition actually draws heavily on that of Bauer, by retaining the catchall categories of "community" and "psychological makeup."[17]

With the triumph of Stalinism in the late 1920s, serious discussion of nationalism virtually ceased. The main source of discussion about the nation therefore passed to non-Marxist political and social scientists, including many who were to be the founding fathers of the academic discipline of International Relations, an orientation that suggests their interests lay in the "state" side of the "nation-state" couplet.[18] Yet although they tended to see nationalism as a movement only emerging from the late eighteenth century, they also accepted that nations—at least the "old historic nations" such as Spain, England and France—long preexisted this period.

THE ANDERSONIAN MOMENT: POLITICAL AND THEORETICAL CONTEXTS

From the 1960s a "modernist" current emerged within the study of na-tionalism that took a much more foreshortened view of its history. Em-phases varied. Of the initial "modernist texts," Kedourie's *Nationalism* (1960) privileged the Enlightenment and Gellner's essay "Nationalism" (1964) the Industrial Revolution as the sources of nationhood. But all "modernists," as the name suggests, saw both nations and nationalism as relatively recent, "modern," creations.[19] The intellectual dominance of modernism only held sway for a relatively brief period, roughly from the late 1970s to the early 1990s, and of the writers identified with it, only Tom Nairn, Eric Hobsbawm and Nigel Harris saw themselves as Marx-ists at the time of writing, as did Anderson.

Anderson is a specialist in East Asian politics. He went to Indonesia in 1962 to study that country's experience during the Second World War, when Japanese occupation supplanted the Dutch colonial presence. As he later commented, his research suggested that there were parallels be-tween the period of resistance to Japan and the returning Dutch, and the 1960s, when the "Guided Democracy" of President Sukarno stood on the edge of a real social radicalization, only to be brought to a bloody end by the coup of 1965.[20] The book that resulted from these researches, *Java in a Time of Revolution* (1972), dealt only in passing with the question of nationalism, but what it does say is interesting in the light of his later preoccupations. Here, Anderson describes the second congress of the youth wing of the Indonesian National Party in 1928:

> At that same congress the participating youth took the historic oath of commitment to one people, the Indonesian people, one nation, the In-

donesian nation, and one language, the Indonesian language. In a real sense the development of nationalism among the educated youths was less the result of their readings in European history or their encounters with racist colonial authorities than of their experience in schools whose raison d'être derived directly from the centralised structure of the Netherlands Indies in the twentieth century. Nationalism was the only explanation that could be given for each student having made the journey from whatever home he had left to enter one classroom with the others. Only nationalism made sense of the new life on which they were collectively embarked. But insofar as this nationalism was a response to experience, it was necessarily limited to those who shared that experience. The politically-minded youth of the 1930s were profoundly isolated from the rest of their contemporaries. It was not until the Japanese period that nationalism spread deeply into small-town and rural Java; and it did so then because of the new experiences encountered there, to which it gave coherent meaning.

In describing the later role of the Barisan Pelopor (Vanguard Corps) during the resistance, Anderson notes: "It was a new nationalism, very different from that of their elders, precisely because it grew out of an unprecedented experience."[21] Many of the themes rehearsed here—the initial growth of nationalism as emerging from the collective experience of an elite group, the sense of nationalism as a means of understanding the world rather than a narrow set of political demands—were to re-emerge in more fully developed form in *Imagined Communities*. Anderson was expelled from Indonesia for displeasing the Suharto regime shortly after the book appeared. "Exile," he later wrote, "had the advantage of pushing my inquiries back into the nineteenth century, and from everyday politics to the transformations of consciousness that made presently existing Indonesia thinkable." There were, however, other factors that led him to write *Imagined Communities*.

In 1978 and 1979 wars had taken place between Vietnam, Cambodia, and China, but "none of the belligerents had made more than the most perfunctory attempts to justify the bloodshed in terms of a recognizable Marxist theoretical perspective." This said something about their character: "Since World War Two every successful revolution has defined itself in national terms . . . and, in so doing, has grounded itself firmly in a territorial and social space inherited from the revolutionary past."[22] But the idea that socialism, or even the transition to socialism, should perpetuate nation-state and nationalism was contrary to all previous Marxist positions. What implications did this have for the Marxist theory of nationalism? There was already a perception that Marxism lacked an adequate theory of nationalism. In 1976 Tom Nairn had claimed that nationalism "represents Marxism's greatest historical failure."[23] As Anderson points out, that implies "the regrettable outcome of a long, self-conscious search for historical clarity." His response was that the problem was rather that this search had never taken place; consequently, "nationalism has proved an uncomfortable *anomaly* for Marxist theory and, precisely for that reason, has been largely elided, rather than confronted."[24] Anderson now reveals that he was more sympathetic to Nairn's position than this suggests and claims that he intended *Imagined Communities* to offer critical support, but also to extend Nairn's critique from Marxism to all other political traditions, which he saw as similarly lacking.[25] What then was his alternative?

ANDERSON'S ARGUMENT

Anderson starts by arguing that nationalism is "a radically changed form of consciousness."[26] To define it, he starts with the reason why the nation has to be imagined: "It is imagined because the members of even the smallest nation will never know most of their fellow-members, meet them, or even hear of them, yet in the minds of each lives the image of their community." Anderson is insistent that "imagined" does not mean "false," because all communities beyond the original gatherer-hunter groups have to conduct a similar act of imagining: "Communities are to be distinguished, not by their falsity/genuineness, but by the style in which they are imagined." Anderson argues that there are three aspects to what is being imagined: limitation, because no nation can encompass the entire world and the boundaries of each are set by other nations; sovereignty, because nations came into existence at the time when the legitimacy once conferred by absolutist divine right was being replaced by that of the state; and community, because the horizontal solidarities of the nation were stronger than vertical oppositions, even those of class.[27]

Anderson identifies "the end of the 18th century" as the period that saw "the spontaneous distillation of a complex 'crossing' of discrete historical forces," and once distilled it was no longer necessary for each potential new nation to have undergone the same experiences. They could be "transplanted, with varying degrees of self-consciousness, to a great variety of social terrains."[28] But the origin of these forces goes much further back in time. Anderson argues that from the late medieval period onward there was the collapse of three key conceptions of the world: the idea that belief systems expressed in particular script languages like those of Christianity and Islam (using respectively Latin and classical Arabic) offered privileged access to truth; the belief that society was naturally organized around and under monarchs who were persons apart from other human beings and who ruled by some form of divine dispensation; and an understanding of the past and present in terms of some creation myth. Such notions rooted human lives firmly in the very nature of things, giving certain meanings to the everyday fatalities of existence (above all death, loss, and servitude) and offering, in various ways, redemption from them. All these conceptions were subverted by economic change, discoveries social and scientific, and the development of increasingly rapid communications: "No surprise then that the search was on, so to speak, for a new way of linking fraternity, power and time together."[29] He is not of course making the absurd suggestion that religion had to decline in importance before nationalism could emerge, contrary to the claims of several of his critics.[30] Given the importance he ascribes to the Reformation, this is clearly a misreading of his argument. What he is suggesting instead is that the nature of what people expected from religion changed, at least in the West.

For Anderson, the solution was provided by the emergence of "print capitalism."[31] This created the possibility of a vast market beyond the tiny minority who could understand Latin. Print-languages "created unified fields of exchange and communication below Latin and above the spoken vernaculars." They "gave a new fixity to language, which in the long run helped to build that image of antiquity so central to the subjective idea of the nation." And they created "languages of power," with certain dialects playing a dominant part in communication through printing. These were "largely unselfconscious processes resulting from the explosive interaction between capitalism, technology and human linguistic diversity."[32]

The remainder of the book sets out how national consciousness spread and was transmuted into nationalism. He argues there were three main kinds of nationalism, arising in successive waves: "creole" nationalism associated with the revolt of the American colonies ("creole" in its

Spanish use means a Latin American of European ancestry); "language" nationalism associated with Western Europe; and "official" nationalism associated with Central and Eastern Europe, and with the Asian and African anticolonial movements. In what is perhaps his boldest innovation, Anderson argues that the "pioneers" of nationalism were the first of these, the colonial states of the Americas. He ascribes the rise of nationalism to the attempt by Madrid to impose greater control, the influence of Enlightenment ideas, and the way in which the South American continent had been divided into particular, territorially delimited administrative units: "In this respect they foreshadowed the new states of Africa and parts of Asia in the mid-20th century ...The original shaping of the American administrative units was to an extent arbitrary and fortuitous, marking the spatial limits of particular military conquests. But over time they developed a firmer reality under the influence of geographic, political and economic factors."[33]

Two necessary internal processes translated the brute fact of territoriality into national consciousness, according to Anderson. There was the self-identification of the descendents of settlers with the colonial territory, in distinction from their European-born equivalents. And there was the emergence of a particular manifestation of print capitalism: the newspaper that "brought together, on the same page, this marriage with that ship, this prince with that bishop," creating "quite naturally, and even apolitically ... an imagined community among a specific assemblage of fellow-readers, to whom these ships, brides, bishops and princes belonged. In time, of course, it was only to be expected that political elements would enter in."[34]

Although vernacular language was critical to the original formation of national consciousness, once nationalism became available as a model, it was no longer necessary for new nations to have this as their basis.[35] The emergence of nationalism was originally associated with the popular masses, but it became available for use for "conservative, not to say reactionary" ends by the state bureaucracies of societies that had not experienced successful popular movements.[36] Anderson argues that the anti-imperialist nationalism, which began to build new states after 1945, drew on both of these aspects. "That is why so often in the 'nation-building' policies of the new states one sees both a genuine, popular nationalist enthusiasm and a systematic, even Machiavellian, instilling of nationalist ideology through the mass media, the educational system, administrative regulations and so forth."[37]

A brief exposition can only hint at the subtlety, complexity, and sophistication of Anderson's arguments. More than any previous writer, Anderson established that the phenomenon of nationalism was constructed and historical, not natural and eternal. Part of the charm of the book lies in the sheer range and novelty of the examples that Anderson musters to illustrate his argument, many of them drawn from areas such as Burma, Thailand, and Indonesia, which do not normally feature in discussions of nationalism. Reading it again, I was struck by how strange a book it is. The strangeness is partly a matter of style. Anderson refers in several places to Walter Benjamin's opposition of "Messianic time" and "empty homogenous time," but the book also reproduces many aspects of the German writer's allusive and disconnected manner.[38] Benjamin was primarily a philosopher and cultural critic, disciplines where an opaque literary technique is not necessarily a disadvantage; in Benjamin's case, the elliptical nature of his writings consciously invokes the fragmentation of the modern consumerism whose birth he recounted in, among other works, *The Arcades Project*.[39]

And yet *Imagined Communities* is one of those books that are of great individual value, but that have ultimately exerted a negative influence on socialist thought. As I suggested earlier, this is due to problems within the book itself, and not just to misreadings. Given that I strongly disagree with several aspects of Anderson's account of nationalism (most in relation to what he *omits*), it is more than usually necessary to state in advance which criticisms of his work or inferences from it I think are wrong or illegitimate.

POSTMODERNIST APPROPRIATION
AND PRIMORDIALIST APPROBATION

Imagined Communities made an immediate impact on publication, but perhaps not in the way that Anderson had hoped. Although other Marxists did find his work useful, it actually provided far greater support for emerging ideologies fixated on questions of identity, above all postmodernism. One of Anderson's more insightful critics, Anthony Smith, noted that, while Anderson's project is not itself a postmodernist reading, "it is the idea of the nation as discourse to be interrogated and deconstructed, that has proved most influential."[40] Anderson does not, of course, suggest that the nation is simply a discourse, but many of his critics have found it convenient to ascribe that view to him. The Scottish writer Murray Pittock, for example, writes, "The weakness of Anderson's notion of the 'imagined community' is that it implies that one can imagine at will, and choose an identity as the postmodern consumer chooses a lifestyle product."[41] Again, this position would be nonsense, but Anderson nowhere argues it; on the contrary, his argument is in the adoption of identities that are only available because of a determinate (although certainly not determined) historical process.

What both Smith and Pittock oppose in Anderson's work is precisely his constructivism, his modernism. But some postcolonial thinkers regard Anderson as *too* materialist. Partha Chatterjee, for example, writes that "the theoretical tendency represented by Anderson certainly attempts to treat the phenomenon as part of the universal history of the modern world." He opposes this in relation to Africa and Asia:

> If nationalisms in the rest of the world have to choose their imagined community from certain "modular" forms already made available to them by Europe and the Americas, what do they have left to imagine? History, it would seem, has decreed that we in the postcolonial world shall only be perpetual consumers of modernity. Europe and the Americas, the only true subjects of history, have thought out on our behalf not only the script of colonial enlightenment and exploitation, but also that of our anti-colonial resistance and postcolonial misery. Even our imaginations must remain forever colonised.

Chatterjee argues that "anti-colonial nationalism creates its own domain of sovereignty within colonial society well before it begins its political battle with the imperial power." This domain is the spiritual one, "an 'inner' domain bearing the 'essential' marks of cultural identity."[42] Anderson did not respond directly to Chatterjee, but in a later article for *New Left Review* he rightly argued that the distinction between Western and Eastern nationalism was relatively unimportant: "The oldest nationalisms in Asia—here I am thinking of India, the Philippines, and Japan—are older than many of those in Europe and Europe Overseas—Corsica, Scotland, New Zealand, Estonia, Australia, Euskadi, and so forth." Anderson has no difficulty in demonstrating that creole, linguistic, and official types of nationalism are as prevalent in the East as in the West. And, as he also notes, "what people have considered to be East and West has varied substantially over time."[43]

Anderson is therefore not vulnerable to criticism on the grounds Chatterjee raises. But he is prevented from making a more vigorous response because of a flaw in his own theory, namely the contingent role it allocates to capitalist development. I will return to the point below, but it is possible here to make a direct answer to Chatterjee. If India had achieved rounded capitalist development early enough, such that it was able to resist British imperialist aggression (an outcome far more conceivable there than in, for example, China), something like nationalism as it is understood in "Western" terms would have emerged because it is a *necessary* superstructural component of capitalist societies. What Chatterjee is proposing is an ahistorical mysticism that, in an interesting example of what Hegel used to call the "interpenetration of opposites," actually reproduces in "postcolonial" guise many of the criticisms raised by more conventional critics.

Smith is one of the main proponents of the "perennialist" view of nations that sees them as rooted in much older ethnic identities. He considers it a problem that, for Anderson, "the nation possesses no reality independent of its images and representations. But such a perspective undermines the sociological reality of the nation, the bonds of allegiance and belonging which so many people feel, and obscures both the institutional, political and territorial constitution of nations, and of the powerful and popular cultural resources and traditions that underpin so many nations and endow them with a sense of tangible identity."[44] Similarly, Pittock wants to defend a conception of Scottish nationalism stretching back to early medieval times: "The idea that identities are mainly chosen, invented or dreamt up is, like the teleological and sometimes Marxian history whence it derives, a judgement on the past in terms of a present agenda: 'be whatever you want to be' may be a sentiment understood by our posterity, but it was inaccessible to our ancestors."[45] Unfortunately, nationalist identities were also inaccessible to our ancestors, whatever fantasies may be entertained about the Declaration of Arbroath, or whatever. In other words, Anderson is being attacked here precisely where his work is strong, not where it is weak.

Nevertheless, as these criticisms demonstrate, the dominance of the modernism to which Anderson belonged was relatively brief. Politically, the latest resurgence of nationalism, and theoretically, the idiocies of post-modern identity politics, have given impetus to a revival of arguments that hold that nations are much older than modernists have claimed. As Pittock notes, "the idea that nations and nationalism cannot predate the French Revolution" is increasingly on the defensive.[46] The final collapse into primordial essentialism was signaled by two works by Emmanuel Todd, *L'illusion Economique* (1998) and *La Diversité du Monde* (1999). Todd's key thesis has been approvingly summarized by Tom Nairn to claim that "nationalism is constitutive of man's social nature."[47] Naturally Nairn has no time for the constructivist interpretation of Anderson: "Peoples have not 'imagined' such communities by chance, or out of ir-rational impulses from the soul. Identities are not aesthetic choices, but ways of existing." He therefore endorses what he takes to be a change of heart by Anderson in a later essay called "The Goodness of Nations."[48]

REIMAGINING THE HISTORY OF THE NATION

Imagined Communities can still play a role in intellectually challenging both postmodernism and primordialism, but only if its themes are inte-grated into a more consistently materialist framework. The book consists of a series of impressionistic studies on particular aspects of nationalism. But the connections between them are often difficult to establish. What is missing is any central dynamic linking them together, except for the concept of print capitalism. Yet the universality of contemporary nation-alism suggests that it was originally produced and subsequently repro-duced by a set of conditions wider and more fundamental than this. Anderson's argument about the coincidence of existential doubt and technological advance in print seems unconvincing as an explanation for something as all-pervasive as nationalism. A more convincing expla-nation might be the more general development of capitalism and, given the way in which antimodernists have attempted to deny *any* necessary relationship between nationalism and capitalism, we might have expected Anderson to argue the contrary.[49] But, like Otto Bauer, Anderson sees a purely contingent relationship between this and the rise of nationalism: "What made the new communities imaginable was a half-fortuitous, but explosive, interaction between a system of production and productive relations (capitalism), a technology of communications (print), and the fatality of human linguistic diversity."[50] He made the same point, even more strongly, in a later essay: "The two most significant factors generating nationalism and ethnicity are both *linked* closely to capitalism. They can be described summarily as mass communications and mass migrations."[51] The connection between national consciousness and capitalism is, however, far more all-embracing than this suggests.[52] In fact, national consciousness took as many centuries to become the dominant form of consciousness as the capitalist mode of production did to become the dominant mode of production, and it did so as a consequence of that. Four main elements combined, reflecting to a greater or lesser extent the impact of capitalism on feudal society.

The first element was the formation of externally demarcated and internally connected areas of economic activity. Europe had emerged from the first crisis of feudalism by the later fifteenth century as a system of states that was still dominated by the feudal mode of production. It was a system, however, increasingly adapted to elements of capitalism. In this context, the importance of capitalist development was less in the domain of production than that of circulation, for it was in the creation of trade networks that merchant capital began to link up dispersed rural communities both with each other and with the urban centers to form an extensive home market.

Linked directly to this element was a second, the adoption of a common language by the communities that were being connected to each other at the economic level. The need to communicate for the purposes of market exchange began to break down the distinctiveness of local dialects, forging a language common, or at least comprehensible, to all. Language in this way began to set the boundaries of the economic networks referred to above, boundaries that did not necessarily coincide with those of medieval kingdoms. Such economic and linguistic unification was far easier in a small centralized kingdom such as England than in a territory such as the German Empire. Indeed, establishment of state frontiers often purely determined the boundary between a dialect of a particular language and another language. And of course Anderson is right that the formation of standard forms of language was immeasurably aided by the invention of printing and the possibilities it presented for the codification of language in mass-produced works. These would not have been produced unless an audience of the literate already existed that understood their contents, but their effect was to extend the size of that audience, since printers could not produce works in every local dialect, only in the one that had emerged as the standard form, or in those that were in competition to do so. The increasing standardization of language then fed back into its original economic formation, as the merchants whose trading networks had originally defined the territorial reach of linguistic comprehensibility increasingly identified themselves with that territory, to the exclusion of rivals who spoke a different language. The rise of the vernacular was accompanied by the decline of Latin as a lingua franca, a process virtually complete by the mid-sixteenth century and expressed in the new profession of interpreter, now necessary to make vernacular diplomatic exchanges mutually comprehensible.

The third element was the character of the new absolutist states. Absolutism was the form taken by the feudal state during the economic transition from feudalism to capitalism. Yet the absolutist states did not arise automatically. The replacement of the estates monarchy of the earlier feudal period by a more centralized apparatus was the political response of the feudal ruling class to the social and economic pressures—different in degree and combination throughout Europe—set in train by the first crisis of the feudal system and the greater significance of capitalist production in the economies that emerged from it. The local jurisdictions that characterized the classic epoch of military feudalism began to give way to greater concentration of state power, notably through the introduction of standing armies and, partly in order to pay for them, regular centralized taxation.

Death and taxes both involve bureaucracies that require a version of the local language comprehensible across the state territory, thus strengthening the "linguistic" element. They also had two unintended effects. The introduction of regular taxation and the adoption of mercantilist policies reinforced the economic unity that had begun to emerge spontaneously from the activities of merchant capitalists. And the military rivalry that characterized the new system necessitated mobilizing the active support of the bourgeois minority as a source of financial backing and administrative expertise. Despite these innovations it is nevertheless important not to mistake the role of absolutism in the birth of nationhood, which was that of a midwife, not that of a mother. The issue is often elided by reference to the influence of "the modern state" in the creation of nations, but this is to dissolve the difference between the absolutist state and its genuinely modern bourgeois successor. The arrival of nationhood coincided not with the establishment of the absolutist states but with their overthrow.

The fourth and final element is local manifestations of a global religious belief. The ideology of absolutism involved stressing the deeds of religious figures such as saints, who were associated with the territory of the realm, but it was the Reformation that made religion more than an ideologically pious enhancement to the image of the ruling dynasty. Wherever Protestantism became the dominant religion within a given territory after 1517 it contributed to the formation of national consciousness by allowing communities of belief to define themselves against the interterritorial institutions of the Roman Catholic Church and the Holy Roman Empire. In part this was through the availability of the Bible in the vernacular, but this in turn depended on the existence of linguistic frameworks in which market transactions and state administration could be carried out. Protestantism acted as a stimulus to national consciousness only to the extent that the development of capitalism had provided it with the framework to do so. Naturally the process went furthest in England, but even there it was not until after the death of Elizabeth in 1603 that Protestantism came to be separated from regnal solidarity with the monarch. It took longer for Catholicism to play the same role.

There is therefore a problem with Anderson's focus on "creole" nationalism as the major formative experience of nationalism. Apart from anything else, he contradicts himself by describing it as drawn from an earlier model: "In effect, by the second decade of the 19th century, if not earlier, a 'model' of 'the' independent national state was available for pirating." He describes this as "a complex composite of French and American elements."[53] But incredibly, this is one of the first occasions that France is mentioned. To ignore the influence of the French Revolution in establishing the "model" seems particularly perverse. The problem here is that even France and the United States are not the first nations. The United Netherlands and England have a stronger claim to priority. To argue that nations only appeared at some stage in the later eighteenth century would be as absurd as arguing that capitalism only appeared at the same period. While Anderson is right to draw attention to cumulative movements, he misses something else, which is the explosive effect of the revolutionary turning points that punctuate capitalist development, and their impact in coalescing hitherto inchoate ideological elements into a national identity. His account is, so to speak, all process and no events.

The success of groups with an emergent national consciousness in the Netherlands and England in elevating this new form of consciousness into political movements led others (first in North America, Ireland, and France, then generally) to aspire to national status, even if their level of social development had not previously allowed national consciousness to arise. The bourgeois revolutions effected the final transformation of the term "nation" to one that stood for "the people" as a community—although one of the most divisive issues within all bourgeois revolutionary movements was precisely how "the people" should be defined. The struggle against absolutism required the mobilization of at least a large minority of "the people" to achieve the expulsion or destruction of the royal dynasty. This could only be done by providing some form of identity that could embrace the often very different forms of opposition to the crown, regardless of whether the ruler in question was foreign (as in the case of Spanish Habsburg dynasty in the Netherlands) or native (as in the case of the Stuart dynasty in England). Nationalism provided this identity.

National consciousness could not flourish, or even take root, unless the conditions for capitalist development were present, and for it to be consolidated across Europe, even if only among the bourgeoisie, there had to be at least one case where it made the transition to nationalism and then became embodied in a nation-state. Only when there were concrete examples of nationhood could different groups know what they were conscious of, regardless of whether they then went on to develop nationalisms of their own or not.

The capitalist nation-state became a permanent feature of the international state system only toward the end of the hundred years between the end of the English Revolution in 1688 and the beginning of the French Revolution in 1789. Thereafter new nations could be manufactured regardless of whether the original elements were present or not—although an economic infrastructure and common language would, of necessity, have to be introduced at some point for a sense of national consciousness to be consolidated. The ideological dominance of nationalism over the population depended, however, on when a particular revolution occurred in the overall cycle of bourgeois revolutions. In the two states where bourgeois revolutions were successfully completed before or during 1688, the Dutch and the English, the existence of national consciousness was directly proportional to the extent that the postrevolutionary state developed a centralized apparatus, rather than a federal or confederal structure. In this respect English nationalism was as far in advance of its Dutch predecessors as it was of its American successor, which similarly remained an alliance of semiautonomous states down to 1865.

After 1848 all ruling classes intent on creating states on the British or French models were forced to embrace nationalism, not because they were personally capitalists, but because all of them—Prussian Junkers, Japanese Samurai, Italian monarchists, and, eventually, Stalinist bureaucrats—were engaged in building industrial societies dominated by the capitalist mode of production. The example of Italy is typical of how ruling classes were faced with the need to diffuse consciousness of being a nation down from elite level into the mass of the population, a large and growing proportion of whom were not the bourgeoisie and petty bourgeoisie who had originally formed the nation, but workers. The difficulties involved should not be underestimated: as late as the 1860s as many as a quarter of the inhabitants of the French state did not speak French.

Class is the great absent theme in *Imagined Communities,* yet no Marxist account can deal with the subject without exploring the role nationalism plays in class relations. National consciousness begins to emerge in the social classes below the rulers of the new nation-states, partly as the result of deliberate indoctrination, but far more so as the by now inevitable pattern of life experience within societies shaped by the nation-state form. Among the working class the existence of reformist class consciousness provides the context within which national consciousness and nationalism develop. Reformist class consciousness was originally a historical product of the social conditions produced by the transition to capitalism or, more precisely, by the process of capitalist industrialization, first in Britain and subsequently elsewhere.

Once the initial shock of industrialization passed, workers came to accept that capitalism was not a passing aberration but a new form of society that might have many years of vitality ahead of it. The apparent permanence of the system forced accommodation and adaptation, however grudgingly, from the new exploited class, whose horizons were anyway limited by the "dull compulsion" to work, raise families, and recover from the savage exertions demanded by the factory system. Although these conditions provoked resistance, the fact that the new system generated its own defensive illusions made the possibility of a generalized revolutionary class consciousness emerging out of these resistance struggles less likely. Under early capitalism exploitation was accompanied by the economic discipline instilled by fear of the poverty that would result from being sacked. The actual process of exploitation, the fact that the worker produced more than that for which she or he was rewarded, was hidden from view. As a result, although workers were usually hostile to their own particular boss, this did not necessarily generalize into opposition to the system as a whole. Although trade unions grew out of worker resistance, the goal of these new organizations, whatever rhetoric was employed about the (invariably distant) overturning of the system, was improving the condition of the working class within the system itself. The resulting contradictory form of consciousness finds its most basic expression in an acceptance by workers of the wages system accompanied by a rejection of the particular level of wages they are being offered, but it extends to all aspects of social life.

What then is the relationship of national consciousness to this reformist consciousness? National consciousness does not compete with revolutionary class consciousness directly for the allegiance of workers, but as a key element in reformist class consciousness. Indeed, one might say that workers remain nationalist to the extent that they remain reformist. And from the point of view of the capitalist class in individual nations it is absolutely necessary that they do so, or the danger is always that workers will identify, not with the "national" interest of the state in which they happen to be situated, but with that of the class to which they are condemned to belong, regardless of the accident of geographical location. Nationalism should not therefore be seen as something that only "happens" during separatist movements on the one hand, or during Fascist and imperialist manifestations on the other. The capitalist system generates nationalism as a necessary everyday condition of its continued existence.

Mass nationalism was therefore initially a product of industrialization, but not simply because it is functional for the ruling class in industrial capitalism. Industrialization and urbanization together produced the changes in human consciousness that made nationalism *possible* (for the subordinate classes), as well as creating societies that made nationalism *necessary* (for the dominant class). They developed new structural capacities, new modes of experience, and new psychological needs in the people who had to work in the factories and live in the cities. Nationalism responds to the need for some collective sense of belonging with which to overcome the effects of alienation, to the need for psychic compensation for the injuries sustained at the hands of capitalist society, in the absence of revolutionary class consciousness, but in conjunction with reformist class consciousness.

The ideological role played by the ruling class in reinforcing nationalism is therefore only possible because nationalism already provides one possible means of meeting the psychic needs created by capitalism. Once a capitalist nation-state has been established, those who control the apparatus always seek to consolidate the hold of nationalism among the people who inhabit its territory. States need conscripts for their armies, citizens to pay taxes, workers to accept that they have more in common with those who exploit them at home than they do with their fellow-exploited abroad. This made it imperative that loyalty to a state be secured, and the nation was the means. Since the eighteenth century British workers have often been asked to accept rises in interest rates, cuts in wages and services, or participation in imperialist wars, but never for the benefit of British capitalism, always for the benefit of the British nation, for "the national interest."

It is not only the state that makes such appeals. The organizations of the working class themselves reinforce reformist class consciousness within a national context. At the most elementary level this is because such organizations are unwilling to challenge the nationalism within which political discourse is conducted, for fear of being labeled unpatriotic. More importantly, however, it is because they seek either to influence or to determine policy within the confines of the existing nation-state. Typically, therefore, nationalism is invested with the contradictory character of the reformist worldview.

CONCLUSION

If nationalism is as intertwined with capitalism as I have suggested, then nationalism today can only ever be progressive in certain limited circumstances, most obviously in relation to movements against national oppression. Marxists cannot be nationalists, nor can they even support nationalisms as such, although they can support particular national demands or movements. This is not Anderson's conclusion, as he hinted in *Imagined Communities* itself: "In an age when it is so common for progressive, cosmopolitan intellectuals (particularly in Europe?) to insist on the near-pathological character of nationalism, its roots in fear and hatred of the other, it is useful to remind ourselves that nations inspire love, often profoundly self-sacrificing love."[54] He made the point more clearly in a lecture given in the Indonesian capital of Jakarta shortly after the overthrow of the Suharto regime. Anderson told his audience that he had "half-jokingly" raised the slogan "Long live Shame!"

> No one can be a true nationalist who is incapable of feeling "ashamed" if her state or government commits crimes, including those against her fellow citizens . . . During the Vietnam War, a good part of the popular opposition came from just this good sense of shame among the American citizenry that "their government" was responsible for the violent deaths of three million people in Indochina, including uncounted numbers of women and children . . . So they went to work in protest, not merely as advocates of universal human rights, but as Americans who loved the common American project.[55]

The distinction between true and false nationalists is dangerous in the extreme and opens up the possibility of collapsing into old Stalinist notions about "reclaiming our history" from the right, "progressive patriotism," and so on.

In the concluding chapter to the original edition, Anderson expressed the forlorn hope that the experience of what he called "inter-socialist wars" would not be repeated: "But nothing can be usefully done to limit or prevent such wars unless we abandon such fictions as 'Marxists as such are not nationalists' or 'nationalism is the pathology of modern development,' and, instead, do our slow best to learn the real, and imagined, experience of the past."[56] Like Nairn before him, Anderson then goes on to invoke Walter Benjamin's image of the Angel of History, propelled into the future by a storm from Paradise, the storm called Progress, while the debris of history gathers beneath him.[57] It is high time we stopped the legacy of this great, if eccentric, Marxist thinker being misappropriated in ways that are quite alien to his thought. Benjamin understood the tragedy of history as few other Marxists have done, but he did not see the future of humanity as necessarily being an endless prolongation of that tragedy. On the contrary, he considered it necessary for there to be a "messianic interruption" of history to bring merely capitalist progress to a halt: "A genuinely messianic face must be restored to the concept of a classless society and, to be sure, in the interest of furthering the revolutionary politics of the proletariat itself."[58] The messianic vision to which Benjamin alludes involves something more than looking for the best in existing nations or seeking to create new ones on a capitalist basis. Anderson's important work, illuminating in so many ways, is ultimately a failure because he remains trapped within the ideological presuppositions of its subject. He has shown us that national consciousness and the nation-state are forms whose beginnings can be found in past history. But because he misunderstands the forces that brought them into being, he fails to recognize that future history may also see them brought to an end.

ᨠᐤ Chapter 8 ᨦᒧ

Walter Benjamin and the
Classical Marxist Tradition[1]

INTRODUCTION

Chris Nineham's article "Benjamin's Emergency Marxism" is less concerned with assessing the work under review, Esther Leslie's book *Walter Benjamin*, than with assessing the work of her subject, Benjamin himself. Given how little Chris says about Leslie's biography, readers of *International Socialism* should be aware that it is an impressive achievement in its own right, as the work of one Marxist considering the life of another. It is a sustained attempt to reconstruct Benjamin's inner life from the "remnants" he left behind: both his literary output—most of which has been available in the German *Collected Works* since 1991—and what Leslie calls "more intimate materials," the photographs, drawings, and objects of all sorts that Benjamin collected throughout his life, some of which appear as illustrations in the book.[2] Leslie maintains an absolutely consistent focus on Benjamin's perspective, never breaking off to contextualize or deliver primers in the period of Central European history during which he lived. Nor are we given the subject's life here, and his work there, for separate consideration: Leslie affords the same status to Benjamin's theoretical writings as to the more conventional biographical sources in diary entries and letters for insights into his consciousness. One of the many pleasures of this book is the way we learn how specific passages in Benjamin's work began in biographical episodes, his response to which he then incorporated into his writing. For example, in his last and greatest essay, "On the Concept of History," Benjamin writes that reformists do not see the working class as "the avenger that completes the task of liberation in the name of generations of the down trodden." Instead: "The Social Democrats preferred to cast the working class in the role of a redeemer of future generations, in this way cutting the sinews of its greatest strength. This indoctrination made the working class forget both its hatred and its spirit of sacrifice, for both are nourished by the image of enslaved ancestors rather than by the ideal of liberated grandchildren."[3] We now learn that the origin of this celebrated passage lies in a ten-day conference at Potnigny in France, during May 1940, which Benjamin attended while waiting for the outcome of his ultimately fruitless attempts to secure a passage to the USA: "Benjamin witnessed a dreadful lecture by Emilie Lefranc of the Confederation Generale du Travail, an example of vulgar Marxism effortlessly serving counter-revolutionary ends. The main theme of the lecture was that workers should not nourish their spirit of revenge, but rather simply be inspired by the struggle for social justice."[4] Leslie does not always draw out these linkages, and making them depends on the reader knowing Benjamin's work as much as the history against which it was written. It is not *A Rebel's Guide to Benjamin* then; but it is the best place to start for anyone wanting to deepen their understanding of his achievements.

Reading Chris's review, however, those unfamiliar with Benjamin's work might wonder whether he *had* any achievements to his credit. His deeply misleading critique judges Benjamin, a philosopher and cultural critic, as if he were a political theorist, then compounds this error by ascribing to him views that in any case he did not hold. Chris implies that, while Benjamin may have coined a few memorable aphorisms or aperçus, there is nothing in his work that requires us to undertake any reconsideration of how Marxists might respond to artistic or cultural production. Where Benjamin sounds a fire alarm for his readers, Chris extends them a comfort blanket. And even where Chris concedes that Benjamin might have insights to offer, he contrives either to reduce them to commonplaces or to give the impression that they are responsible for leading people in wrong directions. The following example shows how this method of criticism works.

First, Chris quotes a passage where Benjamin discusses the possibility that "technological reproducibility" in cinema might allow mass audiences to appreciate new approaches to realism in art, approaches that they would have rejected when presented to them in classic bourgeois forms such as easel painting. ("The reactionary attitude towards a Picasso painting changes into a progressive attitude towards a Chaplin movie.") Chris then claims that time has demonstrated Benjamin's error: "In the era of *Celebrity Big Brother* such enthusiasm sounds naive." Given that Benjamin was discussing Chaplin, one of the great cinematic artists of the twentieth century, it is not entirely clear what the reference to reality TV is doing here. Chris then reveals that, in any case, Benjamin was, after all, quite aware of the dangers of media technology being applied for reactionary ends: "In the essay's epilogue he argues that in the hands of the Nazis the same technology which can politicize culture can also glamorize and corrupt mass politics."[5] Despite this concession, the effect, within the overall context of Chris's piece, is to give the impression that Benjamin's position is questionable in some way, and may even be a precursor to that of the contemporary fantasists of "cultural resistance," for whom watching *Celebrity Big Brother* is an insurrectionary act. In fact, Benjamin's concern about the reactionary use of new technologies was as much inspired by Hollywood as by Nazi propaganda, as can be seen from his response to one of Frank Capra's films, *You Can't Take It with You*. Considered populist and "against plutocracy" at the time, Benjamin complained that the film embodied "inoffensiveness" or "harmlessness" to the point where its supposedly "heart-warming" qualities actually rendered it a new opium of the people and, indeed, complicit with Fascism.[6] This may be an exaggerated verdict on Capra's Popular-Frontism lite, but it scarcely indicates an uncritical attitude to mass-produced culture. Nevertheless, it is his comments on Nazism that perhaps have also to be applied to Big Brother and to reality TV more generally: "[Fascism] sees its salvation in granting expression to the masses—but on no account granting them rights. *Mass reproduction is especially favoured by the reproduction of the masses.* In great ceremonial processions, giant rallies, and mass sporting events, and in war, all of which are now fed into the camera, the masses come face to face with themselves."[7] And what they come face-to-face with, of course, is their own alienated selves under capitalism.

There are a number of other things that could be said in response to Chris; but I want to focus on two. The first is the question of *how* we read Benjamin, what we read him *as*. There is no point in approaching his work, even his most political work, as if it was the *Collected Speeches and Resolutions of the First Four Congresses of the Third International*. To do so is to commit what philosophers call a category mistake, leading to Benjamin being criticized on the basis of what he did not write rather than assessed on the basis of what he did write. The second is to focus on the meaning of "On the Concept of History," specifically to answer the charges of "voluntarism," supposedly exemplified by the famous "emergency brake" metaphor that gives Chris the title of his review, and of placing too great a weight upon history as a motivation for revolutionary action.

WAS BENJAMIN A "WESTERN MARXIST"?

Chris claims that there is a "growing fascination" with Benjamin's work, as part of which "the far left are making great claims" for him.[8] Well, apart from Esther Leslie, some other Marxists like Michael Löwy and Alex Callinicos still take Benjamin seriously; but any objective survey would have to conclude that the peak of his fashionability has long since passed. As Leslie noted in an earlier book, *Walter Benjamin, Overpowering Conformism*:

> A conference held in London to mark Benjamin's hundredth birthday in July 1992 saw intellectual after intellectual testify to Benjamin's failure, when measured against contemporary ambitions: his failure to understand the meaning of law, his failure to comprehend the compassionate stance of modern Judaism and his consequent failure to mourn properly (Gillian Rose); his failure to derive an ethics (Alex Honneth); his failure as a feminist, his failure at (academic) success, due to his outsider status, and his failure to move beyond the autobiographical and micrological (Janett Wolff); his failure to find out what he should have been seeking all along but did not: a notion of experience without a subject (Martin Jay); his failure as the modus operandi of the intellectual (Zygmunt Bauman); his theoretical failure which goes hand in hand with the failure of Marxism, and the resulting failure of contemporary Marxian-Benjaminians to neutralise historical distance and contingency and recognise the superiority of social democracy (Irving Wohlfahrt). In as much as Benjamin was a Marxist he failed.

Leslie continues this catalogue of rejection for several more paragraphs, yet as she points out, hostility to Benjamin's Marxism is not a new phenomenon, reflecting the retreat from socialist commitment attendant on the fall of the Stalinist regimes; it merely brought into sharper focus the distrust that had always been shown toward it, even by erstwhile supporters like Theodore Adorno, Max Horkheimer, or Gershom Scholem.[9] This in turn suggests why we should be interested in him. What kind of Marxist was he?

Isaac Deutscher distinguished between what he called the "Classical Marxist" tradition, "the body of thought developed by Marx, Engels, their contemporaries, and after them by Kautsky, Plekhanov, Lenin, Trotsky [and] Rosa Luxemburg," and that of "vulgar Marxism," "the pseudo-Marxism of the different varieties of European social-democrats, reformists, Stalinists. Krushchevites, and their like."[10] Perry Anderson later added a third variant, which he called "Western Marxism," to signal the shifting geographical axis of Marxist thought from Eastern and Central Europe to Western Europe after the rise of Hitler and consolidation of Stalinism. This tradition, according to Anderson, was "a product of *defeat*," and it represented a version of Marxist theory that was divorced from the working class and had "migrated virtually completely into the universities." The work of Western Marxism moved in the opposite direction to the classical tradition, "from economics and politics towards philosophy," took the form of a 'second-order . . . discourse" or "esoteric discipline," and was characterized by "extreme difficulty of language."[11] Western Marxism is the category to which Benjamin's work has the most obvious affinities, and Anderson certainly regards him as one of its representative figures, in his case the characteristic obscurity of language involving "a gnomic brevity and indirection"—indeed, Anderson says that the famous passage from "On the Concept of History" invoking the Angel of History is expressed in language that would have been "virtually incomprehensible to Marx and Engels."[12] Anderson is simply wrong on the last point. If anything, it was Marx's own use of "sociological poetics" that may have provided Benjamin with one of the sources for his own style. When we consider some of the images that Marx employs—history as a theatrical performance, first tragic then comic; capital as a vampire, sucking the blood of living labor; the capitalist as a sorcerer, conjuring up forces from the nether world that then escape his control—the Angel of History does not seem so outlandish a concept as to present him with difficulties of comprehension.[13] As this suggests, Benjamin does not quite fit the mold of Western Marxism, for four reasons.

First, although he had ambitions to become an academic, he was never successful in obtaining a permanent post, with the result that he was forced to make a living through reviewing, public lecturing, translating, and other forms of intellectual odd-jobbery. In any case there is reason to believe that he would have found the false impartiality and narrow specialization of academic life intolerable. At one point he endorsed the early educational policies of the Russian Revolution: "Only if man experiences changes of milieu in all their variety, and can mobilise his energies in the service of the working class again and again in every new context, will he be capable of that universal readiness for action which the Communist program opposes to what Lenin called 'the most repulsive feature of the old bourgeois society': its separation of theory and practice."[14] Benjamin did publish in scholarly journals when he could, of course, but his non-academic status meant he was always more of a classical "man of letters" than, for example, the German Western Marxists with whom he is most often associated, like Adorno, Horkheimer, or Marcuse. Isaac Deutscher was another Marxist who had to survive in similar ways outside the academy, although his style could scarcely have been more different from that of Benjamin. Their type barely survived the Second World War and hardly exists today. Benjamin foresaw his own demise as a function of the heightening of class conflict in which unattached intellectuals would increasingly have to take sides:

> Today it is official doctrine that subject matter, not form, decides the revolutionary or counterrevolutionary attitude of a work. Such doctrines cut the ground from under the writer's feet just as irrevocably as the economy has done on the material plane. In this, Russia is ahead of Western developments—but not as far ahead as is believed. For sooner or later, with the middle classes who are being ground to pieces by the struggle between capital and Labor, the "freelance" writer must also disappear.[15]

In fact the decline of the man of letters took place for quite different reasons. As Russell Jacoby tells the story for the United States, the assimilation of the wider category of intellectuals until it was virtually synonymous with that of university-based academics was one of the main factors that destroyed this type of writer, along with the end of bohemia and the concomitant rise of the suburbs, which deprived them of a cultural environment, as well as the disappearance of the type of general publication in which they could publish, which deprived them of an audience.[16]

Reference to the US example suggests the group to which I believe Benjamin has the greatest affinities: the left-wing New York intellectuals of the thirties and forties.[17] There are many differences, of course. Their idiom was much clearer and more direct. And while many were also Jewish, even prior to their radicalization in the 1930s they tended to be secular humanist, and insofar as they were concerned with Judaism, it was mainly with defending distinctive aspects of the culture from assimilation. In other respects their outlook was cosmopolitan, and the *doctrines* of Jewish mysticism, which play such a central role in Benjamin's work, were always alien to them.[18] Similarly, although Benjamin was also interested in Trotsky's work and there are several aspects of their writing that overlap, the New Yorkers tended to be closer in organizational terms to actual Trotskyist organizations.[19] Nevertheless, when allowances are made for their respective cultural particularities, it is clear that Benjamin and his New York contemporaries were the same type of intellectuals and that consideration of these affinities might be at least as productive as the attention that is endlessly paid to Benjamin's links with the Frankfurt School.[20]

Second, and partly because of his position outside the academy, Benjamin developed a literary style that was quite distinct from the clotted, constipated prose of the professors. It is not without its difficulties, of course. Michael Löwy notes that Benjamin's thought had three main sources: Jewish mysticism, German Romanticism, and historical materialism.[21] Naturally these also inform his prose, which can be an obstacle to understanding for contemporary readers familiar only with the last. Authors with similar interests to those of Benjamin, such as John Berger or Hans Magnus Enzensberger, have drawn on his fragmented, allusive literary style to good effect; but when writers with quite different cultural formations attempt to adopt Benjamin's for the purposes of political or historical rather than cultural analysis, it can lead to work that is unfocused or incoherent. Whatever its other virtues, Benedict Anderson's celebrated book *Imagined Communities* suffers from precisely these defects.[22] The question, however, is whether or not the style is adequate or appropriate for *Benjamin's* purposes, not those who have followed him. Chris quotes Hannah Arendt and Theodore Adorno's criticism of Benjamin for adopting the cinematic technique of montage in the *Passenger Werke,* now available in English as *The Arcades Project:* "The problem is that montage is an artistic method. It can be effective in the hands of someone sensitive to the half hidden, symbolic significance of appearances, but it does not add up to a method of analyzing how society works or the role of culture within it. At times this was the weight Benjamin tried to place on it."[23] But there is a false assumption here. Benjamin was not concerned with anything so general as "analyzing how society works or the role of culture within it"—and why should criticism confine itself to these enormous themes in any case?—but with something much more specific: capturing an aspect of the experience of capitalist modernity, in microcosm, through a multiple-perspective view on commodity culture in the city where it was most advanced. He evidently believed that that the task of revealing the nature of an environment structured by the sale of commodities could not be undertaken in the same way as the task of critically assessing a novel, a poem, or a film—although, as the *Selected Works* demonstrate, he was perfectly capable of doing so in relatively conventional ways when required. Instead he employs the techniques of modernist novels, poems, and films: "This work has to develop to the highest degree the art of citing without quotation marks. Its theory is intimately related to that of montage." Or again: "Method of this project: literary montage. I needn't *say* anything. Merely show."[24] What this suggests to me, at any rate, is that we should treat *The Arcades Project* as Benjamin intended, as a work of art in its own right. That, in turn, suggests that we should read it as we would Eliot's *The Waste Land* or Burroughs's *Naked Lunch,* rather than as a failed attempt to write something comparable to Lukács's *The Historical Novel* or Trotsky's *Literature and Revolution.*

Third, although Benjamin was interested in what we now regard as high culture—above all in his obsessive, lifelong engagement with the poet Charles Baudelaire—he also opened up entirely new areas for Marxist analysis in relation to folk, popular, and mass cultures.[25] Because the babble about culture is now neverending, and usually utterly valueless, it is important to understand both how innovative Benjamin's work was and how it differed from what followed. Although Benjamin was a modernist, his central emphasis was on the importance of new cultural forms that emerged *after* the ascendance of the bourgeoisie and that bore limited resemblance to the historical novel or the classical symphony. In particular he stressed the need to

> rethink conceptions of literary forms or genres, in view of the technical factors affecting our present situation, if we are to identify the forms of expression that channel the literary energies of the present. There were not always novels in the past, and there will not always have to be; there have not always been tragedies and great epics. Not always were the forms of commentary, translation, indeed even so-called plagiarism, playthings in the margins of literature; they had a place in the literary writings of Arabia and China.[26]

Of his contemporaries, only Gramsci among the classical Marxists and Orwell among the wider socialist movement had comparable interests in wider culture issues.[27] In this respect, Benjamin took positions that were distinct from both the Frankfurt School and the New York intellectuals, both of whom had considerably more pessimistic attitudes to contemporary culture.[28] Benjamin shares some of these perspectives, albeit with interesting differences in emphasis, but his operational conclusions are quite different.

In "The Paris of the Second Empire in Baudelaire," Benjamin focuses on literature rather than, as in Greenberg, on the arts in general, but the origins of the avant-garde are presented in very similar terms:

> Actually, the theory of *l'art pour l'art* assumed decisive importance around 1852, at a time when the bourgeoisie sought to wrest its "cause" from the hands of the writers and poets. . . . At the end of this development, we find Mallarmé and the theory of *la poesie pure*. Here we find the poet has become so far removed from the cause of his own class that the problem of literature without a subject becomes the centre of discussion. This discussion is evident in Mallarmé's poems, which revolve around *blanc, absence, silence, vide*. This to be sure—particularly in Mallarmé—is the face of a coin whose obverse is by no means insignificant. It shows that the poet no longer supports any of the causes pursued by the class to which he belongs. To found a production process on such a basic renunciation of all the manifest experiences of

this class engenders specific and considerable difficulties—difficulties that make this poetry highly esoteric.[29]

Benjamin differs from Greenberg, however, over the possibilities of the avant-garde being harnessed to a revolutionary project, mainly because of the immense difficulties it posed for the working class—or indeed anyone outside of the cultured elites of bourgeois society:

> At no point in time, no matter how utopian, will anyone win the masses over to a higher art; they can be won over only by finding one nearer to them. And the difficulty consists precisely in finding a form for art, such that, with the best conscience in the world, one could hold that it *is* a higher art. This will never happen with what is propagated by the avant-garde of the bourgeoisie. . . . The masses positively require from a work of art (which, for them, has its place in the circle of consumer items) something that is warming. Here the flame that is most readily kindled is hatred.

The "avant-garde of the bourgeoisie" that Benjamin has in mind here either makes no concessions to the sensibilities of the audience or consciously intends to shock them. He is not, however, suggesting that art should not be challenging or require effort; simply that it cannot be deliberately inaccessible or repulsive. As a result, although his definition of kitsch is similar to that of Greenberg—"Kitsch . . . is nothing more than art with a 100 per cent, absolute and instantaneous availability for consumption. Precisely within the consecrated forms of expression, therefore, kitsch and art stand irreconcilably opposed"—he sees it as containing possibilities: "But for developing, living forms, what matters is that they have within them something stirring, useful, ultimately heartening—that they take 'kitsch' dialectically up into themselves, and hence bring themselves nearer to the masses while yet surmounting the kitsch."[30] The final point in this passage returns us to the argument about new forms that could be used for either avant-garde or kitsch purposes but also had the potential to transcend the obscurity of the former and the vulgarity of the latter; the cinema and, to a lesser extent, photography were the most important for Benjamin, but the argument also applies to popular music from jazz onward. What is crucial about these forms for Benjamin is that they involve "alienating the productive apparatus from the ruling class by improving it in ways serving the interests of socialism." Authors, or artists more generally, have two functions in their role as producer: "first, to induce other producers to produce, and, second, to put an improved apparatus [of production] at their disposal." How can we judge whether an apparatus has been improved? "And this apparatus is better, the more consumers it is able to turn into producers—that is, readers or spectators into collaborators."[31] The possibilities of participation in, rather than passive consumption of, culture have yet to be fully absorbed by the Marxist tradition, let alone put into practice, although it is possible to identify works that embody the principles Benjamin endorsed in artistic production.[32]

The fourth area of difference with Western Marxism places him closest to the classical tradition: his commitment to the socialist revolution. For, unlike all Western Marxists, Benjamin never adapted to social democracy, Stalinism, or any variation of socialism from above, nor did he lapse into political pessimism or despair. It is possible to interpret his suicide at the Franco-Spanish border in 1940 as an act of *personal* despair; but as Paul Wood writes, "it was undoubtedly an act of great courage."[33] It can also be interpreted as a final act of self-determination, by actively choosing death rather than surrender and so denying the Gestapo their victim.[34] In any event, Benjamin retained to the end his belief in the possibility of socialist revolution on the basis of working-class self-activity. His final substantial work before his suicide, "On the Concept of History" and its preparatory notes, are the greatest theoretical affirmation, in the face of inconceivable adversity, of the actuality of the revolution in the entire Marxist canon. The difference between this work and the outright renegacy of Horkheimer or even the evasiveness of Adorno could not be starker. Chris claims that this was voluntarism, an act of faith for which Benjamin provides no grounds. I will argue below that this is a misunderstanding; but even to the extent that it does involve an act of faith, Benjamin is far closer to classical Marxism than Chris supposes.

REVOLUTION, HISTORY, AND TRADITION

Chris accuses Benjamin of alternating between determinism and voluntarism, particularly towards the end of his life. But this determinism is of a particularly pessimistic sort, the obverse of the optimistic determinism of social democracy, in which the development of the forces of production will inevitably deliver socialism without conscious human effort.

Instead it points toward the termination of human culture. Indeed, Chris suggests that, for Benjamin, it is not simply the forces of production, but technology more narrowly that is leading toward war. Yet Chris doesn't actually argue the point; he simply offers two quotes from *One-Way Street and Other Writings,* which bear a somewhat tangential relationship to the point he is trying to make.[35] Here is the passage in which Benjamin sets out the most developed version of his argument about technology.

> If the natural use of productive forces is impeded by the property system, then the increase in technological means, in speed, in sources of energy will press towards an unnatural use. This is found in war, and the destruction caused by war furnishes proof that society was not mature enough to make technology its organ, that technology was not sufficiently developed to master the elemental forces of society. The most horrifying features of imperialist war are determined by the discrepancy between the enormous means of production and their inadequate use in the process of production (in other words, by unemployment and the lack of markets). *Imperialist war is an uprising on the part of technology, which demands payment in "human material" for the natural material society has denied it.* Instead of draining rivers, society directs a human stream into a bed of trenches; instead of dropping seeds from airplanes, it drops incendiary bombs over cities; and in gas warfare it has found a new means of abolishing the aura.[36]

If we were to take this literally, it might appear that Benjamin did not merely ascribe a logic of warfare to technology but imagined that the technology itself was turning on us, in the manner of *Terminator 3: The Rise of the Machines.* But what Benjamin means is rather that, in societies dominated by capitalist relations of production, where technology is not used to meet human need but for accumulation, the conflicts that society generates will lead to technology being used for destructive purposes, in ever more complex and inventive ways, as an obscene parody of the creativity that socialism would bring. As a contemporary illustration, we only need to contrast the extraordinary achievement of the US military in constructing a city in the desert from nothing, prior to the opening of the Third Gulf War, with the lack of resources subsequently made available to the Iraqis for reconstruction following the occupation. In short, there is nothing remotely determinist about Benjamin's attitude to technology; it simply describes the reality of imperialism.

A superficially more plausible accusation is that of voluntarism. Unfortunately, if this can be sustained, it is not just Benjamin that stands condemned, but a large part of the Marxist tradition. Here is Chris's charge-sheet in full:

> The truth is that Benjamin never completely solved the problem that haunted him. He correctly warned against blind faith in progress. He knew the potential of the explosive struggles capitalism stores up, but he never arrived at a rounded explanation of how those struggles could develop and mature. Sometimes he fell back on a catastrophe theory of consciousness: "Marx says that revolutions are the locomotives of history. But perhaps it is quite otherwise, perhaps revolutions are an attempt by passengers on this train—namely the human race—to activate the brake." This is characteristically thought provoking, but it is also voluntaristic. It is not clear where the action arises from. Revolutions are always partly a response to a sense of emergency, but Benjamin's own epoch demonstrates all too vividly that impending catastrophe does not automatically mean the brake will be applied. Revolutionary consciousness is made possible by the everyday contradictions of capitalism, and active intervention in them, not just a sense of the horror of its ultimate destination. What we do now to develop it will effect what happens when the train approaches the bumpers.[37]

Chris is perhaps expecting too much from what is, after all, an author's note to himself from a set of preparatory materials. Even so, it should be obvious that "humanity reaching for the emergency brake" is a not a *political program* for how the socialist revolution will be *achieved,* it is a *metaphor* for what the socialist revolution *will be*—the means of averting the disasters that capitalism is preparing for us and that will otherwise occur. Our recently acquired knowledge of the dangers and implications of environmental collapse gives this passage an even greater resonance now than when it was written.[38] And many people, including the present writer, have found it invaluable in helping us conceptualize the meaning rather than the mechanics of the socialist revolution.[39] What then was Benjamin actually trying to convey in "On the Concept of History" and its preparatory materials?[40] Despite the great beauty of the language, there is no doubt that it contains several very difficult passages, and many academic careers have been built, not on clarifying its meaning for readers, but in rendering it even more obscure. At the risk of bending the stick too far in the other direction and oversimplifying, what Benjamin seems to be doing—among other things—is proposing three notions, two of which have been expressed elsewhere in the classical Marxist tradition, the third of which is an original contribution to that tradition.

The first is that of a "wager" on the possibility of revolution. The concept of the wager was first introduced into Western culture by the Roman Catholic philosopher Blaise Pascal during the seventeenth century. Pascal's argument was that since we cannot know for certain whether God exists or not by way of our reason, we have to gamble, to wager, on his existence. Pascal argues that we have everything to gain and nothing to lose from wagering on the existence of God, but everything to lose—that is, eternal life—from wagering the other way.[41] The argument was secularized by Lucien Goldmann in his classic study of Pascal and Racine, *The Hidden God* (1964): "Marxist faith is faith in the future which men make for themselves in and through history. Or more accurately, in the future that we must make for ourselves by what we do, so that this faith becomes a 'wager' which we make that our actions will, in fact, be successful. The transcendental element present in this faith is not supernatural and does not take us outside or beyond history; it merely takes us beyond the individual."[42] The theme was further developed in a discussion of Goldmann by Alasdair MacIntyre:

> But if tragic thought and dialectical thought differ in . . . crucial respects, they also resemble each other at key points. Both know that one cannot first understand the world and only then act in it. How one understands the world will depend in part on the decision implicit in one's already taken actions. The wager of action is unavoidable. . . . Not eternity but the future provides a context which gives meaning to individual parts in the present. The future which does this is as yet unmade; we wager on it not as spectators, but as actors pledged to bring it into being.[43]

As in the case of the theory of culture shared by the Frankfurt School and the New York intellectuals, we appear to be witnessing a parallel intellectual development, where an idea is arrived at independently by different individuals within a shared tradition. Although Benjamin makes several passing references to Pascal in his work, he does not explicitly discuss the wager. Nevertheless, Michael Löwy has plausibly suggested that "On the Concept of History" is also infused with the belief that "the Marxist utopia of an authentic human community is of the order of a Pascalian wager":

> It is the engagement of individuals—or social groups—in an action that involves risk, the danger of failure, the hope of success, but to which one commits one's life. Any wager of this type is motivated by trans-individual values, whether these are immanent and secular, as in the Marxist wager on the achievement of the socialist community, or transcendent and sacred, as in the Pascal's wager on the existence of God, and is not susceptible of scientific proof or factual demonstration.[44]

The notion of the wager may not immediately appear to be compatible with classical Marxism, and the authors cited here may seem marginal to that tradition. Nevertheless, the wager has had a subterranean existence in the work of more central figures. It is surely embodied in Lenin's *practice* between his arrival at the Finland Station and the fall of the Winter Palace in 1917. It surfaces in Gramsci's prison notebooks, particularly in the following passage: "In reality one can 'foresee' to the extent that one acts, to the extent that one applies a voluntary effort and therefore contributes concretely to creating the result 'foreseen.' Prediction reveals itself thus not as a scientific act of knowledge, but as the abstract expression of the effort made, the practical way of creating a collective will."[45] But perhaps it is best and most briefly summed up in a famous aphorism by James Connolly: "For the only true prophets are they who carve out the future which they announce."[46] The central point is that it is possible to lose this wager. After the history of the twentieth century, only the very stupid, the very naive, or those possessed of a religious cast of mind quite alien to Marxism could possibly believe that socialism was inevitable. Trotsky was one of the very few Marxists prepared to look into the abyss that opens up once this is acknowledged, which he did in relation to the fate of the Russian Revolution:

> The historic alternative, carried to the end, is as follows: either the Stalin regime is an abhorrent relapse in the process of transforming bourgeois society into a socialist society, or the Stalin regime is the first stage of a new exploiting society. If the second prognosis proves to be correct, then, of course, the bureaucracy will become a new ruling class. However onerous the second perspective may be, if the world proletariat should actually prove incapable of fulfilling the mission placed on it by the

course of development, nothing else would remain except only to recognise that the socialist programme, based on the internal contradictions of capitalist society, ended as a utopia. It is self evident that a new "minimum" programme would be required—for the defence of the interests of the slaves of the totalitarian bureaucratic society.[47]

MacIntyre subsequently abandoned Marxism, but he continued to endorse Trotsky's rejection of any alternatives to the working class as the agent of revolutionary change and his understanding that no one else would come to the rescue if the working class failed to play its historic role:"One of the most admirable aspects of Trotsky's cold resolution was his refusal of all such fantasies."[48] But the force of Trotsky's argument today is in no way reliant on claims about the inability of the working class to take and retain power. We know that the working class has the innate structural *capacity* to achieve the socialist revolution, but whether it can be realized is another issue altogether, which involves questions of consciousness, leadership, strategy, and the extent to which our enemies possess the same qualities. There is also the question of time: the working class may simply continue to be defeated, as it has been until now, until it is too late to prevent the planet becoming uninhabitable.

The second notion that haunts "On the Concept of History," and to which I have already alluded, is that of the "actuality of the revolution." This first appears in Lukács's *Lenin: A Study in the Unity of His Thought* (1924), where he writes that, to the vulgar Marxist, "the fighters on the barricades are madmen, the defeated revolution is a mistake, and the builders of socialism . . . are outright criminals." Against this, revolutionaries, of whom Lenin was preeminent, work from the principle that "the actuality of the proletarian revolution is no longer only a world historical horizon arching above the working class, *but that the revolution is already on the agenda.*" It is not of course that the revolution "is readily realisable at any given moment," but its actuality was "a touchstone for evaluating all the questions of the day": "Individual actions can only be considered revolutionary or counter-revolutionary when related to the central issue of revolution, which is only discovered by an accurate analysis of the socio-historic whole."[49] The crucial passages on this theme in Benjamin are those that precede the famous metaphor of the emergency brake, in which Benjamin claims that Marxism is a form of "messianism":

In the idea of classless society, Marx secularised the idea of messianic time. . . . Once the classless society had been defined as an infinite task, the empty and homogenous time was transformed into an anteroom, so to speak, in which one could wait for the emergence of the revolutionary situation with more or less equanimity. In reality, there is not a moment that would not carry with it its own revolutionary chance—provided only that it is defined in a specific way, namely as the chance for a completely new resolution of a completely new problem. For the revolutionary thinker, the peculiar revolutionary chance offered by every historical moment gets its warrant from the political situation. But it is equally grounded, for this thinker, in the right of entry which the historical moment enjoys vis-à-vis a quite distinct chamber of the past, one which up to that point has been closed and locked. The entrance into this chamber coincides in a strict sense with political action, and it is by means of such entry that political action, however destructive, reveals itself as messianic. . . . Whoever wishes to know what the situation of a "redeemed humanity" might actually be, what conditions are required for the development of such a situation, and when this development can be expected to occur, poses questions to which there are no answers. . . . But classless society is not to be conceived as the endpoint of historical development. From this erroneous conception Marx's epigones have derived (among other things) the notion of the "revolutionary situation" which, as we know, has always refused to arrive. A genuinely messianic face must be restored to the concept of classless society and, to be sure, in the interest of furthering the revolutionary politics of the proletariat itself.[50]

What both Lukács and Benjamin are saying, in different ways, is not that revolutionaries should be declaring a state of permanent insurrection—which would indeed be voluntarism—but that they should behave in the knowledge that we are in the period where revolution is historically possible and necessary. Benjamin was hostile to the idea of "progress," where this is understood as an inevitable upwards movment through successive modes of production, each one involving growth in the productive forces, until the point is reached where socialism becomes possible. Leaving aside the caricature of human social development that this involves, it also plays an important ideological role for the social democratic and Stalinist bureaucracies, in that the moment when sufficient progress has taken place for socialism to be on the agenda always seems to be beyond the next horizon, the productive forces never quite developed enough (Kautsky), the "democratic stage" still to be achieved (Stalin), and so on. This underlies Benjamin's hostility to the Popular Front. In a recently translated piece from the closing months of his life, Benjamin notes how "the Hitler-Stalin *entente* has knocked away the whole scaffolding of the Popular Front" and refers to "the latter's intrinsic weaknesses."[51] It is also why he has such a heightened awareness of the need to seize the moment. "Definition of basic historical concepts: Catastrophe—to have missed the opportunity."[52] It is worth pausing at this stage to remember that Benjamin was a German Jew—that is, a member of a group on the verge of genocidal oppression from a country that had missed two "opportunities," in 1918–1923 and 1929–1933. It should be obvious that the very concept of an "opportunity" is incompatible with a voluntarist conception of revolution being possible any time, any place, anywhere.

The third notion is the distinctiveness of the Marxist attitude toward history. This is the one most original to Benjamin and also the most difficult to grasp, as Chris inadvertently demonstrates. "Of course, consciousness of history is an important factor in current struggles," he reminds us: "One of the most important roles of the revolutionary party is to keep alive the memory of past struggles that the ruling class want to suppress, and to fight for their revolutionary interpretation." But Benjamin "is asking too much of history": "By itself, or even with the help of the finest historians, history cannot make people struggle."[53] Benjamin certainly makes a number of apparently cryptic utterances about history: "The only historian capable of fanning the spark of hope in the past is the one who is firmly convinced that *even the dead* will not be safe from the enemy if he is victorious. And this enemy has never ceased to be victorious."[54]

This passage reads like poetry, and like poetry, it is not meant to be taken literally. What Benjamin seems to mean is something closer to the party slogan George Orwell has O'Brien make Winston Smith repeat in *Nineteen Eighty-Four:* "Who controls the past controls the future: who controls the present controls the past."[55] The past can be changed to suit the needs of the ruling class and only the victory of socialism will ensure that it remains safe. But where should we look for "the spark of hope" in it? Benjamin's approach involves considerably more than simply referring to a tradition of "past struggles" to inspire contemporary socialists: it is to question the very nature of that tradition.

One aspect of the theory of progress discussed above is an undialectical attitude toward the development of class society, in which those social forces that brought the capitalist world into being, and the culture they created, are treated to uncritical celebration. As Benjamin points out, in one of the greatest passages in all of Marxism, this has certain ideological consequences:

> With whom does the historian actually sympathise? The answer is inevitable: with the victors. And all rulers are the heirs of prior conquerors. Hence, empathising with the victor invariably benefits the current rulers. The historical materialist knows what this means. Whoever has emerged victorious participates to this day in the triumphal procession in which the current rulers step over those who are lying prostrate. According to traditional practice, the spoils are carried in the procession. They are called "cultural treasures," and a historical materialist views them with cautious detachment. For in every case these treasures have a lineage which he cannot contemplate without horror. They owe their existence not only to the efforts of the great geniuses who created them, but also to the anonymous toil of others who lived in the same period. There is no document of culture which is not at the same time a document of barbarism. And just as such a document is never free of barbarism, so barbarism taints the manner in which it was transmitted from one hand to another.[56]

To simply remember the achievements of the bourgeois revolution and bourgeois culture—Cromwell on the one hand, Milton on the other—without also holding in our minds the contradictions of the progress they represent is to forget the "anonymous toil" that made it possible: "It is more difficult to honour the memory of the anonymous than it is to honour the memory of the famous, the celebrated, not excluding poets and thinkers."[57] To put this in concrete terms: the peasants who revolted against the English monarchy in 1381 and their yeoman descendants of the New Model Army who overthrew it in 1649 are not part of *our* tradition; they are the ancestors—in some cases quite distant ancestors—of the present capitalist class, of "the current rulers." Benjamin was of course perfectly aware that the ruling classes suppressed aspects of their rise to power that had become inconvenient to them. Thus in *The Arcades Project* he writes: "The enshrinement or apologia is meant to cover up the revolutionary moments in the occurrence of history. At heart, it seeks the establishment of a continuity. . . . The parts where tradition breaks off—hence its peaks and crags, which offer footing to one who would cross over them—it misses."[58] But the answer to this is not to "claim" bourgeois revolutionaries for the socialist tradition: it is still possible to understand and celebrate their achievements and, in some cases, their heroism and self-sacrifice, without superimposing their struggles onto our own. Our tradition is what Benjamin calls "the tradition of the oppressed," the tradition of those who did not benefit from the victories over the precapitalist order, even though they participated in the struggle against it, and who *could not* have benefited from it, given the impossibility of establishing the socialist order much earlier than Benjamin's own lifetime. I have elsewhere tried to show this distinction between the "tradition of the oppressed" and what we might call "the tradition of the victors" by distinguishing between our bourgeois "equivalents" (Luther, Cromwell, Robespierre) and our plebeian "forerunners" (Munzer, Winstanley, Babeuf).[59] In some cases the distinction is less easy to draw, but without it, celebration of what we might call "the tradition of the victors" simply becomes celebration of the established fact of where history has temporarily come to rest. It is only *after* the socialist revolution that we will able to embrace this tradition without "cautious detachment": "only a redeemed mankind is granted the fullness of its past—which is to say, for only a redeemed mankind has its past become citeable in all its moments."[60] If it is only the actual achievement of the socialist revolution that will finally allow us to *incorporate* previous revolutions into our tradition, it is only the struggle to achieve it that allows us to fully *understand* them. Outside of the future goal of a redeemed humanity the history of which they are part will remain a heap of fragments, the pile of rubbish against which the Angel of History turns its wings: "Without some kind of assay of the classless society, there only a historical accumulation of the past."[61]

But if one aspect of Benjamin's approach is to narrow down the range of our tradition, another is to blow it wide open, to explode the conception of what he calls "empty, homogenous time" and replace it with "messianic, now-time," so that every moment in history is potentially of use to revolutionaries. Benjamin says that "nothing that has ever happened should be regarded as lost to history."[62] Let me try to illustrate what he means with an example from the bourgeois revolution. In a classic passage from "The Eighteenth Brumaire of Louis Bonaparte" Marx describes the ideology of the French Revolutionaries of 1789:

"Camille Desmoulins, Danton, Robespierre, Saint-Just and Napoleon, the heroes of the old French Revolution, as well as its parties and masses, accomplished the tasks of their epoch, which was the emancipation and establishment of modern *bourgeois* society, in Roman costume and with Roman slogans." Marx argues that the "gladiators" of the bourgeois revolution "found in the stern classical traditions of the Roman republic the ideals, art forms and self-deception they needed in order to hide from themselves the limited bourgeois content of their struggles and maintain the enthusiasm at the high level appropriate to great historical tragedy."[63] This assessment is not in dispute, but Benjamin argues that something else is also going on, in addition to the heroic "self-deception" of which Marx writes:

> To Robespierre ancient Rome was a past charged with now-time, a past which he blasted out of the continuum of history. The French Revolution viewed itself as Rome reincarnate. It cited ancient Rome the way a fashion cites a by-gone mode of dress. Fashion has a nose for the topical, no matter where it stirs in the thickets of long ago; it is the tiger's leap into the past.[64]

In other words, the characteristically austere qualities of Republican Rome—civic patriotism, "republican virtue," self-sacrifice, and so on—were *actually* relevant to the French Revolutionaries in their struggle with the absolutist regime and were not—or were not only—a rhetorical ploy with which they sought to disguise their real objectives.

There are major structural differences between the bourgeois and socialist revolutions, above all in the fact that, unlike the bourgeoisie, the working class has to be fully conscious of what it is trying to achieve.[65] Does this mean that Benjamin's demand that we ransack the whole of history for pasts "charged with now-time" is no longer relevant? I believe that it is still relevant, but in a different way. In the context of socialist politics, what Benjamin seems to be saying is that we do not and cannot know which aspects of our tradition or history more widely will be of most use to us in coming struggles. We inherit some general, historically demonstrable conclusions about the limits of reformism, the dynamics of revolution, the role of the revolutionary party, and so on; but although every new situation is in some senses unique, for each there will be a moment or moments in history that help to illuminate them. The point is these moments will not always be the ones we want or expect or have learned to give meetings on. Before the campaign against the poll tax began, I doubt that anyone thought the Glasgow Rent Strikes during the First World War or the squatters' campaigns after the Second would become models for action; but they, and not the struggle against the Industrial Relations Act or the Miners' Strike, proved to be the more relevant. This is not simply a plea for a more comprehensive knowledge of our history, useful though that might be; it is for socialists to make the necessary leaps of the imagination to see what parts of the tradition are genuinely relevant to our current situation. If there is a "Benjaminian" contribution to socialist politics, rather than to cultural theory, this may be what it involves.

Conclusion

Benjamin's central focus on culture and his absence from direct political engagement tend to exclude him from the front rank of the classical Marxist tradition, as is suggested by a comparison with the career of Gramsci, the classical figure with whom he shares the most interests. As we have seen, however, this does not mean that classical themes are completely absent from his work. In addition to those I have already discussed he was also aware of the importance of revolutionary consciousness, writing that "without confidence no class could, in the long run, hope to enter the political sphere with any success. But it makes a difference whether this optimism centres on the active strength of the class or under the conditions under which the class operates."[66] In other words, there is more than one type of "confidence": the objective strength of the working class (numbers, industrial organization), while important, will not lead to improvements in its condition if the class does not have the necessary level of consciousness that can ensure these strengths are effectively used—an observation that still has some relevance today. It is true that Benjamin did not set himself the task of explaining precisely how such consciousness would be obtained. But then, why should he have done? There are texts that do so with which he was quite familiar; one is called *What Is to Be Done?* and another *History and Class Consciousness.* On the other hand, despite the very great achievements of classical Marxism, there are areas that the key figures did not discuss, or to which they devoted less attention than was necessary. Later figures, of which Benjamin was one of the first and most important, may not have had their universal range of interests and insights, but they can still add to our understanding of the world. In other words, we need to see Benjamin's work, not in opposition to the classical tradition, but as a contribution that enriches it, by deepening our understanding of some key themes and addressing others that had hitherto been absent.

Chapter 9

Shock and Awe
Naomi Klein's Interpretation
of Neoliberalism[1]

INTRODUCTION

Authors with both talent and a theme of topical importance are still not guaranteed to seize the public imagination: they also require good timing. More precisely, they require a mass audience predisposed to sympathetically listen to what they have to say. This means that the writers concerned must be, if not exactly ahead of their potential audience, then at least attuned to shifts in popular consciousness that are perhaps not yet fully formed. Several classics of socialist literature appeared, as it were, too early to have immediate impact. George Orwell's *Homage to Catalonia* (1938), for example, is now rightly regarded as one of the outstanding autobiographical accounts of the Spanish Civil War and a merciless critique of the bankruptcy of the Popular Front strategy; but by the time of Orwell's death in 1950 it had failed to sell even the initial print run of 1,500.[2] The very defeats that Stalinism had helped bring out meant that the majority of socialists were simply not open to the arguments it contained. Its popularity came later, in the wake of Orwell's fame as the author of *Nineteen Eighty-Four* and the emergence of a New Left after 1956.

The Canadian radical journalist Naomi Klein has been rather more fortunate in her timing than Orwell. Between 1995 and 1999 Klein worked to expose how giant multinational brands dominated the world economy. The resulting book, *No Logo,* appeared early in 2000, only months after the November 1999 demonstrations against the WTO in Seattle had signaled the coalescence of new forms of collective opposition to capitalist globalization. According to Klein's own account, her book went to the printer's as the protesters took to the streets: "I consider myself lucky that I happened to write a book just at a movement's moment." Klein herself did not fully appreciate the scale and extent of the movement—although to be fair, no one else did either. Indeed, before starting the book she was only aware of "small-scale activism" such as "culture jamming" and "ad busting" and saw these as having an important future only as "an act of faith."[3] *No Logo* itself concludes by listing the fragmented groups that she hoped together might "wrest" globalization "from the grasp of the multinationals": "Ethical shareholders, culture jammers, street reclaimers, McUnion organisers, human-rights activists, school-logo fighters and Internet watchdogs are at the early stages of demanding a citizen-centred alternative to the international rule of the brands."[4] Nevertheless, *No Logo* caught a mood and, once a relatively cohesive movement did emerge, it rapidly achieved classic status among supporters of alternative globalization, elevating Klein to a preeminent position in the movement. Contributors to *International Socialism* have disagreed with her support for decentralization and opposition to the resolution of strategic differences through hard political argument; but there is no doubt that Klein has played a serious participative role, refusing the temptation to become a mere radical celebrity offering detached commentary on events.[5]

Klein's background as a journalist rather than an academic gave her two particular strengths. One was that she was concerned with communicating to large numbers of people in a comprehensible manner, as can be seen by comparing *No Logo* with what was perhaps its main rival for iconic status among the left during this period: Hardt and Negri's *Empire.* The former has exercised more real influence than the latter, despite the greater amount of overearnest citation that *Empire's* often incomprehensible prose has received in the academy. The other was that she was interested in recounting those concrete aspects of capitalist globalization that more pretentious contributions ignored, not least the actual conditions experienced by workers in, say, an Ontario Wal-Mart or a Philippine export processing zone. But her account did more than simply expose hitherto concealed aspects of exploitation. Unlike many accounts of the changes to economic life under capitalist globalization, Klein also conveyed the impact of multinational capitalism on the very textures of everyday life, such as the replacement of hitherto public space with retail outlets in which no activity but consumption is allowed, the rendering identical of cities through the intrusion of an inescapably narrow range of shops and products, and the transformation of people into advertisements for their own exploiters by carrying the corporate brand on their clothing.

Nor was this discussion wholly untheoretical, as some of her more patronizing critics have claimed. In relation to branding, for example, Klein turned her fire not only on the corporations themselves but on postmodern cultural theorists whose obsession with displacing class onto identity politics converged with corporate celebrations of the market as the source of freedom and individual choice. In fact, as Klein explained, neoliberal globalization has two aspects. One was certainly the homogenization of the High Street, but the other it is its inescapable obverse, diversification. Capital has no problem at all with Difference, except as a problem of niche marketing. Indeed, Klein argued that even this had been turned into an opportunity: "The market has seized upon multiculturalism and gender-bending in the same ways that it has seized upon youth culture in general—not just as a market niche but as a source of a new carnivalesque imagery." As she rightly notes, the identity politics of the 1980s and 1990s virtually invited this response from capital: "The need for greater diversity—the rallying cry of my university years—is now not only accepted by the culture industries, it is the mantra of global capital."[6] *No Logo* was therefore not simply a rallying cry against corporate dominance but a polemic against the intellectual complicity of dominant trends within self-proclaimed "radical" thought with fin-de-siècle bourgeois ideology.[7]

FROM GLOBAL BRANDS TO DISASTER CAPITALISM

Seven years lie between *No Logo* and Klein's latest book, *The Shock Doctrine*, during which time her only substantive publication has been a collection of journalism written between the Seattle protests and 9/11.[8] The latter event, and the various responses to it on the left, seem to have been the catalyst for a change in her perspective. In particular, as she recently explained in conversation with the Marxist geographer Neil Smith, she was concerned about the way in which 9/11 divided what had, until then, been a movement finding its way toward opposing the system as a whole:

> There was a really powerful global discussion going on and it wasn't about globalisation, it was actually more and more about capitalism. There's been a lot of activism since that period, but I feel like we on the left and we who were part of that moment, not really a movement but a moment, went in two different directions. Some of the people who were talking about neoliberalism just sort of put their heads down and kept talking about neoliberalism and pretended there weren't wars and terrorism and just stayed on message. . . . They were surprised that there weren't hundreds of people interested in talking about it anymore when they would organise events . . . People were actually interested in what was going on in Iraq and Afghanistan and they wanted an analysis of torture and things changed. The other side of it is that a lot of the energy of that anticorporate, anticapitalist analysis went to just fighting wars, as well it should have. But I think part of the problem was, and it was particularly true in this country [i.e., the United States], was that the promise of a really big movement—a big, popular antiwar, anti-Bush movement—was so seductive to a lot of organisers that there was an idea that we really shouldn't talk about economics because that's divisive. . . . Let's have a big protest saying "Bush is bad and wars are bad" and not talk about the economic agenda that is being served or make connections with what we knew before September 11th.[9]

What Klein is attempting in *The Shock Doctrine* is to integrate events like wars—not least the "Global War on Terror"—but also supposedly "natural" disasters, into an account of how contemporary capitalism works. Although there is some stylistic continuity with her earlier work, notably the incorporation of eyewitness journalism and interviews with victims of the system, *The Shock Doctrine* is in other respects a very different type of book from *No Logo*. Rather than a series of contemporary snapshots, the approach is historical, tracing the enfolding of the neoliberal era from the Chilean coup of 1973 onward, occasionally moving further back in time to search for precedents. But the differences are not merely structural. The vibrant optimism of tone with which she first caught the movement's attention has become much more somber, as if the longer-term perspective she adopts here has brought home precisely the extent of the violence committed against humanity during a period that has now lasted nearly forty years.

We now think of that period as one dominated by neoliberalism, although Klein tends to treat neoliberalism and neoconservatism as interchangeable terms for a particular way of organizing capitalism that she prefers to call "corporatism," characterized by "huge transfers of public wealth to private hands, often accompanied by exploding debt, an ever-widening chasm between the dazzling rich and the disposable poor and an aggressive nationalism that justifies bottomless spending on security."[10] Whatever terminology is employed for the current form of capitalist organization (I will continue to refer to neoliberalism in what follows) Klein rightly distinguishes it from capitalism itself.[11] As we shall see, however, this avoids one error (equating neoliberalism with the system as a whole) only to open up the possibility of another (that "another capitalism is possible" shorn of the inhumanity of neoliberalism). I will return to this point below, but first: what is Klein's argument?

She begins with the way in which theoretical support for free markets was kept alive by a small band of thinkers, above all Milton Friedman (who features as her main intellectual adversary here), after the tide began to turn against free-market capitalism with the Great Crash of 1929: "During these dark days for laissez-faire, when communism conquered the East, the welfare state was embraced by the West and economic nationalism took root in the postcolonial South, Friedman and his mentor, Friedrich Hayek, patiently protected the flame of a pure version of capitalism, untarnished by Keynesian attempts to pool collective wealth to build more just societies."[12] But the coming to power of rulers either searching for economic answers or already committed to market solutions—initially the Chilean military, then the Thatcher and Reagan governments—provided the first opportunities for these ideas to be put into practice. Coincident with the preservation of neoliberal theory at Chicago University by Friedman and his acolytes, a form of electroconvulsive therapy ("electroshock treatment") was being developed by Ewen Cameron at McGill University with CIA funding. Ostensibly to help psychiatric patients, this was in fact used by his paymasters to reduce prisoners to a vegetative state of blankness and receptivity. Klein claims that this form of psychological torture or "coercive interrogation," although in actual use, most recently in the aftermath of 9/11, also acts as a metaphor for a broader social process—or perhaps one might say that there is a "social equivalent" of the individual act of torture: "Like the terrorized prisoner who gives up the names of his comrades and renounces his faith, shocked societies often give up things they would otherwise fiercely protect."[13] Social shock treatment and neoliberal economics have been linked, in the sense that the former has been used to pave the way for the introduction of the latter, in a conjoined process Klein calls "disaster capitalism." She twice quotes Friedman's statement that "only a crisis—actual or perceived—produces real change" and argues that neoliberalism is a "shock doctrine" that takes advantage of disaster ("crisis") in order to impose the idea of the new market order.[14] The notion of "shock" therefore works on three levels, moving from metaphor to reality: first, "countries are shocked—by wars, coups d'état and natural disasters"; second, "they are shocked again—by corporations and politicians who exploit the fear and disorientation of this first shock to push through economic shock therapy"; and third, "people who resist are, if necessary, shocked again—by police, soldiers and prison interrogators."[15]

Putting this argument to work, Klein is able to demonstrate that, contrary to the neoliberal claim that free markets and parliamentary democracy are mutually dependent systems, "this fundamentalist form of capitalism has consistently been midwifed by the most brutal forms of coercion, inflicted on the collective body politic as well as on countless individual bodies." And not only the introduction, but the maintenance of neoliberal regimes requires at the very least the severe curtailment of democracy, in all respects other than the most formal—the bare right to vote for virtually indistinguishable parties. As this suggests, Klein regards neoliberalism from the beginning as a project reliant on state power. Rather than markets being "freed" from the state as the ideology endlessly proclaims, we have instead witnessed the formation of a new but equally close relationship between the two: "In every country where Chicago School policies have been applied over the last three decades, what has emerged is a powerful ruling alliance between a few very large corporations and a class of mostly wealthy politicians—with hazy and ever shifting lines between the two groups."[16] Klein supports her argument with a series of individual country-by-country case studies, ranging from Chile to post-Stalinist Russia, from post-Apartheid South Africa to post-invasion Iraq (which receives the most detailed treatment), from the path of the Southeast Asian tsunami of December 2004 to the wake of Hurricane Katrina in New Orleans during September 2005. These chapters constitute the core of the book and their cumulative power is undeniable, although as we shall see, her demonstration of the way in which neoliberalism has become generalized throughout the system, irrespective of the nominal politics of the regimes that have introduced it, could stand independently of the "shock" metaphor and would actually be stronger without it. Before turning to that critique, however, I want to note some wholly misguided criticisms of Klein from writers who also claim to be critical of the system, or at least aspects of it.

It is unsurprising that the most severe of these attacks have come from self-deluded liberals whose delusion consists precisely in believing that neoliberalism has simply been an unfortunate, if gigantic, mistake. Will Hutton, long-time Keynesian, scourge of "Anglo-Saxon capitalism," and currently director of the Work Foundation, began his review in the *Observer* by claiming: "Naomi Klein is confused"—a confusion apparently demonstrated by the fact that "nowhere does she concede that markets can have good results as well as bad," nor does she "explore . . . why economic freedom is so appealing to so many," nor yet "set out an alternative manifesto for running economies or societies":

> In her delusional, Manichaean world view, privatisation, free markets, private property, consumer freedom, the profit motive and economic freedom are just other terms for corporate self enrichment, denial of voice, limitation of citizenship, inequality and, sometimes, even torture. . . . Nothing good ever came from globalisation, which is just more capitalism. Democracy, however, is a halcyon world of political and economic cooperation, citizen voice and engagement, with a freely-arrived at assertion of the common interest in which most think along the same lines as, say, Naomi Klein.

Following this final sneer (for which there is not the slightest justification in anything Klein has written, either here or elsewhere), Hutton then goes on describe Klein as a "mirror image" of Friedman on account of "the absolutist categories in which they think."[17] The condescension and ignorance on display here are both revealing of Hutton's politics and deeply unfair to Klein. She does not reject markets—indeed, her support for a reformed capitalism is a weakness in her work:

> I am not arguing that all market systems are inherently violent. It is eminently possible to have a market-based economy that requires no such brutality and demands no such ideological purity. A free market in consumer products can coexist with free public health care, with public schools, with a large segment of the economy—like a national oil company—held in state hands. . . . Keynes proposed exactly that kind of mixed, regulated economy after the Great Depression, a revolution in public policy that created the New Deal and transformations like it around the world.[18]

Furthermore, Klein embraces globalization and distinguishes it from capitalism or "corporatism." Finally, as Hutton himself acknowledges in the quote above, she sees democracy as the alternative to markets. The latter issue is what seems to have most irritated Hutton, containing as it does the danger that "the left . . . should conceive of democracy as a surrogate for socialism." Here we can detect his real concern:

> What was wrong about so much shock therapy and brutal introduction of markets that Klein describes was not that societies should have cleaved to a quasi-socialist alternative under the rubric of democracy. It was that they should have paid infinitely more attention to the building of the "soft" institutions of democracy, including universal education and health care, as the vital precondition for successful markets.[19]

I have quoted these comments at some length because it is important to realize that, whatever problems there are with Klein's work, her position is infinitely more realistic about the workings of capitalism, incomparably more sensitive to the enormities its supporters are prepared to commit, than the vacuous waffle about "civil society," "democratic governance," and the like, which Hutton has been promoting to a curiously uninterested audience of capitalists and government ministers for several decades now. Above all, Klein is on the side of those who have suffered from and are fighting back against capitalism; Hutton, on the other hand, is committed to defending the system against which they struggle, despite its "excesses," hence his hysterical response to the popularity of a work that offers at least the possibility of a deeper critique.

In taking sides Klein is quite unsparing of the reputations of organizations that once embodied popular aspirations but that have since capitulated to neoliberalism, like Solidarity in Poland and the ANC in South Africa. Her discussion of the abandonment of the black majority by the latter has inevitably provoked furious defensive responses by ANC apologists. Ronald Suresh Roberts, for example, has accused Klein of condescension toward black South Africans who reelected the ANC with ever-bigger majorities until 2004, who he claims were apparently fully aware the party embodied their best interests. He denounces her main sources (Patrick Bond and William Gamede), for their institutional affiliations and the fact that they may have accepted funding from corporate sources before, in a final absurd reality-reversal, portraying Klein as a dominant figure unfairly victimizing the blameless ANC government: "Klein herself is, of course, a powerful part of the global media, with her well-meaning but stubbornly Orientalist representations of African politics, complete with a 'culture-shocked' Mandela and a chronically paralysed native electorate, falsely unconscious of its own best interests."[20] To argue that criticism of postcolonial regimes is a refusal of solidarity, regardless of what these regimes have done or failed to do after taking power, is a piece of moral blackmail that has been used all too often in the past to whip Western liberals and even some would-be revolutionaries into line; it is to Klein's credit that she refuses to bow to it, rightly understanding that the solidarity we owe is to the exploited and oppressed, not to parties or states that claim to represent them while betraying their interests at every turn.

THE LIMITATIONS OF A METAPHOR

The real problems with *The Shock Doctrine* lie elsewhere. The detail that Klein provides of how neoliberalism has become the dominant form of capitalist organization is far more convincing than the theoretical framework or, more accurately, the organizing metaphor within which it is presented. Klein presents neoliberalism as the manifestation of the inner logic of corporate capitalism (although perhaps not of capitalism itself) and "shock" as the means by which it can be realized. She therefore treats every geopolitical event (using that term in its broadest sense) since 1973 as one either consciously undertaken or opportunistically manipulated to impose neoliberalism, a fixation that inevitably produces unnecessarily conspiratorial undertones to her work. (As Joseph Stiglitz remarks, "there are no accidents in the world as seen by Naomi Klein."[21]) There are three problems with the "shock" metaphor as an aid to understanding contemporary capitalism.

First, how necessary was "shock" to the introduction of neoliberalism? "There are huge third world economies that have been ravaged by neoliberalism that haven't endured 'the shock doctrine,'" notes Alexander Cockburn.[22] He specifically mentions India in this context, but could just as easily have mentioned Mexico or Egypt, neither of which is discussed by Klein, even though they are in the neoliberal vanguard of their respective regions and are at least as important in geopolitical and geoeconomic terms as Chile or Iraq, which receive detailed attention because they appear to confirm her thesis.[23] More damaging still is the absence of credible examples of "shock therapy" in the cases of the two states of the developed world where neoliberalism has taken deepest root: the United Kingdom and the United States.

As far as the United Kingdom is concerned, Klein identifies the Falklands War of 1982 as the decisive moment for Thatcher in implementing her program: "the disorder and nationalist excitement resulting from the war allowed her to use tremendous force to crush the striking coal miners and to launch the first privatization frenzy in a Western democracy."[24] In fact, the popular impact of the Falklands victory was relatively short-lived and did not feature particularly prominently in Conservative electoral material during the 1983 campaign, although it certainly helped to consolidate Thatcher's leadership over her party.[25] The Conservative victory that year had a far less epochal and far more conjunctural basis. In electoral terms, they faced a compromised and incoherent Labour Party, a section of whose voting base had shifted to the newly formed Social Democratic and Liberal Party. As one of Thatcher's earliest and best biographers recounts:

> There was nothing in the nature of Thatcherism, nor any brilliant stratagem in the mind of its leader, which brought these propitious circumstances about. . . . Yet [they] produced among the forces ranged against the most unpopular British leader of modern times, on the one hand a party that was unelectable, on the other a grouping destined merely to be a vote-splitter.[26]

But equally significant was the ideological and organizational situation of a working-class movement already disillusioned by the previous Labour government, weakened by unemployment but offered some relief by the emergence of the economy from the depths of the 1981–82 slump. Far from the Falklands being the shock that made Thatcher's victory over the miners and everything that followed possible, the outcome of the subsequent miners' strike was itself the turning point in establishing the neoliberal regime in Britain, the key to which was not the unleashed power of the state—formidable though that was—but the failure of other unions and the TUC to deliver effective solidarity with the NUM. The short- to medium-term effect, exacerbated by the overlapping onslaught against the print unions, was to thoroughly cow the union bureaucracy, and to shatter the confidence of workers to risk resisting in any generalized way through their workplace organizations, although they fought back in other ways, notably in the campaign against the poll tax. In other words, the British working class had been temporarily defeated in a way that had undoubtedly serious consequences (from which it has yet to fully recover), but it was scarcely shocked into a condition of psychological collapse.

Klein's account of the United States is even more implausible, focusing as it does on the aftermath of 9/11: "What happened in the period of mass disorientation after the attacks was, in retrospect, a domestic form of economic shock therapy. The Bush team, Friedmanite to the core, quickly moved to exploit the shock that gripped the nation to push through its radical vision of a hollow government in which everything from war fighting to disaster response was a for-profit venture."[27] Reading this one might almost believe that the United States had been spared the neoliberal onslaught until the fall of the Twin Towers, whereas it has suffered, from the late 1970s, longer and more intensively than anywhere in the West apart from the United Kingdom. More recently, the Bush administration certainly used the rhetoric of national emergency to feed the military-industrial complex, cut taxation for the wealthy, reduce regulation for business, and attack social provision.[28] But all these moves were continuations of existing policies that were already being implemented. And it was the wars in Afghanistan and Iraq that gave them a blanket of patriotic cover, rather than 9/11 itself. In the case of the United States too the key was the weakening of the labor movement, a task made easier by the fact that the US labor movement did not even enjoy the collective successes of the British in the early 1970s: the retreat started much earlier than the US equivalent of the miners' strike, the defeat of the PATCO air traffic controllers in 1981.[29]

Second, was "shock" always applied for the purpose of introducing neoliberalism? In general, Klein makes far too direct a link between economics and politics. Take, for example, the two central events that dominate *The Shock Doctrine,* which she explicitly links: the Chilean coup of 1973 and the invasion of Iraq in 2003.[30]

Klein is of course right to say that, in Chile, it was only in the aftermath of a violent seizure of power by the military that the neoliberal regime could have been put in place; but this was not the motivation for the coup, which was carried out instead to crush the political aspirations of the working-class movement that had looked to Allende and that was by 1973 beginning to organize on its own behalf. In fact, the generals initially had little idea what economic policies to introduce and in other circumstances might well have looked to the Catholic corporatist model introduced by Franco to Spain after 1939 that had been followed more or less faithfully by previous Latin American dictatorships. In retrospect, the arrival of the "Chicago Boys" to oversee the implementation of Pinochet's program of privatization and deregulation has a wider significance, but initially it appeared to have no resonance elsewhere and subsequent coups to that in Chile did not immediately adopt neoliberalism. Klein herself notes that the Argentinean dictatorship that came to power in 1976 did not follow its Chilean predecessor in privatizing social security or natural resources: in fact these were achieved decades later by the successor civilian governments.[31]

In relation to Iraq, Klein quotes Bush the Father at the head of one chapter denying accusations that Bush the Son "invaded Iraq to open up new markets for US companies," a denial that she regards as self-evidently preposterous.[32] However, painful though it is to admit, the elder Bush is simply speaking the truth: the United States did not invade and occupy Iraq in order to create profit opportunities for private security firms, but for strategic reasons connected to Middle Eastern oil—not to guarantee price or even supply for US use, but to control the supply in relation to competitors, above all those ascendant states, above all China, that have already attained regional power status.[33]

Third, accepting—with the caveats entered above—that neoliberals have opportunistically intervened to take advantage of disaster situations in recent decades, why it was only at a certain stage in postwar history that crises were manipulated to produce these outcomes? Two examples will illustrate the problem.

One is from the core of the world system. At the end of the Second World War it quickly became apparent that Britain had unresolved economic problems. These were not helped by a massive rearmament program that began to erode the welfare state within years of it being initiated. When the Conservative Party was returned to office in 1951, some members of the new administration led by Rab Butler drafted a proposal to float the pound, which would have immediately led to it falling in value against the dollar. The central intention here was to put an end to balance-of-payments difficulties that were already characteristic of the British economy. Exports would be given a massive boost, while at the same time imports would fall; domestic prices would be high, but wages would have to be held down to avoid inflationary pressures, not least by allowing unemployment to rise. In effect, the government would be forced to cut funding of the welfare state, especially the housing program, as well as its overseas military commitments. The plan was dropped, largely as a result of Churchill's nervousness over the likely consequences in electoral terms.[34] Historians have tended to treat this episode as a typical example of the consensual thinking that supposedly prevented deepseated problems from being tackled before the advent of the Thatcher regime.[35] The point, however, is that an experiment of this sort would have been, in capitalist terms, both destructive and unnecessary at this time. Destructive, because it ran contrary to the type of economic structures being put in place in the advanced capitalist West; most obviously, it would have destroyed the Bretton Woods agreement, the only components of which to have been put in place were precisely the fixed exchange rates that British actions would have undone. Unnecessary, because from the end of the Korean War in 1953 the British economy began to take off into a boom that meant that any attempt to limit tradeunion power or redefine the limits of the welfare state could be postponed. British capitalism did indeed have serious underlying problems, but in conditions of generalized expansion, very few members of the British ruling class felt it was necessary to take action. Those who did argue for proto-Thatcherite solutions in the late fifties, like Enoch Powell, were marginalized.

My other example is from the developing world. The Indonesian coup of 1965 was a successful attempt by a section of the local ruling class, backed by the United States and the United Kingdom, to destroy the power of the Communist Party and the left more generally, in what was at that point the most extreme use of counterrevolutionary violence since the Second World War. But neither internal nor external forces sought to impose what was then thought of as a neoclassical economic program on the country, even though this was the perfect opportunity to do so. Klein draws parallels between the group of Indonesian economists trained at the University of California, the so-called Berkeley Mafia who advised the military both before and after the coup, and the "Chicago Boys," who played a similar post-coup role for the Chilean Junta ten years later. She rather elides, however, the nature of the economic policies followed in the former case, which were quite different from the latter.[36] Indonesia under Suharto was regarded as a reliable ally of the West in the Cold War, but continued the strategy of state-led economic development initiated by the pre-coup regime. This was similar to the strategies of the other newly industrializing countries of East Asia, particularly Taiwan, Singapore, and South Korea, although it was accompanied with even greater levels of corruption. Indeed, so far was Indonesia from what were regarded as neoliberal norms that the financial crisis of 1997 and the overthrow of Suharto the following year in a political revolution saw much neoliberal comment on the necessity of dispensing with so-called crony capitalism. No less a neoliberal luminary than Alan Greenspan described Suharto's Indonesia as being a "particularly appalling" example of crony capitalism "in the last third of the twentieth century," that is, the period following the US-backed coup that brought him to power.[37]

What these examples suggest is that neoliberalism was far from being the application of a doctrine that capitalists, state managers, or politicians had been waiting to apply since the introduction of the New Deal in the 1930s or the creation of the postwar welfare states, since when offered the opportunity to do so before the mid-1970s they did not. In other words, if Klein's thesis was correct, the policies we now associate with neoliberalism would have been introduced much earlier in the twentieth

century than they in fact were. Instead, even the most ferociously counterrevolutionary regimes followed the dominant economic model of
state intervention. It is certainly the case that in the global South, the
military repression of regimes reflecting the reformist aspirations of the
working class and the oppressed opened up opportunities for multinational corporations to play a greater role, but the latter have not themselves always pursued neoliberal policies, nor have they always demanded
them from the states with which they have had to deal. Klein writes that
"Friedman's vision coincided with the interests of the large multinationals, which by nature hunger for vast new unregulated markets."[38] But the
interests of the multinationals have changed over time. During the Great
Boom there was general support for state intervention among the larger
businesses and corporations, while small businesses retained their traditional hostility to it—attitudes embodied in the positions taken by their
respective organizations, the Business Roundtable and the US Chamber
of Commerce. These differences expressed the relative security of their
positions within the market: corporations were protected from the worst
exigencies of price competition and were able to plan for longer-term
investment and growth, often in alliance with the state; small businesses
were much more vulnerable, and the state simply represented a source
of demands for predatory taxation and bureaucratic regulation. Neoliberal globalization has changed the relative position of the corporations,
so that all but the largest transnational corporation are in a similar position
in terms of size to the small businesses of the postwar period: "The
process of globalisation has sharply increased the degree of competitive
pressure faced by large corporations and banks, as competition has become a worldwide relationship." Corporations still need a home state to
act as a base, but they require it to behave differently. Increased competition "pushes them towards support for any means to reduce their tax
burden and lift regulatory constraints, to free them to compete more effectively with their global rivals."[39]

EXPLAINING THE NEOLIBERAL MOMENT

In many respects Klein's position is close to David Harvey's. Although
he is only mentioned once in the text (in a footnote about the introduction of neoliberalism to China after the Tiananmen Square massacre),
Klein refers in her acknowledgments to him as one of "several thinkers

and chroniclers of neoliberalism [who] have shaped my thinking."[40] More recently she has said that her object, "using David Harvey's parameters," was to track "the counter revolution against Keynesianism and developmentalism and the period from the 1930s through to the end of the '60s, where there was a period when there was a response to another crisis, which was the market crash of 1929."[41] There is, however, one central problem with the concept of a neoliberal "counterrevolution" shared by Harvey and Klein, which is that it perpetuates the neoliberal myth that socioeconomic developments in the postwar period were fundamentally detrimental to capital, when in fact this was the period when it enjoyed the highest levels of growth in human history. It is certainly true that a number of concessions were granted to the working class, and it is for this reason that the reputation of "the Golden Age" remains high, particularly in contrast to what Eric Hobsbawm calls "the landslide" that followed. It rests on two main factors.[42] One was high, indeed for practical purposes full, employment. The other was the expansion of the "social wage" through the provision of education, health, and social security, particularly unemployment benefits and pensions.[43] Both of these were necessary to capital: to gain the support of the labor force, thus helping to ensure social stability and to aid increases in productivity, thus contributing to international competitiveness. Consequently, these measures were not necessarily dependent for their introduction on social or even liberal democratic governments. As Tony Judt has correctly noted:

> Outside of Scandinavia—in Austria, Germany, France, Italy, Holland, and elsewhere—it was not socialists but *Christian Democrats* who played the greatest part in installing and administering the core institutions of the activist welfare state. Even in Britain, where the post–World War II Labor government under Clement Attlee indeed inaugurated the welfare state as we knew it, it was the wartime government of Winston Churchill that commissioned and approved the Report by William Beveridge (himself a Liberal) that established the principles of public welfare provision: principles—and practices—that were reaffirmed and underwritten by every conservative government that followed until 1979.[44]

Judt's target here is that particularly ignorant type of North American journalist (exemplified by Thomas Friedman) who imagines that the welfare state was socialist in inspiration, but in Britain postwar social welfare was at least partly initiated by the local representatives of social democracy and lies within the recognizable world of European social welfarism. In the United States, although some reforms were directly introduced during the New Deal of the 1930s, above all Social Security, their expansion, let alone the introduction of more general social welfare provisions such as Medicaid and Medicare, was the result of the movements of the 1960s, above all that for black civil rights. But these were implemented not by the Democrats but by the Republicans during Richard Nixon's first term between 1968 and 1972. Nixon's discovery that "we are all Keynesians now" proved quite compatible with the saturation bombing of Cambodia and the targeted assassination of leading members of the Black Panther Party.[45] The fundamental point of all reforms associated with the welfare state in Britain, the New Deal and Great Society programs in the United States, or their analogues elsewhere, is therefore that they were not just compatible with capitalism, but organized in line with its requirements. Edward Thompson made the point powerfully in relation to Britain as the Keynesian era was coming to an end:

> The reforms of 1945 were assimilated and re-ordered within the system of economic activities, and also within the characteristic concepts, of the capitalist process. This entailed a translation of socialist meanings into capitalist ones. Socialised pits and railways became "utilities" providing subsidised coal and transport to private industry. Private practice, private beds in hospital, private nursing-homes and private insurance impoverished the public health service. Equality of opportunity in education was, in part, transformed into an adaptive mechanism through which skilled labor was trained for private industry: the opportunity was not *for* the working class but scholarship boy to escape *from* this class. . . . In short, what was defeated was not each "reform" . . . but the very meaning of reform as an alternative logic to that of private enterprise, profit and the uncontrolled self-reproduction of money.[46]

In short, as Hilde Nafstad and her colleagues write, "welfare states should not be understood simply as a protective reaction against modern capitalism, but as varieties of modern capitalism."[47]

Klein rightly rejects the Soviet Union and its satellites and imitators as a model for the contemporary radical left, but nevertheless considers them to be "post-capitalist" societies, which consequently required an entirely new capitalist class to be created after their demise. (She regards "Venezuela's Hugo Chávez or Cuba's Fidel Castro" as proponents of "socialist government" partly on account of their willingness to expropriate corporate holdings.[48]) However, rather than view these societies as being fundamentally different from those of the West, as was endlessly declared in the Cold War propaganda of both sides, it is better to see them as existing on a continuum of state intervention, with two extremes, the United States and the Soviet Union, at opposite ends of the scale. In Eastern Europe the state itself assumed the role of a "collective capitalist." As Paul Mattick writes: "Arising at the same time as the mixed economy, the state-capitalist system may be regarded as Keynesianism in its most developed and consistent form."[49] Between the two extremes lay many states that combined elements of both, most in the postcolonial world, particularly in those that were to be classified as the newly industrialising countries. Nigel Harris notes that South Korean development "was as state capitalist as any East European economy and as Keynesian as any West European social democracy," and although a major contributor to the growth of world trade, "as regards the role of the state," it was "as 'socialist' as most of the countries that applied that term to themselves."[50] So even though these countries engaged in foreign trade in a way that the Stalinist countries did not, the role of the state was essentially the same in both cases. This raises the question of why the two camps were in such potentially lethal opposition if both were fundamentally capitalist, but the answer is less obscure than is sometimes supposed. Capitalist nation-states, after all, had been known to go to war with each other before the onset of the Cold War, notably in 1914 and 1939. In this case, however, there was an additional reason. Mattick notes that the displacement of "the market system by the planned system" or the complete supersession of private capital by state capital would be experienced by individual capitalists as "their death warrant," and would not be accepted by them without opposition or, as Mattick suggests, "civil war."[51] The same is also true on the other side, as any attempt to reintroduce private capital into wholly state-capitalist economies would mean that some sections of the bureaucratic ruling class would lose their privileged positions in a situation of market competition—as a minority did after 1991, although perhaps as much as 80 percent managed to transform themselves into private capitalists or managers.[52]

It is at the end of this period of exceptional growth that the real roots of neoliberalism are to be found. The precise causes of the return to crisis after 1973 have been widely debated, but some key features are highlighted by most analysts. Increased price competition from West Germany and Japan within the advanced world was made possible by intensive investment in technology and relatively low wages. This forced their hitherto dominant rivals—above all the United States—to lower their own prices in a situation where production costs remained unchanged. US corporations were initially prepared to accept a reduced rate of profit in order to maintain market share but, ultimately, they too undertook a round of new investments, thus raising the capital-labor ratio and increasing the organic composition of capital, leading to consequent further pressure on the rate of profit.[53] As Al Campbell writes, neoliberalism was therefore a solution to "a structural crisis of capitalism" in which "policies, practices and institutions" that had hitherto served capital accumulation no longer did so: "More narrowly, one can say that capitalism abandoned the Keynesian compromise in the face of a falling rate of profit, under the belief that neoliberalism could improve its profit rate and accumulation performance."[54] But the inadequacy of Keynesian policies was itself the result of changes to the nature of the world economy that had taken place during the long boom—an unprecedented threefold expansion of international trade, the advent of cross-border production, the increase in large-scale foreign direct investment, and the creation of "offshore" banking and flows of money capital unlimited by national boundaries—all of which made these policies increasingly difficult to apply with any possibility of success. States had not become completely powerless in the face of markets—that is the myth of globalization assiduously cultivated by politicians seeking to shift responsibility for neoliberal policies onto what T. S. Eliot once called "great impersonal forces" over which they had no control.[55] In that sense neoliberalism represented a choice, but it was a choice increasingly difficult to avoid so long as the goal was the preservation and expansion of capitalism at all costs.

The economic roots of neoliberalism were therefore decisive. The one condition that was universally required in order to impose the neoliberal regime was to eliminate or at least reduce the power of the organized working class. The real reason for the attack on the ability of unions to effectively defend their members was threefold. The first was to ensure that wage costs fell and stayed down, so that the share of profits going to capital was increased. This also extended to the social wage, the expansion of which in the postwar welfare states was also a cost to capital, a drain on investment, which capitalists and state managers were only prepared to pay so long as the system was expanding: when it began to contract, as it did after 1973, these costs had to be reduced. The second was to enable corporate restructuring, the closing of "unproductive" units, and the imposition of "the right of managers to manage" within the workplace. The third, and a more long-term tactical consideration, was to assist social democracy to adapt to neoliberalism by weakening the main source of countervailing pressure from the broader labor movement.

Only very rarely did these attacks involve destroying the trade union movement. The Chilean Coup of 1973, the "other 9/11," is exceptional in this respect and it was only possible on a temporary basis. At the time, however, it was regarded as a tragic reversal of the reformist strategy adopted by Allende and Popular Unity, but not as foreshadowing any new development; Latin America had, after all, experienced numerous coups in the twentieth century, albeit few as violent as this. In the very important case of China, the ruling class was fortunate in that there was no movement to be destroyed: the reality of this so-called workers' state being an atomized labor force presided over by official trade unions that were an arm of the state. (Ironically, the emergence of a genuine labor movement in China has been in response to the regime's neoliberal turn.) In most cases, however, the attack on trade union power involved two strategies.

One was to provoke a decisive confrontation between a state-backed employer and one or two important groups of unionized workers (textile workers in India in 1980, air traffic controllers in the United States in 1981, miners in the United Kingdom in 1984–85) whose defeat would act as an example to the others, against a background of multiplying legal restraints and increasing employer intransigence. In these circumstances politicians gambled that most sections of the trade union bureaucracy would give priority to the continued existence of their organizations, however much reduced in power, rather than mount effective resistance. Looking back at the refusal of other unions, the AFL-CIO, and TUC to give effective support to unions under attack, the bet appears to have involved a limited amount of risk.

The other strategy was to establish new productive capacity, often virtually new industries in geographical areas with low or nonexistent levels of unionization, and prevent the culture of membership from becoming established: the classic example of this strategy being the movement of productive capital from the old "rust belt" industrial regions of the northeastern United States to the southern "sun belt."[56] Actual geographical shifts within nation-states were more common and more damaging to trade union organization than the threatened geographical shifts to locations in the global South, which were often made by employers but far less frequently carried out, not least because of their lack of technological infrastructure and the cost in abandoning fixed capital that such relocations would involve. However, as Graham Turner notes, "it is the threat of relocation that proves just as powerful as the reality of a transfer somewhere cheaper."[57]

The emergence of neoliberalism as a conscious ruling-class strategy, rather than the esoteric ideological doctrine associated with Friedman and company, therefore took place in response to the end of the postwar boom, but in changed conditions created by that boom. Politicians and state managers began to implement some of the policies long advocated by Hayek and Friedman, not because individual opportunities to do so that had previously been missing finally presented themselves, as Klein claims, but because the changed conditions of accumulation required changed strategies; given the limited number of strategies available (assuming these were to be in the interests of capital), it is unsurprising that theory and practice began to overlap. In 1974, the *Economist,* at that time still advocating a more or less Keynesian approach, accused Sir Keith Joseph of being a "follower" of Friedman. Joseph responded saying "the evolution of my views owes little to him":

> On the contrary, it stems primarily . . . from critical re-examination of local orthodoxies in the light of our own bitter experience in the early 1970s. . . . By early this year [1974], we had a historically high rate of inflation, an enfeebled economy, the worst relations with the trade union movement in decades, and a lost election with the greatest fall in our share of the vote since 1929. Surely this was sufficient incentive to rethink—we are practical people who judge ideas and policies by results.[58]

The more credible advocates of capitalist globalization, like Martin Wolf, have been able to emphasize the way in which neoliberalism (although he refuses the term) has been an adjustment to reality rather than an adoption of dogma:

> To many critics, the last two decades of the twentieth century were the age of a manic "neo-liberalism" imposed by ideological fanatics on a reluctant world. This picture is false. The change in politics was, with very few exceptions, introduced by pragmatic politicians in response to experience.[59]

Wolf wants to defend the neoliberal order, but his essential point is correct. As Andrew Gamble writes, neoliberalism as "a global ideology" was less significant than "the competitive pressures of capital accumulation in forcing the convergence of all capitalist models and all national economies towards neo-liberal institutions and policies."[60] Even then, with the exception of the onslaught on the labor movement, neoliberalism as a system only emerged in a piecemeal fashion, after many false starts, accidental discoveries, opportunistic maneuvers, and above all the certainty that no one in mainstream political life—that is, the adherents of social or liberal democracy—would do anything seriously to impede its implementation, and that they would eventually adopt it, in the name of realism, as their own. That is why Wolf, while acknowledging the role of Thatcher and Reagan, is able to add: "But many of the leaders who made most of the difference were far from being committed liberals. Many were on the left."[61] Or perhaps it would be more accurate to say, as Klein so clearly demonstrates, that many were formerly on the left.

CONCLUSION

Neoliberalism is mutating in response to the current crisis. The precise character of this new stage of capitalist organization is not yet settled. We can, however, be sure that, in the absence of a boom comparable to that of the postwar period (which seems unlikely, to say the least), any new formation will prove to be no more beneficial to the working class than its predecessor. Understanding neoliberalism is therefore not a historical issue, but one of urgent practical concern, as it has shaped the conditions under which the working class still has to fight, conditions that extend beyond economic structures, or even the immediate situation in the workplace, to the types of political representation and the forms of consciousness with which workers will enter the struggles to come. Yet despite the crucial importance of the issue, there is no wholly satisfactory account of this most recent period in the history of capitalism. The book that comes nearest from a Marxist perspective is Harvey's *A Brief History of*

Neoliberalism, but theoretically it is highly eclectic and consequently misleading on several key points.[62] Furthermore, although it is markedly more readable than the average work of Marxist political economy (including most of Harvey's earlier works), it presents a formidable challenge to anyone not already familiar with a series of complex theoretical debates.

For this reason alone, *The Shock Doctrine* is an important work. Although, as we have seen, it draws on Harvey in some respects, it presents an argument about neoliberalism in terms far more comprehensible to nonacademic activists than the jargon of, say, "the spatial-temporal fix." The very fact of its popularity does, however, place an onus on Klein's fellow members of the radical left to draw friendly but critical attention to its weaknesses. In the end, these do not stem so much from the metaphor that provides Klein with her title and structure as from the understanding of capitalism that underlies it. Economic crisis barely features here, unless as something consciously created by ruling classes to change economic structures to their advantage. The idea that capitalism enters into involuntary crisis, as a result of the internal mechanisms of the mode of production, is almost entirely absent from *The Shock Doctrine,* yet it is in this fact that hope actually lies.

If neoliberalism was indeed the essence of capitalism, then we would expect the bourgeoisie to endlessly seek to reimpose that model, whenever conditions are apt. This is certainly what Klein expects, based on her response to the outbreak of the current crisis: "During boom times it is profitable to preach laissez-faire, because an absentee government allows speculative bubbles to inflate. When these bubbles burst, the ideology becomes a hindrance, and goes dormant while government rides to the rescue. But rest assured: the ideology will come roaring back once the bail-outs are done."[63] But if this is so, from where is the impetus for her desired Keynesian welfare-state reforms to come? Surely, not from capitalists since, according to Klein, they are merely waiting to reimpose free market conditions. But equally, how can the oppressed and exploited force a change on the capitalist class if the latter have been able to suppress the possibilities of democracy to the extent that her account reveals? Something of this dilemma is apparent in Klein's final chapter, where she offers some tentative reasons for optimism, which (apart from the Lebanese general strike of 2006) mainly amount to small-scale attempts at post-disaster "community reconstruction."[64] Her failure to understand the role of crisis, rather than some omnipresent capitalist urge toward free markets, as the motivation behind neoliberalism, also blinds her to the possibilities that a renewed period of crisis has for both sides in the class struggle. Neoliberalism was founded on the weakening of the labor movement, and if what replaces neoliberalism is to be in the interests of the exploited and oppressed, the labor movement must be rebuilt. That task will have to involve much more than projects of reconstructing what we had before the neoliberal catastrophe. We know, not least because Naomi Klein has shown us in this flawed but immensely valuable book, what our enemies are capable of if we fail.

Chapter 10

Antonio Gramsci's Reception in Scotland[1]

INTRODUCTION

"Gramsci's relevance to Scotland today," wrote one young socialist in 1975, "is in his emphasis that in a society which is both mature and complex, where the total social and economic processes are geared to maintaining the production of goods and services (and the reproduction of the conditions of production), then the transition to socialism must be made by the majority of people themselves and a socialist society must be created within the womb of existing society and prefigured in the movements for democracy at the grass roots."[2] Although the politics of the author have altered somewhat in the intervening years, the absence of punctuation, constipated literary style, and portentous declamation of platitudes remain unchanged and may alert the reader to his identity. The author was, of course, Gordon Brown, then student rector of Edinburgh University, here introducing *The Red Paper on Scotland*, a volume that in many ways represents the climax of the process by which Gramsci's ideas were received in Scotland.

Brown was no revolutionary even then and his appropriation of Gramsci was generic rather than specific to Scotland, since there were few Western societies of which his comments would not have been true.

However, two other contributors, Tom Nairn and Ray Burnett, made far more concrete use of a Gramscian approach. Their writings, together with the earlier work of Hamish Henderson and the later work of Christopher Harvie and James D. Young, established the main ways in which Gramsci would be used to analyze Scottish conditions, to which surprisingly little of any substance has subsequently been added. Angus Calder once claimed that "Gramsci's thought has been especially influential in Scotland."[3] It is difficult to know how influence can be measured, but what Calder seems to have meant is that Gramsci's thought has been applied to distinctively Scottish issues and dilemmas, rather than, as in Britain as a whole or other parts of the English-speaking world, to general problems of hegemony or revolutionary organization.

Why this should be is one of the questions that I hope to answer in this chapter. All of the writers listed in the preceding paragraph drew attention to Gramsci's Sardinian origins, suggesting that this gave his work a special affinity with or applicability to Scotland. For Nairn, the comparisons could be found in their levels of development: "In the past it is clear that the cultural importance of marginal and relatively backward areas of Europe, like Scotland, the Italian Mezzogiorno, Ireland or (in the nineteenth century) Russia, always depended upon a complicated interrelationship of province and metropolitan centres."[4] Henderson thought that both Sardinia and Scotland had retained distinct national characteristics within the larger nations of which they were part and had a common tradition of educating the subaltern classes.[5] (In one respect, however, he saw Scotland as being superior: "It must never be forgotten that both Gaelic and Scots, unlike Sardinian, are proud possessors of a glorious literary tradition."[6]) Language is obviously central to culture and Henderson was fond of citing Gramsci's advice to his sister, Teresina, that she should bring up her son, Franco, to speak their native Sardinian, and not "proper" Italian.[7] In the second issue of his journal, *Calgacus* (1975), Burnett reproduced Henderson's translation of the same letter with an accompanying note: "Those Marxists who would dismiss minority languages and the whole question of folk culture as insignificant may perhaps find some significance in this letter."[8] Young also quoted the letter as an example of both the complexity of "Gramsci's attitude to languages" and how he had "departed from Marxist orthodoxy," before going on to argue for the need to ensure the survival of the Scots and Gaelic languages.[9]

What is most striking about these parallels is how inexact they are. Harvie came closer than the others by noting that, as a Sardinian, Gramsci "came from the Italian equivalent of the Scottish Highlands."[10] In that case the comparison is between Sardinian and Gaelic, not Scots, since—leaving aside the precise status of Scots as a language—it clearly has closer affinities with English than Sardinian has with Italian. In other respects, however, the comparison is between the Italian South as a whole, of which Sardinia was a part, and the Scottish Highlands. What is clearly not sustainable is what is implied, namely that it is possible to compare Sardinia with Scotland as a whole, and that Scotland occupies a position within Britain similar to that which Sardinia, or even the entire Mezzogiorno, occupies within Italy.

This may seem to be a trivial point about the inappropriate use of analogy; in fact it illustrates how a highly selective reading of Gramsci has been used to support certain misleading assumptions about Scotland. The publications and events through which Gramsci's work was disseminated in Scotland produced insight as well as this type of mystification—this is why they are still worth discussing; but any attempt to map the process must therefore also address two questions raised by it: the extent to which the writers responsible were true to Gramsci's own conceptions—where possible by referring to the texts available to them at the time—and, perhaps more importantly, how useful their appropriations were in analyzing Scottish history and society.

TRANSLATION: 1945-1956

There is only one indirect reference to Scotland in Gramsci's writings. In a 1919 survey of the European revolutionary left for the Turin-based paper that he edited, *L'Ordine nuovo*, one passage commends the "tendency represented by John Maclean," although it describes him as being based "in England."[11] Gramsci was probably following Lenin's wartime identification of those key individuals and organizations that could form the basis of a new International.[12] A more tenuous connection can be traced from a reference in his prison notebooks to the Italian liberal educationalist Ferrante Aporti. As the editors of the 1971 *Selections from the Prison Notebooks* point out, Aporti was influenced by Robert Owen's Scottish infant school experiments after the Napoleonic Wars; the extent to which Gramsci was aware of this connection is, however, unclear.[13] Perhaps the most significant connection, though, was the earliest and most intangible: the concept of "civil society" that emerged from the Scottish Enlightenment and was transmitted, via Hegel and Marx, to Gramsci, for whom it became a key concept in the prison notebooks.

The first direct link between the Sardinian revolutionary and Scotland was made by Hamish Henderson during the Second World War. After his death in 2002, Henderson was frequently described as a Communist in obituaries, although his relationship with the Communist Party of Great Britain (CPGB) was complex and, according to his biographer Timothy Neat, there is no evidence that he ever actually joined it.[14] Formal membership was, however, less important than it might appear: Henderson wrote for CPGB journals like *Our Time,* acted as a CPGB spokesman at international events, and, until 1956 when he sided with the party's internal critics, he cleaved to most of the basic tenets of Stalinism. None of which is to imply an absence of independent thought on his part during the forties and early fifties, but this relative orthodoxy had implications for his understanding of Gramsci.

Henderson was first introduced to Gramsci's work by comrades of the Second Partisan Division of the Valtellina while he was serving in Italy with the British Army. He was subsequently sent the first Italian edition of the *Lettere del carcere* by Amleto Micozzi in Rome on their publication in May 1947. This edition did not, however, present the texts as written, but in edited form—partly to avoid making public those aspects of Gramsci's personal relationships that threatened family sensitivities, but also to effectively censor his disagreements with positions taken by the Communist International (CI) and the Communist Party of Italy (PCI) during his incarceration. According to Henderson's own account, he immediately began translating them into English, a process that involved traveling to Italy where he met Gramsci's brother Carlo, and a visit to Cambridge to meet Gramsci's friend and benefactor, Piero Sraffa. He completed the translations in March 1951.[15]

What did Henderson see in Gramsci? His interests are clear from a letter to publisher John Lehmann sent in late 1949 in an attempt to persuade him that Henderson should translate the letters and Lehmann should publish them:

A confirmed theatre goer, the first "critic" to quote and honour Pirandello and his "barn-stormers": Gramsci applauds Ibsen and Andreieff, he anticipated George Orwell by a decade, he recognised the mythological force in Boys Stories, Westerns and Serial Romances. He saw Folk Art as the natural bedrock of all cultural developments. He planned a book on popular taste and studied popular "bad art" because of what all art tells us of the human and social reality. He exemplifies a "quality of civic courage": the quality above all, perhaps, that modern man needs . . . Gramsci was a great man. Possibly one of the very few great men to have lived in this sorry century, he has a strange (Scottish) mixture of hardness and softness . . .

Henderson then compares Gramsci to a number of world figures including the Scots John Maclean, Norman Douglas, Thomas Carlyle, and Hugh MacDiarmid.[16]

Despite Henderson's efforts, his translation remained largely unpublished for over 20 years. Although extracts appeared in the *New Reasoner* during 1959, the first substantial selection only appeared in *New Edinburgh Review* in 1975 and in book form in 1988, by which time Gramsci's other works had become widely available through other sources.[17] Gramsci was therefore first imported into Scotland, not through Henderson's translations, but through the latter's own writings and the enthusiasm they conveyed. His essay assessing the postwar Scottish literary scene, "Flower and Iron of the Truth," for example, contains references to "pluralism of the superstructures" becoming a form of mere "Alexandrian virtuosity" if disconnected from the life of the people.[18] The reference to a plurality of "superstructures" rather than a singular superstructure, as in Marx's own writings, indicates a distinctively Gramscian approach.[19] Henderson also introduced Hugh MacDiarmid to Gramsci—something for which he may or may not be forgiven—in a letter of 1950.[20] MacDiarmid went on to refer to Gramsci in his 1955 poem "In Memoriam, James Joyce," which rather clumsily invokes "That heroic genius, Antonio Gramsci/Studying comparative linguistics in prison."[21]

More important than these passing references, however, was the emphasis Henderson drew from Gramsci's work on the political significance of folklore or what he called "the fostering of an alternative to official bourgeois culture, seeking out the positive and 'progressive' aspects of folk culture."[22] It was this that inspired both his work with the School of Scottish Studies at Edinburgh University and his contribution to the Scottish folk revival.[23] But perhaps his single greatest intervention in this respect was the establishment of the Edinburgh People's Festival in 1951. He later described how it related to Gramsci:

> Attracting people who felt excluded by the International Festival, keeping the prices low and including children—it was Gramsci in action! One of the things that attracted me to Gramsci was his great interest in popular culture. He was a Sardinian, and the Sardinian folk song is rich and bountiful and vigorous to the nth degree. When he was in prison he wrote to his mother and sisters asking for details of their folk festivals. Gramsci in action was the People's Festival.[24]

Speaking on BBC Radio in 1992 Henderson claimed: "What is now the largest and greatest Arts Festival in the world was kicked into being by the Edinburgh People's Festival—by Antonio Gramsci, a dead man—and by the Communist Party."[25] The People's Festival ran parallel to the International Festival of the Arts from 1951 to 1954, until it was sabotaged by Cold War politics: the Scottish TUC placed the festival on its list of proscribed organizations and withdrew financial support, while the Labour Party declared that association with the festival, which it essentially treated as a CPGB front organization, was incompatible with party membership.[26]

Henderson's achievements then, were to identify, over thirty years before extracts from the prison notebooks dealing directly with this subject were published in English, those aspects of Gramsci's work that were primarily concerned with culture and to give them practical application. Use of Gramsci for this purpose was possible, however, not only because of Henderson's personal drive and inventiveness, but because in the postwar period there was in any case a resurgence of interest in folk culture among the Communist parties and their peripheries. In other words, the turn to national folk traditions may have been given a Gramscian inflection in Scotland, but the general approach was not particularly of Gramscian inspiration: the onset of the Cold War saw an assertion of the idea of national culture as a repository of popular "folk" values against the threat of US commercialization and consumerism. In this context, Gramsci's arguments about the importance of culture were assimilated, at a Scottish as much as a British level, to a much more conventional strategy that was profoundly hostile to the very aspects of US-produced mass culture (detective novels, Hollywood films) that he saw as important. Henderson's admirer and fellow-poet, the historian

Edward Thompson, participated in denunciations of "the American threat" in the early 1950s without any recourse to Gramsci.[27] In the prison notebooks, Gramsci links "the loss of [British] naval and economic supremacy" with the fact that "its very culture is menaced by America"; but it is unlikely that he regarded this as a matter for regret.[28] His linkage of imperial with cultural decline should also remind us that Gramsci retained the classical Marxist notion of totality; he did not, in other words, believe that culture could be understood outside of its inner connection to politics and economics.

Henderson was not the first socialist—and he would certainly not be the last—to draw from Gramsci not only inspiration but validation for his existing positions. For, although Gramsci was indeed interested in folk culture, he was also a modernist who critically admired the work of the Italian Futurists, despite the reactionary and, in many cases, Fascist nature of their politics.[29] His desire to see folk culture taught and studied, read and performed, was partly in order to *overcome* what he called "the separation between modern and popular culture," not to preserve the latter as a supposedly untainted expression of subaltern consciousness. In her history of the postwar Scottish folk music scene, Ailie Munro quoted Gramsci (via Henderson's translation) on the significance of folk as "a separate and distinct way of perceiving life and the world": "This profound statement implies some class alignment but goes beyond it, to the idea of the 'man of independent mind' who can fight back against the overpowering tide of mass consumer culture. Yesterday's rebels may be tomorrow's 'officials,' but folk song continues to present the alternative, the nonconformist, the unofficial viewpoint which is perennially necessary for society's health."[30] Yet Gramsci understood the "philosophical" aspect of folklore as an embodiment of "common sense," which he saw as an inherently contradictory worldview partly composed of ruling-class ideas. This was why he counterposed it to "good sense," meaning a world view more consciously constructed on a scientific (i.e., Marxist) basis.[31] As he wrote in a crucial passage in the notebooks: "The philosophy of Praxis does not tend to leave the 'simple' in the primitive philosophy of common sense, but rather to lead them to a higher conception of life."[32]

Nevertheless, when all these qualifications have been made, the extent of Henderson's achievement needs to be recognized. The role of Gramsci as a theoretical mainstay of the cultural studies industry has become so familiar since the 1970s that the exceptional and innovatory nature of Henderson's strategy, in this place (Scotland) and at that time (the early years of the Cold War), tends to be obscured. The People's Festival in particular was not an academic exercise, not a rhetorical invocation of "cultural struggle" that never at any point leaves the seminar room, but a relatively successful public intervention in which large numbers of working-class people participated.

APPLICATION (I): 1956-1968

Henderson was as dependent as everyone else on what Gramsci's successor as leader of the PCI, Palmiro Togliatti, was prepared to authorize for publication, and political sensitivities were even greater in relation to the notebooks than the letters. In a letter to Phil Stein, a friend in the CPGB, Henderson wrote of his "respect for Togliatti himself, worthy heir to the great tradition of Gramsci."[33] But Henderson was unaware that Togliatti had been deeply concerned by the incompatibility of the prison notebooks with Stalinist orthodoxy. "The notebooks of Gramsci, which I have finished studying, contain material which could be utilised only after a proper processing," he wrote to CI head Georgi Dimitrov in 1941: "Without such treatments the material cannot be utilised and, in some parts, if the contents were found in their unexpurgated form, it would not be in the party's best interest."[34] It was in this spirit that Togliatti "oversaw" the editing of the original Italian edition that appeared between 1948 and 1951, as part of a strategy that simultaneously emphasized Gramsci's supposed, but in fact wholly imaginary, adherence to Stalinist doctrine, and his role as a distinctively "native" intellectual ornament for the PCI.

Access to Gramsci's work was even more limited for those reliant on English translations—a narrow selection from work already censored. In the decade after 1956, when interest in non-Stalinist Marxism began to revive, the main works of Gramsci that were available in English were two short US-edited selections of his writings both published in 1957, extracts from Henderson's translation of the prison letters that appeared in the *New Reasoner* during 1959, and rather esoteric extracts from the notebooks on the subject of education published in the *New Left Review* (*NLR*) during 1965.[35] Nor were there a great number of serious com-

mentaries. Gramsci appears in US historian Stuart Hughes's 1958 survey
of European intellectual trends between 1890 and 1930, but is subject
to a relatively sophisticated Cold War treatment emphasizing the supposedly "totalitarian" implications of his theory.[36] A pioneering article
from 1960 on Gramsci's use of hegemony by the Welsh Communist
Gwyn Williams was misleading and subsequently disowned by its author
on these grounds.[37] These two works were drawn on by Edward Thompson in his mid-sixties polemic with Perry Anderson who subsequently
criticized him precisely for relying on such dubious secondary sources.[38]

The second Scot to show any interest in Gramsci was one of Anderson's colleagues on the editorial board of the *NLR*, a young intellectual
called Tom Nairn. In this case too there is a connection with the PCI interpretation of Gramsci's work. Nairn read Gramsci in the original Italian
while studying at the Scuola Normale Superiore in Pisa, during 1957–
58. One of Nairn's first published articles, "La nemesi borghese," appeared
in the PCI's cultural journal *Il Contemporeano* during 1963, but the bourgeoisie whose nemesis he recounted in Gramscian terms was that of England, not Scotland.[39] That the PCI should have exercised an influence on
the hitherto apolitical Nairn was unsurprising: it was the largest Communist party in Western Europe and had the most sophisticated theoretical
approach and a highly developed cultural apparatus, in many ways comparable to that of the Central European Social Democracy before the
First World War: the contrast with the CPGB would have been obvious
even in Nairn's native Fife, which had a strong Communist tradition by
British standards. On his return to the United Kingdom, Nairn maintained his contact with the party as British correspondent for the PCI
daily paper *Unita,* to which Henderson had also contributed, and joined
the editorial board of the *NLR*. His partnership with Anderson produced
the articles that form the basis of their famous "theses" on the backwardness of the English social formation.[40] In "La nemesi borghese" Nairn
had invoked Gramsci's notion of "delegated authority," in the sense of the
bourgeoisie passing responsibility for political rule onto the established
landowning class.[41] It reappears in Anderson's "Origins of the Present
Crisis," where Gramsci is invoked at the beginning of the section on "History and Class Consciousness: Hegemony."[42] In the case of both articles
the key passages from the prison notebooks were those eventually published in English as "Notes on Italian History." Nairn continued to be in-

terested in Gramsci's ideas and would occasionally quote from him in general terms, for example in his comment that the history of a party is really the history of a country from a particular point of view.[43] Nairn would not begin his analysis of Scotland until the late sixties, however, and initially at least, it owed nothing directly to Gramsci.

Nairn knew Henderson, having contacted him after the *New Reasoner* published extracts from the prison letters in 1959. Henderson approached Nairn late in 1966, inviting him to collaborate on the project of translating and publishing the letters in their entirety. According to Timothy Neat, "Nairn gave Hamish help and advice but lacked the resources to do more."[44] It was now fifteen years since Henderson had completed his translation of the letters and the sheer lack of interest in them, except from other left intellectuals who were similarly lacking in institutional support, indicated the how little impact Gramsci had made on Scottish political culture or academic life. This was soon to change.

APPLICATION (2): 1968-1975

The upsurge of Scottish interest in Gramsci had three stimuli. One, general throughout the West, was the opening of a period of global revolution that began with the Vietnamese Tet Offensive in January 1968 and only ended with the sidetracking of the Portuguese Revolution in November 1975. Another, specific to Scotland but in some respects a symptom of the growing crisis, was the emergence of the Scottish National Party (SNP) as a credible electoral force with its victory at the Hamilton by-election in November 1967, although the party had been gradually building support throughout the decade. The third was that, from 1968, the accessibility of material by and about Gramsci in English began to multiply as the new revolutionaries began to explore the buried traditions of pre-Stalinist Marxism. In the immediate aftermath of the French May a collection of articles from *L'Ordine nuovo* dealing with the factory councils was published in the *NLR* and subsequently reprinted as a pamphlet by the Institute for Workers' Control.[45] Some serious biographical and critical works, notably those by Cammett, Pozzolini, and Fiori (translated by Nairn), and articles mainly concerned with exposition began to appear in English, but these were still limited resources for those without Italian.[46] With the appearance of *Selections from the Prison Notebooks* in 1971, however, the English-speaking left had direct access to substantial passages from his later work. This was of particular significance for the anti-Stalinist revolutionary groups that had begun to emerge after 1956 and that had been boosted by the events of 1968 and after. To the extent that they had previously been interested in Gramsci, it had largely been in relation to his views on party organization.[47] In the interim a third protagonist had entered the scene.

Ray Burnett, an Edinburgh-born, working-class Catholic, was a student at Aberdeen University in the late sixties and early seventies. In his own words: "Largely because of their rejection of Labourism and their ostensibly deeper interest in theory and political analysis I gravitated towards and then joined the principal group on the Trotskyist left, the 'International Socialists' [IS]."[48] Burnett had originally been far more concerned with Irish than Scottish issues and traveled to the North at Easter 1969 to take part in the first Belfast to Dublin civil rights march.[49] In the sections of his book, *War and an Irish Town,* devoted to his personal experience of the civil rights movement, Eamonn McCann noted: "With Ray Burnett, a Scottish comrade, then a member of IS, who had been hitching around Ireland and been given a lift in the middle of a riot, I drafted a leaflet which by seven o'clock was being distributed as 'Barricade Bulletin No. 2.'"[50] Burnett subsequently took part in the Derry Defence Committee.[51]

For Burnett, the publication of the *Selections from the Prison Notebooks* encouraged him to look at "the peculiarities of the Scottish for a change, rather than the English."[52] In 1972 the Edinburgh-based cultural magazine, *Scottish International*, published his major contribution to Gramsci studies, "Scotland and Antonio Gramsci."[53] Burnett surveyed the views of Scottish left-wingers toward the question: "What does 'Scotland' mean or what should it mean to him [sic] as an advocate of socialism?" The answer, he thought, would be "very little." Burnett discerned three tendencies within the Scottish left, each with its own way of ignoring the issue. The first, an amorphous "social" tendency around students and the underground, was not concerned with Scotland at all, but with "the global deterioration of life under advanced industrial society" to which it counterposed solutions that essentially revolved around lifestyle politics. The second consisted of those political tendencies, usually of Trotskyist descent, that organized at a British level and did recognize Scottish problems, but only as specific examples of those generally faced by other declining industrial regions in advanced capitalism, "no different from [those of] any other distressed region of England, viz. unemployment and low wages." The third tendency, the left nationalist parties and groups organized at a Scottish level, did indeed recognize a distinct Scottish dimension to politics, but their analysis relied on the myth that Scotland was a colony of England, a position that Burnett rightly rejected. The tendency to which Burnett allocated the greatest proportion of the blame for failing to take the Scottish Question seriously was the second, with which he himself was aligned, since it had the most potential to do so:

> The truth of the matter is that those who formulate the basic theories of the Left in these islands simply do not see anything specific about Scotland other than a geographical district and an ephemeral political movement which can be summed up and dismissed in classic terms with contemptuous ease and a few choice quotes from Lenin.... Rather than face up to the awkward question of what 'Scotland" is, as opposed to what Scottish Nationalism is, the formal left have pretended that it does not exist.[54]

Burnett found that the approach of the IS, although generally more sophisticated than its competitors, had one thing in common with them: "There was some fine writing, some good incisive critique of several aspects of the contemporary social order. But invariably the source material, the statistics, the examples, the references were all derived from the social, political and cultural complexities of England. And for the most part it was accepted. In Aberdeen, as elsewhere, we not only read them, we sold them and promoted them as valid critiques of our situation. In reality they were not." What Burnett calls "a suffocating Englishness" meant more than a refusal to analyze those aspects of the Scottish experience that were distinctive within Britain; it involved an attitude that he found "ferociously anti-Scottish," as if any interest in Scottish conditions was the antechamber to Scottish nationalism—an object of ritual denunciation on the basis of classical (but often contradictory) Marxist texts from time of the First World War.[55]

It was to remedy this situation that Burnett turned to Gramsci and, in particular, the passages that seemed to distinguish between different revolutionary strategies.[56] Burnett's purpose in referring to the famous distinction between a war of position in the West and a war of maneuver in the East, supposedly required because of the greater strength of civil society in the former, was not to advocate a reformist strategy, as he made clear both in this essay and subsequently in *The Red Paper on Scotland*.[57] Rather, it was to draw attention to the need to understand the nature of civil society in Scotland, if this was indeed to be the battleground in a prolonged war of position:

> While we have a homogenous British state it must be noted that the organisations and institutions in civil society which compromise its bulwarks and defences have an azoic complexity the most significant feature of which is for us is that civil society in Scotland is fundamentally different from that in England. What is more, much of our shared "British" ideology, as it manifests itself in Scotland, draws its strength and vigour from a specifically Scottish heritage of myths, prejudices and illusions.

Burnett is thinking in the second quoted sentence about the Scottish contribution to British imperialism and anti-Catholic Irish racism. He then goes on to make a claim that was startling at the time, although it has since become part of the common sense of the left in Scotland: "Furthermore, even political society, the State in its ethico-political sense, does not have the same external façade in Scotland as it does down south."[58] Burnett ended by referring to Gramsci's note "Against Byzantianism," with its call for concrete application of universal theory to specific situations: "Applying this to our own situation, the left must look again at its own practice of using formulae developed elsewhere to combat nationalism in debate instead of defeating it by deflecting these truths through a Scottish prism and thereby presenting a superior understanding of our problems."[59]

Burnett's argument did not involve support for Scottish nationalism or independence, or even for the setting up of a specifically Scottish section of the IS, but rather the adoption of an approach that would both "cherish the diverse contributions of the flowering Makar and the rantin' ploughboy, the radical weaver, the passionate Gael, and the rovin' tinker," and also address the specificities of contemporary Scotland.[60] In the short- to medium-term this made no impact on his erstwhile organization, and Burnett had left the IS by the time it transformed itself into the Socialist Workers Party (SWP) in late 1976, its existing attitude to Scottish issues intact. As Neil Williamson noted in his account of the Scottish revolutionary left after 1968: "Typical . . . was the election campaign leaflet of

Peter Porteus of the SWP in the 1978 Garscadden by-election where the entire issue of devolution, the Assembly and self-determination did not rate a mention in one of his leaflets."[61]

Meanwhile, Burnett took a new initiative. In April 1973 he invited Henderson to speak at a conference he had organized at Marischal College in Aberdeen called "What Kind of Scotland?"

> With the help of some non-aligned friends I put together a "Teach-in on Scottish culture" with over 50 invited contributors and a wide range of questions and topics spread over a weekend. The programme material bears unmistakeable traces of Gramscian influences which is not surprising given the central aim of the exercise was to get the left interested in all the diverse aspects and questions of Scottish culture which the left had almost entirely ignored.

The event received a mixed reception, with the revolutionary left being particularly skeptical; but Burnett later described to Timothy Neat how, as a result of Henderson's intervention from the floor and their subsequent discussions, "he changed my life that day."[62]

Further initiatives, more directly related to Gramsci, were now being taken by others on the left. The first National Day Conference on Gramsci to be held in Britain took place at Edinburgh University in June 1974, and the proceedings were then published along with other papers in three special issues of the *New Edinburgh Review*, under the somewhat eccentric editorship of Maoist anthropologist Charles Keith Maisels. The first two of these issues also carried Henderson's translation of the prison letters in their entirety for the first time.[63] Burnett was, however, increasingly removed from these developments. He subsequently moved to Wester Ross to produce a quarterly journal called *Calgacus,* after the quasi-mythical Pictish warrior whom Tacitus credited with resisting the Romans at the Battle of Mons Gropius. The editorial board (which never met) included Henderson, the playwright John McGrath, and the poet Sorley MacLean; but *Calgacus*'s combination of Celtic nationalism, folk revivalism, and revolutionary socialism lasted for only three issues before succumbing to bankruptcy in autumn 1975.[64]

The CPGB in Scotland, aware that the legacy of Gramsci—a nominally orthodox Communist thinker—was being increasingly appropriated by the revolutionary left, attempted to recuperate him for the British

Road to Socialism. The position was beginning to emerge among the student membership of the party in England that Gramsci might be considered an alternative, rather than a supplement to Leninist tradition as they understood it; but this had no influence in Scotland at this stage. In Neil Rafeek's oral history of Scottish women members of the CPGB, one of his interviewees, Frieda Park, describes her puzzlement while attending the Communist University of London in 1974: "That was the first time I'd come across people who said 'I prefer Gramsci to Lenin.'"[65] Far more typical were these comments from a 1974 article by David Whitfield in *Scottish International*, where Burnett had first launched his appeal for Gramscian analysis two years previously.

First, the author identifies what he sees as the limitations of Burnett's own analysis, namely that it gave "very little indication . . . of the precise nature of Gramsci's insight, or of the specific use to which it might be put in improving an analysis of Scottish politics," then points out that "Scottish legal traditions, religious traditions, educational traditions, recreational traditions, all differ from those of the rest of Britain." Apparently oblivious to the fact that these were precisely the points Burnett had made, Whitfield then continues:

> The struggle to undermine the Scottish hegemony [sic] must therefore take place within its peculiarly Scottish context, and requires a party of the Left aware of and dedicated to the needs of Scotland, allying the demands of nationalism to those of the organised working class. But because the struggle cannot be located exclusively in Scotland, a wider alliance, an international alliance for socialism is necessary. The Scottish hegemony can fall only as the influence of capitalism in Britain as a whole declines.[66]

Here we have the CPGB's standard Popular Frontism refreshed with a barely understood Gramscian terminology, for unless references to "the Scottish hegemony" mean "the exercise of bourgeois hegemony in Scotland," the term is simply meaningless.

Burnett's position did, however, receive support in the same journal from what might at first appear an unexpected source, Tom Nairn, who commended Burnett's work in an open letter to *Scottish International*, describing "Antonio Gramsci and Scotland" [sic] as "one of the best articles you've published" and opining that: "I think that Gramsci today, whether he was considering Scotland or his own Sardinia, would try to set the problem [of nationalism] in a European context."[67] Nairn was to join the editorial board of *Calgacus* for its brief existence, but, more to the point, starting from Burnett's interpretation of Gramsci, Nairn's own work began to reflect the influence of the latter. The context was the decline of Nairn's brief revolutionary enthusiasm and his reconsideration of Scottish nationalism.

Nairn had been highly critical of Trotskyism in general and the IS in particular in "The Left against Europe?"[68] The Trotskyist Burnett had, however, suggested a Gramscian interpretation of Scottish history and society that supported the move Nairn now wanted to make. In his major contribution to *The Red Paper on Scotland*, "Old Nationalism and New Nationalism," Nairn quoted Burnett and extended his analysis in a direction far more sympathetic to Scottish nationalism—or at any rate, Scottish independence—than Burnett's original article.[69] Nairn now argued that, like several other areas in Western Europe, Scotland was experiencing the rise of what he called "neo-nationalism." In the Scottish case, the arrival of US-based oil companies in the North Sea had provided a functional equivalent of the imperialist intrusions that had provoked "modernising," "developmental" nationalisms of which Scotland had previously no need.

Drawing on the same sections of the prison notebooks as Burnett, Nairn goes beyond pleas to recognize the distinctiveness of Scottish culture to make a case for its uniqueness.[70] Nairn starts from Gramsci's distinction between precapitalist and capitalist ruling classes, and the respective relationships between their states and civil society: the former is essentially one of dominance, the latter of hegemony. "The main point about this modern State-society relationship—quite distinct from that of Antiquity or feudalism—is that through it the whole people become part of society, really for the first time." The emergence of capitalist society is characterized by unevenness, resulting from different chronologies of development and respective starting points; but each civil society tended to be, or to become, coterminous with a particular state. Scotland was the exception, an anomaly that retained a distinct national identity within a larger geographical state, rather than being absorbed as a mere province of one or another of the great European powers, as had happened to so many other potential nations. Why was this? It was certainly the case that the majority of the Scottish ruling class welcomed the Union of 1707 as a means of development, but they were the type of "essentially conservative" group Gramsci saw as characteristic of feudalism. The state into which Scotland was absorbed at the behest of this ruling class was quite distinct in Europe at the time in being "post absolutist," "the very prototype of the modern development Gramsci indicates: that 'revolution of the bourgeois class' which involved the progressive 'absorbing of the entire society' into the new State-society relationship emblemized in nationalism." But the absorption of Scottish society into Britain had created a problem of national identity in Scotland, one that was insoluble under the Union. The absence of statehood meant Scotland could not become a nation like others: "The problem of its bourgeoisie therefore became— put in the starkest terms—one of naturalizing or repressing the country's more distinctive and proto-national features."[71] They chose repression and the consequent formation of a "neurotic" culture characterized by grotesque levels of kitsch.

This was undoubtedly a substantial and serious attempt to apply Gramscian concepts to Scottish history. The transformation of Scotland after 1746 was comparable with that of Italy after 1859—the model of "passive revolution" discussed by Gramsci at several points in the notebooks.[72] Nairn was clearly aware of these parallels. In a subsequent discussion of works by Hobsbawm, Smout, and Wallerstein, for example, he referred to how: "The Improvers—lairds, lawyers, clerical moderates, professors entrepreneurs—argued for an undemocratic revolution-from-above; argued and won."[73] Unfortunately Nairn did not develop these insights further. Referring to Burnett's invocation of "our specifically Scottish heritage of myths, prejudices and illusions," he wrote: "All I have tried to do is indicate in some general ways how that heritage is accessible to discussion in the Gramscian terms which he proposed."[74] In effect, his use of Gramsci had been to establish an historical analysis upon which to base the contemporary political position he now wanted to adopt— an emphasis with which there could be no dispute were it not that the analysis itself contained several distortions.

At one point Nairn referred to the role of the Scottish bourgeoisie in achieving the necessary degree of national "repression" and in this context invoked Gramsci again:

What is remarkable in the Scottish case is its success and solidity, and the degree to which it was self-administered. Gramsci used a story, "The Fable of the Beaver," to illustrate the acquiescence of the Italian bourgeoisie in fascism: "The beaver, pursued by trappers who want his testicles from which medicinal drugs can be extracted, to save his life tears off his own testicles . . ." . . . Adapting the fable to our argument one might say: in the 19th century the Scottish bourgeoisie could hardly help becoming conscious of its inherited *cojones* to some extent, its capacity for nationalism: but since this consciousness conflicted with its real, economic interests in an unusual fashion, it was forced to—at least—repress or "subliminate" the impulse itself. [75]

There are two problems with this passage. First, it is evident from Gramsci's discussion after the "Fable" that he is not referring to the Italian bourgeoisie, but to the passivity of the Italian Socialist Party and trade union movement in the face of Mussolini.[76] Second, the comparison that Nairn wants to make here between the Scottish and Italian bourgeoisies is in any case completely misleading, and indicates the direction that his analysis was about to take. Most members of the Italian bourgeoisie welcomed Mussolini as their savior from the socialist threat: they did not "acquiesce" in the face of Fascism but embraced it, at least until the alliance with Germany threatened the destruction of the Italian state from Allied invasion and popular insurrection. Similarly, as Nairn himself made quite clear on other occasions, the nascent Scottish bourgeoisie was not emasculated by the Union; the Union established the conditions for its rise to power. The purpose of this comparison is effectively to naturalize nationalism, so that the failure of the Scottish bourgeoisie to produce a political nationalism represents a form of sickness, a failure that now has to be overcome if health is to be restored. Nairn's claim that entire nations can suffer from neurosis and whole social classes practice sublimation indicates that his theoretical basis has moved some way from Gramsci toward Freud.[77]

Nairn dismissed the earlier optimistic analysis of "The Three Dreams of Scottish Nationalism" as based on "two misjudgements": "the left had pinned too much faith on the rationality of working class based struggle (understood as a potentially international force), and far too little upon the non-rational strengths of nationalism." For Nairn, socialists had little option but to accept the continued influence of nationalism: "In my view it has become totally inadmissible to oppose such tendencies in the name of an abstract internationalism, a universal socialist or class struggle which exists only in aspiration."[78] By now Gramsci has vanished from the horizon altogether. In the prison notebooks he had argued that revolutionaries had a responsibility to actively participate in bringing about the socialist world they wished to see: "In reality one can 'foresee' to the extent that one acts, to the extent that one applies a voluntary effort and therefore contributes concretely to creating the result 'foreseen.' Prediction reveals itself thus not as a scientific act of knowledge, but as the abstract expression of the effort made, the practical way of creating a collective will."[79] The failure of the class struggle in the early 1970s to achieve socialism might, in these terms, have involved a failure of the left, including Nairn himself, to "contribute concretely to creating the result foreseen," rather than the structural incapacity of the working class to free itself from nationalist influence. But Nairn increasingly saw Scottish nationalism as a substitute for the inability of the working class to destroy the British state: "More than any other factor, more even than the miners' strikes of 1972 and 1974, it has exposed the senility of the old consensus and its two party system."[80]

These hyperbolic claims for the significance of Scottish nationalism did not, however, involve any sympathy for Scottish culture. Perry Anderson once revealed how Isaac Deutscher had described his and Nairn's treatment of English history and society as involving the "rhetoric of deprecation" amounting in his eyes to a form of "national nihilism."[81] But there is a sense in which Nairn treats Scotland in the same way, as more conventional, less instrumentalist nationalists have complained.[82] If Henderson and to a lesser extent Burnett exaggerated the oppositional qualities of folk culture, Nairn barely recognizes that they exist. With the exception of works of High Modernism such as MacDiarmid's *A Drunk Man Looks at the Thistle* (1926), which Nairn invokes positively on several occasions, he treats Scottish culture as if it were nothing but the *Sunday Post* and *Dr Finlay's Casebook* writ large.[83] If for Henderson popular culture is the Voice of the People, hostile to bourgeois culture, for Nairn it is the Voice of D. C. Thompson, trapped within it. There is no sense in either position that culture is a field of contradiction and conflict played out in consciousness, but the latter is the most immediately debilitating by way of its pessimism. "Nationalism could only have worked," Nairn wrote later in 1975, "because it actually did provide the masses with something real and important—something that class consciousness postulated in a narrowly intellectualist mode could never have furnished, a culture which however deplorable was larger, more accessible, and more relevant to mass realities than the rationalism of our Enlightenment inheritance."[84] Here again the echoes are not of Gramsci but of Althusser, with his insistence on the inescapability of ideology.[85] For Gramsci, the subaltern class cannot already spontaneously possess complete nonideological knowledge of the world under capitalism, but from its existing partial, contradictory understanding it *can* achieve it and it is the task of revolutionaries is to assist in this: "If [Marxism] affirms the need for contact between intellectuals and simple [i.e., the term used by the Roman Catholic Church for the masses] it is not in order to restrict scientific activity and preserve unity at the low level of the masses, but precisely in order to construct an intellectual-moral bloc which can make politically possible the intellectual progress of the mass and not only of small intellectual groups."[86] For Nairn this aspiration had become a utopia.

Application (3): 1975-1979

The publication of *The Red Paper on Scotland* in February 1975 was closely followed by that of Michael Hechter's *Internal Colonialism*, a discussion of Scotland and the other nations belonging to what the author called the British "Celtic fringe." Hechter's work was unique in a Scottish context, both at that time and since, in that, although it mentions Gramsci only in passing, it does so in relation to an important work written prior to his imprisonment, "Some Aspects of the Southern Question" (1926), referring to the 1957 edition of *The Modern Prince*. Hechter offered Gramsci's discussion of the Mezzogiorno as an early example of the concept of internal colonialism.[87] Yet he also added that the term fitted less well in Scotland than in Ireland, or even Wales, as a consequence of a much more complex situation, a point that he emphasized more strongly in a 1982 retrospective on the debates of the previous decade.[88] In another respect, however, Hechter's book was the first sign of what was to come. Although he identified with a particularly US type of non-Marxist radical sociology (Immanuel Wallerstein and Charles Tilly are both acknowledged in the preface), he wrote as an academic and published under the highly respectable imprint of Routledge and Kegan Paul: this was a wholly different environment from *Scottish International*, or even the *NLR*.

Yet the same trend was under way in Scotland. 1977 saw the publication of both Nairn's *The Break-Up of Britain,* which incorporated a revised version of "Old and New Nationalism," and Christopher Harvie's *Scotland and Nationalism,* which continued the debate opened by Burnett and continued by Nairn. Harvie later described the participants, including himself, as "aggressive rationalists who didn't really know the kind of material we had to deal with": "*Scotland and Nationalism* was really a book written at the end of a period. It reeked of 'the lessons of 1968'; it assumed that libertarian-Marxist intellectuals purged of false doctrine were going to ride the horse of nationalism as a new governing elite."[89] There were, however, several important differences between Harvie's work and that of all his predecessors, which this retrospective assessment rather elides. His engagement with Gramsci did not take place at a time of optimism and opportunity for the left, which in their various and overlapping ways 1945, 1956, and 1968 had been for Henderson, Nairn, and Burnett, but at the end of the revolutionary period symbolized by the latter date—something already recognized by Nairn, although his default pessimism led him to announce the onset of the downturn before it had really begun. But by 1977 the situation had clearly changed: only two years on from the publication of *The Red Paper on Scotland,* Harvie was already treating it as a historical document, recording the vanished illusions of a time now past: "The university intellectuals who contributed to the *Red Paper* had moved to a position of political involvement. But their prospective allies were far from evolving the conscious proletarian intelligentsia of Gramsci's vision." Instead "the people of the tower blocks and bleak estates" were turning to nationalism.[90] Although Harvie refers here to "university intellectuals who contributed to *The Red Paper,*" less than half the contributors (fourteen out of twenty-nine) fell into this category at the time of publication, and these did not include many of the most radical (Burnett and Nairn, but also McGrath).[91] Indeed, the Scottish Gramscians had only limited, tenuous, and uncertain relationships with higher education: Henderson and Nairn were intermittently or peripherally employed there and Burnett worked as a school teacher rather than a university lecturer. Harvie, on the other hand, progressed through the conventional academic route and was employed as a history lecturer with the Open University at the time *Scotland and Nationalism* was published. He remained a political activist, particularly in relation to the question of devolution that loomed large in Scottish politics as the decade staggered to an end. In occupational location, however, he was closer to Hechter, and this in turn suggests the process by which the "men of letters" or freelancing intellectuals, such as those who had originally brought Gramsci to Scotland, were beginning to be replaced by professional academics—although this was of course a general process across the West.[92]

Harvie was also at this time a member of the Labour Party. So too, of course, was Gordon Brown—but although Brown enabled the publication of authors attempting to discuss Gramsci's work, he made no serious attempt to do himself. Harvie was therefore the first of Gramsci's Scottish interlocutors not to have belonged to the far left, in one form or another. Of course, in a small country with a highly concentrated population and relatively few media outlets like Scotland, the boundaries between the different sections of the left have always been relatively fluid: Harvie was, for example, later to share editorial board duties with Nairn on the short-lived *Bulletin of Scottish Politics* (1980–81), a journal that published figures from both the SNP left like Stephen Maxwell and then-Trotskyists like George Kerevan. Harvie's intervention signaled two changes in Gramsci's reception in Scotland, both indicative of the way in which the mainstreaming of Gramsci, the Leninist and revolutionary, was becoming a suitable case for academic citation and reformist appropriation. How did he put Gramsci to use?

Early in his book, Harvie argues that the historical relationship of the Union to Scottish nationalism "underline[d] many of the insights of one European political thinker whose influence on the reorientation of socialist thought has been considerable, not least in Scotland": "Influenced by Croce as well as Marx, [Gramsci] challenged the latter's crude generalisations about nationalism. He was preoccupied by the way in which the masses were persuaded to accept 'civil society' (a phrase originated in eighteenth-century Scotland) which sustained the dominant political and economic groups, and he attributed the critical function to the intellectuals. Intellectual history thus becomes, in Gramsci's view, as in mine, the key to understanding why nationalist movements emerge."[93] Even this short extract suggests that the new academic context did not necessarily lead to greater levels of understanding or accuracy. Harvie has written a number of valuable historical works, of which in many ways *Scotland and Nationalism* is one, but his grasp of Marxist theory has always been somewhat tenuous, to say the least. The masses are not "persuaded" to accept "civil society," since civil society is simply those noneconomic social relationships that are outside the state—the masses are *part* of civil society; the question for Gramsci was how they were persuaded to accept the capitalist system, and even then only partially ("contradictory consciousness"). How, in other words, does the bourgeoisie achieve and maintain its hegemony? In part the problem here is simply the type of slapdash formulation that recurs throughout Harvie's writings; but there are deeper misunderstandings at work. He retrospectively described himself as working, like Nairn, under the influence of the "Marxist contagion." More specifically:

> Both Nairn and I depended on Gramsci's notion of the balance of "organic" and "traditional" intelligentsias. Like Marx, Gramsci saw political praxis occurring where intellectual "understanding" combined with the desperation of the proletariat. Arguing to some extent from Britain in 1848, where the intellectuals inhibited rather than furthered revolutionary change, he divided them into two: an "organic" intelligentsia who were essentially the experts of the industrial economy, whose ethic could affect the proletariat in the course of its work; and a "traditional" intelligentsia which, in education, law and medicine, served the conservative order. The latter can change (its commitment to "values" may even make it— or some of its members—a radical force in a crisis) but it usually influences its less focussed "organic" intellectuals in a conservative direction.[94]

It is true that Gramsci believed intellectuals could be divided into traditional and organic groups, but the rest of this passage involves a distortion of what he meant by them. As Peter Thomas puts it: "These 'traditional intellectuals' were, in fact, the organic intellectuals of a previously emergent and now consolidated and dominant class, unwilling, at best, or, at worst, unable, to recognise their continuing political function."[95] Ruling classes do not generally require organic intellectuals except in the period when they are still struggling for dominance: once installed in power, the organic will become the traditional in their turn. In relation to the bourgeoisie-in-power, a partial exception might be made for those periods in which a major reconstruction or reorientation of capital is required, such as the shift to neoliberalism in the 1970s: here the role of intellectual advocacy on the part of free-market think tanks had a supporting role, but the decisive factor was in every case the application of state power.

Harvie writes of how "in the twentieth century Gramsci marvelled at the way in which the 'traditional intelligentsia' of the British professions had pre-empted the role of the 'organic intelligentsia' produced by industrial capitalism."[96] In fact, members of the "British professions" acted as organic rather than traditional intellectuals. The crucial distinction is not one of different occupations, but of social roles. Harvie's misunderstandings in this respect led to several misconceptions about Scottish history. In relation to the Reformation we are told: "In Scotland . . . the 'traditional intelligentsia' that Calvinism created anticipated the 'organic' managerial intelligentsia of capitalism."[97] Similarly, in relation to the Enlightenment (here Harvie is summarizing the argument of *Scotland and Nationalism* in a later essay): "During the Enlightenment the traditional intelligentsia—clergy, lawyers, and landowners—pre-empted the functions of the organic intelligentsia. Their expertise in the social sciences, invention and entrepreneurship, thus inoculated the country against any awkward radicalism on the part of this group."[98] The Calvinist clergy did not "anticipate," nor did the Enlightenment intelligentsia "pre-empt" the functions of the organic intellectuals—they *were* the organic intellectuals of their respective periods. Gramsci saw the organic intellectual as being a revolutionary category, which meant that, in the context of his own time, he mainly thought of them in relation to the working class.[99] This is why he writes of how "*Ordine Nuovo* worked to develop certain forms of new intellectualism and to determine its new concepts . . . since such a conception corresponded to latent aspirations and conformed to the development of real forms of life. The mode of being of the new intellectual can no longer consist in eloquence . . . but in active participation in practical life, as constructor, organiser, 'permanent persuader' and not just a simple orator."[100]

Harvie's misconceptions were minor, however, compared to the phantasmagoric claims made at the end of the decade in James Young's *The Rousing of the Scottish Working Class* (1979). Here we learn, for example, that "the contradictions in Gramsci's thought which led him to advocate 'civilising' and emancipating the workers from 'vicious habits like alcoholism' at the same time as he thought to use populism, social banditry, mysticism and millenarianism as weapons in the struggle to overthrow capitalism."[101] Young was a long-term socialist activist who had been associated with several organizations, which briefly included the forerunners to IS, the Socialist Review Group, and was at this point working as History lecturer at Stirling University. Drawing on Hechter's work he wrote that "Scottish society [was] pushed into a subordinate role [as] a victim of 'internal colonisation' with an economy peripheral to the core of British capitalism, and with institutions dominated by the 'conquering metropolitan elite.'"[102] Young did attempt to establish a more direct connection with Gramsci by linking the concept of internal colonialism to that of hegemony, quoting the classic exposition from the prison notebooks: "The 'normal' exercise of hegemony on the now classical terrain of the parliamentary regime is characterised by the combination of force and consent, which balance each other reciprocally, without force predominating excessively over consent. Indeed, the attempt is always made to ensure that force will appear to be based on the consent of the majority, expressed by the so-called organs of public opinion—newspapers and associations—which, therefore, in certain situations, are artificially multiplied."[103] Young then applies this general formula to Scotland: "However, as Scotland was an internal colony without its own State apparatus, it was necessary for the possessing class to depend on ideological indoctrination and consensus to a much greater extent than occurred in most other, industrial societies."[104] This passage consists of a series of non-sequiturs. Why would the bourgeoisie in Scotland *need* its own apparatus when it had that of the British state? Would it not be more plausible for an "internal colony" to require *greater* exercise of force than consent? And, without in any way accepting the internal colony thesis, is it not the case that, historically, Scotland *was*—initially at least—subject to greater exercise of force than England, both in the suppression of the Radical movement of the 1790s and the shop stewards' movement during the First World War?

In retrospect, the work of Harvie and Young, with all its confusions, represents the last moment in Gramsci's introduction into Scotland by native thinkers on the left. The decade that had opened so promisingly had not ended with Gramsci's ideas being assimilated in any serious way. When the Trotskyist writer Neil Williamson came to give an assessment of the Scottish revolutionary left in the decade since 1968, one of his reflections was that "there must have been few who thought that these Gramscian plants produced around 1973 would find the Scottish left such stony soil."[105] Yet, looking back from the other side of the eighties in 1994, Lindsay Paterson could note: "The writings of Antonio Gramsci . . . became popular among the Scottish left."[106] Which ideas had become popular and why?

DIFFUSION: 1979-?

During the 1970s Gramsci had been used by the PCI to promote the turn toward Eurocommunism, in much the same way as he had been used to promote all its previous strategic turns since 1943. In this case, however, it signalled something qualitatively different: the open acceptance of reformist positions that had traditionally been associated with social democracy. As Nairn's former colleague Perry Anderson pointed out in a celebrated article from 1976, this distorted Gramsci's Leninist insistence on the need to overthrow bourgeois state power; but Anderson also argued that certain ambiguities in Gramsci's own formulations had allowed the distortion to be carried out with some credibility.[107] Anderson may have been less than fair to Gramsci in the latter respect, but his concern for how Gramscian concepts were increasingly being used was only too well founded.[108]

In Britain, the main instrument for transforming Gramsci into a vulgar liberal was the organ of the Eurocommunist wing of the CPGB, *Marxism Today*. Prior to the 1980s ascendancy of this journal, the very few discussions of Scotland by party members that used Gramscian terms went little beyond the historical arguments advanced by Nairn. In the collectively written volume *Scottish Capitalism*, produced by CPGB academics in 1980, the argument draws on the same passages from "State and Civil Society" as Nairn had done to argue essentially the same case for the specificity of Scotland within the Union.[109] Nor did this change, as Neil Rafeek notes: "The reformers who identified with *Marxism Today* and who emphasized the importance of Gramsci [in England] did not have counterparts in Scotland."[110] What occurred instead was that the *Marxism Today* interpretation of Gramsci, rendered in its most sophisticated form by Stuart Hall, entered Scottish political life in a much more diffuse way, the various elements being accepted as (and here the term is used in Gramsci's sense) the "common sense" of the left on the subject.[111]

Henderson, for example, whose formal links with the CPGB had been severed many decades before, was broadly supportive of the project, writing: "Mention must be made of the role of *Marxism Today* in applying Gramscian methods of political and cultural analysis to the concrete situation in Thatcher's Britain."[112]

It was in culture and art that this particular interpretation of Gramsci loomed largest. Pat Kane, one half of pop duo Hue and Cry, noted of their first hit, "Labor of Love," from 1987: "'Withdraw my labor of love,' the hookline, was a straight Leftist metaphor, the summit of my argument derived from Gramsci (and shamelessly cribbed from *Marxism Today*) about how Thatcherism was exercising 'hegemony' over the working classes: 'loved you putting me down in a totally new way,' said the song's speaker, a reference to the way Thatcher's rhetoric of individualism was a new a subtle exercise of authority over the popular consensus."[113] The influence extended to more traditional art forms. Also during 1987, for example, the exhibition *The Vigorous Imagination: New Scottish Art* opened at the Gallery of Modern Art in Edinburgh in August and included Ken Currie's "The Self-Taught Man," in which a Clydeside shipyard worker is depicted reading a book with word "Gramsci" on the front cover. In another painting ("Glasgow Triptych: Young Glasgow Communists") a young woman sits on a pile of books, one of which is by Gramsci, addressing her male comrades. According to Currie's own commentary, this represents a rejection of "traditional" methods of struggle in favor of a "totally new approach" based on "adherence to the new and controversial ideas of Gramsci."[114] Henderson saw it as deeply significant: "That a Scottish working-class intellectual—a stubborn survivor in Thatcher's Britain—should be interested in Gramsci's thought in the 1980s is readily comprehensible."[115] Yet as Calder noted of Currie: "His famous image of the Self-Taught Man reading Gramsci has in the background the neon lights which typify the Glasgow night culture of pubs, boxing and gambling which Currie (who, without sectarianism, sees virtues in the Calvinist tradition) holds in moral contempt."[116]

Currie's work embodies a more general problem. In a critique of Currie's aesthetics, Paul Wood extended the argument to embrace the entire interpretation of Gramsci that had come to be dominant by the late eighties. Pointing out the fact that Gramsci was "a leader of factory occupations, a Bolshevik supporter, and a delegate to the International," Wood noted that these central elements of his life and work had been ignored or suppressed by a Communist movement increasingly bound to national and reformist roads to socialism, but intent on using Gramsci as left cover for the abandonment of revolutionary politics. Wood recognized that there was a "positive side" to the way Gramsci was being used, notably "an address to the specific and particular conditions of local cultures," but:

> This aspect of the legacy of Gramsci, particularly in countries like Wales and Scotland, requires very careful debate. It reaches beyond the academic or artistic into areas of real strategy and policy: that is into areas where people's lives are affected directly. There is no question that more or less sophisticated advocacy of arguments about the production of national-popular culture has been a powerful pole of attraction in the recent period; not least because that period has witnessed a cyclical downturn in class-based militancy; and not least in Scotland. It is fairly common to find sections of the left arguing for the need to re-appropriate patriotism from the Right, for the articulation of a Left nationalism against, e.g., the depredations of multi-national capital. It is the terms of any such national-popular culture of resistance which require close scrutiny.[117]

There was nothing particularly Scottish about most of the themes involved, whether the critique of so-called economism, the emphasis on the construction of political identity, the need for class alliances, the prioritization of culture and ideology as sites of contestation, or the endlessly invoked "struggle for hegemony"; but in the context of the Thatcher regime and the rise of support for devolution in Scotland as a means of escaping it, one particular aspect of this new Gramsci had a more political resonance, to which Wood alludes: the "national-popular." The editors of the *Selections from the Prison Notebooks* had cannily warned in 1971 that Gramsci intended this as "a cultural concept . . . radically alien to any form of populism or 'national-socialism.'"[118] However, in a topsy-turvy context where an essentially political concept like hegemony could be treated as cultural, it made perfect sense for an essentially cultural concept like the national-popular to be to be treated as political.

There were of course variations, depending on whether writers were using Gramsci to support classically reformist positions or those of the SNP left. Here for example is the conclusion to an article by Paul Tritschler, one of the editors of the left journal *Radical Scotland*, in 1986:

"To take a national approach . . . is not at variance with socialist objectives. Indeed, the party, for Gramsci, must pose the solution to the oppression of the working class and social movements within the context of the nation's particular cultural orientations and traditions."[119] The "party" here—although Tritschler acknowledges its current failings—is the Labour Party. But here is a very similar argument from two adherents of a short-lived socialist current within the SNP, now entirely extinct, which appeared in print under the rubric of "national popular publications": "National relations are the result of a combination which is original and unique and . . . the struggle must therefore exist within its own historical, cultural and geographic boundaries."[120] The actual text by Gramsci that is partially quoted prior to the first passage and that evidently inspired the second (which misquotes it without attribution) reads as follows:

> To be sure, the line of development is towards internationalism, but the point of departure is "national"—and it is from this point of departure that one must begin. Yet the perspective is international and cannot be otherwise. Consequently, it is necessary to study accurately the combination of national forces which the international class [the proletariat] will have to lead and develop, in accordance with the international perspective and directives [i.e. those of the Comintern]. The leading class is in fact only such if it accurately interprets this combination . . . [121]

A complex, even quite tortuous argument, relating to internal debates within the CI about the precise role of national factors in achieving the international working-class revolution, is therefore turned into a simple celebration of the national. These conclusions cannot be legitimately derived from either Gramsci's life or work. Gramsci's own consistent position, from the moment of his adherence to Marxism, is not open to doubt. In "The Lyons Thesis" (1926), a crucial preprison work cowritten with Togliatti and almost totally ignored on the Scottish left, they write that the initial revolt of the working class against capitalism

> took a different form in each nation, which was a reflection and consequence of the particular national characteristics of the elements which, originating from the petty bourgeoisie and peasantry, contributed to forming the great bulk of the industrial proletariat. Marxism represented the conscious, scientific element, superior to the particularism of the various tendencies of a national character and origin; and it waged a

struggle against these, both in the theoretical field and in the field of organisation. . . . After the victory of Marxism, the tendencies of a national character over which it had triumphed sought to manifest themselves in other ways, re-emerging within Marxism as forms of revisionism.[122]

As virtually all his major biographers and interpreters have noted, Gramsci increasingly abandoned his initial Sardinian nationalism as he became more involved in the socialist movement.[123] The much-cited letter to Teresina indicates his continued support for Sardinian culture: "Nevertheless my culture is fundamentally Italian," he wrote to his sister from prison, "and this is my world; I have never felt torn between two worlds."[124] But neither was he an Italian nationalist, for "it is one thing to *be* particular and another to *preach* particularism." The error here is to assume that national consciousness automatically translates into nationalism: "Goethe was a German 'national,' Stendhal a French 'national,' but neither of them was a nationalist."[125]

Scottish Marxist academics otherwise continued to use Gramscian concepts in their analysis, often to good effect. In particular, two excellent studies of the labor movement in Edinburgh, by Robert Gray and John Holford, both made exemplary use of the concept of "contradictory consciousness."[126] But more commonly there is little sense that they have anything specific to say about Scotland; in other words, they use the concepts to discuss features of Scottish society that are indistinguishable from those of English or even Western society in general. The effect is often of theoretical throat-clearing, which is no longer restricted even to Marxists of any description: Sean Damer uses "the intellectuals," "hegemony," and "common sense" in discussing the Moorepark housing scheme in Glasgow; Grant Jarvie uses "hegemony" in relation to the significance of Highland Gatherings and Games; David McCrone uses "ideology" in relation to a discussion of nationhood.[127]

More often, however, the concepts are simply trivialized—although there is of course no specifically Scottish way of trivializing Gramsci. For example, in Colin McArthur's generally very illuminating analysis of Hollywood representations of Scotland, he informs us of how Gramsci's work was important in shifting the attention of Marxists to culture, "particularly in relation to his concept of *hegemony*, which he deployed to explain how ruling blocs retain control mainly by consent rather than coercion." I am less interested here in the misreading this involves (ruling blocs retain control by consent *and* coercion) than in what follows. McArthur writes of one position that became popular in the early eighties: "To apply the terms of this analysis, the anti-Tartanry/Kailyard position became, in the 1980s and 1990s and at least as far as the Scottish intelligentsia is concerned, *hegemonic*."[128] The idea that the popularity of a particular notion among a group of academics and media professionals can be equated with the exercise of "hegemony" as a means of securing class rule simply means that the term has effectively been rendered meaningless.

The most explicit abandonment of Gramsci came, however, at the hands of the thinker who did most to naturalize his thought within Scotland in the first place. In April 1997, shortly before the New Labour dispensation began at Westminster, Tom Nairn gave a talk, appropriately enough at the Italian Department of University College, London. In the main, his argument was about the uselessness of the concept of civil society, both historically and in relation to contemporary debates—an argument with which I am in broad agreement.[129] In passing, however, Nairn makes a number of comments about his one-time influence, which begin by noting the obvious attractions that Gramsci had for the New Left, as it emerged between 1956 and 1968:

> Those reared within the political stultification and conservative oppression of the Cold War discovered a new icon, an apparently non-dogmatic and anti-economistic forerunner who spoke to them in ironic, frequently sarcastic undertones utterly different from the loud brass of official Marxism-Leninism. Furthermore, his interests were obviously in what they found to be a sympathetic direction: literature, the unexpected undersides of public displays, the minutiae of popular culture and fashion, the world of implications sometimes discernible in small or unpretentious phenomena. All this could not but appeal to a generation undergoing the socio-cultural and lifestyle revolution of the late 1950s and 1960s. And part of its glamour was the Gramscian representation of "civil society" as a sphere which not only counted but maybe mattered more than the arid gymnastics of statism, whether in the practice of the East or the aspirations of communist parties in the West.

But Nairn's critique goes deeper than the rejection of a particular aspect of his theory; he declares that the entire fixation with Gramsci by the left had been a mistake:

What this ignored was Gramsci's actual dour view of society. Non-state society was not rediscovered or enjoyed for its own sake, but with an absolutely statist redemption in mind. . . . The circumstances of censored notebook composition compelled a detour through pluralism, and the avoidance of overtly anti-statism, and anti-national rhetoric. But the point of it was to lay the foundations for the standard proletarian-internationalist state of Third International times: il moderno principe or radically Leninist polity within which society would be reconfigured to suit the vision of a commanding elite.[130]

Nairn at least recognizes that, whatever his innovations, Gramsci remained a Leninist throughout the composition of the prison notebooks and to the end of his life. Not for him the type of incomprehension displayed, for example, by Allan Harkness, who asserts that: "Gramsci's is an argument for pluralist liberal democracies."[131] Nor does he display the astonishment of his former colleague Lindsay Paterson in the face of Gramsci's unwavering belief in the need to destroy the state: "Even Gramsci—nowadays thought of as an apostle of a liberal communism—believed that the end of the state would be the dawn of the merely regulated society."[132] For Nairn, Gramsci's rejection of liberal democracy is precisely the problem: "To ethical betrayal there corresponded a policy of ethical recovery which demanded a ferocious Redeemer: the modern prince of Machiavellianism reborn. In the collective form of the Party, this radical force was supposed to reinstate the class struggle and render it immune to further betrayals—by putting down firmer roots in 'civil society.'"[133] Nairn does note, in passing, that Gramsci was in fact opposed to the direction in which Stalin took the Soviet Union and the CI during the 1920s and 1930s, and that this was one of the reasons why socialists in the 1960s were attracted to his work. Nairn now revealed that they were mistaken: "Behind any disenchantment with 'crude' Russian hegemony lay a more powerful will towards, in [Neil] Harding's words, 'a transcendent tactic and sublime goal' in the sky of the new proletarian enlightenment."[134] Gramsci is therefore said to have harbored a monolithic "statist" agenda behind the superficially open concepts employed in his prison notebooks. Here we have effectively returned to Cold War interpretations of Gramsci that were virtually the only ones available at the time Nairn first encountered Gramsci's work in Italy, in for example Stuart Hughes's discussion from 1958 of "hegemony": "As happened so often in Gramsci's writings, a totalitarian thought was clothed in liberal guise." At least Hughes allows that Gramsci was "innocent": "Like Marx himself, he failed to draw the final implications of his own thinking, and quite sincerely believed he was aiming at human liberation."[135] Nairn is not even this generous. The irony is that, despite Nairn's newfound hostility, he has more accurately discerned the revolutionary core of Gramsci's thought than most of his predecessors, including his own younger self. What attitude one takes toward Gramsci therefore depends on how valid one still regards the revolutionary project for which he gave his life.

CONCLUSION

Hamish Henderson, the first man to bring Gramsci to Scotland, died on March 8, 2002. On May 4 Angus Calder and George Gunn unfurled a gigantic banner of Gramsci at the summit of Ben Gulabin, before scattering Henderson's ashes near the Glenshee Water.[136] It is tempting to see in this gesture a symbol for the abandonment of any attempt to apply Gramsci's thought to Scottish conditions. The original Scottish Gramscians had, by the late 1970s, produced an impressive if flawed body of work, the main focus of which was on the cultural distinctiveness of Scotland. This was necessary and, initially at least, probably unavoidable, given the lack of interest hitherto shown in the subject, above all on the revolutionary left. As the left entered the era of defeat and neoliberal ascendancy, however, it proved all too easy for these positions to be assimilated to a reformist interpretation of Gramsci that saw him primarily, or even exclusively, as a theoretician of the cultural and ideological superstructures. Nairn and Burnett briefly raised the possibility of using Gramsci for other purposes: the former to establish an interpretation of Scottish history that might explain the origins of our national discontents, the latter to develop a specifically Scottish politics for the revolutionary left. Nairn's was the more extended argument, but neither found any successors willing to develop their insights.

Burnett thought that the revolutionary left would be able to meet the challenge of making a Gramscian analysis of the Scottish situation. It did not do so then and is further away from doing so now, partly because of its current fragmentation, partly because many of the groups and individuals have adopted a form of "left nationalism" that does not require any form of Marxist analysis, Gramscian or otherwise—indeed, this "left nationalism" is actively hostile to any other left that does not immediately and unconditionally affirm the goal of Scottish independence. Independence may be a necessary tactical objective for the Scottish left—I believe that it is—but unless it is treated as part of a wider strategic conception, it is unlikely to deliver the results expected of it. Even under the present conditions of devolution, however, it should be clear that the difference between Scotland and the other nations of the United Kingdom is *political*, not cultural, and that this is likely to increase. This divergence is precisely why Gramsci remains a potentially important theoretical resource for the left. As the translation of the complete prison notebooks into English proceeds and we also have access to a wider selection of the preprison writings, we can see more clearly the continuities in Gramsci's thought, the most consistent of which is his relentless focus on the political. Whether elements of the Scottish left will be capable of Gramsci's revolutionary Marxism, for both historical analysis and socialist strategy, is an open question. If it can, then it has the experience of the pioneers discussed in this article to draw upon: we can learn from their mistakes and build on their achievements.

✍ Chapter II ✍

Women and the Lost World of Scottish Communism
Neil Rafeek's Communist Women in Scotland[1]

A decade ago Steven Fielding concluded a highly critical review of Noreen Branson's *History of the Communist Party of Great Britain, 1941– 1951* (1997)—the fourth volume of the party's "official" history—by asking:"how much attention does an organisation whose official membership never exceeded 56,000 actually merit?" Fielding then went on to accuse the book of unwarranted "self-importance," given that it was dealing with a party that, even at its most successful,"remained a marginal force," and recommended a posture of "humility"; after all, he asked, "how different would Britain have been without the CPGB?"[2] For most of its existence, including the period when it was a genuinely revolutionary organization, the CPGB had considerably fewer members than the 56,000 it achieved during the Second World War: 4,000 at the beginning in 1920, 4,742 at the end in 1991.[3] The numbers do not tell the whole story and to suggest that it would have made no or little difference whether or not the CPGB had existed suggests, at the very least, rather limited knowledge of the British labor movement. For better or worse, sometimes for better *and* worse, the CPGB was never irrelevant.

For this reason alone, the late Neil Rafeek's posthumously published book, *Communist Women in Scotland*, is of considerable interest to anyone concerned with attempts to build left-wing organizations outside the Labour Party. Based on his PhD thesis, the first to be awarded for oral history at the University of Strathclyde, Rafeek's book is constructed around interviews with forty-one, mainly female, former members of the CPGB in Scotland conducted between 1994 and 1999.[4] The resulting work covers the entire period from the party's formation in the aftermath of the Russian Revolution to its final self-immolation in 1992, following the collapse of the regimes in Eastern Europe and the Soviet Union. The main chronological focus is, however, on the period following the Second World War, an emphasis no doubt partly determined by the availability of surviving interviewees, but also the result of a conscious choice by Rafeek, who saw this period in the party's history as having been "undervalued," a judgment that he hoped to overturn on the basis of material "which reveals, in Scotland at least, the extent to which the party was still active and in some areas very relevant."[5] Rafeek's point is valid, since this foreshortening of the CPGB's period of influence continues unabated. In his recent biography of Hamish Henderson, for example, Timothy Neat writes of how in 1959 his hero was "delighted to be invited to become a member of the Fife Socialist League," while the CPGB, to which he had hitherto belonged, "floundered into obscurity."[6] At the very least judgments of this sort read back later developments onto a period to which they are inapplicable. Nevertheless, a proper acknowledgment that the CPGB continued to be an important component of socialist politics in Scotland well into the postwar period does not mean this period was when the organization exercised its greatest positive influence. As we shall see, Rafeek's essentially uncritical attitude to orthodox Communism and his acceptance of its own self-image means that he has no sense that the CPGB might have become a different *kind* of party in 1951 than it was in 1921. I will return to these issues below, but it is important to state first that, whatever criticisms may be leveled at it, the book is important for two reasons.

First, as I have already suggested, Rafeek reminds us of how important the CPGB was as part of the labor movement, not only nor even mainly in great set-piece trade union struggles, but in myriad small-scale types of local activity in which the "Communist women" that form his subject were more likely to participate. One episode in which female party activists played a major role, for example, was in campaigning for better screening procedures for cervical cancer in the 1950s and 1960s—the type of unglamorous but essential activity that extended welfare provision from below, but that would not have been as effective without the involvement of politically conscious activists that the CPGB supplied in numbers quite disproportionate to the size of the organization.[7] Rafeek is therefore correct to rhetorically inquire: "Had the CP not existed one might wonder how many reforms attributed to action by the labour movement would have been achieved."[8] What he also brings out strongly in relation to this kind of activity is the way in which members of the CPGB were embedded in their local communities, at least until the 1960s. This is one reason why the influence of the CPGB in Scotland went far beyond those who agreed with all its politics. William McIlvanney, for example, testified to this when he wrote, in the year of the organization's demise, that "Scottish Communism has remained its own animal, less bear than beast of social burden, helping hurt lives in the small ways that it could, given its continuously enfeebled state." And, in relation to its members, McIlvanney spoke for many others in saying: "Disagreeing with their theory, I have found myself time and time again replenished by their practice and renewed in my belief in a more habitable vision of the future."[9]

Second, the book also provides a permanent testament to several generations of mainly working-class female activists whose recollections of their political experience would otherwise have remained unheard by anyone outside their immediate circles. What is immediately striking, from the perspective of the early twenty-first century, is how some forms of socialist activity remain essentially the same today, even with the advance of electronic communication.[10] Take, for example, the eternal staple activity of every revolutionary: Selling the Paper. Mary Docherty recalls how "we used to go canvassing for the *Daily Worker* nearly every Saturday or we organized areas to sell the *Daily Worker* and we had members of the party that went out on a regular Saturday round with extra papers on a Saturday."[11] A similar approach, prioritizing personal rather than public sales, was taken with publications specifically produced for women: "You went from *door to door*, it's a lot simpler in a small village going from door to door; you know people physically, it's not as hard as in the city running up and down tenements, and you go down a street in no time, unless you blethered of course, which happened pretty often, and we used to sell about 100 *Women Today* for instance, which was the party publication at the time."[12] Beyond any particular forms of activity, the sense of "the party" as a self-contained "virtual" community in its own right, emphasized by many of those interviewed here, is one that even today members of any organization to the left of the Labour Party will recognize. There is continuity then; but what has changed is equally striking. The cultural context in which many of Rafeek's interviewees became involved in politics—those belonging to the earliest generations in particular—has completely disappeared. The world in which Socialist Sunday Schools, the Clarion Scouts, or the Woodcraft Folk were mass working-class organizations, and formed a common background not only for members of the groups that initially formed the CPGB but also for the Independent Labour Party (ILP), now seem almost unimaginably distant.[13] Yet despite the book's undoubted usefulness as a documentary record, the fundamental organizing concepts around which Rafeek structured his book—the distinctiveness of being Scottish, the specific experience of women, and the politics of Communism—all reveal problems with his approach.

Rafeek criticizes Pamela Graves for ignoring what is specific to Scotland in a book (*Labour Women*) supposedly dedicated to the British experience as a whole. It is not clear to me, however, that his book engages with this subnational dimension either, other than by setting geographical limits to his interview base.[14] Interesting aspects of this theme emerge from the testimony of his interviewees but are largely left unexplored. One of these concerns the level of regional unevenness *within* Scotland, particularly in cultural terms. It is clear from comments by Aberdonian members of the party that they regarded their Glaswegian comrades as expressing attitudes that the former found overbearing and arrogant. The Aberdonians go on to explain these contrasts, in admirably materialist terms, as arising from the fact that the working class was longer established, more highly industrialized, and more confident of its organizational strength in the Southwest than the Northeast, where workers were still often second- or even first-generation migrants from the countryside.[15]

More significant perhaps, but completely untouched by Rafeek, is the tension between the Scots as a whole and the English. Yet this was an issue, as the Scottish writer Jackie Kay recalls in another collection based on the experiences of the generations brought up in Communist families: "Scottish Communists didn't identify with England: even with English party members, they would be criticised for thinking London was the centre of the universe. The London party was thought to be very chauvinistic."[16] What is more puzzling is the absence of any discussion of the party's attitude to what has successively been described as "home rule," "self-government," and "devolution," even though the CPGB supported the establishment of a Scottish Parliament from the turn of the century to the Popular Front in the mid-thirties onward.[17] It could be argued that this has nothing particularly to do with the Communist women who are his main subject; but Rafeek devotes a chapter to Communist attitudes toward the Soviet Union and its satellites, and there is nothing gender-specific about that subject either. In particular, devolution became a central demand after the work-in at Upper Clyde Shipbuilders in 1971–72, an episode to which Rafeek rightly devotes several pages of discussion but says nothing on this aspect.[18]

This omission may be because the subject raises several difficult questions concerning Communist policy. One long-standing criticism of the CPGB (to which the present author subscribes) is that it consistently embraced what might be called "lower-case" Scottish nationalism to the detriment of the labor movement, in two respects. One was to give priority to a Popular Front politics of pan-national "class alliances" over strike action whenever faced with any major industrial crisis, such as a plant closure. The other was that, even in situations where industrial action proved unavoidable, the arguments against closures or job losses tended to be framed in terms of the defense of "Scotland's industries" or "Scotland's jobs."[19] The disastrous consequences of this were most starkly apparent during the Miners' Strike of 1984–85, a dispute that Rafeek rightly sees as crucial in setting the context for subsequent working-class politics. "Unfortunately for the mining communities and labour movement, the dispute ended in defeat for the strike and wholesale rundown of the mining industry."[20] All true, but one of the reasons for the defeat was that, at a crucial point in the dispute, when the case was made by striking miners for mass picketing to close down Ravenscraig Steelworks, members of the CPGB with positions in both the National Union of Mineworkers and the Iron and Steel Trades Confederation opposed the strategy on the grounds that this might cause long-term damage to "Scotland's steel industry," when it should have been obvious that if the miners did not win, the steel industry would follow the coal industry into oblivion—which is of course what happened within a decade.

Insofar as a distinctive aspect to CPGB politics in Scotland emerges from these interviews, it is that the Scots were generally more accepting of the leadership positions. Susan Galloway, a member of the Young Communist League from Manchester, described the political divisions within the CPGB in England from the 1970s as essentially falling along class lines, with the Eurocommunists being "professional, middle class, academic" and the "Marxist-Leninists" with whom she aligned herself being "trade union communists and the working class." In Scotland, however, where the class composition of the party was far more weighted toward the working class, there was still support for the Eurocommunist-dominated Executive Committee, but for different reasons: "You had the phenomena of the party loyalists, large sections of the party who were working class and they just didn't accept the political developments there had been in the party and they saw it was important to be loyal to the executive committee and that was their view and for a long, long time, even when there was expulsions and everything, they stuck to that position."[21] This account is not particularly flattering to the CPGB in Scotland, particularly when we learn, from Rafeek himself, that Scotland "was a party district whose delegates at congresses customarily supported the party executive, usually unanimously, and were placed where all delegates could see them."[22] Tom Nairn once wrote: "Just as there was no Old Tory like a Scotch Old Tory, so there would be no Gladstonian Liberal like a Scotch one, no Imperialist like the North British variety, and no Labourite like the Glasgow Faithfuls."[23] It would appear that there was no Stalinist like a Scottish Stalinist either—although, as we shall see, Rafeek refuses the term.

To what extent then was the fact of gendered difference significant to female members of the CPGB, at least insofar as they saw themselves as Communists? In other words, is the entire category of "Communist women" misleading? Rafeek himself writes: "I need to emphasise that the women I interviewed did not see gender and the role of women as a reason to join the CP. . . . Their primary aim was to fight for socialism. Although some might have felt gender constraints, they were really interested in a collective approach to the class struggle and building the CP into the vanguard party in Britain."[24] Rafeek sees the lack of direct engagement with what was known as "the women question" as largely positive, although occasionally his comments reveal some of the underlying tensions: "Although some [women] may have been disappointed by the inflexibility in family difficulties and women's domestic responsibility, this era also reflects the united stand behind party policy and the common goal of socialism that came before all else."[25] What did "family difficulties" and "domestic responsibility" involve? On the basis of his own evidence, it was that women generally had to carry out their social roles as wives, mothers, and carers in addition to party activity, but that even the latter tended to involve the necessary but less political aspects of Communist life—quite literally making tea and sandwiches in some cases. As Rafeek puts it with rather excessive restraint: "Although fund raising was hugely important for the party, there seemed to be an over reliance on women members to do the most mundane and, as far as political results were concerned, less rewarding tasks."[26] Only those women who were unmarried escaped the double burden. Mary Park, for example, is quoted as saying:

> I never saw any reason to become involved in women's politics; to me it was the political situation and what needed to be done and how we could advance to a better socialist system of society. . . . I probably should have been more involved in the women's side of things, but I just accepted that I was an equal part of the organization and at that time I didn't have children and I wasn't tied down, I was free to do whatever I wanted to do. . . . [27]

Rafeek notes that women did not suddenly become aware of their oppression in the 1960s, with the advent of the modern women's liberation movement; they were aware, but that awareness was subordinated to the need for socialism. "From the developing feminist viewpoint, the argument 15 years later was the other way round: there could be no change towards socialism until all communists recognised the need to end discrimination in the party."[28] Two points need to be made here. First, if the following comments made by Katy Campbell are more generally applicable, then the women-only debates opened up under the impact of the women's movement of the 1970s were a genuinely liberating experience for women members; this in turn suggests that they had been less satisfied with their situation than Rafeek claims. Campbell recalls that "*everybody* spoke but *everybody*, I mean people you never heard open their mouths at party meetings. So interesting and so much of it reflective, I mean years of reflection coming out about life in general in the world that the party men would never hear."[29]

Second, while it is certainly the case that the issue of sexual inequality within the party became a live issue at this time, the dividing line politically went deeper than this. By the early 1980s, the key argument, advocated by Beatrice Campbell among others, was that the achievement of socialism would not in itself liberate women and that, along with the end of racism and other forms of oppression, it had to be fought for as a separate if related goal. As with the national question, the key issue here is political: how was it that, once the question of women's liberation was no longer possible to avoid, the alternative to treating it as a second-order "after socialism" issue was the adoption of essentially bourgeois feminist positions.

This takes us, finally, to the core politics of the CPGB, the subject upon which Rafeek maintains his deepest silence. This is not a Scottish, or British, issue. The inescapable context for any discussion of the CPGB, the factor without which there would have been no Communist Party in Great Britain or anywhere else, is the Russian Revolution and the destiny of the state that emerged out of it. The CPGB perished in the same year as the Soviet Union, and this, to use an expression well known to readers of the party's literature, Is No Accident. At this point anyone reviewing a book about the CPGB (or any other Communist party) has to declare their position. Put bluntly, the attitude one takes to the overall politics of the CPGB as an organization will depend on the attitude one takes to the Soviet Union and the Communist International. In partic-ular, it depends on whether one believes that during the 1920s these in-stitutions either preserved or reversed the achievements of 1917, whether they maintained or abandoned Leninist politics. My own position is that by 1928 at the latest, the Stalinist bureaucracy had effectively led a counter-revolution that in terms of content had destroyed every element of socialism in the Soviet Union while retaining continuity with 1917 only in terms of the outward forms of observance. Connoisseurs of the British left will recognize in this the position associated with the Inter-national Socialist tradition. Early on in his book Rafeek makes clear that he has no time for Trotskyist criticisms of any sort, however unorthodox, as can be seen from his comment on the histories of the CPGB by Bronstein and Richardson, Dewar, Woodhouse and Pearce, and other Trotskyists: "These histories justify the Trotskyite line yet fail to acknowledge the CPGB's achievements, most notably why it still managed to attract politically conscious workers in noticeable numbers compared with the comparative (even absolute) failure of other left-wing parties that espoused revolutionary politics."[30] Rafeek then goes on to quote Kevin Morgan on the motivations behind membership of the CPGB and the complexity of the allegiances that it involved—issues about which Trotskyists were allegedly either ignorant or uninterested.[31]

This is a caricature, of course. A common position among most Trotskyists of whatever variety is that the formation of the CPGB was a major step forward for the revolutionary left in Britain, overcoming the fragmentation that had formerly existed among groups like the British Socialist Party and the Socialist Labour Party, as well as the combination of sectarian and propagandist tactics that characterized their politics. But even in relation to the period after the CPGB ceased to be a revolutionary organization, it should be clear from this review that I recognize and respect the commitment and activism of the membership; no one joined the CPGB for a quiet life or a position of bureaucratic security, when they could instead realistically expect to be jailed, blacklisted, witchhunted, or subject to the attention of the security services.[32] The point is not the personal integrity of the members but the political degeneration of their organization—unavoidable when the ideal of socialist society it upheld was in reality a murderous bureaucratic dictatorship based on systematic repression of the working class, slave labor, and national oppression of minority peoples.

Much recent writing on the CPGB by sympathetic academics, a body of work to which Rafeek's book belongs, has claimed on the one hand that the CPGB reflected native British socialist traditions and on the other that it operated more independently of Moscow than is usually thought. Rafeek, for example, refers to membership disagreement with the Nazi-Soviet Pact of 1939 as an importance example of dissidence before the greater upheavals caused by Khrushchev's Secret Speech and the suppression of the Hungarian Revolution.[33] The first claim can be sustained, although, mutatis mutandis, it could be made of all the Communist parties. It was not, however, unequivocally positive since the emphasis on national traditions all too often collapsed into a form of left nationalism (discussed above in relation to Scotland) that was actively encouraged by the Communist International following the turn to the Popular Front in 1935. Neither does it necessarily support the claims for independence from Moscow, which are unsustainable, at least before the late 1960s by which point the leadership of the CPSU no longer required the unquestioning obedience of its "sister" parties. Individual members had always had personal sticking points when some new outrage, often involving Russian foreign policy, brought an accumulation of discontents to a head and made continued membership impossible. These occurred both before and after 1956 and in Scotland involved figures as important as Harry McShane, but the leadership of the party and the bulk of the membership accepted them. Formed in the context of the Russian Revolution, shaped by the shifting balance of power with the Russian party and state, the CPGB could not have escaped the degeneration that befell them during the 1920s without breaking with Stalinism. This interpretation of the fate of the Communist parties is not, incidentally, exclusive to Trotskyism, but one that was shared by many other socialists who remained unconvinced by the Stalinist myth. In the late 1930s, Franz Borkenau, a member of the Communist Party of Germany between 1921 and 1929, wrote an important history of the Communist International, from an essentially social democratic viewpoint, in which he identified three periods in its development: the first (1919–1923) in which it was a genuine revolutionary organization; the second (1923–1928) by which time it had become an extension of the faction struggle within the CPSU; and a third (1928–1943) by which time it had been turned into a component of Russian foreign policy.[34]

How did the interests of Russian foreign policy affect CPGB activity? Rafeek mentions detailed critical discussions of CPGB's industrial policy during the Second World War, which was to support the British and, by extension, the Russian war effort, but fails to say what the nature of that criticism is, let alone attempt to answer it. There were, for example, two important wartime strikes in Glasgow about equal pay for women engineers, one at Rolls Royce at Hillingdon and the other at Barr and Stroud at Anniesland. In relation to the first, Rafeek recounts the experience of Agnes MacLean, a leading figure in the action: "Despite recent attempts to paint a more cynical and derogatory view of the CP in Scotland during the war, Agnes McLean had no doubts about why she came to join it." Rafeek quotes McLean: "I found that the people who were ready to support the women and back them and stand by them and never let them down were Communist Party members." Rafeek adds: "It was during the industrial action that Agnes and her colleagues received full support from communists."[35]

Things were, however, more rather more complex than this picture of unambiguous backing suggests. In an article that Rafeek dismisses without actually discussing, the late Peter Bain notes the overall context of CP policy:

> The CP had resolutely opposed strikes since the Nazi invasion of the Soviet Union in June 1941, and with a claimed membership of 600–700 in the Scottish Rolls-Royce factories, Party members filled many leading union positions and controlled Hillington's negotiating committee. Thus, no doubt sincere support for improving women's wages was constrained by an overriding commitment to attain advances without recourse to strikes. Whilst this was the "Party line" inevitably this led to internal tensions. For example, Hillington convenor Andrew McElroy was reported to have resigned from the CP after the defeat of his motion to financially support the C2 block strikers in August. . . . During the strike a CP leaflet called for a return to work on the basis of the steward's proposals and the AEU call to speed up the negotiating machinery.[36]

A similar contradictory position, which ultimately emphasized the need to curtail the action before all the women's demands were met, characterized the Anniesland strike: "The Communist Party also leafleted the Anniesland plant to urge an immediate end to the strike, and it was a CP member who moved the return to work. The *Daily Worker* first mentioned the dispute on December 29th (the strike started on December 11th), and devoted a total of only around 300 words in three brief factual reports during the month the women were on strike."[37] The differences of interpretation over this episode suggest one of the inherent dangers of oral history, which Rafeek does not always overcome. The necessary desire to allow the speaker to register his or her memory of events without prompting by the historian can lead, where the memories are not at least compared with other accounts that might contradict them, to an unreflective acceptance of their testimony as the truth: did the CP argument for going back to work constitute "full support"? It clearly did not for everyone involved in the Hillington strike. The fact that Rafeek was predisposed to uncritically accept Agnes MacLean's version means that he does not inquire whether it was (for example) retrospectively informed by her subsequent lifelong membership of the Communist Party and a valedictory desire to emphasize the positive role it played in the labor movement.

Throughout, Rafeek is hostile to other left parties and groups outside the Labour Party, and although he does not quote his interviewees on the subject, there is no reason to suspect that the majority would disagree with his views. There were certainly was no credible alternatives to the CPGB until very late in the period covered by his book. As Rafeek writes: "After the war CP members were able to look at various ultra-left groups that seemed eternally anti-Soviet and whose undistinguished impact suggested the CP must be doing *something* right, for it remained the largest party to the left of the Labour Party."[38] And even after 1956, which saw the first major wave of resignations from the party, rival left groups did not immediately gain memberships beyond the hundreds at best and tens in the case of most. Rafeek notes of the failure of the Fife Socialist League, the one wholly Scottish New Left organization, to establish itself on a permanent basis: "There was no room in British politics for an organised political alternative to fit between the Labour Party's social democracy and the CP's radical Marxism."[39] But this is precisely the point. Particularly after 1968, the idea that the CPGB represented "radical Marxism" was increasingly regarded as a joke outside its own ranks, except among employees of MI5 or leader columnists for the *Scottish Daily Express*. Members of the CPGB were of course still to the left of mainstream Labour politics. A revealing episode is recalled by Alice Milne in which the sainted Donald Dewar, lobbied by members of the Aberdeen Peace Committee about the Vietnam War, is as evasive and patronizing toward them as he is deferential and exculpatory toward the United States.[40] But although the CPGB and the Labour Party stood on opposite sides of the Cold War, in terms of domestic politics, the former was much closer to the latter than it was to, say, the Vietnam Solidarity Campaign (VSC), which was dominated by the despised "ultra-left," and it was the groups inside VSC that were attracting the young.

Rafeek tacitly recognizes the way in which the focus for left activity began to slip away from the CPGB, but only in relation to the great industrial struggles of the early 1970s: "The denouement for the establishment must have been a fear of union militancy seeping through to young minds, which it did to the extent that even the CP was seen as slightly old hat."[41] In a collection of interviews with mainly Scottish women conducted in the mid-1970s, Jean McCrindle and Sheila Rowbotham found that those born during the Second World War, and for whom the Labour Party was intolerable, now had a range of organizational alternatives beyond the CPGB, either in Trotskyist groups like the International Socialists or in broader campaigns like those of the women's liberation movement.[42] In effect, these took over the type of activity that used to be dominated by the CPGB, as was recognized by many former members who gravitated to their campaigns. But for many older former members no party could take the place of the CPGB. Jean McCrindle herself expresses the views of that generation in an interview with Rafeek: "The party was our life, it really was. I've never experienced politics again like that except in the women's movement actually, when it becomes your life again. But as a political party I've never had that again."[43]

But it is also important to realize that this was not true of everyone with this history. In his autobiographical account of the campaign against the poll tax during the late 1980s, Tommy Sheridan recalls that some of the people who took part had been involved in Communist politics:

> Jack Jardine raved about these meetings. He said it reminded him of his childhood in Govan. A communist called Peter McIntyre held big meetings from the fountain of the cross. . . . Jack himself was a leader of the apprentices' strike which began on Clydeside in 1952 when he was seventeen. . . . The Young Communist League leafleted for the strike and one of its members, Jimmy Reid, was a spokesman on the committee. . . . One of the first people elected on our committee was Meg Callaghan . . . a Rolls Royce widow. As it turned out, she had been brought up in the ILP. She remembers marching beside Manny Shinwell and Jimmy Maxton as a child. Her parents sent her to Socialist Sunday School. . . . There were lots of people like Meg across Pollock who saw this as a reminder of the radicalism of their youth. Grace Moran, then a forty-year-old cleaner, was one of the names on our phone tree. She's soft-spoken and describes herself as not wanting to go to extremes. It turned out she had been a member of the Young Communist League in her teens.[44]

Some indication that former Communists did not simply mourn their old organization but got involved in new forms of activity whose inspiration lay elsewhere would have undermined the elegiac mood, but might also have indicated that, important though the CPGB was as a mobilizing force, its passing has not left the gap that his interviewees claim. This also suggests a broader point, which is that just as books dealing with the history of the Labour Party cannot ignore the impact of the Communist Party on its members, particularly in relation to trade union activity, neither can books about the CPGB ignore the way in which the revolutionary left after 1968 was able to successfully attract people who would previously have been drawn to it.

When the CPGB voted to transform itself into the Democratic Left in November 1991 it was already a historical relic, of direct significance mainly to an older generation of activists. As Jackie Kay comments: "It is not a loss for our generation in the same way but I do feel it is very sad on my parents' behalf."[45] Although other works drawing on interviews have since appeared, we will increasingly have to rely on written sources.[46] We should therefore be grateful that Rafeek captured the memories of these party members while it was still possible. It would have been perhaps expecting too much for someone so much in sympathy with the politics of his subjects to provide a critical account, but as a source book and testament *Communist Women in Scotland* will be of lasting value.

Eric Hobsbawm's Unanswered Question[1]

INTRODUCTION

Eric Hobsbawm is now the only survivor of an entire generation of British Marxist historians born in the second and third decades of the twentieth century. The roll-call of those who have predeceased him gives some indication of the extraordinary range of talent involved: George Rudé and Edward Thompson (both died 1993), Geoffrey de Ste. Croix (2000), Rodney Hilton (2002), Christopher Hill (2003), Brian Manning (2004), Victor Kiernan and John Saville (both 2009).[2] Yet, remarkably for someone born in the same year as the Russian Revolution, Hobsbawm has only recently given up public speaking and he is still regularly sought out by the British media for commentary on current affairs, most recently on the Arab Spring.[3] Nevertheless, it is likely that his latest collection, boldly entitled *How to Change the World*, will be his last. Appropriately enough it deals with the subject of Marxism itself and provides us with the opportunity to assess his own relationship to it, which has been far from straightforward.

For Hobsbawm, as for Hill, Hilton, Kiernan, Saville, and Thompson, the roles of Communist Party militant and Marxist intellectual were originally inseparable. Unlike these contemporaries, they remained so:

301

he retained his membership of the Communist Party of Great Britain (CPGB) almost until the organization dissolved itself following the collapse of the Stalinist regimes in 1989–91. Hobsbawm has written that his Marxism "was, and to some extent still remains, that acquired from the only texts then easily available outside university libraries, the systematically distributed works and selections of 'the classics' published (and translated in heavily subsidised local editions) under the auspices of Marx-Engels Institute in Moscow."[4] Despite this declaration, Hobsbawm's Marxism, at least as expressed in his historical works, has never been confined by the mechanical formulae of Stalinist orthodoxy, which may explain why—as he has noted with evident pique more than once—his historical works were not translated into Russian nor, Hungarian and Slovenian apart, into the majority of the other Eastern European languages until after the fall of the Berlin Wall.[5] Hobsbawm has argued that for several reasons the general approach of the Historians Group of the CPGB was not as marked by "dogmatism" as it might have been: outside of contemporary political issues that potentially conflicted with the views of the party leadership there were genuine attempts to explore historical issues; in the case of British history there was in any case no particular line; and group members specifically attempted to connect their work as Marxists with analysis of earlier radical traditions.[6] Nevertheless, he candidly acknowledged the personal constraints imposed on his own work:

> I myself became essentially a nineteenth-century historian, because I soon discovered—actually in the course of an aborted project of the CP Historians' Group to write a history of the British labor movement—that, given the strong official Party and Soviet views about the twentieth century, one could not write about anything later than 1917 without the likelihood of being denounced as a political heretic. I was ready to write about the century in a political or public capacity, but not as a professional historian. My history finished at Sarajevo in June 1914.[7]

Yet in two of his most substantial late works, *Age of Extremes* (1994) and now this new collection, Hobsbawm has become precisely what he once denied himself from being—a historian of the twentieth century. But as the evasions and refusals of these texts reveal, there remain limits to Hobsbawm's capacity to deal with certain historical periods and problems that were not simply the result of bureaucratic fiat, but his own personal political beliefs.

TREATING CAPITALISM AS A TOTALITY

Before turning to these issues it may be worth reminding ourselves of the methodological strengths of Hobsbawm's Marxism, for it is one of the paradoxes of his career that, the legacy of Stalinism notwithstanding, Hobsbawm has remained more aligned with the classical Marxist tradition than comparably famous historians like Hill and Thompson who shared his formative Communist background. Thompson in fact makes an interesting comparison. It is not necessary to be a Marxist to produce important historical work, of course, as the names Bloch, Braudel, or Ginzburg testify, and this is also the case with Thompson. Although his work was explicitly informed by a socialist identification with the oppressed and exploited there is little distinctively Marxist about his theoretical framework, even in *The Making of the English Working Class*. This is frustrating, because "The Peculiarities of the English," one of the few works where he did attempt to marry his own deep historical knowledge with an explicit Marxist theoretical position, is one of the greatest historical essays written in Britain since the Second World War. Thompson's individual talents took him very far without a firm theoretical basis, but given the absence of those talents among most of his followers (Peter Linebaugh is the main exception), his influence has been catastrophic.[8] Unlike Thompson, Hobsbawm refused to abandon his membership of the CPGB after 1956. This decision can be politically criticized on a number of levels, but it was accompanied, in his case, with the retention of some of the fundamental Marxist propositions that Thompson came to dismiss.

It is sometimes argued that his classicism is primarily demonstrated by his adherence to the base-superstructure metaphor.[9] It would be more accurate to say that Hobsbawm accepts that the relationship between the social organization of production and other aspects of human life that is encapsulated in the metaphor is the necessary starting point for understanding history; he has never regarded it as a *substitute* for doing so.[10] The format of the individual volumes in his quartet on the history of capitalism may appear superficially comparable to those conventional historical surveys that conclude with perfunctory chapters on culture or the arts, the leftovers that can be dealt with once more important economic and political matters have been dealt with. In fact, Hobsbawm did something quite different: consciously structuring his work to ascend from those aspects of human life most immediately involved in the material reproduction of society to those concerned with its ideological representation, and these different moments are not autonomous from each other but linked through a series of mediations. Indeed, what distinguishes Hobsbawm as a Marxist historian is his insistence—usually implicit, since he rarely engages in theoretical muscle-flexing in his substantive works—that capitalism and earlier class societies form a totality that is ever present no matter how microscopic the aspect that the historian may subject to scrutiny.[11] This insistence has manifested itself in his work in two particularly important ways.

One is that since capitalism emerged as a system, which for Hobsbawm was signaled by the crisis of the seventeenth century, it has been international in character.[12] Hobsbawm had very little time for Trotsky or his ideas, so there is a certain irony in the fact that his historical work has always been guided by a perspective similar to that of the latter, which treated capitalist world economy not simply as the sum total of its individual component nation-states but as possessing an influential existence in its own right. One of the pleasures of reading the *Age* quartet in sequence is the way in which the reader can follow the expanding geographical boundaries of capitalism as the project unfolds, from the essentially European setting of *The Age of Revolution* through to the truly global reach of *Age of Extremes.*

The other is that lives of the exploited and oppressed cannot be understood in isolation from those of the people who are exploiting and oppressing them. This may seem obvious, but even though Hobsbawm is rightly regarded with Rudé as one of the founders of "history from below" his work has never involved the kind of social history that is concerned simply with exploring the texture of everyday experience. Endless repetition of Thompson's expressed desire to "rescue the poor stockinger, the Luddite cropper, the 'obsolete' hand-loom weaver, the 'utopian' artisan, and even the deluded follower of Joanna Southcott from the enormous condescension of history" has obscured the fact that, in hands other than those of Thompson or similarly committed writers, there is nothing specifically Marxist or even necessarily left wing about this approach.[13]

Indeed, it can often simply involve a kind of microscopic antiquarianism about what Thomas Gray memorably called "the short and simple annals of the poor."[14] Hobsbawm has never been interested in this kind of history from below, but has focused instead on actual movements—no matter how apparently eccentric or removed from the mainstream of labor history—such as the millenarian sects and social bandits he investigated in the 1950s and 1960s.[15] And he never regarded these movements in isolation, but in relation to the social forces to which they were opposed: for Hobsbawm totality necessarily involves history from above, as much as from below, even if it is the subjects of the latter that claim our retrospective sympathy or solidarity.

We turn to *How to Change the World* then to find some insight into the Marxism that has inspired his achievements as a historian. The book is highly uneven in terms of both style and quality, as is likely to be the case with any collection spanning fifty-three years (the earliest piece dates from 1957, the latest from 2010) and drawn from quite disparate sources. The sixteen chapters break down as follows: six contributions to the Italian book series *Storia del Marxismo*—only three of which have previously appeared in English—and a previously unpublished further chapter ("Marxism in Recession, 1983–2000") apparently conceived as a coda to these; three introductions to works by Marx and/or Engels; five selections from journals or edited collections; and one lecture. But contrary to the book's subtitle, these are very much tales of Marx (and Engels) rather than of Marxism. The second part of the book, devoted to the latter subject, deals with it in very general terms indeed and, as Hobsbawm himself notes: "The only post–Marx/Engels Marxist specifically discussed in this book is Antonio Gramsci."[16] The problems with the second half of the book, at least in the sections dealing with the period after 1914, are not however simply their lack of specificity, nor are they a result of the unevenness typical of essay collections; but of the conflict between Hobsbawm's historical materialism and his Stalinism.

The first part of *How to Change the World*, on "Marx and Engels," is by far the stronger. The greatest and longest essay reproduced here as chapter 7, which alone would justify the appearance of this collection, is Hobsbawm's introduction to extracts from the *Grundrisse* ("Pre-capitalist Economic Formations"), first published in 1964–65. Here, he not only delineates the trajectory of Marxist theory but also makes his own contribution to it. The notoriously elliptical form of Marx's notebooks has given rise to multiple and often mutually inconsistent interpretations; but Hobsbawm's, perhaps the earliest to appear in English, remains one of the most convincing. Hobsbawm writes of "Marx's refusal to separate the different academic disciplines," noting:

> Such mechanical divisions are misleading, and entirely contrary to Marx's method. It was the bourgeois academic economists who attempted to draw a sharp line between static and dynamic analysis, hoping to transform the one into the other by injecting some "dynamising" element into the static system, just as it is the academic economists who still work out a neat model of "economic growth," preferably expressible in equations, and relegate all that does not fit into the province of the "sociologists." The academic sociologists make similar distinctions on a rather lower level of scientific interest, the historians on an even humbler one. But this is not Marx's way. The social relations of production (i.e. social organisation in its broadest sense) and the material forces of production, to which they correspond, cannot be divorced.

The warning that "Marx must not be divided up into segments according to the academic specialisations of our time" is well made, since these are artificial and arbitrary, and encourage an understanding of the world that is fragmentary and incoherent.[17] The fact that it is regularly ignored by Marxist intellectuals is at least partly due to the fact that, as Hobsbawm notes in another essay reproduced here, since the Second World War they—or perhaps I should say, we—have operated largely in an academic context where identification with a specific discipline is virtually a condition of employment, ritual genuflections toward multi- or inter-disciplinarity notwithstanding.[18] Marx himself may have emphasized certain aspects of the social world rather than others, but the latter are, as it were, merely off-stage for the duration, their presence still felt in the action, not relegated to a different performance altogether. Hobsbawm adhered to this approach. It is difficult, reading his books and essays, to say at which point the historian has given way to the anthropologist (*Primitive Rebels*), the historical sociologist ("Revolution"), the social geographer ("Labor in the Great City"), or the cultural critic (*Behind the Times*).

More substantively, Hobsbawm in the same chapter deals sensibly with the claim that Marx believed in a universal succession of more advanced societies, each based on a more complex mode of production, as supposedly outlined in the 1857 Preface to *A Contribution to the Critique of Political Economy*. In fact, as Hobsbawm points out: "The statement that the Asiatic, ancient, feudal and bourgeois formations are 'progressive' does not ... imply any simple unilinear view of history, nor a simple view that all history is progress. It merely states that each of these systems is in crucial respects further removed from the primitive state of man."[19] Seen in this way, the only universal transition is from primitive communism to the various forms of pre-capitalist class society: "Feudalism appears to be an *alternative* evolution out of primitive communism, under conditions in which no cities develop, because the density of population over a large region is too low."[20] But feudalism was the only mode of production whose own internal contradictions, as opposed to external pressures, have led to the emergence of capitalism. That there would be a *further* universal transition, namely from capitalism to socialism, would have been axiomatic for Hobsbawm in the mid-1960s; as we shall see, this is no longer the case.

Hobsbawm's admiration for the *Grundrisse* does not lead him to claim that Marxism remained an incomplete project until the notebooks were written, or even later. In a chapter originally published as an introduction to the "Manifesto of the Communist Party" he points out that, in economic terms at least, "Marx wrote the *Manifesto* less as a Marxian economist than as a communist Ricardian." But, contrary to the position upheld in different ways by both Althusserians and Political Marxists, he argues that in most other respects historical materialism was essentially established as an explanation for transformative social change by 1848: "Unlike Marxian economics, the 'materialist conception of history' which underlay this analysis had already found its mature formulation in the middle 1840s. It remained substantially unchanged in later years. In this respect the *Manifesto* already was a defining document of Marxism. It embodied the historical vision, though its general outline remained to be filled in by fuller analysis."[21] The study devoted to Gramsci also has many thought-provoking passages. As with Marx, Hobsbawm restores to sanity discussions that had become quite unnecessarily confused. In particular, his assessment that Gramsci did not propose a "war of position" for societies in the West as opposed to a "war of manoeuvre" in the East seems to me to be soundly based:

He did not in fact commit himself in principle to any particular outcome
of the lengthy "war of position" which he predicted and recommended.
It might lead directly into a transition to socialism, or into another phase
of the war of manoeuvre and attack, or to some other strategic phase.
What would happen, must depend on the changes in the concrete situation.... In short, the "war of position" had to be systematically thought
through as a fighting strategy rather than simply as something for revolutionaries to do when there was no prospect of building barricades.[22]

Hobsbawm treats Gramsci as someone whose thought can still inform the strategic decisions that socialists are required to make today; the
founders of historical materialism much less so.

HEIRS TO MARX?

In the chapters on Marx and Engels he is rightly concerned to historicize
his subjects and to refuse any sense that we can treat them as contemporaries from whom "lessons" can be learned about appropriate political
action. In this connection Hobsbawm claims, correctly in my view, that
it is "virtually impossible to derive from the classic writings anything like
a manual of strategic and tactical instructions, dangerous even to use them
as a set of precedents, though they have nevertheless so been used. What
could be learned from Marx was his method of facing the tasks of analysis
and action rather than ready-made lessons to be derived from classic
texts."[23] Yet at several points he takes this position so far that the reader
might doubt whether Marx and Engels had any fixed or definitive political views at all, other than supporting the formation of working-class
parties committed to socialism. Indeed, Hobsbawm explicitly argues
against any attempts to establish a Marxist tradition involving policies as
opposed to methods:

> It is . . . vain to seek in Marx for the anticipation of such later contro-
> versies as those between "reformists" and "revolutionaries," or to read
> his writings in the light of the subsequent debates between right and
> left in the Marxist movement. . . . The issue for Marx was not whether
> labor parties were reformist or revolutionary, or even what these terms
> implied. He recognised no conflict in principle between the everyday
> struggle of the workers for the improvement of their conditions under
> capitalism and the formation of a political consciousness which envisaged
> the replacement of capitalist by socialist society, or the actions which led

to this end. . . . It is an anachronism to identify Marx with either a "right" or a "left," "moderate" or "radical" wing of the international or any other labor movement. Hence the irrelevance as well as the absurdity of arguments about whether Marx at any point ceased to be a revolutionary and became a gradualist.[24]

In another chapter Hobsbawm effectively turns this position on its head (although the end result is the same) by refusing to distinguish between any of Marx's successors on the grounds that *all* can claim an equally legitimate lineage:

> We should . . . reject the idea that there is a sharp difference between a "correct" and an "incorrect" Marxism. His mode of enquiry could produce different results and political perspectives. Indeed it did so with Marx himself, who envisaged a possible peaceful transition to power in Britain and the Netherlands, and the possible evolution of the Russian village community into socialism. Kautsky and even Bernstein were heirs to Marx as much (or, if you like, as little) as Plekhanov or Lenin.[25]

This is intended to be provocative, but it is in one major respect simply wrong. Earlier I agreed with Hobsbawm that that in most respects other than the economic (the dual nature of the commodity, the distinction between labor and labor power) historical materialism was a finished doctrine by the 1847–8. There is however one very important exception to this: the nature of the state and specifically that of the capitalist state. In 1848, Marx and Engels argued for the proletariat to seize control of the existing state and "wrest, by degrees, all capital from the bourgeoisie . . . centralise all production in the hands of the state, i.e. of the proletariat organised as a ruling class." Only in the future ("in the course of development"), after a period in which we have "swept away the conditions for the existence of class antagonisms and of classes generally," will we have "an association, in which the free development of each is the condition of the free development of all."[26] Their position changed again after the experience of the revolutions of 1848–9; but as Hal Draper writes of *Class Struggles in France, 1848–1850,* where this change is first registered: "This summary look into the future includes the abolition of classes but does not specifically mention elimination of the state."[27] The change in attitude to the state indicated by the Paris

Commune—"the political form at last discovered under which to work out the economical emancipation of labor"—is decisive here.[28] As Engels was later to confirm:"One thing was proved by the Commune, viz. that 'the working class cannot simply lay hold of the ready-made state machinery, and wield it for its own purposes.'"[29]

Yet Hobsbawm passes over the Paris Commune in a handful of pages without giving any sense of how fundamental the experience was in reshaping Marx and Engels's attitude to the state.[30] Insofar as Marx did believe that a peaceful transition was possible in countries like Britain and the Netherlands, it reflected a failure to consistently apply his own theoretical discovery concerning the nature of the capitalist state, not a retreat from it. In any case, over a hundred years of experience in Britain, the Netherlands and indeed everywhere else has surely demonstrated the impossibility of peaceful transitions to power. The point is that the attitude toward the state adopted by post-Marx Marxists is broadly indicative of their fidelity to his views in other respects. In this crucial respect Lenin is an heir to Marx in a way that Bernstein and the later Kautsky and Plekhanov are not.[31]

POSTREVOLUTIONARY SOCIETY

One suspects that Hobsbawm's vagueness over the nature of postrevolutionary forms of working-class rule ("whatever its precise form") is informed by the vast chasm between the character of the Paris Commune and the Russian workers' councils of 1905 and 1917 on the one hand, and the Stalinist states on the other. He obliquely alludes to the latter in a passing reference on the danger of postrevolutionary state entrenchment, but down to the early 1980s at any rate still seems to have regarded them as genuine socialist institutions.[32] It is in this context that we can see the theoretical damage that Stalinism has inflicted on his work as a historian of the twentieth century. I noted earlier that Hobsbawm treats capitalism as a totality. In relation to what he takes to be socialism, however, he abandons this position. At the end of his reflections on Gramsci, Hobsbawm lamented the way in which the Stalinist states had concentrated on economic transformation at the expense of developing "political and legal institutions, and processes": "Quite apart from the other disadvantages of this neglect of politics, how can we expect to transform human life, to create socialist *society* (as opposed to a socially owned and managed economy), when the mass of the people are excluded from the political process, and may even be allowed to drift into depoliticisation and apathy about public matters?"[33] How indeed? Seven years later, the "serious weaknesses" identified by Hobsbawm saw the mass of the people either participate in revolutions against the states from which they had been excluded or at least refuse to defend them.

The echoes of Althusser are very strong here, particularly his claims that "a revolution in the *structure* does not *ipso facto* modify the existing superstructures and particularly the *ideologies* at one blow (as it would if the economic was the *sole determinant factor*), for they have sufficient of their own consistency *to survive beyond their immediate life context,* even to recreate, to 'secrete' substitute conditions of existence temporarily."[34] I am not accusing Hobsbawm of sympathy for Althusser, a thinker for whom he has always displayed a healthy scepticism.[35] The point is rather that anyone who wishes to argue that the Stalinist states were based on a socialist economic base while simultaneously criticizing their lack of democracy is effectively forced to retreat into a non-Marxist pluralism in which any sense of mediated totality has been abandoned. Gramsci made the point in general terms in his prison notebooks: "Between the economic structure and the state with its legislation and its coercion stands civil society, and it is this latter which has to be radically transformed, in concrete terms and not just as it appears in statutes and learned books. The state is the instrument for bringing civil society into line with the economic structure, but the state has to 'want' to do that, i.e. the representatives of the change that has already come about have to be in control of the state."[36] By the late 1920s in the case of Russia and from the very beginning in the case of the other Stalinist regimes, the "representatives of the change that has come about" had brought civil society in line with the economic structure: lack of democracy was not an aberration or a residue, it was the necessary condition for accumulation and industrialization to take place under conditions of bureaucratic state capitalism. There have been times when Hobsbawm has come close to accepting this. Interviewed in the immediate aftermath of the fall of the Berlin wall, he said of the Soviet Union that it "obviously wasn't a workers' state . . . nobody in the Soviet Union ever believed it was a workers' state, and the workers knew it wasn't a workers' state."[37] In one of the most recent essays reproduced here he notes of state planning and ownership: "There is nothing exclusively socialist about this."[38] Yet this acknowledgment has not affected the sense of loss that Hobsbawm has expressed on several occasions for the collapse of the selfsame non-workers' state. How to explain this disjunction?

ASSESSMENT OF THE POPULAR FRONT

The answer, I think, lies not in what Hobsbawm thinks the Soviet Union *was,* but rather in what he believes that it *did,* above all to contribute to the victory over Fascism. "It is an elementary observation of Marxism that thinkers do not invent their ideas in the abstract," he writes in one of the essays reproduced here, "but can only be understood in the historical and political context of their times."[39] This comment, made of Gramsci, is equally applicable to its author. Hobsbawm's own historical and political context was the Popular Front against Fascism and War—broadly, 1935–1939, then 1941–45—and adherence to the politics of the Popular Front has been a constant in his politics ever since.[40] It is difficult for those born afterwards to fully appreciate, for many of those becoming socialists at that time, just how deeply the Stalinist tactics of the period became a touchstone for politics as such, almost a form of Gramscian "common sense." For this reason, Hobsbawm has always had a problem in dealing with the Popular Front as a historian.[41] What we get instead is a recycling of Stalinist propaganda, mercifully minus the accusation that contemporary dissenters were actual Fascist agents. Here, this approach is represented in a truly dreadful chapter, "In the Era of Anti-fascism, 1929–1945," central to which is the Spanish Civil War:

> What sacrifices ought revolutionaries to make in the necessary cause of rolling fascism back? Was it not conceivable that victory over fascism could be won—but at the cost of postponing the revolution, or even reinforcing non-fascist capitalism? . . . the radical element took the utopian road of denying any contradiction between anti-fascism and immediate proletarian revolution. Even those who did not reject the broad anti-fascist front altogether as an unnecessary betrayal of revolution (as Trotsky did, misled by his hostility to the Stalinist Comintern which was the main advocate of such a front), called for its conversion into insurrection at any suitable moment . . . at the time these utopian arguments carried little weight. They may even account for the isolation and lack of influence of those who propounded them, such as the Trotskyite

and other dissident Marxist groups. People who fought with their backs to the wall against the encroaching forces of fascism gave priority to the immediate struggle. If it was lost then the revolution of tomorrow—even, in Spain, the revolution of today—had no chance.

"What alternative to the communist policy of fighting the Spanish Civil War was there? Then as now the answer must be: none."[42] In fact, given that Communist policy led to total defeat in the Spanish Civil War, the only way that Hobsbawm can ascribe any success to the Popular Front is to stretch the category to include the Second World War after the entry of the USSR and the establishment of the People's Democracies in Eastern Europe and the Balkans after 1943.[43] Hobsbawm's discussion of Spain shows all too clearly the destructive influence of his politics on his historiography. First, it was not the case in Spain that the war was taking place and well-meaning but mistaken ultra-lefts were arguing for a policy of revolution that would have inadvertently obstructed or sabotaged the Republican military effort—*the revolution had already begun*, with the popular seizure of land and factories, collectivization from below, and so on; the great historic crime of the Spanish Communists and their Russian advisers was to reverse it, often though violent repression. Those who argued that the war could only be won by deepening the revolution did at any rate have one fairly important historical example on their side, that of Russia itself: "We must recall once again that if the October Revolution was able to triumph in a war of three years duration over countless enemies, including the expeditionary forces of the mightiest imperialist powers, it was only because this victory was assured above all by the fact that *during the war* the peasants had gained possession of the land while the workers held the mills and factories."[44]

Thus Trotsky, after Franco's victory in 1939; but there is no need to rely on Trotsky (whom Hobsbawm frequently criticizes, but never quotes), or his supporters, or even eyewitnesses or participants like George Orwell or Franz Borkenau. The point has been made by figures much closer to Hobsbawm's own politics. Hobsbawm is aware of the work of the Spanish Communist Fernando Claudin, whom he cites in another connection.[45] But Claudin, a leader of the Spanish Communist Youth at the time of the Civil War and subsequently a member of the PCE's Central Committee and Political Bureau until his expulsion in

1965, also conducted his own research into the role of Russia in the Civil War. His conclusion? "Stalin helped the Spanish Republic in order that it might prolong its existence and arrive at a compromise solution acceptable to the 'Western democracies,' within the framework of a system of anti-Hitlerite alliances, and not in order that it might *win*." Claudin argues that this conclusion was "forced" on him by an analysis of the facts, even though he accepts that at the time most anti-Fascists would have regarded it as a "monstrous calumny": "Subsequent events showed, nevertheless, clearly enough, that Stalin was not one to hesitate in sacrificing to *raison d'etat* not merely the possibility of revolution but an actual revolution, even when this occurred close to the Soviet frontier and there were no 'technical' difficulties in the way of supplying the aid needed to oppose imperialist intervention."[46]

CONCLUSION

Perhaps it is expecting too much of Hobsbawm to change his assessment of the Popular Front at this stage in his life: it seems to be an integral part of his—in my view, admirable—refusal to renege on his Communist beliefs in the face of neoliberal demands for recantation such as those regularly issued by the likes of Niall Ferguson.[47] His desire to establish a world of free and equal human beings is separable from his ambiguities concerning the Russian experience; but the nature of that experience cannot simply be written off as *sui generis,* as an experiment doomed to failure about which nothing can be said. Strangely perhaps, the problem emerges most acutely not in Hobsbawm's historical discussion but in his reflections on the future:

> Since the 1980s it has been evident that the socialists, Marxist or otherwise, were left without their traditional alternative to capitalism, at least unless or until they rethought what they meant by "socialism" and abandoned the presumption that the (manual) class would necessarily be the chief agent of social transformation. But the believers in the 1973–2008 *reductio ad absurdum* of market society are also left helpless. . . . Paradoxically, both sides have an interest in returning to a critique of both capitalism and the economists who failed to recognise where capitalist globalisation would lead, as predicted by him in 1848. . . . Once again the time has come to take Marx seriously.[48]

The difficulty here is that the supposed symmetry of failure between Stalinist state capitalism and neoliberal market capitalism is liable to two interpretations. One is for a return to the type of social democratic compromise typical of the advanced West during Hobsbawm's Golden Age between 1945 and 1973. Unfortunately this position has been taken by virulent enemies of Marxism and the socialist left more generally. In 2006, Tony Judt wrote "that moribund, system-building explanations of the Left may indeed be due for a revival—if only as a counterpoint to the irritating over confidence of contemporary free-marketeers of the Right." The twenty-first century is thus characterized by two fantasies. One is the "smug, irenic insistence" of the neoliberal "policy consensus," while the second "is the belief that Marxism has an intellectual and political future: not merely in spite of Communism's collapse but because of it. Hitherto found only at the international 'periphery' and in the margins of academia, this renewed faith in Marxism—at least as an analytical tool if not as a political prognostication—is now once again, largely for want of competition, the common currency of international protest movements." Both fantasies, according to Judt, result from "a common failure to learn from the past." With a classically liberal evenhandedness, Judt denounces both those who celebrate "the triumph of the market and the retreat of the state" and "those who dream of rerunning the Marxist tape, digitally remastered and free of irritating Communist scratches," who "would be well advised to ask sooner rather than later just what it is about all-embracing 'systems' of thought that leads inexorably to all-embracing 'systems' of rule."[49] In a generally warm and respectful obituary article, Hobsbawm notes both Judt's personal attacks on his own work and Judt's "essentially social democratic liberalism," but fails to grasp the central if unwelcome point of similarity with his own position.[50]

The other interpretation would involve not the synthesis of two failed models of capitalist development—failed from the perspective of the majority, that is, not that of the ruling classes—but transcendence: a resumption of the revolutionary project that so concerned Judt in his final years. Whether Hobsbawm thinks this is possible is unclear. The title of his uneven, infuriating, and sporadically brilliant book is a statement: how to change the world; but in fact it is better understood as a question, which he leaves his readers to answer.

POSTSCRIPT[51]

Eric Hobsbawm died on October 1, 2012, a little over a week after the review article of *How to Change the World* reproduced above first appeared in the Mumbai *Economic and Political Weekly*. It was obvious—as I rather tactlessly suggested in the first paragraph—that this book was likely to be his last (another volume of essays is in fact scheduled to appear in 2013).[52] Some of his right-wing critics, like Michael Burleigh, argue in their obituaries for Hobsbawm that his historical work must be rejected because of his support for the Soviet Union and the other Stalinist states.[53] Others, like Niall Ferguson, are aware that books such as *The Age of Empire* cannot simply be dismissed on a priori political grounds, but nevertheless treat his work as quite unrelated to his Marxist theory of history: from this perspective Hobsbawm may have held dangerous and objectionable views, but as a professional historian he did not, at least until his final works, allow these to seriously influence his analysis.[54]

Hobsbawm himself always argued that his historiography was inseparable from his Marxism and, indeed, only made possible by it. I argue above that he was essentially right in this judgment. For those of us on the anti-Stalinist left Hobsbawm's orthodox Communism meant that his political judgments—his extraordinarily narrow conception of the working class, for example, or his belief that nationalism could be harnessed for progressive ends—had to be treated with deep suspicion; but much of his historical writing has to be afforded a great deal more respect.

Now that his life is over and his body of work complete, it is only fair to Hobsbawm that his critical admirers take time to assess his output as a whole, free from the demands of instant assessment required by obituaries. I am confident, however, that relatively little of his serious historical output is irredeemably tainted by the political tradition to which he belonged; most of it is a lasting contribution, not only to the culture of the left, but far beyond it. And can those critics of the right who endlessly demanded that he recant the views that informed his entire life and work point to any historians with their beliefs who entered the public consciousness to anything like the same degree?

The Posthumous Adventures
of Adam Smith[1]

INTRODUCTION

On the High Street section of the Royal Mile in Edinburgh stands a statue of Adam Smith. Sculpted by Alexander Stoddard and unveiled on July 4, 2008, the only statue of the great man to be erected in the Scottish capital at first seems unexceptional—a worthy memorial to one of the great figures of the Scottish Enlightenment. It is certainly a more impressive work than the travesty of David Hume, also by Stoddard, on the other side of the High Street. Hume appears in classical garb and looking rather slimmer than contemporary memoirs and paintings of the philosopher would leave us to believe. Smith is at least represented in the costume of his age, standing in front of a scythe and sheaf of corn, symbols that rightly reflect the agricultural focus of *The Wealth of Nations*. Viewed from the back, however, the statue displays the difficulties we still face in coming to terms with Smith and his work.

On the plinth is a plaque containing the names of the subscribers who paid for the statue, the first of which is that of Dr. Eamonn Butler. In one respect this is appropriate, since the organization that he heads, the Adam Smith Institute, commissioned Stoddard to carry out the work, collected the subscriptions that paid for it, and negotiated the site with

Edinburgh City Council. But in another respect Dr. Butler's imprimatur is not appropriate at all; for the Adam Smith Institute is a body whose views bear as much resemblance to those of Smith as the views of the former Soviet Institute of Marxism-Leninism bore to those of Marx and Lenin. In both cases some phrases are brandished—a "hidden hand" here, a "dictatorship of the proletariat" there—to disguise the infidelity of these institutions to their supposed sources of inspiration.

The Adam Smith Institute (henceforth ASI) was established in 1976, the bicentenary of the publication of *The Wealth of Nations,* by Butler and two fellow-graduates of St. Andrews University, Stuart Butler and Madsen Pirie, as a think tank that would focus on developing policies that could be adopted by sympathetic governments, the type of policies we now think of as characteristic of neoliberalism.[2] At one point in 1994 the ASI ran a mock-interview with Smith from beyond the grave in which, speaking through the medium of one Edwin G. West, he called for the abolition in the United States of "minimum wages, tariffs, export subsidies, agricultural marketing boards, taxes on capital, 'free' education at government schools and the whole US system of central banking."[3] To be fair—although there is no obvious reason why we should be fair to the people responsible for devising the poll tax—the ASI is obviously aware that it is unable to use Smith as a ventriloquist's dummy for its own views in every case, so it also includes a cautionary note on its website: "While Adam Smith is our inspiration, we do not pretend that he was right about everything."[4] The issues about which Smith was wrong, one gathers, were those on which he would have disagreed with the ASI.

Jacob Viner once wrote that "an economist must have very peculiar theories indeed who cannot quote from the *Wealth of Nations* to support his special purposes."[5] There are indeed passages in Smith's work that can be used to support neoliberal conclusions, if contradictory passages and the context in which they were written are ignored. But if neoliberals are the most egregious offenders in relation to making selective and dehistoricized interpretations of Smith, these are typical of almost *all* of the interpretations of his work currently on offer. This is, however, not a new development: the battle for Adam Smith began almost as soon as his body was interred in the Canongate churchyard in Edinburgh.

THE REPUTATION OF A POLITICAL ECONOMIST

Smith died on July 17, 1790—a death that, as Emma Rothschild writes, "was the subject of little interest, in England and even in Scotland."[6] The previous year, Thomas Malthus withdrew the 1784 edition of *The Wealth of Nations* from his college library to find that he was only the third person to have done so.[7] As Richard Teichgraeber has pointed out, when Dugald Stewart was appointed as the first professor of political economy at Glasgow in 1793, he "talked of a hope that 'in due time' Smith's example would be followed by other students of political economy. Yet only ten years later, Francis Horner, a former pupil of Stewart and a founder of the *Edinburgh Review*, spoke of a "superstitious worship" that had come to be attached to Smith's name.[8] What had happened in the intervening period to elevate his reputation from relative obscurity to one surrounded with quasi-religious reverence?

Around the time of Smith's death, a year into the French Revolution, Nicolas de Condorcet published a 220-page summary of *The Wealth of Nations*, which he described as one of those books "which does most honor to Great Britain."[9] In his *Elements of the Philosophy of the Human Mind* (1792) Stewart drew attention to the parallels between Smith's work and that of his French Enlightenment contemporaries like Condorcet, pointing out also how they had mutually influenced each other. Here and in his other writings of the time, Stewart attempted to maintain a balance between rejecting revolutionary interpretations of Enlightenment doctrine and urging the timely reform of the conditions that made such interpretations attractive to the unwary.[10] Arguments of the latter sort, which would have passed unnoticed in enlightened publications fifty years earlier, or even during the American War of Independence, now bore the mark of the Jacobin beast and Stewart was swiftly forced to recant. His retreat had an impact on his theoretical approach to political economy, for Stewart became the person primarily responsible for deradicalizing Smith, above all in his biographical "Account of the Life and Writings of Adam Smith LL.D" published in 1794. As John Saville writes: "It was Adam Smith the conservative theorist whom Stewart presented in his university lectures, and it happened that among the generations of students who listened to him were many who were to become important in British political life. . . . From Stewart they absorbed what was becoming the economic 'commonsense' of middle-class Britain."[11]

Not all aspects of Smith's original thought were universally admired in revolutionary France. *The Theory of Moral Sentiments* had begun to attract attention there during the economic debates in the Assembly of Notables during 1788, mainly from readers of *The Wealth of Nations* who wanted to explore his ideas further, yet they identified a contradiction. In the former work he claimed that humans act from sympathy with or altruism toward their kind, whereas in the latter he appeared to argue that they act from selfish motives, or at least the pursuit of individual self-interest, although this will have beneficial effects.[12] It is usually said that the inconsistency between the anthropological accounts of human nature offered in his two main works—the so-called "Adam Smith Problem"—was first identified by his German interlocutors during the 1840s.[13] But in 1793 the industrial capitalist, lawyer, and Jacobin Pierre-Louis Roederer had already undertaken a critique of *The Theory of Moral Sentiments* in which he identified this alleged inconsistency. Although an admirer of Smith, Roederer was unhappy with the central argument in his first book, precisely because Smith claimed in it that human beings were motivated by impulses that had their origin outside of self-interest. In lectures delivered two months after the execution of Louis XVI, Roederer opposed the idea that, through the exercise of sympathy, men and women could empathize with others and vicariously enjoy or suffer their experiences, on two grounds. First, it was a dangerous doctrine, because it presented false arguments for both social inequality and admiring riches: not sympathy but the desire for emulation was the key, otherwise why should Frenchmen not admire the parasitic nobility who had contributed nothing toward their own wealth and who were now engaged in counterrevolution? Second, it had political implications, for if, as Smith suggested, the principle of sympathy inclined toward monarchy (albeit on the English model established in 1688), then what was to prevent a new or restored dynasty emerging, even if, as in France, the king was executed and monarchy abolished?[14]

For Roederer then, the author of *The Wealth of Nations* was both insufficiently hostile to the nobility and—astonishing as this now seems—insufficiently committed to the market. In Britain, the generation of British Whig thinkers who rose to prominence after 1800, particularly those associated with the *Edinburgh Review*, and who found some of Smith's arguments useful, identified the same problem, but adopted a different strategy: rather than drawing attention to the contradiction they simply pretended that it did not exist. As Teichgraeber notes, in economic terms only one of his themes really interested them:

> They focused almost entirely on his argument for free trade—especially as it applied to monopolies and the Corn Laws—because this was what they took to be the most interesting and useful aspect of the *Wealth of Nations.* As a result, when "free trade" emerged in the 1780s as a matter of practical politics, more people of different types gave the book greater attention and respect. This delayed recognition of Smith's achievement, however, also had a second and unintended result—namely, the reduction of the *Wealth of Nations* to a book whose single overarching concern was seen to be driving home the doctrine of free trade.[15]

It is interesting, in the light of later developments discussed below, that those who were busy reducing Smith's work to a doctrine of free trade were both aware of what they were doing and unwilling to criticize Smith openly. The letter by Horner mentioned above is particularly revealing in this respect:

> I should be reluctant to expose S[mith]'s errors before his work had operated its full effect. We owe much at present to the superstitious worship of S[mith]'s name; and we must not impair that feeling, till victory is more complete. . . . Until we can give a correct and precise theory of the origin of wealth, his popular and plausible and loose hypothesis is as good for the vulgar as any others.[16]

Yet the interpretation of Smith associated with the ideologists of industrial capitalism was not the only one. Radicals were initially more attentive to and supportive of his work than either Whigs or Tories, as is demonstrated by the tribute paid to him by Robert Burns—anonymously—in the September 1790 edition of the *Gentleman's Magazine:*

> *Death* and *Hermes* of late in Elysium did boast,
> That each would bring hither what earth valued most:
> Smith's *Wealth of Nations* Hermes stole from his shelf;
> *DEATH* just won his cause—he took Smith himself.[17]

The radicals were not opposed to the market. In first part of *Rights of Man,* published the following year, Thomas Paine invoked the superiority of Smith's method to that of Edmund Burke, but remained as supportive of competition as his opponent.[18] The differences at this stage were over politics rather than economics. As Edward Thompson summarized the radical position:"In political society every man must have equal rights as a citizen: in economic society he must naturally remain employer or employed, and the State should not interfere with the capital of one or the wages of the other. The *Rights of Man* and the *Wealth of Nations* should supplement and nourish each other."[19] But the radicals of the 1790s did not necessarily accept all of Smith's philosophical positions. Smith had written in *The Theory of Moral Sentiments:* "If we saw in the light in which others see us, or in which they could see us if they knew all, a reformation would generally be unavoidable."[20] It is sometimes claimed that Burns effectively endorses this position in his poem, "To a Louse."[21] In fact, Burns flatly denies the possibility of what Smith suggests and in that sense his is a more pessimistic conception than Smith's own:

> O wad some Pow'r the giftie gie us
> To *see ourselves as ithers see us!*
> It was frae monie a blunder free us,
> An' foolish notion:
> What airs in dress an' gait wad lea'e us
> An' ev'n Devotion![22]

By the end of the Napoleonic Wars the emergent working-class movement also began to draw theoretical sustenance from *The Wealth of Nations,* but from markedly different sections of the book than those admired by the bourgeoisie. "As a result," writes David McNally, "by the 1820s, 'Smithian' apologists for industrial capitalism confronted 'Smithian socialists' in a vigorous, and often venomous, debate over political economy."[23] An excellent example of this conflict can be found, inevitably, in the *Edinburgh Review.* "Mr Spence is an acute man; but undoubtedly quite ignorant of the principles of political economy," began a critique of William Spence's *Agriculture the Source of the Wealth in Britain,* a book that was admittedly directed against the Edinburgh Reviewers in general and James Mill in particular. It continued: "If the persons who have bought five editions of Mr Spence's pamphlet could only be persuaded to look into the *Wealth of Nations,* they would need fewer cautions of ours; and if Mr Spence would take the trouble of understanding that cel-

ebrated work, we have so good an opinion of his sagacity, as to be persuaded, that he would either cease to write upon economical subjects,
or write to retract and atone for his first publications."[24]

In stark contrast to his successors like David Ricardo and—above
all—Malthus, Smith continued to be invoked by working-class radicals
until the early days of the Chartist movement at least.[25] By the 1850s
this was no longer the case. If Smith continued to be read by working-
class people it appears to have been in the spirit approved of by their
rulers. The government commissioner for the coalfields in Newcastle
and Durham, John Leifchild, ventured north of the border mid-decade
to comment approvingly on the reading habits of the Scottish miners
and the healthy attitudes that this revealed:

> Many of them read such books as Adam Smith's "Wealth of Nations,"
> and are fond of discussing the subjects he treats of.... Such men can be
> reasoned with about anything belonging to their calling and they know
> very well why wages cannot at particular times be higher than a certain
> standard. They see at once, by the price current in this market, what is
> the fair portion to go to the workman as wages, according to the cir-
> cumstances of the pit, and the general state of the trade. Such men will
> have nothing to do with the Union. They scorn to read the penny and
> two penny publications current in other places. They are ready, after their
> work, to read and enjoy a chapter of the "Wealth of Nations."[26]

The plausibility of the picture conjured here—a compliant workforce
sagely conceding the need for lower wages after imbibing the Principles
of Political Economy from the pages of *The Wealth of Nations*—is, to say
the least, challenged by the fact that unionization had been increasing in
the West of Scotland coalfields since 1850 and, in 1856 when Leifchild's
book appeared, the biggest strike in Scottish mining history down to
that year took place, precisely against attempts by the masters to reduce
pay.[27] The point is not that the type of deferential worker celebrated by
Leifchild did not exist, but that Smith was now being used to support
such attitudes to the employers, rather than to oppose them.

By this time Marx had spent over a decade in his prolonged engagement with Smith's thought and in many respects proved himself to be
his forebear's most faithful reader. Marx valued Smith as "the *interpreter*
of the frankly bourgeois upstart" who "speaks the language of the still

revolutionary bourgeoisie, which has not yet subjected to itself society, the State, etc."[28] But Marx was not engaged in attempting to claim one or other aspect of Smith's thought to be his "real" position, but rather to subject it to a critique that reveals those aspects that are scientific ("esoteric") and those that are apologetic ("exoteric"). For Marx, the fact that Smith's thought contains both elements means that it is marked above all by "perpetual contradiction":

> On the one hand he traces the intrinsic connection existing between economic categories or the obscure structure of the bourgeois economic system. On the other, he simultaneously sets forth the connection as it appears in the phenomena of competition and thus as it presents itself to the unscientific observer just as to him who is actually involved and interested in the process of bourgeois production. One of these conceptions fathoms the inner connection, the physiology, so to speak, of the bourgeois system, whereas the other takes the external phenomena of life, as they seem and appear and merely describes, catalogues, recounts and arranges them under formal definitions. With Smith both these methods of approach not only merrily run alongside one another, but also intermingle and constantly contradict one another. With him this is justifiable (with the exception of a few special investigations, [such as] that into money) since his task was indeed a twofold one. On the one hand he attempted to penetrate the inner physiology of bourgeois society but on the other, he partly tried to describe its externally apparent forms of life for the first time, to show its relations as they appear outwardly and partly he had even to find a nomenclature and corresponding mental concepts for these phenomena, i.e., to reproduce them for the first time in the language and [in the] thought process. The one task interests him as much as the other and since both proceed independently of one another, this results in completely contradictory ways of presentation: the one expresses the intrinsic connections more or less correctly, the other, with the same justification—and without any connection to the first method of approach—expresses the *apparent* connections without any internal relation.[29]

The area in which these contradictions appear most explicitly is in Smith's version of the labor theory of value, with its dangerous claim that the socially necessary labor required to produce commodities was also the objective measure of their value—the very position for which Smith was admired by the early labor movement. In the notebooks published as *Theories of Surplus Value* Marx first notes the advances made by Smith in this field:

> Adam Smith rightly points out that only the part of the labor (value) which the workman newly adds to the material resolves itself into wages and profit, that is to say, the newly-created surplus-value in itself has nothing to do with the part of the capital which has been advanced (as materials and instruments). Adam Smith . . . has thus reduced profit to the appropriation of the unpaid labor of others. . . . Here it is only important to stress that Adam Smith very clearly recognises, brings out and expressly emphasises the contradistinction between his view of the origin of profit and [the] apologist view.[30]

But later Marx identifies parts of Smith's argument where he retreats from these insights. In discussing what he calls "this peculiar train of thought in Adam Smith's book" he writes:

> First the value of the commodity is examined, and in some passages correctly determined—so correctly determined that he traces out in general form the origin of surplus-value and of its specific forms, hence deriving wages and profit from this value. But then he takes the opposite course, and seeks on the contrary to deduce the value of commodities (from which he has deduced wages and profit) by adding together the natural prices of wages, profit and rent. It is this latter circumstance that is responsible for the fact that he nowhere correctly explains the influence of oscillations of wages, profit, etc., on the price of commodities—since he lacks the basis [for such an explanation].[31]

But in some respects Marx found Smith to be guilty, not merely of inconsistency or confusion, but of omission. In *The Wealth of Nations* Smith discussed the "original accumulation" of capital in terms of the capacity of capitalists to save, in passages notable for their uncharacteristic evasiveness and self-delusion. He fails, for example, to acknowledge the necessity of "primitive" accumulation for capital and refers instead to the "previous accumulation of stock," a position that Marx described as a form of "insipid childishness" that "is everyday preached to us in the defence of property."[32] By contrast, it was the former Jacobite, Sir James Steuart, who presented a frank and unflinching vision of the process as involving the forcing of the peasantry off the land, compelling them into wage labor, and freeing the land for productive investment. For Steuart recognized that the role of force cannot be restricted only to breaking the social and political dominance of the lords—it must also be exercised against those over whom they had previously ruled: "That revolution must then mark the purging of the lands of superfluous mouths, and forcing those to quit their mother earth, in order to retire to towns and villages, where they may usefully swell the numbers of free hands and apply to industry."[33] Marx's engagement with Steuart was more concentrated and occupied far less space in his collected works than that with Smith, but overall it may have been more wholeheartedly appreciative. In particular, the emphasis Marx places in *Capital* on the necessity of "primitive accumulation" is drawn directly from Steuart, as he acknowledged in this and similar passages: "He examines the process [of the genesis of capital] particularly in agriculture; and he rightly considers that manufacturing proper only came into being through this process of separation in agriculture. In Adam Smith's writings the process of separation is assumed to be already complete."[34] Unsurprisingly, modern defenders of Smith tend, or possibly pretend, to see nothing in Steuart's work other than his mercantilist errors: Iain McLean dismisses one of Smith's greatest achievements (the law of value) but otherwise elevates him above Steuart, at one point drawing parallels between Smith and Mozart on the one hand and Steuart and Salieri on the other.[35] As Michael Perelman has pointed out, some of the historical truths of primitive accumulation revealed by Steuart are still too unwelcome to achieve widespread acceptance.[36]

From the last third of the nineteenth century in particular, the intellectual defenders of capitalism show far less interest in Smith. Interestingly, this is increasingly because they began to regard as legitimate the claims that the left made on his legacy and this shift represents the second turn in Smith's posthumous reputation. Key here is the emergence of neoclassical economics, above all the marginalist reaction against both the classical political economy of Smith and the Marxist critique that sought to build on what he had accomplished. In economic theory marginalism represented the final retreat from the kind of scientific inquiry undertaken by Smith, however imperfect, into ideological justification. It was signaled by the abandonment of the law of value. The tenets of marginalism were first set out by Léon Walras in his *Elements of Pure Economics* (1874) and ultimately codified by Alfred Marshall in his *Principles of Economics* (1890), although they have a long prehistory dating back at least to the 1830s.[37] As Murray Milgate and Shannon Stimson have written: "We might conclude that we live in a future, imagined or real, informed as much, or indeed more, by subsequent nineteenth-century neoclassical economic thought and practise as it is by the thought of Smith . . . and that we understand the conceptual resources of today's economic and political discourse to flow almost exclusively from the marginalist approach to economics introduced in the last quarter of the nineteenth century."[38] In relation to neoliberalism, the most important neoclassical thinkers have been those of the Austrian school, above all, Carl Menger, Ludwig von Mises, and Friedrich von Hayek. Their attitude to Smith is instructive, if surprising, for it more or less accepts the radical and early labor movement interpretation of his work.

Smith undoubtedly presented a problem for the neoclassical school: Walras saw his work as being tainted by "unscientific" social and moral considerations; Menger regarded it as flawed because of Smith's insistence that national economy was not simply an abstraction—a view incompatible with the "atomism" or methodological individualism of the marginalists.[39] Menger was only exaggerating slightly when he wrote in 1891: "Smith placed himself in all cases of conflict of interest between the strong and the weak, *without exception* on the side of the latter." Indeed, in 1883 he had explicitly criticized Smith for his "one-sided rationalistic liberalism" and his "effort to do away with what exists," which Menger claimed "inexorably leads to socialism."[40] Nevertheless, the marginalists needed, for reasons of ideological continuity, to claim Smith as a forerunner whose work they had completed, above all in relation to his advocacy of the market, which they removed from any historical context. "It was only the 'marginal revolution' of the 1870s," wrote Hayek, "that produced a satisfactory explanation of the market processes that Adam Smith had long before described with his metaphor of the 'hidden hand.'"[41] Indeed, starting with Menger in his *Investigations into the Methods of the Social Sciences* (1888), if there is one idea that the marginalists did derive from Smith, then it is the metaphor of the hidden hand—one that was not original to Smith and that had not previously received any attention until its usefulness in reinforcing the notion of a spontaneous economic order became apparent.[42]

As we have seen, in 1803 Francis Horner had proposed that criticisms of Smith should be withheld until "victory is more complete"; by the latter decades of the nineteenth century these criticisms were now being made—not because of the completeness of the capitalist victory, but because it was under threat from "the vulgar," or more precisely a growing labor movement whose socialist objectives the neoclassical economists feared could be supported by Smith's arguments. There was some truth in this: as late as the 1920s some workers still found it possible to treat Smith and Marx (and Darwin) as complementary thinkers:

> One might assume that Adam Smith and Charles Darwin gave aid and comfort to unbridled capitalism, but they were also read enthusiastically (and very differently) by the partisans of the Plebs League and the NCLC [National Council of Labor Colleges]. Smith, Darwin, and Marx all offered materialist theories of evolution based on struggle and exploitation. They all suggested that the existing social order was not ordained, but had progressed according to certain scientific laws. Once those laws were understood, society could be reconstructed along different lines. For Dunfermline housepainter James Clunie (b. 1889) Das Kapital and The Wealth of Nations both demonstrated that industrialism inevitably increased economic inequality, the exploitation of labor, and class conflict.[43]

The advent of the postwar boom and attendant triumph of Keynesianism in the economics discipline seemed to signal the final reduction of Smith to purely historical figure, and one confined to the history of economics rather than of sociology or moral philosophy at that. The prevailing attitude to Smith's work has been admirably summed up by James Buchan: "His books now, were long and Scotch and close-printed. They were no more use to the modern economist and politician than sixpenny tracts of eighteenth-century medicine to a General Practitioner or MD."[44] Yet from the mid-1970s on Smith's reputation began to experience an extraordinary revival. More extraordinary still was that the people responsible for this third reputational shift were largely the intellectual descendants of—and in the case of Hayek, actual members of—the very neoclassical school that had previously shown no great enthusiasm for his work.

WILL THE REAL ADAM SMITH PLEASE STAND UP?

In 1976, at the moment of formation of the AIS, Milton Friedman gave a speech at Saint Andrews University that included the following claims:

"Adam Smith was a radical and revolutionary in his time—just as those of us who today preach laissez faire are in our time. He was no apologist for merchants and manufacturers, or more generally other special interests, but regarded them as the great obstacles to laissez faire—just as we do today."There was one respect, however, in which Friedman believed contemporary free-marketeers would have to extend their categories, broadening "the 'tribes' of 'monopolists' to include not only enterprises protected from competition but also trade unions, school teachers, welfare recipients, and so on and on."[45] In a particularly audacious move, the neoliberals attempted to resolve the Adam Smith Problem by presenting the difference between *The Theory of Moral Sentiments* and *The Wealth of Nations* not as a contradiction but a problem that could only be resolved by adhering to the prescriptions contained in the latter work. During the same conference at which Friedman gave the speech quoted above, Ronald Coase argued that the existence of benevolence and other feelings not driven by self-interest were an obstacle to the market order if they extended much beyond immediate family, friends, and possibly close work colleagues. Any wider application would simply lead to politicians and bureaucrats acting on behalf of supporters or client groups and thus jeopardizing the blind working of the market, the unintended outcomes of which were the only guarantee of beneficial effects.[46] The sheer perversity of this reading—the exact opposite of Smith's clearly stated meaning—is so audacious as to produce a degree of admiration; it is certainly a match for attempts by Stalinist ideologues to "explain" that, for example, when Lenin talked about the abolition of the state he really meant strengthening it to an unprecedented degree.

In a sense these interpretations involved a return to the original distortions of Smith that arose immediately after his death, but now in the context of the crisis of Keynesianism and state capitalism, and a resurgence of ideas about "free" markets as the alternative. Unsurprisingly, the neoliberal attitude to Smith is well expressed by one of its political leaders, AIS heroine Margaret Thatcher, who noted with bemusement in her autobiography the failure of her "revolution" to win hearts and minds in Scotland, "home of the very same Scottish Enlightenment which produced Adam Smith, the greatest exponent of free enterprise economics till Hayek and Friedman."[47] Thatcher's concern may be unwarranted: in Smith's homeland the more openly promarket figures in the Scottish

National Party, like Michael Russell, have similar reasons for admiring Smith: "Adam Smith was the father of modern capitalism and it is high time that his own people rediscovered his genius, particularly as, in his own land, that genius is currently tarnished by the half-baked economic models espoused by most of our political parties."[48] As two of Smith's more acute recent interpreters have written: "It is no longer thought necessary to examine how and why Smith argued in favour of the market, nor indeed how he qualified his case."[49]

Yet many on the left accept neoliberal nostrums at face value and merely reverse their value judgments. For the German Marxist Elmar Altvater: "Some of the most striking ingredients of neoliberal intellectual approaches can be traced back to the origins of liberal thinking in the early 18th century," among whose proponents he of course includes Smith.[50] On the occasion of Smith's appearance on the £20 banknote in 2007, one Scottish historian, the late James Young, claimed in the pages of the *Herald* that "Adam Smith was a pioneer of the vicious anti-humanist economics of capitalism" and linked him, somewhat implausibly, "with all the other advocates of anti-gay entrepreneurship; aggressive immoral and naked capitalism; and post-modernism."[51] As Young's ravings suggest, the socialist left often ascribe extreme positions to Smith that are even less plausible than those of the neoliberal right. Some have gone so far as to accuse him of deliberately and dishonestly ignoring actual economic developments in his own work because these undermined his argument. Perelman, for example, finds the absence of any discussion of the Carron Iron Works in *The Wealth of Nations* to be deeply suspicious since, as he rightly says, the Carron Company was in the vanguard of the Industrial Revolution in Britain and was situated relatively near to Kirkaldy, where Smith was writing his great work; but Perelman has an explanation for Smith's omission:

> Smith's reluctance to discuss the Carron works makes sense in terms of his enthusiasm for individualism . . . the Industrial Revolution is absent in Smith's writings. By now, the reason for this is obvious. Although Smith's liberalism seemed liberating, from a different perspective it must have been disempowering to people who were toiling in the Carron works. Presenting such people as isolated individuals would have accurately conveyed their powerlessness.[52]

There are, however, two respects in which Smith *has* exercised an influence on the radical left.[53] One is through his argument that the expansion of trade is the prime mover in generating capitalist development or, as he saw it, the dominance of commercial society. Hence, Robert Brenner might therefore have a case for describing those thinkers who agree with Smith on this question—notably Paul Sweezy, Andre Gunder Frank, and Immanuel Wallerstein—as "neo-Smithian" Marxists.[54] At least one of them, Wallerstein, specifically denies being a Smithian, on the grounds that Smith believed capitalism was an integral part of human nature and he does not, and that Smith understood capitalism to be based on the operation of a free market and he understands it to be based on proletarianization of labor and the commercialization of land.[55] Neither of these arguments deals with the importance or otherwise of trade in generating proletarianization and commercialization, but this is not the main difficulty. "The division of labor," wrote Smith, "is the necessary, though very slow and gradual, consequence of a certain propensity in human nature ... to truck, barter, and exchange one thing for another."[56] This famous passage is frequently cited to "prove" that Smith believed capitalism was intrinsic to human nature.[57] Now, as David Graeber has shown, Smith was wrong to claim that humans have always engaged in barter.[58] Nevertheless, identifying a propensity to do so is very far from claiming that this inevitably leads to the type of capitalist society that currently exists. As I will discuss in more detail below, Smith was not an advocate of capitalism but of "commercial society." The latter term was not a synonym—the former was not in use in Smith's day—but describes a different system entirely.[59] Smith distinguishes between "those original principles of human nature" ("of which no further account can be given") and "the necessary consequence of the faculties of reason and speech" and claims it is "more probable" that the propensity to barter belongs to the latter set of properties.[60] As Dogan Göçmen has written, Smith's refusal to place it alongside such "original principles" as "compassion and sympathy" means that he "formulates a hierarchical order" between these two conceptions of human nature in which the propensity to barter is situated lower down as a product of history, of our social being rather than what Marx called our species being.[61]

If we turn to Smith's other influence on the radical left then we find a much greater acceptance of the distinction between commercial society and capitalism. Indeed, his arguments for commercial society are used as a means of criticizing contemporary neoliberal globalization. Some of the writers involved in making this critique overlap with the "neo-Smithian Marxists": the late Giovanni Arrighi, for example, claimed that that the market system envisaged by Smith can be distinguished from capitalism and that the former exists now in China, or perhaps East Asia more generally, where a "market-based growth" distinct from "capitalist growth" is supposedly embedded.[62] But attempts to discern in Smith's work a model of a "real free market" that has been violated by "the global corporate system" extend far beyond these adherents of World Systems Theory. John McMurty writes, *"every one of Smith's classical principles of the free market has been turned into its effective opposite."*[63] David Korten sets out what these principles were:

> Thus [Adam Smith's] vision of an efficient market was one composed of small owner-managed enterprises, located in the communities where the owners resided. Such owners would share in the community's values and have a personal stake in its future. It is a market that has little in common with a globalised economy directed by massive corporations without local or national allegiance, managed by professionals who are removed from real owners by layers of investment institutions and holding companies.[64]

This is an attractively counterintuitive idea that challenges the neoliberals on their own terms and also has the advantage of being true: Smith's vision of what he called "commercial society" *was* quite different from contemporary neoliberal globalization. There are however major difficulties with it, not least over the geographical and temporal location of this alternative. If, for Arrighi, it can be found in post-Maoist China, for Korten it existed in the economic, social, and political arrangements characteristic of the postwar boom, where he claims that, in the West at least, a proper balance was maintained between the total state dominance exercised in the Stalinist East—which he misidentifies as "Marxism"—and the supposedly unconstrained market of the current neoliberal era:

> Thus, the neoclassical economists left out Smith's considerations of the destructive role of power and class, and the neo-Marxists left out the beneficial functions of the market. Both advanced social experiments on a massive scale that embodies a partial vision of society, with disastrous

results. . . . Contrary to the boastful claims of corporate libertarians, the West did not prosper in the post–World War II period by rejecting the state for the market. Rather it prospered by rejecting extremist ideologies of both Right and Left in favour of democratic pluralism: a system of governance based on a programmatic institutional balance among the forces of government, market and society.[65]

From our present situation it is understandable why the late Eric Hobsbawm could describe the period between 1948 and 1973 as "the Golden Age."[66] But whatever else might be said for it, the structure of Western capitalism during these years did not resemble anything described by Smith either in *The Wealth of Nations* or in his other writings. Furthermore, contrary to the claims made by both neoliberals and many of their critics, they were not years in which capitalism was in any sense constrained, but that instead saw the greatest sustained growth in the history of the system.[67] In any event, the unique conditions that made the postwar boom possible are unlikely to ever be repeated.

Those on the social-democratic or center-left have essentially accepted the neoliberal economic order.[68] They still, however, wish to maintain some distance from what I call vanguard neoliberalism by insisting on the need for policies with which to ameliorate the consequences of privatization, deregulation, and the rest while leaving them in place. The ideological uses of Smith are indispensible in this context. In 2002 the then–Chancellor of the Exchequer Gordon Brown gave a lecture in which he asked "whether Adam Smith would feel more at home in the right-of-centre Adam Smith Institute or in the left-of-centre (John) Smith Institute, named after my good friend John Smith, the leader of the Labour Party." Unsurprisingly, Brown opined that the latter would have proved the more congenial to his fellow native of Kirkcaldy.[69] In a work intended to support and elaborate Brown's position, Iain McLean argues that to describe Smith as "a man of the Left" would be anachronistic as the terms left and right did not acquire their political meanings until the French Revolution.[70] This seems unnecessarily concerned with labels rather than attitudes, since "left" is a relative concept that can be retrospectively discerned in most historical situations.[71] We can identify what would later be left-wing positions prior to 1789, for example in the English Civil War. What is genuinely inapt is to ascribe, as McLean does to Smith, positions associated with social democracy—

a much more historically specific term from an even later date than "left": "It favours government intervention to counter market failure; redistributive taxation; and trade liberalisation for the benefit of all including the poor of the world. It does not favour producer groups; public ownership of trading enterprises (where there are no market failure issues); or protection, either in rich or poor countries."[72]

The central claim here is not that Smith's position in *The Wealth of Nations* is wrong, merely incomplete. As Brown writes, "I have come to understand that his *Wealth of Nations* was underpinned by his *Theory of Moral Sentiments,* his invisible hand dependent on the existence of a helping hand."[73] Once again, however, there is disagreement over how exactly these two works relate to each other. Early in 2008 the Chinese premier Wen Jiabao gave an interview with Fareed Zakaria for CNN, in which he invoked the authority of Smith to justify the combination of market capitalism and state direction characteristic of China's development since 1978: "*The Wealth of Nations,* said Wen, highlights the need for the invisible hand of the market, while *The Theory of Moral Sentiments* shows the need for the visible hand of government, in the interests of social equity and harmonious development."[74]

What the Scottish and Chinese politicians were both trying to do was bypass the "Adam Smith Problem." In many respects they simply reverse the neoliberal argument about relationship between Smith's two books. It is however equally self-serving to argue that they are simply constitutive parts of a greater whole, the one unintelligible without the other. Roederer was right in 1793: there is a contradiction between them. Here again Göçmen's discussion is invaluable, for the contradiction is not between altruism on the one hand and individualism on the other, but between "an anthropological conception of human beings, which regards human beings as social individuals" and "a critical account of the situation of human beings in commercial society, which describes them as egoistic beings." The resulting contradiction, however, "cannot be ascribed to Smith": "it is a real historical contradiction prevailing in commercial society, which Smith criticizes implicitly and explicitly in different contexts."[75]

FROM COMMERCIAL SOCIETY TO CAPITALISM

Neoconservative and neoliberal writers have a habit of ascribing visionary powers to Smith. For P. J. O'Rourke: "Smith was fostering free enterprise, and he was also nurturing—just in time—resistance to social-ism."[76] Resistance to socialism—in 1776. O'Rourke is a humorist and here he is, as they say, having a laugh. But the ahistorical stupidity of these remarks indicates a more widespread misconception summed up by this comment on the Bank of England website: "Adam Smith's explanations of the society he observed in the 18th century are as relevant today as they were then."[77] The essential error is repeated even by those who dis-agree as to the nature of his relevance, as in this "social-democratic" per-spective by Ryan Hanley: "Insofar as the conditions of contemporary capitalism are in many respects similar to those debated by commercial society's founding fathers, those engaged in the project to ameliorate those conditions stand to gain much from the effort to develop our an-swers to today's problems in light of their efforts."[78] My objection to this kind of argument is simply this: Adam Smith is not "relevant" to our contemporary problems—and such relevance as his work does possess is precisely the extent to which it demonstrates the vast *difference* between his vision and our reality. Anachronistic misconceptions concerning his work could of course be corrected by the radical expedient of actually reading *The Wealth of Nations* and *The Theory of Moral Sentiments*, prefer-ably after situating them in their historical context, namely Scotland's emergence from feudalism.

One of his objections to feudalism was precisely that it had delayed the emergence of commercial society and was consequently "unnatural." "According to the natural course of things," he wrote, "the greater part of the capital of every growing society is, first, directed to agriculture, af-terwards to manufactures, and, last of all, to foreign commerce. . . . But though this natural order of things must have taken place in some degree in every such society, it has, in all the modern states of Europe, been in many respects entirely inverted."[79] When Smith attacked unproductive labor, he was not making some timeless critique of state employees, but thinking quite specifically about Highland clan retainers. When Smith opposed monopolies, he was not issuing a prophetic warning against the nationalization of industries in the twentieth century, but criticizing those companies that relied for their market position on the possession of ex-clusive royal charters in the eighteenth. Above all, unlike his modern epigones, he did not see the market as a quasi-mystical institution that should be made to penetrate every aspect of social life; but rather as a limited mechanism for liberating humanity's economic potential from feudal and absolutist stagnation.

But were impersonal market forces themselves capable of overthrowing feudalism? It should come as no surprise by now to find that Smith appears to express contradictory views at different stages of his career, or at least emphasize very different aspects of the process. In *The Wealth of Nations* he seems to suggest that they can, writing that "what all the violence of the feudal institutions could never have effected, the silent and insensible operation of foreign commerce and manufactures gradually brought about." In particular this was due to the unintended consequence of actions taken by two social groups, "who had not the least intention to serve the public," feudal landowners and those we would now call capitalists: "To gratify the most childish vanity was the sole motive of the great proprietors. The merchants and artificers, much less ridiculous, acted merely from a view to their own interest, and in pursuit of their own pedlar principle of turning a penny wherever a penny was to be got. Neither of them had either great knowledge or foresight of that great revolution which the folly of one, and the industry of the other, was gradually bringing about."[80] Yet in his lectures at the University of Glasgow during the previous decade Smith argued that the self-transformation of the noble proprietors could not be relied upon, and that the violent suppression of their feudal power was essential for the rise of commercial society: "The power of the nobles has always been brought to ruin before a system of liberty has been established, and this indeed must always be the case. For the nobility are the greatest opposers and oppressors of liberty that we can imagine. They hurt the liberty of the people even more than an absolute monarch." Absolute monarchy at least protected the people from the "petty lords" of their domains: "The people therefore never can have security in person or estate until the nobility have been greatly crushed."[81] These are not necessarily incompatible positions—in Marxist terms the former corresponds to the socioeconomic transition to capitalism and the latter to the sociopolitical bourgeois revolution necessary to consolidate it at the level of the state— but Smith himself does not attempt to reconcile them. Nevertheless, his attitude was clear, so that in 1818 Henri de Saint-Simon could legitimately describe the "immortal Smith" as being responsible for "the most vigorous, most direct, and most complete critique ever made of the feudal regime."[82]

Even so, Smith's advocacy for commercial society was very conditional indeed. Long before industrialization began in earnest he intuited that it would lead to massive deterioration in the condition of laborers and their reduction to mere "hands." Understood in the context of the Scottish Enlightenment conception of human potential, the description of pin manufacture at the beginning of *The Wealth of Nations,* reproduced from 2007 on £20 banknotes, not only celebrates the efficiency of the division of labor, but also shows the soul-destroying repetition that awaited the new class of wage laborers.[83] Smith himself provided the context for his discussion of pin-making in his Glasgow University lectures from the early 1760s, once again providing a fuller, more complex, and more radical perspective than that which appears in *The Wealth of Nations:*

> The labor and time of the poor is in civilized countries sacrificed to the maintaining the rich in ease and luxury. The landlord is maintained in idleness and luxury by the labor of his tenants, who cultivate the land for him as well as for themselves. The monied man is supported by his exactions from the industrious merchant and the needy who are obliged to support him in ease by a return for the use of his money. But every savage has the full enjoyment of the fruits of his own labors; there are there no landlords, no usurers, no tax gatherers. We should expect therefore that the savage should be much better provided than the dependent poor man who labors both for himself and for others. But the case is far otherwise. The indigence of a savage is far greater than that of the meanest citizen of anything that deserves the name of a civilized nation. There is another consideration which increases the difficulty in accounting for this. If we should suppose that labor was equally proportioned to each, the difficulty would cease. That is, if we should suppose that of the 10,000 whose labor is necessary to the support of one individual, each was maintained by the labor of the rest, there would here be the reciprocal proportion of the labor of 1 to 10,000 and 10,000 to 1, so that everyone would have the labor of one bestowed upon him. But in no civilized state this is the case. Of 10,000 families which are supported by each other, 100 perhaps labor not at all and do nothing to the common support. The others have them to maintain besides themselves, and besides [those] who labor have a far less share of ease, convenience, and abundance than those who work not at all. The rich and opulent merchant who does nothing but give a few directions, lives in far greater state and luxury and ease and plenty of all the conveniencies and delicacies of life than his clerks, who do all the business. They too, excepting their confinement, are in a state of ease and plenty far superior to that of the artisan by whose labor these commodities

were furnished. The labor of this man too is pretty tolerable; he works under cover protected from the inclemency in the weather, and has his livelihood in no uncomfortable way if we compare him with the poor laborer. He has all the inconveniencies of the soil and the season to struggle with, is continually exposed to the inclemency of the weather and the most severe labor at the same time. Thus he who as it were supports the whole frame of society and furnishes the means of the convenience and ease of all the rest is himself possessed of a very small share and is buried in obscurity. He bears on his shoulders the whole of mankind, and unable to sustain the load is buried by the weight of it and thrust down into the lowest parts of the earth, from whence he supports all the rest. In what manner then shall we account for the great share he and the lowest of the people have of the conveniencies of life? The division of labor amongst different hands can alone account for this. Let us consider the effects this will have on one particular branch of business, and from thence we may judge on the effect and from the effects it will have on the whole. We shall take for this purpose an instance frivolous indeed, but which will sufficiently illustrate it; this is pin-making.[84]

This is the point at which *The Wealth of Nations* begins, but even in Book V of that work, in contrast to the more frequently cited Book I, Smith explicitly considered the way in which the division of labor, while increasing the productivity of the laborers, did so by narrowing their intellectual horizons:

The man whose whole life is spent in performing a few simple operations, of which the effects, too, are perhaps always the same, or very nearly the same, has no occasion to assert his understanding, or to exercise his invention, in finding out expedients for removing difficulties which never occur. He naturally loses, therefore, the habit of such exertion, and generally becomes as stupid and ignorant as it is possible for a human creature to become. The torpor of his mind renders him not only incapable of relishing or bearing a part in any rational conversation, but of conceiving any generous, noble, or tender sentiment, and consequently of forming any just judgment concerning many even of the ordinary duties of private life. Of the great and extensive interests of his country he is altogether incapable of judging; and unless very particular pains have been taken to render him otherwise, he is equally incapable of defending his country in war.... His dexterity at his own particular trade seems, in this manner, to be acquired at the expense of his intellectual, social, and martial virtues. But in every improved and civilized society this is the state into which the laboring poor, that is, the great body of the people, must necessarily fall, unless government takes some pains to prevent it.[85]

Smith contrasts this unhappy state of affairs with that existing under earlier modes of subsistence—modes that, remember, he was committed to transcending:

> It is otherwise in the barbarous societies, as they are commonly called, of hunters, of shepherds, and even of husbandmen in that rude state of husbandry that precedes the improvement of manufactures, and the extension of foreign commerce. In such societies, the varied occupations of every man oblige every man to exert his capacity, and to invent expedients for removing difficulties which are continually occurring. Invention is kept alive, and the mind is not suffered to fall into that drowsy stupidity, which, in a civilized society, seems to benumb the understanding of almost all the inferior ranks of people. . . . Every man, too, is in some measure a statesman, and can form judgments concerning the interest of the society, and the conduct of those who govern it.[86]

It was uneasy anticipations such as these, which Smith shared with James Steuart and Adam Ferguson, that later informed Hegel's conception of alienation and, through him, that of Marx.[87] In response he calls for the state to intervene to raise the educational level of the common people to that fitting of a "civilized and commercial society": "For a very small expense, the public can facilitate, can encourage, and can even impose upon almost the whole body of the people, the necessity of acquiring those most essential parts of education." Here he has before him the example of his own country, in one of the few occasions it features positively in *The Wealth of Nations:* "In Scotland, the establishment of such parish schools has taught almost the whole common people to read, and a very great proportion of them to write and account."[88] And this was only one of the areas in which he was prepared to see state intervention or direction.[89]

It was therefore possible for Smith to approve of commercial society while disapproving of the activities of actual capitalists. Indeed, in a passage that does prefigure Marxist analysis, he specifically denies that they represent society as a whole: "the clamour and sophistry of merchants and manufacturers easily persuade [the public] that the private interest of a part, and of a subordinate part of the society, is the general interest of the whole."[90] It is this, entirely realistic, attitude that allows him to make his most famous comment: "People of the same trade seldom meet together, even for merriment and diversion, but the conversation ends in a conspiracy against the public, or in some contrivance to raise prices."[91] Smith's view of the central function of the state was also clear-sighted: "Civil government, so far as it is instituted for the security of property, is in reality instituted for the defence of the rich against the poor, or of those who have some property against those who have none at all." The worst form of civil government would therefore be one actually run by the rich themselves, above all by a certain type of capitalist, as in these reflections on the East India Company: "The government of an exclusive company of merchants is, perhaps, the worst of all governments for any country whatsoever."[92]

But what would become of the arguments for commercial society if these excrescences turned out to be instead the essence of the new system? His argument in *The Wealth of Nations* can be seen, in McNally's words, as a defense of "agrarian-based capitalist development in a landed commonwealth ruled by prosperous and public-spirited country gentlemen" against the emergent "industrial and commercial capitalists" whose amorality Smith distrusted. In relation to his native Scotland, McNally notes: "Smith hoped that commercial forces could be used to hurry the development of an agrarian-based capitalism guarded by a state run by a natural aristocracy of landed gentlemen."[93] This was not what took place. Even before the process of agrarian improvement imposed on the Scottish Lowlands after 1746 was completed—and it was far advanced even by the time *The Wealth of Nations* was published—it was clear that the class of tenant farmers required to underpin such a system was in terminal decline, leaving occupation of the land divided between the great landowners and large capitalist farmers on the one hand and landless laborers on the other: consolidation and concentration, not a competitive but stable multiplicity of small producers, was the order of the day.[94]

"How realistic was Smith's vision?" Perelman asks this question then answers it with a hypothetical example: "In a small, isolated village in which industry only consisted of artisans producing on a small scale, a market society might have worked the way Smith suggested." In historical terms, however, he concludes: "Such an economy has probably never existed."[95] There is however one society in which it is claimed that such an economy did exist: the thirteen North American colonies of the British Empire, which Smith discussed in the most glowing terms, and whose demands he supported, albeit in a typically moderate style.[96] Michael Merrill argues that this was where Smith's views had genuine traction:

> Free trade, for these men opportunistic of the doctrine, meant the ability to make as much money as possible; it did not mean, as it did for Smith, the abolition of all those restrictions on property and trade that disadvantaged the rich at the expense of the poor. Not surprisingly, Smith's own views found a more congenial home among the coalition of small farmers, artisans, merchants, and lawyers in North America, where the widespread distribution of property gave rise to an economic order that most clearly resembled Smith's ideal type, and whose democratic revolution had swept an aristocratic ruling class from power.[97]

In 1772 Benjamin Franklin compared the situation of the rural population in Scotland (and Ireland) with that in his own country: "I thought of the Happiness of New England, where every man is a Freeholder, has plenty of good Food and Fuel, with whole Clothes from Head to Foot, the Manufactory perhaps of his own Family. Long may they continue in this situation!"[98] Franklin was one of the sources for Smith's information on the American colonies and his somewhat idealized view may well reflect Franklin's influence.[99] His picture did not go unchallenged. Thomas Pownall, a former governor of Massachusetts, wrote to Smith following the publication of *The Wealth of Nations* pointing out that his arguments were based on logical deduction rather than empirical evidence: "You advance upon the ground of *probable reasons for believing only*, you prove by probable suppositions only; yet most people who read your book, will think you mean to set up an absolute proof, and your conclusion is drawn as though you had." As Nicholas Phillipson, who quotes this passage, points out: "It was a response of a critic who understood Smith's method better than most and was in a good position to question the way in which he had used America as the illustration on which the credibility of a vast system had come to depend."[100] Yet, over and above any errors of fact that Smith may have committed, and leaving the precise nature of the slave colonies of the South to one side, the northern colonies did indeed come closest to Smith's ideal of commercial society; but they were not capitalist societies. We need not accept Charles Post's

notion of independent household production as the definition of relations of production ("social property relations," in his terms) in farming
communities, but he is undoubtedly right that these are far removed
from capitalist ones.[101]

CONCLUSION

Albert Hirschman once argued that the first supporters of commercial
society believed it would tame the disastrous warlike passions inherent
in feudalism, but not because they held to an imbecilic faith in the ability
of markets to resolve all human difficulties:

> The passions that needed bridling belong to the powerful, who are in a
> position to do harm on a huge scale and who were believed to be par-
> ticularly well endowed with passions in comparison with the lesser or-
> ders. As a result the most interesting applications of the theory show how
> the willfulness, the disastrous lust for glory, and, in general, the passionate
> excesses of the powerful are curbed by the interests—their own and
> those of their subjects.[102]

For Hirschman, it is Smith who first breaks this line of reasoning, upheld
in Scotland by Steuart and John Millar: "The main impact of *The Wealth
of Nations* was to establish a powerful *economic* justification for the un-
trammelled pursuit of individual self-interest, whereas in the earlier literature . . . the stress was on the *political* effects of this pursuit."[103] As we
have seen, this was not the case. As John Dwyer has shown, the attempt
to distinguish Smith from his contemporaries, "thereby transforming
Smith into a much more revolutionary thinker than he really was," is by
far the weakest part of Hirschman's argument. As Dwyer writes,
Hirschman "reinforces the commonplace image of Smith as the prophet
of individualism who makes the 'ordinary mortal' rather than the statesman or aristocrat, the model of social analysis." But this is to misunderstand his subject: "Smithian analysis cannot be applied to our notion of
the average man. Instead, it referred to landed society, particularly the
gentry and yeomanry, and included those middle-class men who served
the public in a wide variety of bureaucratic functions. Most interestingly,
it typically disparaged those individuals who lived by the profits of commerce and manufacturing, and whose unbridled self-interest could destroy national stability.[104]

Smith based his support for commercial society on a hypothesis concerning its likely positive effects compared to those associated with feudal absolutism. As Joseph Cropsey wrote long ago, "Smith advocated capitalism because it makes freedom possible—not because it *is* freedom."[105] Now that the consequences of "actually existing capitalism" have been experienced for more than two hundred years, and it is clear that, for the majority of humanity, the dehumanizing effects of the division of labor already identified by Smith were not an unfortunate by-product but actually constitutive of the system, there is less excuse for such misrecognition. Political economy was the central discipline of the Enlightenment, the greatest intellectual achievement of the bourgeois revolutions. The expectations that Smith had of capitalism have been disappointed; the predictions he made for it have been falsified; to defend capitalism now, to further claim him in support of such a defense while ignoring the discrepancy between his model and our reality, is to attack Enlightenment values quite as comprehensively as did the feudal obscurantists to whom Smith was opposed.

It took until the early twenty-first century, but at last we have a fine statue of Adam Smith, author of *The Theory of Moral Sentiments* and *The Wealth of Nations*, on Edinburgh High Street; but these works, which should forever be read, need to be read for what they tell us about his century, not ours.

Notes

These notes contain several references to the work of Antonio Gramsci. Where these refer to passages from the published selections of his prison notebooks, or to the complete edition of them currently in progress, I have followed the convention of also giving their source in the original notebook (Q) and note (§) after the publication page number.

Preface

1. Vladimir I. Lenin [1913], "The Three Sources and Component Parts of Marxism," in *Collected Works*, vol. 19, *March–December 1913* (Moscow: Foreign Languages Publishing House, 1963), 23–24.
2. See, for example, Eric J. Hobsbawm, "In the Era of Anti-Fascism, 1929–4," in *How to Change the World: Tales of Marx and Marxism, 1840–2011* (London: Little, Brown, 2011), 283, 285, 298–99.
3. See, for example, Naomi Klein, "What's Next? The Movement against Global Corporatism Doesn't Need to Sign a Ten-Point Plan to Be Effective," in *Fences and Windows: Dispatches from the Front Lines of the Globalization Debate* (London: Harper Perennial, 2005), 26–27.
4. Alex Callinicos, "The Dynamics of Revolution," *International Socialism* 2:137 (Winter 2013), 127.
5. Tom Nairn, "The Question of Scotland," in *Faces of Nationalism: Janus Revisited* (London: Verso, 1997), 189.
6. Neil Davidson, *How Revolutionary Were the Bourgeois Revolutions?* (Chicago: Haymarket Books, 2012), 436–39, 446–65; Alex Callinicos, *Trotskyism* (Milton Keynes: Open University Press, 1990), chapters 4 and 5. Callinicos discusses Max Shachtman, C. L. R. James, and Cornelius Castoriadis in a chapter called "Heresies" and devotes a separate chapter to Tony Cliff and his cothinkers called "Reorientations." Although I agree that Cliff did more than anyone else to defend the revolutionary core of Trotsky's thought, in several areas by abandoning or revising specific positions or predictions, I prefer to see these thinkers (and Raya Dunayevskaya) as existing on a continuum or spectrum of "heretical reorienteers" with Castoriadis at one end and Cliff on the other. It is only in the light of Cliff's reversion to aspects of orthodox Trotskyism between 1968 and

1975–particularly in terms of party organization and economic catastrophism–that his relationship to these other thinkers has been obscured.

7. Daniel Bensaïd [2002], "Who are the Trotskyists?," in *Strategies of Resistance and "Who Are the Trotskyists?"* (London: Resistance Books, 2009), 96.

8. Walter Benjamin [1940], "On the Concept of History," in *Selected Writings,* vol. 4, *1938–1940,* edited by Howard Eiland and Michael J. Jennings (Cambridge, MA: The Belknap Press of Harvard University Press, 2003), 391.

9. Frederick Engels [1877], *Anti-Dühring: Herr Eugen Dühring's Revolution in Science,* in *Collected Works,* vol. 25 (London: Lawrence and Wishart, 1987), 145; Walter Benjamin [1940], "Paralipomena to 'On the Concept of History,'" in *Selected Writings,* vol. 4, 402.

Chapter 1: Tom Nairn and the Inevitability of Nationalism

1. Originally published in *International Socialism* 2:82 (Spring 1999) as "In Perspective: Tom Nairn."

2. The major works in order of appearance were: Tom Nairn, *The Break-Up of Britain: Crisis and Neo-Nationalism* (London: New Left Books, 1977); Hugh Seton-Watson, *Nations and States: An Enquiry into the Origins of Nations and the Politics of Nationalism* (London: Taylor and Francis, 1977); John Breuilly, *Nationalism and the State* (Manchester: Manchester University Press, 1982 and 1993); Ernest Gellner, *Nations and Nationalism* (Oxford: Blackwell, 1983); Benedict Anderson, *Imagined Communities: Reflections on the Rise and Spread of Nationalism* (London: Verso, 1983, 1991, and 2006); Anthony D. Smith, *The Ethnic Origins of Nations* (Oxford: Basil Blackwell, 1986); Eric J. Hobsbawm, *Nations And Nationalism Since 1780: Programme, Myth, Reality* (Cambridge: Cambridge University Press, 1990); Nigel Harris, *National Liberation* (Harmondsworth: Penguin, 1990); Anthony D. Smith, *National Identity* (Harmondsworth: Penguin, 1991); Liah Greenfield, *Nationalism: Five Roads to Modernity* (Cambridge, Massachusetts: Harvard University Press, 1992); and Ernest Gellner, *Nationalism* (London: Weidenfeld and Nicolson, 1997). The books by Anderson, Harris, and Hobsbawm, and the first by Gellner, were reviewed in Chris Harman, "The Return of the National Question," *International Socialism* 2:56 (Autumn 1992), 41–49.

3. Tom Nairn [1975], "The Modern Janus," in *The Break-Up of Britain: Crisis and Neo-Nationalism* (Second, expanded edition, London: Verso, 1981), 329.

4. Tom Nairn, *Faces of Nationalism: Janus Revisited* (London: Verso, 1997).

5. For an example of the first, see Nicolai Gentchev, "Lambs to the Slaughter?," *Socialist Review* 218 (April 1998), 29–30; for an example of the second, see Ian Bell, "Spirit of Nationhood Alive and Kicking as the World Goes Global," *The Scotsman* (February 9, 1998).

6. "The fortunes of the SNP have of course affected the intensity of national consciousness, but such consciousness is greater than the number of votes won by that party at elections. It is not necessarily concerned, as is the SNP with national self determination, or with political devolution. It is rather an expression of Scottishness on the part of an amorphous group of interests and individuals, whose identity is caught up with that of Scotland." James G. Kellas [1973], *The Scottish Political System* (Second edition, Cambridge: Cambridge University Press, 1975), 119.

7.   Tom Nairn, "The Question of Scotland," in *Faces of Nationalism,* 189.

8.   Willie Thompson, "Tom Nairn and the Crisis of the British State," *Contemporary Record* 6, no. 2 (Autumn 1992), 308. This interesting if over-reverential article is based in part on an interview with Nairn conducted on December 17, 1991, and is a useful source of information about his career. See also Perry Anderson, "Foreword," *English Questions* (London: Verso, 1992), 3.

9.   Tom Nairn [1977], "The Twilight of the British State," in *The Break-Up of Britain,* 75.

10. Leon D. Trotsky [1931–2], *The History of the Russian Revolution* (London: Pluto Press, 1977), 27; [1925], "Where is Britain Going?," in *Collected Writings and Speeches on Britain,* vol. 2, edited by R. Chappell and Allan Clinton (London: New Park Publications, 1974), 14, 39–40.

11. Alex Callinicos, "Exception or Symptom? The British Crisis and the World System," *New Left Review* I/169 (May-June 1988), 103.

12. The literature on the "Nairn-Anderson thesis" is too vast to be listed here. Virtually the only contribution to the debate to treat Nairn as seriously as it did Anderson was the first, Edward P. Thompson's "The Peculiarities of the English" (1965). This great (and extremely funny) essay is best savored in the complete version published in *The Poverty of Theory and Other Essays* (London: Merlin Press, 1978). A brief but pointed critique of the "thesis" from a perspective similar to mine can be found in Callinicos, "Exception or Symptom?" Various misconceptions about working-class politics during the nineteenth century are corrected in Chris Bambery, "Myth and Reality in British Working Class Struggle," in *Essays on Historical Materialism,* edited by John Rees (London: Bookmarks, 1998), although Bambery takes Anderson rather than Nairn as the starting point for his discussion.

13. Jack Brand, *The National Movement in Scotland* (London: Routledge and Kegan Paul, 1978), 258–262.

14. Tom Nairn, "The Three Dreams of Scottish Nationalism," *New Left Review* I/49 (May-June 1968), 7.

15. Ibid., 13.

16. Ibid., 16.

17. Ibid., 18.

18. David Caute, *Sixty-Eight: Year of the Barricades* (London: Paladin Books, 1988), 308–10. See also the documents assembled in Students and Staff of Hornsey School of Art, *The Hornsey Affair* (Harmondsworth: Penguin Books, 1969).

19. Tom Nairn [1968], "Notes towards the Definition of Anti-Culture," in *The Hornsey Affair,* 24.

20. Tom Nairn, "Why it Happened," in Angelo Quattrocchi and Tom Nairn, *The Beginning of the End: France, May 1968* (London: Panther Books, 1968), 123, 126. Nairn's contribution is dated: "July 1968. Hornsey College of Art, London, in the sixth week of the student occupation, in a classroom where I was once paid to explain this century to those too young to understand it." See ibid., 173. A review of the Verso reissue of this book by Jonathan Neale recommends that readers "skip the second half of the book, by Tom Nairn." See "1968: The Year the Monolith Cracked," *Socialist Review* 219 (May 1998), 17. It is true that in comparison with Quattrocchi's Situationist fireworks Nairn's contribution seems

rather drab, but in comparison with the latter's other work, both before and since, it positively soars.

21. Tom Nairn, "The Three Dreams of Scottish Nationalism," in *Memoirs of a Modern Scotland,* edited by Karl Miller (London: Faber and Faber, 1970), 52, 53–54.

22. Ibid. The reference is of course to the phrase often ascribed to Voltaire: "All the great ones of the earth and all nobles should be hanged, and strangled with entrails of the priests." These words were actually written by Jean Meslier (1664–1729), the parish priest of Etrepigny in the Champagne district of France. They appear in a testament found after he had starved himself to death during a dispute with the feudal superior, which reveals him to have held atheist and, indeed, virtually Communist views. Parts of the manuscript were published by Voltaire in 1762 as *Extrait des sentiments de Jean Meslier* and it is from this publication that the association with him derives.

23. Tom Nairn, "The Left against Europe?," *New Left Review* I/75 (September-October 1972), 116–19.

24. Tom Nairn [1974], "Scotland and Europe," in *The Break-Up of Britain,* 99, 96.

25. Tom Nairn, "Old Nationalism and New Nationalism," in *The Red Paper on Scotland,* edited by Gordon Brown (Edinburgh: Edinburgh University Student Publications Board, 1975), 47, 49; *The Break-Up of Britain,* 179. The majority of the quoted passages were not included in the later version of this essay.

26. Nairn, "Old Nationalism and New Nationalism," 24; *The Break-Up of Britain,* 130.

27. For an example of the first: "After the dark, the unspeakable 17th century, it was 1688 which marked the real dawn in Scotland." See *The Break-Up of Britain,* 109. For an example of the second, see: "[Kailyard culture] is recognisably intertwined with that prodigious array of Kitsch symbols, slogans, ornaments, banners, war-cries, knick-knacks, music-hall heroes, icons, conventional sayings and sentiments (not a few of them 'pithy') which have for so long resolutely defended the name of 'Scotland' to the world. Annie Swan and [A J] Cronin provided no more than the relatively decent outer garb for the vast tartan monster. In their work the thing trots along doucely enough, on a lead. But it is something else to be with it (e.g.) in a London pub on International night, or in the crowd at the annual Military Tattoo in front of Edinburgh Castle. How intolerably vulgar! What unbearable, crass, mindless philistinism! One knows that Kitsch is a large constituent of mass popular culture in every land: but this is ridiculous!" See *The Break-Up of Britain,* 162. On second thought, given the success of *Braveheart,* and the recent announcement that April 6 is henceforth to be celebrated in the USA as "Tartan Day," perhaps Nairn does not exaggerate too grossly after all.

28. Craig Beveridge and Ronald Turnbull, "Scottish Nationalist, British Marxist: the Strange Case of Tom Nairn," in *The Eclipse of Scottish Culture* (Edinburgh: Polygon Books, 1989), 59, 60.

29. Nairn, "The Twilight of the British State," 89–90.

30. Nairn, "The Modern Janus," 339–340, 348–349, 354.

31. Tom Nairn, "The National Question," internal SLP document, cited in Henry M. Drucker, *Breakaway: the Scottish Labor Party* (Edinburgh: Edinburgh University Student Publications Board, 1978), 124.

32. Andrew Marr, *The Battle for Scotland* (Harmondsworth: Penguin Books, 1992), 162.

33. Nairn, *Faces of Nationalism,* 227 note 1.

34. Tam Dalyell, *Devolution: The End of Britain?* (London: Jonathan Cape, 1977), 306.

35. Eric Heffer, *Never a Yes Man* (London: Verso, 1991), 165. Heffer records how his views were received in parliament: "In the Commons I made speeches drawing attention to what the Austro-Marxists and [Rosa] Luxemburg had argued. They cut little ice." It is part of the tragedy of his political career that he ever imagined they would in this setting.

36. Tom Nairn, "Postscript 1981: Into Political Emergency," in *The Break-Up of Britain,* 288, 397–398.

37. See ibid., 402–404 and, more optimistically, an article called, inevitably, "The Crisis of the British State," *New Left Review* I/130 (November-December 1981), 41–44. Words, like currency, lose value through inflation. Thanks to Nairn, the word "crisis," especially when conjoined to the phrase "British state," is worth about as much as a Weimar deutschmark.

38. Thompson, "Tom Nairn and the Crisis of the British State," 320. Ironically, Anderson himself abandoned the classical Marxist perspective shortly afterwards. His own account dates this from the mid-1980s. See Perry Anderson, "Foreword," in *A Zone of Engagement* (London: Verso, 1992), xii-xiii.

39. Tom Nairn, "Cities and Nationalism," in *Faces of Nationalism,* 123.

40. Tom Nairn, "Introduction: On Studying Nationalism," in *Faces of Nationalism,* 10–11.

41. Ibid., 13.

42. Ibid., quoting Steve Jones, *In the Blood: God, Genes and Destiny* (London: Houghton Miffin, 1997), ix.

43. Tom Nairn, "Does Tomorrow Belong to the Bullets or the Bouquets?," *New Statesman and Society* (June 19, 1992), 31.

44. Pat Kane, "Scotland by Starlight," in *Tinsel Show: Pop, Politics, Scotland* (Edinburgh: Polygon Books, 1992), 198.

45. Tom Nairn [1993], "Demonising Nationality," in *Faces of Nationalism,* 63.

46. Tom Nairn [1996], "The Curse of Rurality: Limits of Modernization Theory," in *Faces of Nationalism,* 90–92, 101–102, 109–110.

47. Tom Nairn, "Reflections of Nationalist Disasters," *New Left Review* I/230 (July/August 1998), 149.

48. Zygmunt Bauman [1989], *Modernity and the Holocaust* (Second edition, Cambridge: Polity Press, 1991), 46, 61.

49. Geoff Eley, "The British Model and the German Road: Rethinking the Course of German History before 1914," in David Blackbourn and Geoff Eley, *The Peculiarities of German History* (Oxford: Oxford University Press, 1984), 154.

50. Norman Stone, *Europe Transformed: 1878–1919* (Glasgow: Fontana Books, 1983), 160.

51. Bauman, *Modernity and the Holocaust,* x.

52. Nairn, "The Curse of Rurality," 149.

53. Tom Nairn [1994–6], "Micro-States," in *Faces of Nationalism,* 143–149.

54. Tom Nairn [1990], "The Owl of Minerva," in *Faces of Nationalism,* 52.

55. Nairn, "Demonising Nationality," 57–58.

56. Bob Arnot and Kirill Buketov, "The Political Economy of Russian Labor: From

Acquiescence to Action?," *Abertay Sociology Papers* 1, no. 2 (Dundee: University of Abertay, 1998), 7, 9.

57. Tom Nairn, "The Question of Scale," in *Faces of Nationalism,* 134.

58. Tom Nairn [1980], "Internationalism: A Critique," in *Faces of Nationalism,* 32.

59. Ibid., 30.

60. Ibid., 35.

61. Even this apparent recognition that internationalism once sprung unforced from a prelapsarian proletariat is designed to emphasize the supposed extent of the subsequent fall. In fact, even in their formative years, most proletarians have had to overcome reformist consciousness, strategy, and organization–of which nationalism is inevitably a component.

62. Nairn, "Internationalism," 30–31.

63. Ibid. 32–33, 36.

64. Ibid., 39, 41, 45.

65. Alex Callinicos, *Theories and Narratives: Reflections on the Philosophy of History* (Cambridge: Polity Press, 1995), 179.

66. Smith, *The Ethnic Origins of Nations,* 11–12.

67. Ibid., 8.

68. Gellner, *Nationalism,* 7–8.

69. Nairn, "Introduction: On Studying Nationalism," 7. This is a good example of one of Nairn's most annoying habits: quoting an argument against one of his positions in a knowing kind of way, then carrying on without actually answering the point.

70. Tom Nairn [1995], "Union and Empire," in *Faces of Nationalism,* 209.

71. In particular, Ernest Gellner, "Nationalism," in *Thought and Change* (London: Weidenfeld and Nicolson, 1964). See the references in *The Break-Up of Britain,* 96, 99, 133, 317, 338, 342 and 358. As we saw above, his attitude to the Gellner thesis has now undergone a significant alteration.

72. Nigel Harris, *Of Bread and Guns: The World Economy in Crisis* (Harmondsworth: Penguin Books, 1983), 24.

73. Anderson, *Imagined Communities,* 36.

74. Harman, "The Return of the National Question," 42, 43.

75. The problem for both Anderson and Nairn may have been their incomprehension at the conflicts between supposedly socialist–or at least "post-capitalist"–states in Indochina from 1978 onward. Compare Anderson, *Imagined Communities,* xi, 1–2, and Nairn, "Postscript 1981," 371.

76. George Kerevan, "The Origins of Scottish Nationhood: Arguments within Scottish Marxism," *The Bulletin of Scottish Politics* 1, no. 2 (Spring 1981), 118–119.

77. Occasionally the mask slipped even prior to 1989. When Khieu Samphan, one of the leaders of the Khmer Rouge, was interviewed in January 1981, his response was rather different: "No more socialism. No more socialist revolution. Our ideal is the survival of Cambodia. As for Communism, we saw it as the way to lead Cambodia to independence and survival means only, not the ideal. Now, through the flesh and blood of people, we have been given the experience to know that we cannot follow this way." Quoted in Grant Evans and Kevin Rowley, *Red Brotherhood at War: Vietnam, Cambodia and Laos since 1975* (London: Verso, 1984), 251.

78. This was true even during the First World War, which Nairn repeatedly cites as an example of spontaneous national feeling. The issue has been dealt with in Megan Trudell, "Prelude to Revolution: Class Consciousness and the First World War," *International Socialism* 2:76 (Autumn 1997), 71–85, supplemented by Ian Birchall, "The Vice-Like Hold of Nationalism? A Comment on Megan Trudell's 'Prelude to Revolution,'" *International Socialism* 2:78 (Spring 1978).

79. The following two paragraphs are based on information and–in the case of the first–analysis contained in Alex Callinicos and Mike Simons, *The Great Strike, International Socialism* 2:27/28 (Spring/Summer 1985), 84–92, and Keith Aitken, *The Bairns O' Adam: The Story of the STUC* (Edinburgh: Polygon Books, 1997), 273–281. The latter is a semiofficial history of the Scottish TUC.

80. Quoted in *Miners 1984–1994: A Decade of Endurance,* edited by Joe Owens (Edinburgh: Polygon Books, 1994), 91. The editor and the interviewee are not the same person.

81. Aitken, *The Bairns O' Adam,* 292.

82. Ibid., 295.

83. Alex Law, "Neither Colonial nor Historic: Worker's Organization at Rosyth Dockyard, 1945–1995," in *The History of Work and Labor Relations in the Royal Dockyards,* edited by Anna Day and Kenneth Lunn (London: Mansell, 1999). One the TGWU stewards was Alex Falconer, who became the Labor MEP for Fife and Mid-Scotland in 1984.

84. John Pilger, "The Dockers," in *Hidden Agendas* (London: The New Press, 1998), 351.

85. Nairn, "From Civil Society to Civic Nationalism," 87, 88. My emphasis.

86. Ibid., 84.

87. Tom Nairn [1991], "Identities in Scotland," in *Faces of Nationalism,* 187.

88. Ibid., 193.

89. Ray Burnett, "Socialists and the SNP," in *The Red Paper on Scotland,* 121.

90. *The Scotsman* (June 5, 1998).

91. Joyce McMillan, "Foreign Lesson in Pressing for Home Rule," *Scotland on Sunday* (August 22, 1993).

92. *The Scotsman* (July 1, 1998).

93. See Neil Davidson and Keir McKechnie, "Riotous Assembly?," *Socialist Review* 219 (May 1998), 4–5.

94. Tom Nairn [1997], "Sovereignty after the Election," in *Faces of Nationalism,* 221.

95. Ibid., 223. The reference here to "recalling" Parliament presumably alludes to the feudal estates that dissolved themselves on 28 April 1707!

96. Tom Nairn, "British Sovereignty since the Election," *Scottish Affairs,* special issue, *Understanding Constitutional Change* (1998), 36. Nairn's contribution began with an unseemly grovel to the late Donald Dewar, "our last and greatest Scottish Secretary of State," who had preceded him on the platform: so much for the iniquities of the Labour Party. See ibid., 13.

97. William Ferguson, *The Identity of the Scottish Nation: A Historic Quest* (Edinburgh: Edinburgh University Press, 1998), 316.

98. Paul Surridge, Lindsay Patterson, Alice Brown, and David McCrone, "The Scottish Electorate and the Scottish Parliament," in *Scottish Affairs,* special issue, *Understanding Constitutional Change,* 43.

99. Nairn, "Empire and Union," 208.
100. "Scots Awa," *Economist* (May 26–June 1, 1990), 18–19.
101. Andrew Gowers, "L'Ecosse Libre," *Financial Times* (August 14, 1998).
102. Andrew Neil, "Scotland the Self-Deluded," *Spectator* (August 15, 1998), 12. I am unable to recall the source of this memorable piece of Nairnian invective– aimed for once at a deserving target–but it springs to mind every time Neil's sanctimonious features loom out over one of his odious op-ed pieces in *The Scotsman,* a paper that regularly falls, under his regime as editor-in-chief, to new lows of right-wing hysteria.
103. Tom Nairn, "Race and Nationalism," *Faces of Nationalism,* 121.
104. Nairn, "Why it Happened," 173.
105. Nairn, "The Three Dreams of Scottish Nationalism," in *Memoirs of a Modern Scotland,* 54.
106. Leon D. Trotsky [1933], "The Tragedy of the German Proletariat: the German Workers Will Rise Again–Stalinism, Never!," in *The Struggle against Fascism in Germany,* edited by George Breitman and Merry Maizel (New York: Pathfinder Books, 1971), 377.

Chapter 2: Marx and Engels on the Scottish Highlands

1. Originally published in *Science and Society* 65, no. 3 (Fall 2001).
2. The only existing attempt to list all the references by Marx and Engels to the Scottish Highlands is in Fraser Grigor, "Marx and Engels on the Highlands," *Scottish Marxist* 13 (Spring 1977), 40–45, although it is incomplete.
3. James D. Young, *Racism, the Origins of Inequality and Socialism* (Glasgow: Clydeside Press, no date identified), 22.
4. Ibid.
5. Christopher Harvie, *Scotland and Nationalism: Scottish Society and Politics, 1707 to the Present* (London: George Allen and Unwin, 1977), 26. Harvie is not primarily concerned with attacking Marxism, which he–along with the vast majority of contemporary intellectuals–seems to regard as being long past its sell-by date. Indeed, his lack of interest in the subject is indicated by the impressive error rate in the sentence quoted above. It was, of course, the Duchess rather than the Duke of Sutherland whom Marx specifically attacked and his comments are to be found in *Capital* vol. 1 rather than vol. 2. See also the dismissive comments in "Modern Scotland: Remembering the People," in *Why Scottish History Matters,* edited by Rosalind Mitchison (Edinburgh: Saltire Society, 1991), 80.
6. Alan Armstrong, "Back to the Future–Part Two: 1492 and 1992–Redemption, Improvement and Progress," *Cencrastus* 51 (Spring 1995), 36, 37.
7. John Strawson, "Culture and Imperialism," *Socialist History* 14 (1999), 113–114.
8. Robert J. C. Young, *White Mythologies: History Writing and the West* (London: Routledge, 1990), 3. There are writers on the left who agree that this was the position taken by Marx and Engels, but find it commendable. The most comprehensive statement of this position was given by Bill Warren in his critique of the Marxist theory of imperialism in its Leninist form: "Perhaps the least important reason for such a reevaluation is that the bulk of current Marxist analyses of and propaganda about imperialism actually reverse the views of the

founders of Marxism, who held that the expansion of capitalism into pre-capitalist areas of the world was desirable and progressive." Not the least difficulty with this completely undialectical position is the way in which it justifies the charges of Eurocentrism regularly leveled against the Marxist tradition as a whole by writers like Strawson and Robert Young. See Bill Warren, *Imperialism: Pioneer Of Capitalism* (London: Verso, 1980), 3.

9. Eric J. Hobsbawm, "Introduction," in Karl Marx, *Pre-Capitalist Economic Formations* (New York: International Publishers, 1965), 50.

10. Teodor Shanin, "Late Marx: Gods and Craftsmen," in *Late Marx and the Russian Road*, edited by Teodor Shanin (London: Routledge and Kegan Paul, 1983), 6–8, 15.

11. Franklin Rosemont, "Karl Marx and the Iroquois," *Arsenal/Surrealist Subversion* 4 (1989), 210. Rosemont is followed in this assertion by Peter Fryer, "Engels: A Man of His Time," in *The Condition of Britain: Essays on Frederick Engels,* edited by John Lea and Geoff Pilling (London: Pluto Press, 1996), 149–150 and by Young, *Racism, the Origins of Inequality and Socialism,* 13–14, 41. Armstrong and Young both refer, with Shanin, to an "early," "middle," and "late" Marx, although only Armstrong cites Shanin in this connection.

12. Friedrich Engels [1845], *The Condition of the Working Class in England: From Personal Observations and Authentic Sources,* in *Collected Works,* vol. 4 (London: Lawrence and Wishart, 1975), 319.

13. Friedrich Engels [1848], "Extraordinary Revelations–Abd-El-Kader–Guizot's Foreign Policy," in *Collected Works,* vol. 6 (London: Lawrence and Wishart, 1976), 471–472.

14. Friedrich Engels [1849], "The Magyar Struggle," in Karl Marx, *Political Writings,* vol. 1, *The Revolution of 1848* (Harmondsworth: Penguin/New Left Review, 1974), 221–22, 225–26.

15. Friedrich Engels [1866], "What Have the Working Classes To Do With Poland?," in Karl Marx, *Political Writings,* vol. 3, *The First International and After* (Harmondsworth: Penguin/New Left Review, 1974), 383.

16. John Stuart Mill [1861], *Representative Government,* in *Collected Works,* vol. 19 (London: Routledge and Kegan Paul, 1965), 556.

17. Eric J. Hobsbawm, *Nations and Nationalism since 1780: Program, Myth, Reality* (Cambridge: Cambridge University Press, 1990), 34–35.

18. Mathew Arnold [1866], "On the Study of Celtic Literature," in *The Complete Prose Works of Matthew Arnold,* vol. 3, *Lectures and Essays in Criticism,* edited by R. H. Super (Ann Arbor: University of Michigan Press, 1962), 296–297, 384. In fairness to Arnold, we should note the defense by Russell Jacoby of his "aggressive defence of public education and social equality [and] his assault on the market." See *The End of Utopia: Politics and Culture in an Age of Apathy* (New York: Basic Books, 2000), 67–68, 89–99.

19. Engels to Bernstein, 22 and 25 February 1882, in *Collected Works,* vol. 46 (London: Lawrence and Wishart, 1992), 206.

20. Karl Marx and Friedrich Engels [1845–46], *The German Ideology: Critique of Modern German Philosophy According to Its Representatives Feuerbach, B. Bauer and Stirner, and of German Socialism According to Its Various Prophets,* in *Collected Works,* vol. 5 (London: Lawrence and Wishart, 1975), 146.

21. Karl Marx [1847], *The Poverty of Philosophy: Answer to* The Philosophy of Poverty *by M. Proudhon, in Collected Works,* vol. 6 (London: Lawrence and Wishart, 1976), 173.

22. Karl Marx [1853], "Elections–Financial Clouds–the Duchess of Sutherland and Slavery," in *Collected Works,* vol. 11 (London: Lawrence and Wishart, 1979); [1853] "Forced Emigration–Cossack and Magyar–the Refugee Question–Election Bribery in England–Mr. Cobden," in *Collected Works,* vol. 11; [1853] "The War Question–Financial Matters–Strikes," 7 October 1853, in *Collected Works,* vol. 12 (London: Lawrence and Wishart, 1979); [1854] "Attack Upon Sebastopol–Clearing of Estates in Scotland," in *Collected Works,* vol. 13 (London: Lawrence and Wishart, 1980).

23. Marx, "Elections–Financial Clouds–the Duchess of Sutherland and Slavery," 494.

24. Karl Marx [1867], *Capital: a Critique of Political Economy,* vol. 1 (Harmondsworth: Penguin Books/New Left Review, 1976), 890.

25. Young, *Racism, the Origins of Inequality and Socialism,* 22.

26. Karl Marx [1853], "The British Rule in India," in *Political Writings,* vol. 2, *Surveys from Exile* (Harmondsworth: Penguin Books/New Left Review, 1974), 306–07. Like many of their contemporaries Marx and Engels often used the term "England" in place of "Britain" (which in turn means "England and Wales and the Scottish Lowlands"). Since this substitution occurs several times in subsequent quotations, readers should simply take "England" to mean "Britain," unless the context makes it clear that a more restricted usage is intended.

27. James Mill [1818], *The History of British India,* vol. 1 (Fifth edition, London: James Madden, 1858), 218, 320.

28. Karl Marx [1853], "The British India Company–Its History and Prospects," in *Surveys from Exile,* 310.

29. Edward Said, *Orientalism* (Harmondsworth: Penguin Books, 1985), 155.

30. John Carstairs Matheson, "Socialism and Nationalism," *Socialist* (November 1910). The inspiration for this passage is not Marx, but Lord Macaulay, who makes a very similar comparison in his *History of England,* which began publication in 1848: "Few people seemed to be aware that, at no remote period, a MacDonald or a MacGregor in his tartan was to a citizen of Edinburgh or Glasgow what an Indian hunter in his war paint is to an inhabitant of Philadelphia or Boston. Artists and actors represented Bruce and Douglas in striped petticoats. They might as well have represented Washington brandishing a tomahawk, and girt with a string of scalps." Thomas B. Macaulay [1848–54], *The History of England from the Accession of James II,* vol. 2 (London: Dent, 1906), 451.

31. Ephraim Nimni, "Marx, Engels and the National Question," *Science and Society* 53, no. 3 (Fall 1990), 314, 324.

32. Marx, "Forced Emigration–Cossack and Magyar–the Refugee Question–Election Bribery in England–Mr. Cobden," 529.

33. Macaulay, *The History of England from the Accession of James II* , vol. 2, 493.

34. Engels, *The Condition of the Working Class in England,* 319, 391.

35. Ibid., 559.

36. Nimni, "Marx, Engels and the National Question," 314.

37. Roman Rosdolsky [1948], *Engels And the "Non-Historic Peoples": The National Question in the Revolution of 1848,* edited by John-Paul Himka, *Critique* 18/19

(1986), 129.

38. Neil Davidson, *The Origins of Scottish Nationhood* (London: Pluto Press, 2000), 72–74.

39. Tom Nairn [1975], "Old and New Scottish Nationalism," in *The Break-Up of Britain*, 147.

40. Even Rosdolsky, in an otherwise perceptive passage, makes too many concessions to the notion of a Highland nation before 1746, noting that "the reactionary conduct of the Highland Scots ... proceeded ... not from the reactionary character of their *nationality*, but from specific social, economic and political conditions that drove this 'national refuse' into opposition to the revolution (and so their very nationality became an *expression* of this opposition)." See *Engels and the "Non-Historic Peoples*," 12.

41. Friedrich Engels [1878–82], ["On the Early History of the Germans"], in *Collected Works*, vol. 26 (London: Lawrence and Wishart, 1990), 30. According to Anthony D. Smith, primordialists "claim that nations and ethnic communities are the natural units of history and integral elements of human experience." See *The Ethnic Origins of Nations* (Oxford: Basil Blackwell, 1986), 11.

42. Friedrich Engels [1884], "The Decay of Feudalism and the Rise of Nation States," in *Collected Works*, vol. 26, 559–561.

43. Davidson, *The Origins of Scottish Nationhood*, 28–37.

44. Karl Marx [1855], "Ireland's Revenge," in *Collected Works*, vol. 14 (London: Lawrence and Wishart, 1980), 80.

45. Engels to Marx, 23 May 1856, in *Collected Works*, vol. 40 (London: Lawrence and Wishart, 1983), 50. Earlier in the same letter Engels refers to the low productivity of land, with one notable exception: " ... towards Limerick, the hills are excellently cultivated, mostly by Scottish farmers." These were the descendants of the Protestant settlers from the Lowlands.

46. Friedrich Engels [1865], "Plan of Chapter Two, and Fragments for *The History of Ireland*," in *Collected Works*, vol. 21 (London: Lawrence and Wishart, 1985), 312.

47. Marx to Meyer and Vogt, 9 April 1870, in *The First International and After*, 168–169.

48. Friedrich Engels [1870], "[*The History of Ireland*]," in *Collected Works*, vol. 21, 147–48.

49. Engels to Kautsky, 7 February 1882, in *Collected Works*, vol. 46, 193.

50. Engels, "The Magyar Struggle," 217.

51. James D. Young, "Letter to *Cencrastus*," *Cencrastus* 52 (Summer 1995), 23; Young, *Racism, the Origins of Inequality and Socialism*, 21.

52. Karl Marx [1856], "Speech at the Anniversary of *The People's Paper*," in *Surveys from Exile*, 299–300.

53. Aijaz Ahmad, "Marx on India: A Clarification," in *In Theory* (London: Verso, 1992), 226.

54. Alex Callinicos, *Theories and Narratives: Reflections on the Philosophy of History* (Cambridge: Polity Press, 1995), 154.

55. Ahmad, "Marx on India," 241, 227–228.

56. Karl Marx [1853], "The Future Results of the British Rule in India," in *Surveys from Exile*, 319, 323, 324–25.

57. Callinicos, *Theories and Narratives*, 154–60.

58. Karl Marx [1881], "[Third Draft]," "[Drafts of the Letter to Vera Zasulich]," in

Collected Works, vol. 24 (London: Lawrence and Wishart, 1989), 365.

59. Engels to Kautsky, 7 February 1882, in *Collected Works,* vol. 46, 322–23.

60. Marx, *Capital,* vol. 1, 889–95.

61. Grigor, "Marx and Engels on the Highlands," 44–45.

62. Karl Marx [1857–58], *Grundrisse: Foundations of the Critique of Political Economy (Rough Draft),* (Harmondsworth: Penguin Books/New Left Review, 1973), 133.

63. Thomas M. Devine [1987], "The Highland Clearances," in *Exploring the Scottish Past* (East Linton: Tuckwell Press, 1995), 140.

64. Roy H. Campbell, "Too Much on the Highlands? A Plea for Change," *Scottish Economic and Social History* 14 (1994), 58–64.

65. Armstrong, "Back to the Future–Part Two," 36–37.

66. Karl Marx [1877], "[Letter to *Otechesivenniye Zapiski*]," in *Collected Works,* vol. 24, 199, 200.

67. Marx to Zasulich, 8 March 1881, *Collected Works,* vol. 46, 72.

68. Karl Marx and Friedrich Engels [1882], "Preface to the Second Russian Edition of *The Manifesto of the Communist Party,*" in *Collected Works,* vol. 24, 42.

69. Friedrich Engels [1884], *The Origin of the Family, Private Property and the State: In the Light of the Recent Researches of Lewis H. Morgan,* in *Collected Works,* vol. 26 (London: Lawrence and Wishart, 1990), 232, 235.

70. Although of Irish descent, Connolly was born in Edinburgh in 1868 and lived there until he went to Ireland in 1882 as a private in the King's Liverpool Regiment. He returned in 1889 and only left permanently in 1896. See C. Desmond Greaves, *The Life and Times of James Connolly* (London: Lawrence and Wishart, 1961), 17–25.

71. The SDF became the British Socialist Party in 1912 after merging with some dissident branches of the Independent Labor Party.

72. John Maclean [1920], "Literary Note," in *In the Rapids of Revolution,* edited by Nan Milton (London: Alison and Busby, 1978), 221.

73. John Maclean [1920], "All Hail, the Scottish Workers' Republic!," in *In the Rapids of Revolution,* 218.

74. John Maclean [1920], "Irish Stew," in *In the Rapids of Revolution,* 219.

75. *The Origin of the Family* was in fact one of the few complete works by Marx or Engels available in Britain before the Russian Revolution of 1917 (the English-language edition was published in 1902). The availability of English-language works by Marx and Engels down to 1933 is given in Stuart MacIntyre, *A Proletarian Science: Marxism in Britain, 1917–1933* (London: Lawrence and Wishart, 1986), 91–92. For the publication history of the letter to Zasulich, see David Ryazanov, "The Discovery of the Drafts (1924)," in *Late Marx and the Russian Road,* 127–33.

76. Marx, "Elections–Financial Clouds–the Duchess of Sutherland and Slavery," 491.

77. Friedrich Engels, "Afterword (1894) [to *On Social Relations in Russia*]," in *Collected Works,* vol. 27 (London: Lawrence and Wishart, 1990), 421–22.

78. The influence of the Scottish Enlightenment also entered their work indirectly from a source usually taken to be one of the other "sources and component parts" of Marxism: the writings of Hegel. For the influence of the Scottish Enlightenment on Hegel, with special reference to the division of labor, see Norbert Waszek, "The Division of Labor: From the Scottish Enlightenment to

Hegel," *The Owl of Minerva* 15 (Fall 1983). The link had previously been made in Georg Lukács [1938], *The Young Hegel* (London: Merlin Books, 1975) and Alasdair MacIntyre, *Marxism: An Interpretation* (London: Student Christian Movement Press, 1953), 27.

79. Walter Scott [1817], "Author's Introduction," in *Rob Roy* (London: Dent, 1986), 330.

80. Scott to Lord Dalkeith, 23 November 1806, in *The Letters of Sir Walter Scott 1787–1807*, edited by H. J. C. Grierson (London: Constable, 1932), 385.

81. Eleanor Marx [1895], "Recollections of Mohr," in *Marx and Engels on Literature and Art*, edited by Lee Baxandall and Stephan Morawski (New York: International General, 1974), 150.

82. Paul Lafargue [1890], "Reminiscences of Marx," in *Marx and Engels on Literature and Art*, 152.

83. Engels, *The Origin of the Family, Private Property and the State*, 235.

84. Lewis H. Morgan [1877], *Ancient Society, or Researches in the Lines of Human Progress from Savagery through Barbarism to Civilization* (Chicago: Charles H. Kerr, 1903), 386.

85. Their other major source was William F. Skene, *The Highlanders of Scotland: Their Origins, History and Antiquities* (London: John Murray, 1837). See *The Ethnological Notebooks of Karl Marx: Studies of Morgan, Phear, Maine, Lubbock*, edited by Lawrence Krader (Assen: Van Gorcum, 1972), 307.

86. Morgan, *Ancient Society*, 318.

87. Armstrong has attempted to classify Highland clan society as an example of the tributary mode: "Like many other societies such as the 'mir' in Russia, Scottish clan society was based on the community working the land." Both societies were supposedly characterized by the fact that "chieftains and their immediate kin exacted various tributes from those working the land." They exacted tributes; therefore this must have been . . . a "tributary" society! Armstrong appears to be drawing too literally on the references by Marx to "tribute" in " . . . the Duchess of Sutherland and Slavery." See "Back to the Future—Part Two," 38. In fact, as Chris Wickham has argued, the tributary mode involves a "state class" based on a public institution, with political rights to extract surplus from a peasantry that it does not tenurially control. Far from being dominated by a centralized state bureaucracy, Highland society was characterized by an extreme fragmentation and localism that made it the precise opposite of states like Byzantium for whom the tributary mode is the most appropriate analytic tool. See "The Uniqueness of the East," *Journal of Peasant Studies* 12, no. 2/3 (January/April 1985), 170–71.

88. T. C. Smout [1969], *A History of the Scottish People, 1560–1830* (Glasgow: Fontana Books, 1972), 33.

89. Michael H. Brown, "Scotland Tamed? Kings and Magnates in Late Medieval Scotland: A Review of Recent Work," *Innes Review* 45, no. 2 (Autumn 1994), 126–146.

90. Robert A. Dodgson, *Land and Society in Early Scotland* (Oxford: Oxford University Press, 1981), 153–54.

91. Max Weber [1919–20], *General Economic History* (London: George Allen and Unwin, 1923), 15.

92. Robert A. Dodgson, "'Pretence of Blude' and 'Place of Their Dwelling': The

Nature of the Scottish Clans, 1500–1744," in *Scottish Society, 1500–1800,* edited by Robert A. Houston and Ian D. Whyte (Cambridge: Cambridge University Press, 1989), 187.

93. Engels, "Afterword (1894) [to *On Social Relations in Russia*]," 423, 424, 425–26, 431. Shanin has claimed that twentieth-century revolutions in backward or developing societies (he cites Russia 1905 and 1917, Turkey 1906, Iran 1909, Mexico 1910, China 1910, 1927 and 1949) have vindicated the position that Marx tentatively outlined with respect to Russia in his letter to Zasulich. See Shanin, "Late Marx," 24, 25. They do not. It would take us too far afield to discuss the nature of these revolutions, but as Trotsky pointed out, first for Russia, then more generally, the very possibility of socialism emerging depended on the existence of a working class, and hence on that of capitalism and the prior *dissolution* of the peasant commune. This is in line with the last comments of Engels quoted above, and not that of the Populists, whose position was that socialism could be built on the *basis* of the peasant commune.

94. James D. Young, "Marxism, Liberalism and the Process of Industrialization," *Survey* 70–71 (1969), 215 and Young, "Letter to *Cencrastus*," 23.

95. Jeffrey Vogel, "The Tragedy of History," *New Left Review* I/220 (November/December 1996), 56, 58.

96. The reasons for that failure lie far beyond the scope of this article, although the weakness of trade unions in Scotland during the nineteenth century is obviously one factor. Marx himself wrote in 1867 that: "The formation since the close of 1865 of a Trades' Union among the agricultural laborers at first in Scotland is a historic event." See Marx, *Capital,* vol. 1, 363. Another factor was obviously the attitude of socialists like Carstairs Matheson. What would have been required would have been a Lowland attitude to the Highlanders comparable to that which Antonio Gramsci urged on Northern Italian workers in relation to Southern Italian peasants. See [1926] "Some Aspects of the Southern Question," in *Selections from the Political Writings (1921–1926),* edited by Quentin Hoare (London: Lawrence and Wishart, 1978), 448–49.

97. James Hunter [1976], *The Making of the Crofting Community* (Second edition, Edinburgh: John Donald, 2000), 27.

Chapter 3: The Prophet, His Biographer, and the Watchtower

1. Originally published in *International Socialism* 2:104 (Autumn 2004) as a review of Isaac Deutscher[1954], *The Prophet Armed: Trotsky: 1879–1921*; [1959], *The Prophet Unarmed: Trotsky: 1921–1928*; and [1963], *The Prophet Outcast: Trotsky: 1929–1940* (London: Verso, 2003).

2. Edward P. Thompson, "The Poverty of Theory: Or an Orrery of Errors," in *The Poverty of Theory and Other Essays* (London: Merlin Press, 1978), 193.

3. Therefore, although I agree with Matt Perry that "[a] host of Marxist biographical portraits could be assembled," I am not at all convinced that these represent the best Marxism has to offer in historical writing—a judgment that tends to be supported by the shortness of his own list of examples and the fact that biography fails to reappear anywhere else in his otherwise useful introductory text. See *Marxism and History* (Houndmills: Palgrave Macmillan, 2002), 9.

4. See Tony Cliff, *Lenin* (4 volumes, London: Pluto Press, 1975–9) for an example

of the first and Charles Van Onselen, *The Seed is Mine: The Life of Kas Maine, a South African Sharecropper, 1894–1985* (New York: Hill and Wang, 1996) for an example of the second.

5. David Horowitz, "David Horowitz Versus Christopher Hitchens," History News Network, hnn.us/articles/893.html.

6. Martin Amis, *Koba the Dread: Laughter and the Twenty Million* (London: Jonathan Cape, 2002), 251, 252.

7. Deutscher died before he could complete a projected volume on the third, Lenin, although the early sections were published as *Lenin's Childhood* (London: Oxford University Press, 1970).

8. Where not otherwise specified, details on Deutscher's life are taken from Daniel Singer, "Armed with a Pen," in *Isaac Deutscher: The Man and His Work*, edited by David Horowitz (London: Macdonald, 1971); Perry Anderson, "Preface," in *Isaac Deutscher, Marxism, Wars and Revolutions* (London: Verso, 1984), i–vi; and Tamara Deutscher, "Isaac Deutscher, 1907–1967," Deutscher Prize website, www.deutscherprize.org.uk.

9. Deutscher, *The Prophet Outcast,* 341.

10. Ibid., 176.

11. Peter Sedgwick, "The Tragedy of a Tragedian: An Appreciation of Isaac Deutscher," *International Socialism* 1:31 (Winter 1967/8), 11.

12. Perry Anderson, *Considerations on Western Marxism* (London: Verso, 1976), 99–101.

13. See Michael Ignatieff, *Isaiah Berlin: A Life* (London: Chatto and Windus, 1998), 235.

14. Ibid., 93. For a rather less adoring picture of Berlin, see Hywel Williams, "An English Liberal Stooge," *The Guardian* (April 14, 2004).

15. Deutscher variously compared Trotsky as a historian to Marx, Churchill, and Carlyle. See Deutscher, *The Prophet Outcast,* 177–78, 189. Marx apart, the most appropriate comparison for Trotsky is fact Thomas Babington Macaulay. His *The History of England from the Accession of James VII* bears a startling structural resemblance to *The History of the Russian Revolution*. Both begin with a sweeping summary of national history to the eve of the revolution, before narrowing the focus to an almost day-by-day account. Both display the same depth of characterization in dealing with the historical actors. Both are infused with a distinct theory of history–Macaulay's Whiggism is as important an organizing principle as Trotsky's Marxism. Trotsky followed Marx in not having a particularly high opinion of the political content of Macaulay's work ("sometimes interesting but always superficial"), but the parallels are there all the same. See Leon D. Trotsky [1925], "Where is Britain Going?" in *Collected Writings and Speeches on Britain,* vol. 2, edited by R. Chappell and Alan Clinton (London: New Park, 1974), 90.

16. Deutscher, *The Prophet Armed,* 428.

17. Deutscher, *The Prophet Outcast,* 94–95.

18. Ibid., 141–46, 157–58.

19. Deutscher, *The Prophet Armed,* 216–17. This passage is a good example of how Deutscher can distill the essence of his source materials. Compare Trotsky's own account of his performances at the Modern Circus in [1930] *My Life: An Attempt at an Autobiography* (Harmondsworth: Penguin, 1975), 306–07, 349.

20. Deutscher, *The Prophet Unarmed*, 22.
21. Ibid, 235–36.
22. Deutscher, *The Prophet Outcast,* 148–149. The speech itself is reproduced in Leon D. Trotsky [1932], "In Defence of the Russian Revolution," in *Leon Trotsky Speaks* (New York: Pathfinder, 1972).
23. Sedgwick, "The Tragedy of a Tragedian."
24. Leon D. Trotsky [1924], *Literature and Revolution* (London: Bookmarks, 1991), 272. For Babeuf, see Ian H. Birchall, *The Spectre of Babeuf* (Houndmills: Macmillan, 1997).
25. Trotsky, *My Life*, 604.
26. Deutscher, *The Prophet Armed*, ix.
27. For Deutscher's views on Wolfe, see *The Prophet Outcast*, 460, note 102.
28. Deutscher, *The Prophet Unarmed*, 76–77.
29. Pierre Broué, "Trotsky: A Biographer's Problems," in *The Trotsky Reappraisal,* edited by Terry Brotherstone and Paul Dukes (Edinburgh: Edinburgh University Press, 1992), 20–21.
30. Compare Deutscher, *The Prophet Unarmed,* 308–310 and *The Prophet Outcast,* 49–65 with Michael Reiman [1978], *The Birth of Stalinism: The USSR on the Eve of the "Second Revolution"* (London: I. B. Tauris, 1987), 22, 27–28, 54–55; Vadim Z. Rogovin, *1937: Stalin's Year of Terror* (Oak Park: Mehering Books, 1998), 374–392; and Boris Starkov, "Trotsky and Ryutin: From the History of the Anti-Stalin Resistance in the 1930s," in *The Trotsky Reappraisal.*
31. Dmitri Volkogonov, *Trotsky: The Eternal Revolutionary* (New York: HarperCollins, 1996), xxiv.
32. Daniel Singer, "The Prophet Vulgarised," *Nation* (March 25, 1996).
33. Isaac Deutscher, "1984: The Mysticism of Cruelty," in *Heretics and Renegades and Other Essays* (London: Hamish Hamilton, 1955); reproduced in *Marxism, Wars and Revolutions.*
34. Isaac Deutscher, "The Ex-Communist and His Conscience," in *Heretics and Renegades and Other Essays, 20; Marxism, Wars and Revolutions,* 57–58.
35. Tony Cliff, "The End of the Road: Deutscher's Capitulation to Stalinism," *International Socialism* 1:15 (Winter 1963), 20; *Trotsky*, vol. 4, *The Darker the Night the Brighter the Star, 1927–1940* (London: Bookmarks, 1993), 304–307.
36. Deutscher, *The Prophet Outcast,* 45–49, 342–348. See, for example, his response to criticism from the American SWP in Deutscher, *The Prophet Unarmed,* 449, note 64.
37. Leon D. Trotsky [1935], *Trotsky's Diary in Exile* (London: Faber and Faber, 1958), 54.
38. Deutscher, *The Prophet Outcast,* 210.
39. Perry Anderson, "Trotsky's Interpretation of Stalinism," *New Left Review* I/139 (May/June 1983), 49–54; Alasdair MacIntyre [1963], "Trotsky in Exile," *Against the Self-Images of the Age* (London: Duckworth, 1971), 54–55.
40. Tony Cliff [1948], "The Nature of Stalinist Russia," *Selected Writings*, vol. 3, *Marxist Theory after Trotsky* (London: Bookmarks, 2003), 3–4. Writing in 1918, Lenin argued that five different types of economy operated in Russia: patriarchal, small commodity, private capitalist, state capitalist, and socialist. See Vladimir I. Lenin [1918], "Left Wing Childishness and the Petty Bourgeois Mentality,"

in *Collected Works,* vol. 27, *February–July 1918* (Moscow: Progress Publishers, 1965), 335–36.

41. Leon D. Trotsky [1939], "The USSR in War," in *In Defence of Marxism (Against the Petty-Bourgeois Opposition)* (London: New Park Publications, 1966), 9–11.

42. Deutscher, *The Prophet Outcast,* 266.

43. Deutscher, *The Prophet Armed,* x.

44. Deutscher, *The Prophet Outcast,* 241.

45. Isaac Deutscher, *The Great Contest: Russia and the West* (London: Oxford University Press, 1960), 21–22.

46. Deutscher, *The Prophet Unarmed,* 429, note 69. See also Isaac Deutscher, "Russia in Transition," in *Ironies of History* (Berkeley: Ramparts Press, 1971), 44–46.

47. Isaac Deutscher, *The Unfinished Revolution: Russia, 1917–1967* (London: Oxford University Press, 1967), 22.

48. The point was very forcibly made at the time by Max Shachtman [1949], "Isaac Deutscher's *Stalin*," in *The Bureaucratic Revolution: The Rise of the Stalinist State* (New York: Donald Press, 1962), 229–34. See also Neil Davidson, *Discovering the Scottish Revolution, 1692–1746* (London: Pluto Press, 2003), 9–15, 290–95; and Alex Callinicos, *Making History* (Houndmills: Polity, 1987), 229–33 and "Bourgeois Revolutions and Historical Materialism," *International Socialism* 2:43 (Summer, 1989), 122–27.

49. Deutscher, *The Unfinished Revolution,* 27; Isaac Deutscher, *Stalin: A Political Biography* (London: Oxford University Press, 1949), 174–76.

50. Deutscher, *The Prophet Unarmed,* 10.

51. Deutscher, *Stalin,* 565–66.

52. Leon D. Trotsky [1940], *Stalin: An Appraisal of the Man and His Influence,* edited by Charles Malamuth (London: Hollis and Carter, 1947), 413.

53. Deutscher, *The Prophet Armed,* 372.

54. Ibid., 434. See Christian Rakovsky [1928], "The 'Professional Dangers' of Power," in *Selected Writings on the Opposition in the USSR, 1929–30,* edited by Gus Fagin (London: Allison and Busby, 1980).

55. Deutscher, *The Prophet Outcast,* 369.

56. Ibid., 189.

57. Ibid., 80–81.

58. Leon D. Trotsky [1932], "What Next? Vital Questions for the German Proletariat," in *The Struggle against Fascism in Germany* (Harmondsworth: Penguin, 1975), 228.

59. Deutscher, *The Prophet Unarmed,* 368. In the early 1960s Perry Anderson and Tom Nairn advanced their famous "thesis" on the supposedly incomplete nature of the English Revolution and weakness of the bourgeois society that it produced–a weakness that they claimed was inherited by the English proletariat. Anderson once wrote that Deutscher "dissented from our judgment on English capital, but agreed with our view of English Labor." See "Foreword," *English Questions* (London: Verso, 1992), 5. Yet it is difficult to think of a single national proletariat that Deutscher thought able to challenge its bourgeoisie on a consistent, let alone revolutionary, basis.

60. Leon D. Trotsky [1930–2], *The History of the Russian Revolution* (London: Pluto Press, 1977), 343–44. See also Trotsky, *Trotsky's Diary in Exile,* 53–54.

61. Deutscher, *The Prophet Outcast,* 197, 198, 201.
62. Ibid., 422–23.
63. Deutscher, *The Prophet Armed,* viii.
64. Duncan Hallas, "The Fourth International in Decline: From Trotskyism to Pabloism, 1944–1953," *International Socialism* 1:60 (July 1973), 17–18; Noreen Branson, *History of the Communist Party of Great Britain, 1941–1951* (London: Lawrence and Wishart, 1997), 252.
65. Raymond Williams, *Politics and Letters: Interviews with New Left Review* (London: New Left Books, 1979), 49, 402.
66. John Saville, "The Communist Experience: A Personal Appraisal," *The Socialist Register 1991,* edited by Ralph Miliband and Leo Panitch (London: Merlin Press, 1991), 21.
67. MacIntyre, "Trotsky in Exile," 59.
68. John Dewey et al., *The Case of Leon Trotsky: Report on Hearings on the Charges Made against Him in the Moscow Trials* (London: Martin Secker and Warburg, 1937), 2.
69. George Orwell [1939], "Review of *Russia under Soviet Rule* by N. de Basily," in *The Collected Essays, Journalism and Letters of George Orwell,* vol. 1, *An Age Like This, 1920–1940,* edited by Sonia Orwell and Ian Angus (Harmondsworth: Penguin Books, 1970), 419.
70. Quoted in Raymond Ross, "Trotsky among the Scots," *Cencrastus* 28 (Winter 1987/8), 30.
71. Trotsky wrote in his diary on June 8, 1935, after receiving the invitation: "Only in England, perhaps by now only in Scotland, would such an extravagant idea as entering my candidacy for the post of University Rector be possible." See *Trotsky's Diary in Exile,* 129.
72. Deutscher, *The Prophet Outcast,* 353. For an excellent account of this group, see Alan Wald, *The New York Intellectuals: The Rise and Decline of the Anti-Stalinist Left from the 1930s to the 1980s* (Chapel Hill: University of North Carolina Press, 1987).
73. Deutscher, *The Prophet Armed,* viii.
74. Nicolas Krasso, "Trotsky's Marxism," *New Left Review* I/44 (July–August 1967), 85. The same issue also contains an interview with Deutscher in which he makes several perceptive observations on the crisis in the Middle East: "On the Arab-Israeli War."
75. Deutscher, *The Prophet Outcast,* 261.
76. David Widgery, "Ten Years for Pandora," *Socialist Review* 2 (May 1978), 21.
77. Lawrence Daly, "A Working Class Tribute," in *Isaac Deutscher,* 89.
78. Tariq Ali, *Revolution from Above: Where Is the Soviet Union Going?* (London: Hutchison, 1988), ix.
79. David Widgery, *The Left in Britain, 1956–1968* (Harmondsworth: Penguin, 1976), 525. Apparently the other two were *The Autobiography of Malcolm X* and Hal Draper's *Berkeley: The New Student Radicals.*
80. David Horowitz, "Reality and Dream," *Frontpage,* May 7, 1989, www.frontpagemag.com/Articles/ReadArticle.asp?ID=3948.
81. Tony Cliff, *A World to Win: Life of a Revolutionary* (London: Bookmarks, 2000), 67.
82. Anderson, "Trotsky's Interpretation of Stalinism," 57. Compare Deutscher, *The*

Prophet Outcast, 373.

83. Anderson, "Preface," *Marxism, Wars and Revolutions,* xix.

84. Mike Davis, "Nuclear Imperialism and Extended Deterrence," in *Exterminism and Cold War,* edited by *New Left Review* (London: Verso, 1982), 44.

85. Horowitz, "Reality and Dream."

86. Fred Halliday, "The Ends of the Cold War," *New Left Review* I/180 (March/April 1990), 12.

87. Christopher Hitchens, "Left-Leaning, Left-Leaving," *Los Angeles Times* (November 16, 2003). Mercifully, the introduction by Hitchens to *The Prophet Armed* that was once threatened in the advance publicity has not materialized. A large part of the audience for these books will be from the new generation of activists against imperialist war and capitalist globalization, and nothing would have been more calculated to repel them than association with an ex-socialist turned warmonger and American super-patriot. Hitchens was once—as he occasionally likes to remind his readers—"literary editor" of *International Socialism.* See, for example, *Regime Change* (Harmondsworth: Penguin, 2003), 89–90. His support for imperialism over the invasion and occupation of Iraq (and, come to think of it, virtually every other conflict going back to the Falklands, with the exception of the first Gulf War) therefore renders him more culpable than other B52 liberals like Aaronovitch, Cohen, or Wheen, none of whom had a theoretical perspective to lose in the first place. At one point Hitchens writes that "only a few Trotskyists like my then-self were so rash as to describe the Cold War as, among other things, an inter-imperial rivalry." Ibid., 30. So it was. Why then is Hitchens supporting the imperial power that emerged victorious? The answer comes in an interview in which he also explains why he ceased to be a socialist: "There is no longer a general socialist critique of capitalism—certainly not the sort of critique that proposes an alternative or a replacement. There just is not and one has to face the fact, and it seems to me further that it's very unlikely, though not impossible, that it will again be the case in the future." See "Free Radical," *Reason,* November 2001, www.reason.com. Hitchens is the James Burnham of the post-1968 generation—or possibly the Max Eastman, since his journalism now regularly expresses the kind of view characteristic of a journal that Eastman used to edit: *The Reader's Digest.*

88. Horowitz, "David Horowitz Versus Christopher Hitchens."

89. Quoted in Steven Unger, "Deutscher and the New Left in America," in *Isaac Deutscher,* 215, 218–19.

Chapter 4: There's No Place Like the United States Today

1. Originally published in *International Socialism,* 2:109 (Winter 2005/06) as a review of Victor G. Kiernan [1978], *America: The New Imperialism from White Settlement to World Hegemony* (London: Verso, 2005) and Neil Smith, *The Endgame of Globalization* (New York: Routledge, 2005); with apologies to the late Curtis Mayfield for borrowing the title of his classic 1975 album.

2. Eric J. Hobsbawm, "Preface," in Kiernan, *America,* vii.

3. See Victor G. Kiernan, "A Banner with a Strange Device: The Later Covenanters," in *Covenant, Charter and Party,* edited by Terry Brotherstone (Aberdeen: Aberdeen University Press, 1989) and "The Covenanters: A Problem of Creed

and Class," in *Poets, Politics and the People* edited by Harvey G. Kaye (London: Verso, 1989). Among the rare discussions of Scotland by other members of the Historians Group are: Eric. J. Hobsbawm, "Scottish Reformers of the Eighteenth Century and Capitalist Agriculture," in *Peasants in History,* edited by E. J. Hobsbawm et al. (Calcutta: Oxford University Press, 1980) and Brian Manning, *Revolution and Counter-Revolution in England, Ireland and Scotland, 1658– 60* (London: Bookmarks, 2003), 97–106.

4. His interest in imperialism was not only theoretical: as a member of the CPGB Kiernan was an active anti-imperialist campaigns and he appears to have done work for the party in India (while in the British Army) during the 1940s. As late as 1990 this writer remembers canvassing support among Scottish intellectuals and public figures for an open letter opposing the coming Iraq War that eventually appeared in *The Scotsman;* Kiernan was one of the first to respond. The essays can be found in *Marxism and Imperialism: Studies* (London: Edward Arnold, 1974) and *Imperialism and Its Contradictions,* edited by Harvey J. Kaye (London: Routledge, 1985). A companion volume to *America: The New Imperialism* dealing with Europe is *European Empires from Conquest to Collapse, 1815–1960* (New York: Pantheon Books, 1982). Hobsbawm's much shorter considerations on the subject are, however, far closer to the classical Marxist tradition. See *The Age of Empire, 1875–1914* (London: Weidenfeld and Nicolson, 1975), chapter 3.

5. The contrast is marked with the elegant but somewhat abstract formulations of his first book [1984], *Uneven Development: Nature, Capital and the Production of Space* (Third edition, London: Verso, 1984).

6. See, for example, Leo Panitch and Sam Gindin, "Superintending Global Capital," *New Left Review* II/35 (September/October 2005), 108–18, 121–22.

7. Kiernan, *America,* 3.

8. Ibid., 75.

9. Ibid., 279.

10. Ibid., 29–46, 70–104.

11. This type of writing style is not necessarily an obstacle to presenting a rounded picture of imperialism. For a work by a writer with a similar literary approach to Kiernan (albeit with a different political background) that succeeds in doing this, see Angus Calder, *Revolutionary Empire: The Rise of the English-Speaking Empires from the 15th Century to the 1780s* (London: Jonathan Cape, 1981).

12. Victor G. Kiernan, *The Lords of Human Kind: European Attitudes to the Outside World* (London: Weidenfeld and Nicolson, 1969). By the second edition (1988) the subtitle had changed to *Black Man, Yellow Man, and White Man in an Age of Empire.*

13. Kiernan, *America,* 340–41.

14. See, for example, Jonathan Neale, *The American War: Vietnam, 1960–1975* (London: Bookmarks, 2001), 176–77. The slander that antiwar protesters in the United States were only opposed to the war for reasons of their personal safety was attacked at the time in blistering style by Alasdair MacIntyre, "Le Rouge et Noir," *New Statesman* (November 22, 1968), 714.

15. Kiernan, *America,* xv–xvi.

16. The extent of this error does not mean that we should go to the opposite ex-

treme and accept that US imperialism is the first fully capitalist imperialism, since all previous variants, even the British, continued to exploit their colonial subjects in precapitalist ways. See Panitch and Gindin, "Superintending Global Capital," 103–04 and Ellen Meiksins Wood, *The Empire of Capital* (London: Verso, 2003), 151–54. For critique of this position, see Alex Callinicos, "Imperialism and Global Political Economy," *International Socialism,* 2:108 (Autumn 2005).

17. Smith, *The Endgame of Globalization*, 25.

18. Kiernan, *America,* 107–08. Kiernan is equally bemused by the internationalization of capital: "Over much of the globe today there is so complex a crisscrossing of American capital in Arabia and Japan, Arab and Japanese investment in America, Dutch syndicates buying real estate in the Scottish Highlands, British in Germany, that Lenin would be hard put to say which is the imperialist, who is subjugating whom." See ibid., 273. But since Lenin was one of the first theorists to identify one aspect of imperialism as the movement of capital beyond national borders, he would neither have been bemused nor reduced the question to one of "subjugation" in the first place.

19. Smith, *The Endgame of Globalization,* 48–49.

20. Neil Smith, *American Empire: Roosevelt's Geographer and the Prelude to Globalization* (Berkeley: University of California Press, 2003), 9–25, 454–57.

21. Smith, *The Endgame of Globalization,* 203–04.

22. Ibid, 188.

23. Kiernan, *America,* 312.

24. Smith, *The Endgame of Globalization,* 114, 115.

25. See, above all, Niall Ferguson, *Colossus: The Price of America's Empire* (London: Allen Lane, 2004), 298–302. But compare his forthright demand for America to recognize and assume the responsibilities of empire with the small masterpiece of equivocation and bad faith that is Christopher Hitchens, "Imperialism," in *Regime Change* (Harmondsworth: Penguin Books, 2003), 30–33.

26. Smith, *The Endgame of Globalization,* 175 and 170–76 more generally.

27. Kiernan, *America,* 349.

28. Smith, *The Endgame of Globalization,* 25. But see also Mike Davis [1984], "The Political Economy of Late-Imperial America," in *Prisoners of the American Dream: Politics and Economy in the History of the US Working Class* (London: Verso, 1986), 183, where the idea that Kautsky's vision might be inadvertently realized under US auspices was first raised.

29. Smith, *The Endgame of Globalization*, 209, 210.

Chapter 5: Carnival, March, Riot

1. Originally published in *International Socialism* 2:112 (Autumn 2006) as a review of David Renton, *When We Touched the Sky: The Anti-Nazi League, 1977–1981* (Cheltenham: New Clarion Press, 2006).

2. Renton, *When We Touched the Sky,* 175.

3. Ibid., 23, 174.

4. Quoted in ibid., viii.

5. See David Widgery, *Beating Time: Riot 'n' Race 'n' Rock 'n' Roll* (London: Chatto and Windus, 1986). To be fair, the book was not intended to be a scholarly or

objective account. See David Widgery, "*Beating Time*–a Response to Ian Birchall," *International Socialism* 2:35 (Summer 1987).

6. It is possible to exaggerate the distinction between the two organizations. If my own experience in Aberdeen is anything like typical, then in many parts of the country the same people probably ran them both, as two aspects of essentially the same operation.

7. Renton, *When We Touched the Sky*, 3. Renton admires Widgery's work, without necessarily accepting all his conclusions. See ibid, 47–50, 181–82 and David Renton, "David Widgery," in *Dissident Marxism* (London: Zed Books, 2004), 217–27.

8. David Renton, *Fascism: Theory and Practice* (London: Pluto Press, 1999); *Fascism, Anti-Fascism and Britain in the 1940s* (Houndmills: Macmillan, 2000); and *"This Rough Game": Fascism and Anti-Fascism in European History* (Stroud: Sutton Publishers, 2001).

9. Renton, *When We Touched the Sky*, 175–80.

10. Paul Gilroy, *There Ain't no Black in the Union Jack: the Cultural Politics of Race and Nation* (Second edition, London: Routledge, 2002), 174.

11. Renton, *When We Touched the Sky*, 105, 106, and 102–06 more generally.

12. Maxine Williams, Stephen Palmer, and Gary Clapton, "Racism, Imperialism and the Working Class," *Revolutionary Communist* 9 (June 1979), 41, 42.

13. Renton, *When We Touched the Sky*, 104, 118. Gilroy's other main argument is that the ANL retreated into a patriotic Britishness based on memories of the Second World War to oppose the NF. In fact, the main ANL slogan was "Never Again!" Contrary to what Gilroy appears to believe, this was a reference to the Holocaust, not the Battle of Britain. See the discussion by Renton in ibid., 126–27.

14. For the Stop the War Coalition as a form of United Front, see Andrew Murray and Lindsey German, *Stop the War: The Story of Britain's Biggest Mass Movement* (London: Bookmarks, 2005), 3–5, 47–63.

15. Renton, *When We Touched the Sky*, 180.

16. Ibid., 183.

Chapter 6: Alasdair MacIntyre as a Marxist

1. Previously unpublished in this form, but based on "Alasdair MacIntyre as a Marxist, 1953–1968," in *1956 and All That*, edited by Keith Flett (Newcastle: Cambridge Scholars Publishing, 2007); "Introduction: The Unknown Alasdair MacIntyre" (with Paul Blackledge), in *Alasdair MacIntyre's Engagement with Marxism: Selected Writings, 1953–1974*, edited by Paul Blackledge and Neil Davidson (Leiden: E. J. Brill, 2008); and "Alasdair MacIntyre and Trotskyism," in *Virtue and Politics: Alasdair MacIntyre's Revolutionary Aristotelianism*, edited by Paul Blackledge and Kelvin Knight (Notre Dame, Indiana: University of Notre Dame, 2011). I have also drawn on two unpublished papers delivered at consecutive annual conferences of the International Society for MacIntyrean Inquiry: "Alasdair MacIntyre in 1968: the Road from Marxism?," Saint Meinrad University, Indiana (July 30, 2008); and "MacIntyre on Capitalist Managers and Marxist Revolutionaries," University College Dublin (March 9, 2009).

2. Kelvin Knight, "Revolutionary Aristotelianism," in *Contemporary Political Studies*, vol. 2, edited by Ian Hampsher-Monk and Jeffrey Stanyer (Nottingham: Political

Studies Association of the United Kingdom, 1996); *Virtue and Politics,* chapter 2. For MacIntyre's endorsement of this term, see [1997], "Politics, Philosophy and the Common Good," in *The MacIntyre Reader,* edited by Kelvin Knight (Cambridge: Cambridge University Press, 1998), 235.

3. "The Expert's Expert: Philosophers," *Observer Magazine* (January 8, 1989), 10–11.

4. Alasdair MacIntyre [1958–9], "Notes from the Moral Wilderness," in *The MacIntyre Reader,* 31–49; "Bibliography," ibid., 295.

5. *After MacIntyre: Critical Perspectives on the Work of Alasdair MacIntyre,* edited by John Horton and Susan Mendas (Cambridge: Polity Press 1994), 305–18; *Alasdair MacIntyre,* edited by Mark C. Murphy (Cambridge: Cambridge University Press, 2003), 202–06.

6. Peter McMylor, *Alasdair MacIntyre: Critic of Modernity* (London: Routledge, 1994), 3–73, 178, note 28, 212–13.

7. Kelvin Knight, "Editor's Introduction," in *The MacIntyre Reader,* 2.

8. Alasdair MacIntyre, "Introduction," in *Against the Self-Images of the Age: Essays on Ideology and Philosophy* (London: Duckworth, 1971), vii.

9. Alasdair MacIntyre [1972], "Hegel on Faces and Skulls," in *Selected Essays,* vol. 1, *The Tasks of Philosophy* (Cambridge: Cambridge University Press, 2006).

10. McMylor, *Alasdair MacIntyre,* 4–5. Lest this sound too much like infantile regression, McMylor also notes that this is not merely a return to the starting point since "the long journey of movement and return has been an enormously enriching one."

11. Knight, "Editor's Introduction," 2–4.

12. See, for example, John Saville, "The Politics of Encounter," *The Socialist Register 1964,* edited by Ralph Miliband and John Saville (London: Merlin Press, 1964), 192–199. For the actual details see Christopher Lasch, "The Cultural Cold War: A Short History of the Congress for Cultural Freedom," in *The Agony of the American Left: One Hundred Years of Radicalism* (Harmondsworth: Penguin Books, 1973) and Frances Stonor Saunders, *Who Paid the Piper: The CIA and the Cultural Cold War* (London: Granta Books, 1999), 165–89, 368–90.

13. Chris Harman, personal communication to Paul Blackledge, October 26, 2004; Harman was involved in organizing the meetings.

14. Robin Blackburn, "MacIntyre, the Game Is Up," *Black Dwarf* (January 16, 1970), 11. MacIntyre's critique of Marcuse caused particular offense to the 1968 New Left. Even by the mid-1980s, the attack evidently still rankled. "MacIntyre's account of critical theory is extremely superficial, and his 'summaries' of Marcuse's books are simple-minded, reductionist and uninformed. . . . whatever valid criticisms MacIntyre may have are lost in hyperbole . . . supercilious attacks . . . or idiotic counter-examples." See Douglas Kellner, *Herbert Marcuse and the Crisis of Marxism* (Berkeley: University of California, 1984), 421, note 24. As we shall see, there are a number of problems with the book entitled *Marcuse,* but these do not include MacIntyre's views on Marcuse.

15. Tariq Ali, *The Coming British Revolution* (London: Jonathan Cape, 1972), 203, note 35.

16. Perry Anderson, *Arguments within English Marxism* (London: Verso, 1980), 108. According to Anderson the other philosopher cited "most frequently and

warmly" by Thompson was Leszek Kolakowski.

17. Perry Anderson, "A Culture in Counterflow–II," *New Left Review* I/182 (July/August 1990), 104, 106.

18. Alasdair MacIntyre, "Symposium III: Going into Europe," *Encounter* 22, no. 2 (February 1963), 65.

19. Peter Sedgwick, "The Ethical Dance: A Review of Alasdair MacIntyre's *After Virtue*," *The Socialist Register 1982,* edited by Ralph Miliband and John Saville (London: Merlin Press, 1982), 260, 261.

20. Edward P. Thompson, "An Open Letter to Leszek Kolakowski," *The Socialist Register 1973,* edited by Ralph Miliband and John Saville (London: Merlin Press, 1973), 50, 57–58, 60–61 and the associated endnotes.

21. Martin Shaw, *Marxism Versus Sociology: A Guide to Reading* (London: Pluto Press, 1974), entries 1.6 ("Breaking the Chains of Reason"), 3.25 (*Marcuse*) and 16.5 (*Marxism and Christianity*).

22. David Widgery, *The Left in Britain, 1956–1968* (Harmondsworth: Penguin Books, 1976), 14. See also references to MacIntyre's work in the bibliography, 511 and 519. Widgery reproduces MacIntyre's "The Strange Death of Social Democratic England," in the same volume, 235–40.

23. Chris Harman, "Philosophy and Revolution," *International Socialism* 2:21 (Autumn 1983), 62.

24. Alex Callinicos, *Marxism and Philosophy* (Oxford: Oxford University Press, 1983), 5, 159, note 10.

25. Paul Blackledge, "Socialist Humanism and Revolutionary Politics in the British New Left," in *1956 and all that;* "Freedom, Desire and Revolution: MacIntyre's Early Marxist Ethics," *History of Political Thought* 26, no. 4 (Autumn 2005); "Morality and Revolution: Ethical Debates in the British New Left," *Critique* 35, no. 2 (May 2007); "Alasdair MacIntyre: Marxism and Politics," *Studies in Marxism* 11 (2007); "Alasdair MacIntyre's Contribution to Marxism: A Road Not Taken," in *Revolutionary Aristotalianism: Ethics, Resistance and Utopia,* edited by Kelvin Knight and Paul Blackledge (Stuttgart: Lucius and Lucius, 2008); "Alasdair MacIntyre: Social Practices, Marxism and Ethical Anti-capitalism," *Political Studies* 57, no. 4 (2009); "Leadership or Management: Some Comments on Alasdair MacIntyre's Critique of Marx(ism)," in *Virtue and Politics.*

26. *Who's Who* (London: Oxford University Press, 2004), 1400.

27. His supervisor and later collaborator, Dorothy M. Emmet, claims that MacIntyre was on the verge of obtaining a candidature to become a minister in the Church of Scotland. Given MacIntyre's adherence to Anglicanism, this seems unlikely, unless Emmet is referring to the Episcopalian Church in Scotland that, as it boasts, is "in full communion with the Church of England." See *Philosophers and Friends: Reminiscences of Seventy Years in Philosophy* (London: Macmillan, 1996), 86.

28. Alasdair MacIntyre [1991], "An Interview with Giovanna Borradori," in *The MacIntyre Reader,* 256. MacIntyre also refers to Thompson's work in [1968], *Marxism and Christianity* (Harmondsworth: Penguin Books, 1971), 81–82.

29. Louis Althusser [1965], "Introduction: Today," in *For Marx* (London: Verso, 2005), 31–38.

30. Alasdair MacIntyre, *Marxism: An Interpretation* (London: Student Christian

Movement Press, 1953), 61, 70, 89–91, 95–96, 98, 117.

31. Alasdair MacIntyre, "Review of T. B. Bottomore and M. Rubel, *Karl Marx: Selected Works on Sociology and Social Philosophy* and P. Laslett, ed., *Philosophy, Politics and Society*," *Sociological Review*, new series, vol. 4, no. 2 (December 1956), 266. Tom Stoppard's play, *Rosencrantz and Guildenstern are Dead*, was first performed ten years later, at the 1966 Edinburgh International Festival.

32. Alasdair MacIntyre [1956], "Marxist Tracts," in *Alasdair MacIntyre's Engagement with Marxism*, 25

33. MacIntyre, *Marxism*, 102–03, 104–08.

34. Leon D. Trotsky [1937], "Stalinism and Bolshevism: Concerning the Historical and Theoretical Roots of the Fourth International," in *Writings of Leon Trotsky [1936–37]*, edited by Naomi Allen and George Breitman (Second edition, New York: Pathfinder Press, 1978), 423.

35. Leon D. Trotsky [1903], *Our Political Tasks* (London: New Park Publications, 1904), 77; Rosa Luxemburg [1904], "Organizational Questions of Russian Social Democracy," in *Rosa Luxemburg Speaks*, edited by Mary-Alice Waters (New York: Pathfinder Press, 1970), 114–22.

36. See, for example, Franz Borkenau [1938], *World Communism: A History of the Communist International* (Ann Arbor: University of Michigan Press, 1962), 12–13, 39–56, 87–89.

37. MacIntyre, *Marxism*, 103.

38. See the examples in chapter 3 of this volume.

39. See, for example, Michael Hardt, "An Interview with Michael Hardt," *Historical Materialism* 11, no. 3 (2003), 135.

40. Alasdair MacIntyre [1962], "An Open Letter to a Right-Wing Young Socialist," in *Alasdair MacIntyre's Engagement with Marxism*, 215.

41. Peter Sedgwick, "The New Left," *International Socialism* 1:17 (August 1964), 15–18.

42. See, for example, the personal testimony in Raymond Williams, *Politics and Letters: Interviews with* New Left Review (London: New Left Books, 1979), 365.

43. Alasdair MacIntyre, "The Irrelevance of the Church of England," *Listener* (June 26, 1958), 1055.

44. Alasdair MacIntyre [1959], "Hume on 'Is' and 'Ought,'" in *Against the Self-Images of the Age*, 116.

45. Ibid.

46. Alasdair MacIntyre, "On Not Misrepresenting Philosophy," *Universities and Left Review* 4 (Summer 1958); "The Algebra of the Revolution," *Universities and Left Review* 5 (Autumn 1958).

47. Edward P. Thompson, 'Socialist Humanism," *New Reasoner* 1 (Summer 1957).

48. Harry Hanson, "An Open Letter to Edward Thompson," *New Reasoner* 2 (Autumn 1957).

49. Alastair MacIntyre, "Notes from the Moral Wilderness," in *Alasdair MacIntyre's Engagement with Marxism*, 46–47, 57, 60, 66.

50. Alasdair MacIntyre [1958], "The Algebra of the Revolution," in *Alasdair MacIntyre's Engagement with Marxism*, 43–44.

51. James Baker, "The Need for Developing Revolutionary Theory: The Case of Alasdair MacIntyre," *Labour Review* 7, no. 2 (Summer 1962), 65, 68.

52. Alasdair MacIntyre, "Marcuse, Marxism and the Monolith," *The New Reasoner* 9 (Summer 1959).

53. Duncan Hallas, "Building the Leadership," *International Socialism* 1:40 (October/November 1969), 20; Harry Ratner, *Reluctant Revolutionary: Memoirs of a Trotskyist, 1936–1960* (London: Porcupine Books, 1994), 207.

54. Contributors to the discussion included Jim Allen, the playwright, who was at this time still working as a miner, and Pat Arrowsmith of the Direct Action Committee against Nuclear War.

55. *Newsletter* 2, no. 127 (November 21, 1959), 331.

56. Alasdair MacIntyre [1960], "Communism and the British Intellectuals," in *Alasdair MacIntyre's Engagement with Marxism,* 116–17.

57. Cliff Slaughter, "The 'New Left' and the Working Class," *Labour Review* 4, no. 2 (July-August 1959).

58. Alasdair MacIntyre [1959], "The 'New Left,'" in *Alasdair MacIntyre's Engagement with Marxism,* 87, 89, 90.

59. Alasdair MacIntyre [1960], "Freedom and Revolution," in *Alasdair MacIntyre's Engagement with Marxism,* 131–34.

60. Cliff Slaughter, "What is Revolutionary Leadership?," *Labour Review* 5, no. 3 (June/July1960), 107, 111.

61. Alasdair MacIntyre, letter in *The Listener* (March 17, 1960), 500.

62. Baker, "The Need for Developing Revolutionary Theory," 65.

63. Callaghan, *British Trotskyism,* 78.

64. Alasdair MacIntyre, "Breaking the Chains of Reason," in *Alasdair MacIntyre's Engagement with Marxism,* 150–53.

65. Compare Michael Kidron [1968], *Western Capitalism since the War* (Revised edition, Harmondsworth: Penguin Books, 1970), chapter 3, with Cornelius Castoriadis [1961], "Modern Capitalism and Revolution," in *Political and Social Writings,* vol. 2, *1955–1960: From the Worker's Struggle against Bureaucracy to Revolution in the Age of Modern Capitalism,* edited by David Ames Curtis (Minneapolis: University of Minnesota Press, 1988), 233–57.

66. Compare Maurice Brinton (i.e. Christopher Pallis) [1960], "Socialism Reaffirmed," in *For Worker's Power: The Selected Writings of Maurice Brinton,* edited by David Goodway (Edinburgh: AK Books, 2004), 19 and Tony Cliff [1960], "Trotsky on Substitutionism," in *Selected Writings,* vol. 1, *International Struggle and the Marxist Tradition* (London: Bookmarks, 2001), 129.

67. See, for example, Paul Cardan, "Socialism and Capitalism," *International Socialism* 1:4 (Spring 1961); "Martin Grainger" [i.e. Maurice Brinton], "The Murder Machine," *International Socialism* 1:2 (Autumn 1960); Jean-Francois Lyotard, "Algeria," *International Socialism* 1:13 (Summer 1963).

68. George Thayer, *The British Political Fringe* (London: Anthony Blond, 1965), 142.

69. Cliff's subsequent revision of this and another passage in the 1969 edition of *Rosa Luxemburg* were the result of his reconsideration of the nature of the revolutionary party in the aftermath of the French events of May 1968. The version in Cliff's *Selected Works* contains both original and revised passages. See [1959], "Rosa Luxemburg," in *International Struggle and the Marxist Tradition,* 113. For the impact of the May events on his thought see Ian H. Birchall and Tony Cliff [1968], "France–The Struggle Goes On," in *International Struggle and the*

Marxist Tradition, 209–13; and Tony Cliff, *A World to Win: Life of a Revolutionary* (London: Bookmarks, 2000), 98–104.

70. Michael Kidron, "Two Left Feet," *International Socialism* 1:2 (Autumn 1960), 32.

71. Alasdair MacIntyre, "Is a Neutralist Foreign Policy Possible?," *International Socialism* 1:3 (Winter 1960).

72. *International Socialism* 1:6 (Autumn 1961), 20.

73. Alasdair MacIntyre [1961], "Marxists and Christians," in *Alasdair MacIntyre's Engagement with Marxism*, 179, note 1.

74. MacIntyre, "Breaking the Chains of Reason," 166.

75. Alasdair MacIntyre [1963], "Trotsky in Exile," in *Alasdair MacIntyre's Engagement with Marxism*, 274.

76. Ibid., 272–73, 275.

77. Alasdair MacIntyre, "Trotsky," *International Socialism* 1:8 (Spring 1962), 33.

78. MacIntyre, *Marxism and Christianity*, 90–91.

79. Leon. D. Trotsky [1933–5], "The Notebooks in Translation," in *Trotsky's Notebooks, 1933–1935: Writings on Lenin, Dialectics, and Evolutionism* (New York: Columbia University Press, 1986), 92.

80. MacIntyre, "Trotsky," 33.

81. Alasdair MacIntyre [1961], "Rejoinder to Left Reformism," in *Alasdair MacIntyre's Engagement with Marxism*, 190.

82. Alasdair MacIntyre [1963–4], "Labour Policy and Capitalist Planning," in *Alasdair MacIntyre's Engagement with Marxism*, 284, 289.

83. MacIntyre, "The 'New Left,'" 90.

84. Alasdair MacIntyre [1961], "Culture and Revolution," in *Alasdair MacIntyre's Engagement with Marxism*, 178.

85. Alasdair MacIntyre [1959], "What is Marxist Theory For?," in *Alasdair MacIntyre's Engagement with Marxism*, 102.

86. Alasdair MacIntyre [1963], "Prediction and Politics," in *Alasdair MacIntyre's Engagement with Marxism*, 260–61.

87. Alasdair MacIntyre [1962], "C. Wright Mills," in *Alasdair MacIntyre's Engagement with Marxism*, 244.

88. MacIntyre, "Rejoinder to Left Reformism," 195.

89. Alasdair MacIntyre [1962], "Sartre as a Social Critic," in *Alasdair MacIntyre's Engagement with Marxism*, 206.

90. Karl Marx [1864], "Documents of the First International, 1864–70: Provisional Rules of the International Working Men's Association," in *Political Writings*, vol. 3, *The First International and After*, edited by David Fernbach (Harmondsworth: Penguin Books/New Left Review, 1974), 82.

91. MacIntyre, "Rejoinder to Left Reformism," 189.

92. Alasdair MacIntyre [1961], "The Man Who Answered the Irish Question," in *Alasdair MacIntyre's Engagement with Marxism*, 172.

93. Chris Harman, "Party and Class," *International Socialism* 1:35 (Winter 1968/9), esp. 27–30. This essay was the most significant advance in the discussion of the revolutionary party since the MacIntyre/Slaughter contributions eight years earlier. (The equivalent French text is Daniel Bensaïd and Alain Naïr, "A propos de la question de l'organisation: Lénine et Rosa Luxemburg," *Partisans* 45 (December 1968/January 1969)). Harman was the first British Marxist since Slaugh-

ter to make serious use of Gramsci in this context and it is regrettable that Mac-Intyre himself does not seem to have encountered his work. This is particularly frustrating since, in several articles written during his membership of IS, Mac-Intyre raises themes that were to later to be popularized with the partial translation into English of the prison notebooks, notably that of contradictory consciousness. "All sorts of facts may limit social consciousness," wrote MacIntyre in 1963. "But false consciousness is essentially a matter of partial and limited insight rather than of simple mistake." See MacIntyre, "Prediction and Politics," 252–253. Compare Antonio Gramsci [1929–1935], "The Study of Philosophy," in *Selections from the Prison Notebooks,* edited by Quintin Hoare and Geoffrey Nowell Smith (London: Lawrence and Wishart, 1971), 333, Q11§12.

94. Compare Leon D. Trotsky [1923], "The Lessons of October," in *The Challenge of the Left Opposition (1923–25),* edited by Naomi Allen (New York: Pathfinder Press, 1975), 252 with [1940], "Manifesto of the Fourth International on the Imperialist War and the Proletarian World Revolution," in *Writings of Leon Trotsky [1939–40],* edited by Naomi Allen and George Breitman (Second edition, New York: Pathfinder Press, 1973), 215.

95. MacIntyre, "Prediction in Politics," 255.

96. Ibid., 252.

97. Alasdair MacIntyre [1967], "How Not to Write about Stalin," in *Alasdair MacIntyre's Engagement with Marxism,* 351.

98. *International Socialism* reprinted several works by these authors during the mid-1960s. See Georg Lukács [1919–23], "What is Orthodox Marxism? 1," *International Socialism* 1:24 (Spring 1966); "What is Orthodox Marxism? 2," *International Socialism* 1:25 (Summer 1966); and Lucien Goldmann, "Is There a Marxist Sociology?," *International Socialism* 1:34 (Autumn 1968).

99. Lucien Goldmann, *The Hidden God: A Study of the Tragic Vision in the Pensées of Pascal and the Tragedies of Racine* (London: Routledge, 1964), 90.

100. Alasdair MacIntyre [1964], "Pascal and Marx: On Lucien Goldmann's *Hidden God,"* in *Alasdair MacIntyre's Engagement with Marxism,* 314.

101. Antonio Gramsci [1929–1935], "Problems of Marxism," in *Selections from the Prison Notebooks of Antonio Gramsci,* 438, Q11§15; Michael Löwy, *Fire Alarm: Reading Walter Benjamin's "On the Concept of History"* (London: Verso, 2005) 4, 114, 137 note 15.

102. Alasdair MacIntyre [1965], "Marxist Mask and Romantic Face: Lukács on Thomas Mann," in *Alasdair MacIntyre's Engagement with Marxism,* 319–20.

103. Castoriadis, "Modern Capitalism and Revolution," 226–30.

104. MacIntyre, "Prediction and Politics," 256–58.

105. MacIntyre, "Rejoinder to Left Reformism," 195–96.

106. Alasdair MacIntyre [1964], "Marx," in *Alasdair MacIntyre's Engagement with Marxism,* 298.

107. "Cardan Debate," *Solidarity* 3, no. 10 (August 1965), 22.

108. Ibid., 23–24.

109. Ian Birchall, personal communication to Neil Davidson, August 24, 2000.

110. MacIntyre, "Marx," 297.

111. Alastair MacIntyre, *Secularization and Moral Change* (Oxford: Oxford University Press, 1967), 75.

112. Alasdair MacIntyre, *A Short History of Ethics: A History of Moral Philosophy from the Homeric Age to the Twentieth Century* (London: Macmillan, 1966), 210–14.

113. Ibid., 268–69.

114. Timothy O'Hagan, "Searching for Ancestors," *Radical Philosophy* 54 (Spring 1990), 19.

115. MacIntyre, *A Short History of Ethics,* 214.

116. For Marxist and post-Marxist examples, see, respectively, Alasdair MacIntyre, "Against Utilitarianism," in *Aims in Education: The Philosophic Approach,* edited by T. H. B. Hollins (Manchester: Manchester University Press, 1964) and "Utilitarianism and Cost-Benefit Analysis: An Essay on the Relevance of Moral Philosophy to Bureaucratic Theory," in *Values in the Electric Power Industry,* edited by Kenneth Sayre (Notre Dame, Indiana: Notre Dame University Press, 1977).

117. MacIntyre, *Marxism and Christianity,* 96–98.

118. Alasdair MacIntyre [1968], "How to Write about Lenin–and How Not To," in *Alasdair MacIntyre's Engagement with Marxism,* 360.

119. See, for example, MacIntyre, "Philosophy and Ideology," 92–93.

120. "An Interview with Giovanna Borradori," 259; "An Interview for *Cogito,*" in *The Macintyre Reader,* 267.

121. MacIntyre, *Marxism and Christianity,* 87.

122. "Letter to Readers," *International Socialism* 1:33 (Summer 1968), 17.

123. David Renton, "David Widgery: The Poetics of Propaganda," in *Dissident Marxism* (London: Zed Books, 2004), 207–10.

124. David Widgery, "Ten Years for Pandora," *Socialist Review* 2 (May 1978), 20.

125. Alan M. Wald, *The New York Intellectuals: The Rise and Decline of the Anti-Stalinist Left from the 1930s to the 1980s* (Chapel Hill: University of North Carolina Press, 1987), 267–365.

126. Perry Anderson, *In the Tracks of Historical Materialism* (London: Verso, 1983), 28–30, 32; Dominique Lecourt, "Dissidence or Revolution?," in *The Mediocracy: French Philosophy since 1968* (London: Verso, 2001), 151–75.

127. Milton Fisk, *Socialism from Below in the United States* (1977): available at www.marxists.de. For an article that suggests that Draper's underlying reason may have been his dissatisfaction with the organizational forms taken by the left, see Hal Draper, "Towards a New Beginning–on Another Road: A Political Alternative to the Micro-Sect" (1971), available at www.marxists.org.

128. Gregory Elliot, *Althusser: The Detour of Theory* (London: Verso, 1987), 235–244.

129. Esther Leslie, "Introduction to Adorno/Marcuse Correspondence on the German Student Movement," *New Left Review* I/235 (January/February 1999), 118–23.

130. MacIntyre, "Breaking the Chains of Reason," 166.

131. Colin Rodgers, Rick Coates, and Mike Gonzalez, "There's Something Wrong with Essex," reproduced in Widgery, *The Left in Britain,* 326–27.

132. Quoted in David Caute, *Sixty-Eight: The Year of the Barricades* (London: Paladin Books, 1988), 305.

133. Alasdair MacIntyre, "Le Rouge et Noir," *New Statesman* (November 22, 1968), 714.

134. Alasdair MacIntyre, *Marcuse* (London: Fontana, 1970), 89.

135. "Contrary to bourgeois belief, H. Marcuse did not greatly inspire the British

student movement; bestsellers on the LSE bookstall in 1966 were instead *The Autobiography of Malcolm X* ... Hal Draper's *Berkeley: The New Student Revolt* ... and Isaac Deutscher's anthology of Trotsky, *The Age of Permanent Revolution*." Widgery, *The Left in Britain,* 525.

136. MacIntyre, *Marcuse,* 91.

137. Alasdair MacIntyre, "Review of *Confrontation, University in Turmoil* and *Higher Education in Social Psychology,*" *American Journal of Sociology* 75, no. 4, part 1 (January 1970), 564.

138. MacIntyre, *Marcuse,* 71–72.

139. MacIntyre, *Marcuse,* 88–89. MacIntyre had of course encountered such infantile leftism in Essex. See, for example, the following idiocies by one (subsequently ennobled) student leader: "What we should do, if the situation were to arise again, would be to behave as provocatively as necessary and to effectively sanction the University to the extent that they *need* to use force, probably the police." David Triesman, "Scanner–1: Essex," *New Left Review* I/50 (July–August 1968), 71.

140. Alasdair MacIntyre [1968], "The Strange Death of Social Democratic England," in *Alasdair MacIntyre's Engagement with Marxism,* 366–67.

141. MacIntyre, *Marcuse,* 43.

142. Alasdair MacIntyre [1968], "In Place of Harold Wilson," in *Alasdair MacIntyre's Engagement with Marxism,* 371.

143. Richard Kuper, "Decline and Fall," *International Socialism* 1:42 (February/March 1970), 35.

144. Alasdair MacIntyre [1995], "1953, 1968, 1995: Three Perspectives," in *Alasdair MacIntyre's Engagement with Marxism,* 417.

145. MacIntyre, *Marxism and Christianity,* 101.

146. Ibid., 100–04.

147. Ibid., 90–91.

148. Georg Lukács [1923], "The Changing Function of Historical Materialism," in *History and Class Consciousness: Studies in Marxist Dialectics* (London: Merlin Books, 1971), 228, 229. For similar remarks by a contemporary of Lukács, see Karl Korsch [1923], "Marxism and Philosophy," in *Marxism and Philosophy* (New York: Monthly Review Press, 1970), 56.

149. Paul Cardan [1961–1964], *History and Revolution* (London: Solidarity, 1971); Cornelius Castoriadis [1961–1964], "Marxism and Revolutionary Thought," in *The Imaginary Institution of Society: Creativity and Autonomy in the Social-Historical World* (Cambridge: Polity Press, 1987).

150. MacIntyre, *Marcuse,* 61.

151. Ibid., 42, 43. Open statements of working-class incapacity are actually quite rare in the writings of ex-Trotskyists, but for an earlier rejection of Marxism on these grounds, see Jean Vannier (i.e. Jean van Heijenoort), "A Century's Balance Sheet," *Partisan Review* 15, no. 3 (March 1948).

152. MacIntyre, *Marxism and Christianity,* 105.

153. Alasdair MacIntyre, "Ideology, Social Science and Revolution," *Comparative Politics* 5, no. 2 (April 1973), 340–42.

154. Alasdair MacIntyre [1969], "Marxism of the Will," in *Alasdair MacIntyre's Engagement with Marxism,* 376.

155. Alasdair MacIntyre, *After Virtue: A Study in Moral Theory* (Third edition, Notre

Dame, Indiana: Notre Dame University Press, 2007), 262.

156. Leon D. Trotsky [1939], "The USSR in War," in *In Defence of Marxism (Against the Petty Bourgeois Opposition)* (London: New Park Publications, 1971), 11.

157. MacIntyre, "Trotsky in Exile," 271.

158. MacIntyre, *After Virtue,* 262.

159. Tony Cliff [1948], "The Nature of Stalinist Russia," in *Selected Writings,* vol. 3, *Marxist Theory after Trotsky* (London: Bookmarks, 2003), 130.

160. MacIntyre, "The *Theses on Feuerbach:* A Road Not Taken," in *The MacIntyre Reader,* 232.

161. MacIntyre, "1953, 1968, 1995," 411–16.

162. MacIntyre, "Introduction," in *Against the Self-Images of the Age,* viii.

163. See, for example, MacIntyre, *A Short History of Ethics,* 2, 8 and Alasdair MacIntyre, "'Ought,'" in *Against the Self-Images of the Age,* 142–56.

164. "Interview with Giovanna Borradori," 258.

165. Alasdair MacIntyre, "Preface," in *After Virtue,* xvi.

166. "Interview with Giovanna Borradori," 265.

167. Alasdair MacIntyre, "The Spectre of Communitarianism," *Radical Philosophy* 70 (March/April 1995), 35.

168. Alasdair MacIntyre, "*After Virtue* and Marxism: A Response to Wartofsky," *Inquiry* 27, no. 3 (September 1984), 252.

169. Walter Benjamin, "Paralipomena to 'On the Concept of History,'" in *Selected Works,* vol. 4, *1938–40,* edited by Howard Eiland and Michael W. Jennings (Cambridge, Massachusetts: The Belknap Press of Harvard University Press, 2003), 401–411. In his novel imagining a meeting between Ludwig Wittgenstein, Nikolai Bahktin, James Connolly, and . . . Leopold Bloom, Terry Eagleton puts several passages by Benjamin into Connolly's mouth: "Revolution isn't a runaway train; it's the application of the emergency brake." See [1987], *Saints and Scholars* (London: Futura Publications, 1990), 100.

Chapter 7: Reimagined Communities

1. Originally published in *International Socialism* 2:117 (Winter 2008/9) as a review of Benedict Anderson [1983–91], *Imagined Communities: Reflections on the Rise and Spread of Nationalism* (Third, revised edition, London: Verso, 2006).

2. Anderson, *Imagined Communities,* 228.

3. Josep R. Llobera, *The God of Modernity: The Development of Nationalism in Western Europe* (Providence, Rhode Island: Berg, 1994), 103.

4. Alasdair MacIntyre [1998], "Poetry as Political Philosophy: Notes on Burke and Yeats," in *Selected Essays,* vol. 2, *Ethics and Politics* (Cambridge: Cambridge University Press, 2006), 161.

5. Anderson, *Imagined Communities,* 207, note 1.

6. Phillip Spencer and Howard Wollman, *Nationalism: A Critical Introduction* (London: Sage, 2002), 37.

7. Anderson, *Imagined Communities,* 227.

8. Karl Marx and Friedrich Engels [1875], "For Poland," in *Political Writings,* vol. 3, *The First International and After,* edited by David Fernbach (Harmondsworth: Penguin Books/New Left Review, 1974), 389.

9. Friedrich Engels [1866], "What Have the Working Classes to Do with Poland?,"

in *The First International and After*, 381–85.

10. The claim by Engels that these nations were intrinsically "non-historic" was a piece of Hegelian baggage quite unnecessary to their critique of Pan-Slavism. For the problems with the concept of nonhistoricity, and the extent to which Engels later abandoned it, largely as a result of his analysis of the Irish situation, see chapter 2 in this volume.

11. George Haupt, Michael Löwy, and Claudie Weill, *Les Marxists et la question nationale, 1848–1914: Etudes et textes* (Paris: Maspero, 1974); *Lenin's Struggle for a Revolutionary International: Documents: 1907–1916, The Preparatory Years*, edited by John Riddell (New York: Monad Press, 1984), 348–83; *Workers and Oppressed Peoples of the World, Unite! Proceedings and Documents of the Second Congress, 1920*, vol. 1, edited by John Riddell (New York: Pathfinder Press, 1991), 211–90; *Workers and Oppressed Peoples of the World, Unite! Proceedings and Documents of the Second Congress, 1920*, vol. 2, edited by John Riddell (New York: Pathfinder Press, 1991), appendix 2, 846–885; *To See the Dawn: Baku, 1920—First Congress of the Peoples of the East*, edited by John Riddell (New York: Pathfinder Press, 1993), 137–171; *Theses, Resolutions and Manifestos of the First Four Congresses of the Third International*, edited by Alan Adler (London: Pluto Press, 1983), 328–31 and 409–19.

12. Karl Kautsky, "The National Question and Autonomy," in *The National Question: Selected Writings by Rosa Luxemburg*, edited by Horace B. Davis (New York: Monthly Review Press, 1976), 126, 129; Vladimir I. Lenin [1914], "The Right of Nations to Self-Determination," in *Collected Works*, vol. 20, *December 1913-August 1914* (Moscow: Progress Publishers, 1964), 396.

13. Otto Bauer [1907], *The Question of Nationalities and Social Democracy* (Minneapolis: University of Minnesota Press, 2000), 3, 17, 121.

14. Ephraim Nimni, *Marxism and Nationalism: Theoretical Origins of a Political Crisis* (London: Pluto Press, 1991), 143, 181–84.

15. Lenin, "The Right of Nations to Self-Determination," 308.

16. Joseph V. Stalin [1913], "Marxism and the National Question," in *Works*, vol. 2 (Moscow: Foreign Languages Publishing House, 1953), 307.

17. Eric van Ree, "Stalin and the National Question," *Revolutionary Russia* 7, no. 2 (April 1994), 228.

18. The classic works include: Carlton J. H. Hayes, *The Historical Evolution of Modern Nationalism* (New York: Richard A. Smith, 1931); Hans Kohn, *The Idea of Nationalism* (London: Collier Macmillan, 1944); Alfred Cobban, *National Self-Determination* (Oxford: Oxford University Press, 1945); Edward H. Carr, *Nationalism and After* (London: Macmillan, 1945); and Karl W. Deutsch, *Nationalism and Social Communication: An Inquiry into the Foundations of Nationality* (New York: Wiley, 1953).

19. Elie Kedourie, *Nationalism* (London: Hutchinson University Library, 1960); Ernest Gellner, "Nationalism," in *Thought and Change* (London: Weidenfeld and Nicolson, 1964).

20. Benedict Anderson, *Java in a Time of Revolution: Occupation and Resistance, 1944–1946* (Ithaca: Cornell University Press, 1972), xi–xiv.

21. Ibid., 18–19, 30.

22. Anderson, *Imagined Communities*, 1–2. See also xi, from the preface to the 1991 edition. The same conflicts are also discussed by Nairn in "Into Political Emergency: A Retrospect from the 1980s," in *The Break-Up of Britain*, 371.

23. Tom Nairn, "The Modern Janus," *New Left Review* I/94 (November/December 1975), 3; *The Break-Up of Britain,* 329.

24. Anderson *Imagined Communities,* 3.

25. Anderson, *Imagined Communities,* 208–09.

26. Ibid., xiv.

27. Ibid., 6–7.

28. Ibid., 4.

29. Ibid., 36.

30. See, for example, Umut Özkirimli, *Theories of Nationalism: A Critical Introduction* (Houndmills: Macmillan, 2000), 153.

31. Anderson, *Imagined Communities,* 44–45.

32. Ibid., 36.

33. Ibid., 52.

34. Ibid., 62.

35. Ibid., 133 and 135.

36. Ibid., 110.

37. Ibid., 113–114.

38. See, for example, Anderson, *Imagined Communities,* 24. For the original distinction, see Walter Benjamin [1940], "On the Concept of History," in *Selected Writings,* vol. 4, *1938–1940,* edited by Howard Eiland and Michael W. Jennings (Cambridge, Massachusetts: Belknap Press of Harvard University Press, 2003), 395–97.

39. Walter Benjamin [1927–1940], *The Arcades Project,* edited by Rolf Tiedemann (Cambridge, Massachusetts: The Belknap Press of Harvard University Press, 2002).

40. Anthony D. Smith, *Nationalism and Modernism: A Critical Survey of Recent Theories of Nations and Nationalism* (London: Routledge, 1998), 142.

41. Murray J. Pittock, *Celtic Identity and the British Image* (Manchester: Manchester University Press, 1999), 140.

42. Partha Chatterjee [1993], "Whose Imagined Community?," in *Mapping the Nation,* edited by Gopal Balakrishnan (London: Verso, 1996), 216–17.

43. Benedict Anderson, "Western Nationalism and Eastern Nationalism," *New Left Review* II/9 (May/June 2001), 31, 32.

44. Smith, *Nationalism and Modernism,* 137.

45. Pittock, *Celtic Identity and the British Image,* 129–30.

46. Ibid., 102–03.

47. Tom Nairn, *Pariah: Misfortunes of the British Kingdom* (London: Verso, 2002), 156. Here Nairn specifically follows Emmanuel Todd, *L'illusion economique: essai sur la stagnation des sociétés développées* (Paris: Gallimard, 1998), but essentially as a theoretical justification for a position he had been moving toward for several years beforehand. See chapter 1 in this volume.

48. Tom Nairn, "Ukania: The Rise of the Annual Report Society," in Tom Nairn and Paul James, *Global Matrix: Nationalism, Globalism and State-Terrorism* (London: Pluto Press, 2005), 137; Benedict Anderson, "The Goodness of Nations," in *The Spectre of Comparisons: Nationalism, Southeast Asia, and the World* (London: Verso, 1998).

49. For example: "There is no elective affinity between capitalism and nationalism,

unless we equate the former to modern society in general, and not to a mode of production, *senso strictu.*" Llobera, *The God of Modernity*, 215.

50. Anderson, *Imagined Communities,* 42–43.

51. Benedict Anderson, "The New World Disorder," *New Left Review* I/193 (May/June 1992), 7. My emphasis.

52. The remainder of this section is based on Neil Davidson, *The Origins of Scottish Nationhood* (London: Pluto Press, 2000), chapter 2.

53. Anderson, *Imagined Communities*, 81 and note 34.

54. Anderson, *Imagined Communities*, 141.

55. Benedict Anderson, "Indonesian Nationalism Today and in the Future," *New Left Review* II/235 (May/June 1999), 17. The final sentence has ominous echoes of Richard Rorty's famous declaration that white American liberals should help oppressed blacks, not because they are "fellow human beings," but because "it is much more persuasive, morally as well as politically, to describe them as our fellow Americans—to insist that it is outrageous that an American should live without hope." See *Contingency, Irony and Solidarity* (Cambridge: Cambridge University Press, 1989), 191.

56. Anderson, *Imagined Communities,* 160–61. The quotations are from Hobsbawm and Nairn, respectively.

57. Ibid., 161. This chapter is called "The Angel of History" after the famous passage in Benjamin's "On the Concept of History." The title was also used by Nairn for the last section of "The Modern Janus," the essay to which *Imagined Communities* was partly a response. See *The Break-Up of Britain,* 359–63.

58. Walter Benjamin, "Paralipomena to 'On the Concept of History,'" *Selected Writings,* vol. 4, 402, 403. See also Michael Löwy [2001], *Fire Alarm: On Reading Walter Benjamin's "On the Concept of History"* (London: Verso, 2005), 60–68.

Chapter 8: Walter Benjamin and the Classical Marxist Tradition

1. Originally published *International Socialism* 2:121 (Winter 2009) as a response to Chris Nineham, "Benjamin's Emergency Marxism," *International Socialism* 2:119 (Summer 2008).

2. Esther Leslie, *Walter Benjamin* (London: Reaktion, 2007), 9–13. Many of these remnants are now accessible in *Walter Benjamin's Archive: Images, Texts, Signs,* edited by Ursula Marx, Gudrun Schwarz, Michael Schwarz, and Erdmut Wizisla (London: Verso, 2007).

3. Walter Benjamin [1939], "The Paris of the Second Empire in Baudelaire," in *Selected Writings,* vol. 4, *1938–1940,* edited by Howard Eiland and Michael W. Jennings (Cambridge, Massachusetts: The Belknap Press of Harvard University Press, 2003), 394.

4. Leslie, *Walter Benjamin,* 201–202.

5. Nineham, "Benjamin's Emergency Marxism," 113. See Walter Benjamin [1939], "The Work of Art in the Age of Its Technological Reproducibility (Third Version)," in *Selected Writings,* vol. 4, 264, for the most recent translation of the passage from which Chris quotes. The myth of Benjamin's naivety is widespread. As Leslie reports: "Generations of students are confused by the idea of the aura: taught to them simplistically detached from the axis of revolutionary possibility and capitalist actuality, they believe Benjamin to be the naïf soul, who thought

this odd quality really was abolished and photography and film really had instituted democracy, when clearly aura still persists, art has not gone away and photography and film could be put to use by fascists." Leslie, *Walter Benjamin,* 220.

6. Leslie, *Walter Benjamin,* 203. See also Howard Eiland and Michael W. Jennings, "Chronology, 1938–1940," in *Selected Writings,* vol. 4, 437.

7. Benjamin, "The Work of Art in the Age of Its Technological Reproducibility (Third Version)," 269, 28, note 47.

8. Nineham, "Benjamin's Emergency Marxism," 111, 116.

9. Esther Leslie, *Walter Benjamin: Overpowering Conformism* (London: Pluto Press, 2000), 225–27.

10. Isaac Deutscher [1965], "Marxism in Our Time," in *Marxism in Our Time,* edited by Tamara Deutscher (Berkeley: Ramparts Press, 1971), 18.

11. Perry Anderson, *Considerations on Western Marxism* (London: New Left Books, 1976), 42, 49–50. Anderson's otherwise helpful discussion is nevertheless flawed by some of the individuals he includes, above all Gramsci, Lukács, and Korsch, although he acknowledges that these three were initially leaders of their respective Communist parties. Gramsci died a representative of the classical tradition, obscurity of expression forced on him by conditions of Fascist imprisonment and concerns over losing support from the PCI by unambiguously stating his opposition to Stalinist orthodoxy. And whatever we think of the positions Lukács and Korsch took then or subsequently, until the late twenties both men had at least a critical relationship with the tradition. Leaving aside any consideration of content, the comprehensibility of *Lenin: A Study in the Unity of His Thought* or *Marxism and Philosophy* puts them in a different category from *For Marx* or *One Dimensional Man.*

12. Anderson, *Considerations on Western Marxism,* 54, 89–90.

13. Karl Marx and Friedrich Engels [1848], "Manifesto of the Communist Party," in *Political Writings,* vol. 1, *The Revolution of 1848,* edited by David Fernbach (Harmondsworth: Penguin/New Left Review, 1973), 72; Karl Marx [1852], "The Eighteenth Brumaire of Louis Bonaparte," in *Political Writings,* vol. 2, *Surveys from Exile,* edited by David Fernbach (Harmondsworth: Penguin/New Left Review, 1973), 147–49; Karl Marx [1867], *Capital: A Critique of Political Economy,* vol. 1 (Harmondsworth: Penguin/New Left Review, 1976), 342.

14. Walter Benjamin [1929], "A Communist Pedagogy," in *Selected Writings,* vol. 2, part 1, *1927–1930,* edited by Michael W. Jennings, Howard Eiland, and Gary Smith (Cambridge, Massachusetts: The Belknap Press of Harvard University Press, 1999), 274.

15. Walter Benjamin [1927], "Moscow," in *Selected Writings,* vol. 2, part 1, 38.

16. Russell Jacoby, *The Last Intellectuals: American Culture in the Age of Academe* (New York: Basic Books, 1987), 3–27.

17. For a selection of their writings, see Neil Jumonville (ed.), *The New York Intellectuals Reader* (London: Routledge, 2007). Although this collection is too heavily weighted toward those who later became neoconservatives, it does include, side by side, the great essays by Meyer Shapiro ("Nature of Abstract Art") and Clement Greenberg ("Avant-Garde and Kitsch") that represent their outstanding contributions to the Marxist theory of art. See 121–62.

18. Alan Wald, *The New York Intellectuals: The Rise and Decline of the Anti-Stalinist Left*

from the 1930s to the 1980s (Chapel Hill: University of North Carolina Press, 1987), 27–31, 42–45.

19. For more on the affinities between Benjamin and Trotsky, see Terry Eagleton, *Walter Benjamin: Or, Towards a Revolutionary Criticism* (London: Verso, 1981), 173–79 and Leslie, *Walter Benjamin: Overpowering Conformism,* 228–34.

20. Etienne Balibar is right to say that, despite some formal similarities in approach, in relation to Adorno et al., Benjamin "was merely a reticent, little understood 'fellow traveller.'" See [1995], *The Philosophy of Marx* (London: Verso, 2007), 86.

21. Michael Löwy [2001], *Fire Alarm: On Reading Walter Benjamin's "On the Concept of History"* (London: Verso, 2005), 4.

22. For specific references to Benjamin in this work, see Benedict Anderson [1983], *Imagined Communities: Reflections on the Origin and Spread of Nationalism* (London: Verso, 2006), 161 and chapter 7, "The Angel of History," more generally, which is named after thesis nine of Benjamin's "On the Concept of History." See also chapter 7 in this volume.

23. Nineham, "Benjamin's Emergency Marxism," 116.

24. Walter Benjamin [1927–1940], "Convolute N: [On the Theory of Knowledge, Theory of Progress]," in *The Arcades Project* (Cambridge, Massachusetts: The Belknap Press of Harvard University Press, 1999), 458, 460.

25. For the benefit of any readers on "proletarian culture" lookout duty, it should be noted that Benjamin specifically endorsed the position taken by Trotsky on this question in *Literature and Revolution*. See [1929], "Surrealism," in *Selected Writings,* vol. 2, part 1, 217.

26. Walter Benjamin [1934], "The Author as Producer," in *Selected Writings,* volume 2, part 2, *1931–1934,* edited by Michael W. Jennings, Howard Eiland, and Gary Smith (Cambridge, MA: The Belknap Press of Harvard University Press, 1999), 771.

27. Compare the subjects discussed in Antonio Gramsci [1929–1935], *Selections from the Cultural Writings,* edited by David Forgacs and Geoffrey Nowell-Smith (London: Lawrence and Wishart, 1985) with those in Benjamin's *Selected Works.* Orwell's collection *Inside the Whale and Other Essays* (1939) was extraordinarily innovative in its time. No other writer would have thought of treating the subject matter of two key essays, "Charles Dickens" and "Boys Weeklies," in the same place and, in the case of the latter, of treating them seriously at all. Yet his cultural criticism, of which the latter essay is a good example, now tends to be treated rather patronizingly, where it is not dismissed entirely. According to Martin Barker, for example, Orwell merely "refers" to comics: "it would be too kind to say that that he analyses them." See *Comics: Ideology, Power and the Critics* (Manchester: Manchester University Press, 1989), 13–14. This uncharacteristic condescension apart, Barker's book is a stimulating study that contains a very useful and comprehensible introductory discussion of another important cultural thinker, the Russian Marxist Valentin Volosinov. See ibid., 263–74.

28. It is often asserted that the New York intellectuals were collectively and individually influenced by the Frankfurt School in relation to their analysis of culture. One of Clement Greenberg's biographers, for example, has claimed that he drew on "the anti-fascist Frankfurt school–Theodore Adorno, Georg Lukács, Walter Benjamin." See Florence Rubenfield, *Clement Greenberg: A Life* (New

York: Scribner, 1997), 56. Another writer describes Greenberg specifically as "echoing" Benjamin. See Martha Bayles, *Hole in Our Soul: The Loss of Beauty and Meaning in American Popular Music* (New York: The Free Press, 1994), 79. But there is no evidence that Greenberg or his contemporaries ever read Benjamin or the others at this time, not least because most of their work was simply unavailable; they certainly do not refer to them. Greenberg's early work in particular has interesting parallels to that of Adorno, but unless we subscribe to the view that no American could possibly have an intelligent opinion unless it was formulated by a Central European intellectual first–which I do not–there is no reason to doubt that their positions were arrived at independently.

29. Benjamin, "The Paris of the Second Empire in Baudelaire," 65–66.

30. Benjamin, "Convolute K: [Dream City and Dream House, Dreams of the Future, Anthropological Nihilism, Jung]," in *The Arcades Project*, 395.

31. Benjamin, "The Author as Producer," 774, 777.

32. For a Benjaminian analysis of one of the greatest Scottish films of recent years, Lynne Ramsay's *Ratcatcher*, from a political position close to that outlined here, see Alex Law and Jan Law, "Magical Urbanism: Walter Benjamin and Utopian Realism in the Film *Ratcatcher*," *Historical Materialism* 10, no. 4 (2002).

33. Paul Wood, "Marxism and Modernism: An Exchange between Alex Callinicos and Paul Wood," *Oxford Art Journal* 15, no. 2 (1992), 124.

34. There is a parallel here with Trotsky, who, in a different context, wrote in his Testament that "threatened with a long-drawn out invalidism . . . I reserve the right to determine for myself the time of my death." Leon D. Trotsky [1940], "Testament," in *Trotsky's Diary in Exile* (London: Faber and Faber, 1959), 140–41.

35. Nineham, "Benjamin's Emergency Marxism," 117.

36. Benjamin, "The Work of Art in the Age of Its Technological Reproducibility (Third Version)," 270. Benjamin's italics.

37. Nineham, "Benjamin's Emergency Marxism," 118; Benjamin [1940], "Paralipomena to 'On the Concept of History,'" 402

38. See, for example, Jonathan Neale, *Stop Global Warming: Change the World* (London: Bookmarks, 2008), especially 260–61.

39. Neil Davidson, "Is There a Scottish Road to Socialism?," in *Is There a Scottish Road to Socialism?*, edited by Gregor Gall (Glasgow: Scottish Left Review Press, 2007), 118.

40. In addition to the "Paralipomena," many of the themes of "On the Concept of History" appear in "Convolute N" in *The Arcades Project*, 456–88.

41. Blaise Pascal [1657–62], *Pensées* (Harmondsworth: Penguin, 1966), 121–26.

42. Lucien Goldmann, *The Hidden God: A Study of the Tragic Vision in the Pensées of Pascal and the Tragedies of Racine* (London: Routledge 1964), 90.

43. Alasdair MacIntyre [1964], "Pascal and Marx: On Lucien Goldmann's *Hidden God*," in *Alasdair MacIntyre's Engagement with Marxism*, 314.

44. Löwy, *Fire Alarm*, 114.

45. Antonio Gramsci [1929–1935], "Problems of Marxism," in *Selections from the Prison Notebooks of Antonio Gramsci*, introduced and edited by Quintin Hoare and Geoffrey Nowell Smith (London: Lawrence and Wishart, 1971), 438, Q11§15.

46. James Connolly [1915], "The Re-Conquest of Ireland," in *Collected Works*, vol.

1 (Dublin: New Books, 1987), 263.

47. Leon D. Trotsky [1939], "The USSR in War," in *In Defence of Marxism (Against the Petty Bourgeois Opposition)* (London: New Park Publications, 1971), 11.

48. Alasdair MacIntyre, *After Virtue*, 262.

49. Georg Lukács [1924], *Lenin: A Study in the Unity of His Thought* (London: New Left Books, 1970), 12–13.

50. Walter Benjamin, "On the Concept of History," in *Selected Writings*, vol. 4, 401–403.

51. Walter Benjamin [1940], "Survey of French Literature," *New Left Review*, II/51 (May/June 2008), 39. Leslie invokes the notion of "midnight in the century" to describe the moment at which Benjamin composed "On the Concept of History." Leslie, *Walter Benjamin*, 211. Ironically, in the same article by Benjamin referred to here, he is rude about the literary qualities of the novel by Victor Serge from whence the term derives: "His book has no literary value, and holds the attention only for its picturesque descriptions of Stalinist terror." No doubt this will damn him still further in some quarters. See Benjamin, "Survey of French Literature," 44 and Leslie, *Walter Benjamin*, 209.

52. Walter Benjamin, "Convolute N," 474.

53. Nineham, "Benjamin's Emergency Marxism," 117–18.

54. Benjamin, "On the Concept of History," 391.

55. George Orwell [1949], *Nineteen Eighty-Four* (Harmondsworth: Penguin, 1954), 199.

56. Benjamin "On the Concept of History," 392.

57. Benjamin, "Paralipomena to 'On the Concept of History,'" 406.

58. Benjamin, "Convolute N," 474.

59. For a more detailed discussion see Neil Davidson, *Discovering the Scottish Revolution, 1692–1746* (London: Pluto Press, 2003), 290–94. For an explicit reference to Benjamin, see 299–301.

60. Benjamin, "On the Concept of History," 390.

61. Benjamin, "Paralipomena to 'On the Concept of History,'" 407.

62. Benjamin, "On the Concept of History," 390. Ironically, given Benjamin's distaste for at least some of Victor Serge's novels, "nothing is ever lost" was also a favorite slogan of the latter writer. See [1931], *The Birth of Our Power* (London: Writers and Readers, 1977), 182 and chapter 23 more generally.

63. Marx, "The Eighteenth Brumaire of Louis Bonaparte," 147, 148.

64. Benjamin, "On the Concept of History," 395.

65. Neil Davidson, "How Revolutionary Were the Bourgeois Revolutions? (contd.)," *Historical Materialism* 13, no. 4 (2005), 38–47.

66. Walter Benjamin [1937], "Edward Fuchs, Collector and Historian," in *Selected Writings*, vol. 3, *1935–1938*, edited by Howard Eiland and Michael W. Jennings (Cambridge, MA: The Belknap Press of Harvard University Press, 2002), 273.

Chapter 9: Shock and Awe

1. Originally published in *International Socialism* 2:124 (Autumn 2009) as a review of Naomi Klein, *The Shock Doctrine: The Rise of Disaster Capitalism* (London: Allen Lane, 2007).

2. Peter Davison, editorial note to George Orwell, *Homage to Catalonia*, in *Com-*

plete Works, vol. 11, *Facing Unpleasant Facts, 1937–1939* (London: Secker and Warburg, 1998), 135.

3. Naomi Klein, "This Much I Know," interview by Stephanie Morritt, *Observer* (June 1, 2008).

4. Naomi Klein, *No Logo: Taking Aim at the Brand Bullies* (London: Flamingo, 2000), 445–46.

5. See, for example, Chris Harman, "Anti-Capitalism: Theory and Practice," *International Socialism* 2:88 (Autumn 2000), 53–56.

6. Klein, *No Logo,* 115.

7. In this respect her arguments converge with an equally impressive journalistic polemic by Thomas Frank that appeared almost simultaneously, although he is more sensitive to the ways in which the ideology of the market is used to justify contemporary capitalism. For the similarities between their critiques of what Frank elsewhere calls "the commodification of dissent," compare Klein, *No Logo,* 63–85, 106–124 with Thomas Frank, *One Market under God: Extreme Capitalism, Market Populism and the End of Economic Democracy* (London: Secker and Warburg, 2001), 252–306.

8. Naomi Klein, *Fences and Windows: Dispatches from the Front Lines of the Globalization Debate* (London: Harper Perennial, 2002).

9. Naomi Klein and Neil Smith, "*The Shock Doctrine:* A Discussion," *Environment and Planning D: Society and Space* 26, no. 4 (August 2008), 589–90.

10. Klein, *The Shock Doctrine,* 14–15. See also ibid., 253.

11. Neoconservatism is often wrongly regarded simply as a US foreign policy doctrine based on military intervention. In fact, it is the inescapable domestic complement to neoliberalism across the capitalist world, in the sense that the social division and fragmentation caused by the marketization, commodification, privatization, and the rest require massive increases in the repressive and surveillance apparatus of the state, in the name of restoring social discipline. For that reason, although the two ideologies are inextricably linked, we should maintain an analytic distinction between them.

12. Klein, *The Shock Doctrine,* 17.

13. Ibid., 17.

14. Ibid., 6–7, 140–141.

15. Ibid., 24–25, 71.

16. Ibid., 15.

17. Will Hutton, "Her Ranting Obscures Her Reasoning," *Observer* (September 23, 2007).

18. Klein, *The Shock Doctrine,* 20. Klein is of course not alone on the left in seeing Keynesian solutions as the only realistic alternative to neoliberalism, either from principle or because of the supposed impossibility of making more radical change under current conditions. Compare the liberal Joseph Stiglitz, *Globalization and Its Discontents* (Harmondsworth: Penguin, 2002), 249–50 with the Marxist David Harvey, *A Brief History of Neoliberalism* (Oxford: Oxford University Press, 2005), 183–84, 206.

19. Hutton, "Her Ranting Obscures Her Reasoning."

20. Ronald Suresh Roberts, "Beware Electrocrats: Naomi Klein on South Africa," *Radical Philosophy* 150 (July/August 2008), 7. Roberts has written an authorized

biography of former ANC leader Thabo Mbeki, the general tone of which would not have been out of place at the court of the Emperor Justinian, even down to a defense of his hero's unforgivable attitude to the AIDS epidemic. Since Roberts's hagiography was partly bankrolled by the South African banking group Absa, he should perhaps be more cautious in accusing Klein's sources of accepting tainted funding.

21. Joseph Stiglitz, "Bleakonomics," *New York Times* (September 30, 2007).
22. Alexander Cockburn, "On Naomi Klein's *The Shock Doctrine,*" *Counterpunch* (September 22–23, 2007), available at www.counterpunch.org.
23. India and Mexico receive one passing reference each; Egypt receives none. See Klein, *The Shock Doctrine,* 399, 452.
24. Ibid., 10. See also 136–40.
25. David Sanders, David Marsh, and Hugh Ward, "Government Popularity and the Falklands War: A Reassessment," *British Journal of Political Science* 17, no. 3 (July 1987).
26. Hugo Young, *One of Us: A Biography of Margaret Thatcher* (London: Macmillan, 1989), 298.
27. Klein, *The Shock Doctrine,* 298.
28. Francis Fox Piven, *The War at Home: The Domestic Costs of Bush's Militarism* (New York: The New Press, 2004), 13–88.
29. Kim Moody, *US Labor in Trouble and Transition: The Failure of Reform from Above, the Promise of Revival from Below* (London: Verso, 2007), 106–114.
30. Klein, *The Shock Doctrine,* 7–8.
31. Ibid., 88, 165–68.
32. Ibid., 308.
33. Zbigniew Brzeżinski, *The Grand Chessboard: American Primacy and Its Geostrategic Imperatives* (New York: Basic Books, 1997), 158–173; Alex Callinicos, *The New Mandarins of American Power* (Houndmills: Polity, 2003), 93–8; David Harvey, *The New Imperialism* (Oxford: Oxford University Press, 2003), 18–25, 74–86. To these "external" foreign determinants can also be added one "internal" domestic issue as a motive for war: the need to retain the unified support of Republican voting constituencies that were not only diverse but, in many respects, incompatible. See Piven, *The War at Home,* 27–29.
34. Peter Hennessey, *Having It So Good: Britain in the Fifties* (London: Allen Lane, 2006), 199–217.
35. See, for example, Andrew Marr, *A History of Modern Britain* (London: Macmillan, 2007), 131.
36. Klein, *The Shock Doctrine,* 67–70.
37. Alan Greenspan, *The Age of Turbulence: Adventures in a New World* (Harmondsworth: Penguin, 2008), 275. See also Martin Wolf, *Why Globalization Works: The Case for the Global Market Economy* (New Haven: Yale University Press, 2004), 72, 291.
38. Klein, *The Shock Doctrine,* 57.
39. David Kotz, "The State, Globalisation and Phases of Capitalist Development," in *Phases of Capitalist Development: Booms, Crises and Globalisations,* edited by Robert Albritton, Makoto Itoh, Richard Westra, and Alan Zuege (London: Palgrave, 2001), 104.

40. Klein, *The Shock Doctrine,* 190, 532.
41. Klein and Smith, "*The Shock Doctrine:* A Discussion," 583.
42. Eric J. Hobsbawm, *Age of Extremes: The Short Twentieth Century, 1914–1991* (London: Allen Lane, 1994), 403–416.
43. Although, as Perry Anderson rightly remarks, the period since 1973 has seen dramatic, if uneven, improvements in the living conditions of millions in the global South who were excluded from the prosperity of the Long Boom. See [1994], "The Vanquished Left: Eric Hobsbawm," in *Spectrum: From Right to Left in the World of Ideas* (London: Verso, 2005), 301.
44. Tony Judt, "Introduction: The World We Have Lost," in *Reappraisals: Reflections on the Forgotten Twentieth Century* (London: William Heinemann, 2008), 10.
45. Robert Brenner, "The Paradox of Social Democracy: The American Case," in *The Year Left 1985,* edited by Mike Davis, Fred Pfeil, and Mike Sprinkler (London: Verso, 1985), 55–59; Piven, *The War at Home,* 66–67.
46. Edward P. Thompson, "An Open Letter to Leszek Kolakowski," in *The Socialist Register 1973,* edited by Ralph Miliband and John Saville (London: Merlin Books, 1973), 53.
47. Hilde Nafstad et al., "Ideology and Power: The Influence of Current Neo-Liberalism in Society," *Journal of Community and Applied Social Psychology* 17, no. 4 (2007), 314.
48. Klein, *Fences and Windows,* xix.
49. Paul Mattick, *Marx and Keynes: The Limits of the Mixed Economy* (London: Merlin Books, 1971), 279–80.
50. Nigel Harris, *The End of the Third World: Newly Industrialising Countries and the Decline of an Ideology* (Harmondsworth: Penguin, 1986), 42.
51. Mattick, *Marx and Keynes,* 284.
52. Michael J. Haynes, *Russia: Class and Power, 1917–2000* (London: Bookmarks, 2002), 210–14.
53. Chris Harman, *Explaining the Crisis: A Marxist Analysis* (London: Bookmarks, 1984), 99–102; Robert Brenner, *The Economics of Global Turbulence: The Advanced Capitalist Economies from Long Boom to Long Downturn, 1945–2005* (London: Verso, 2006), 99–101. Harman argues that an increase in the organic composition of capital (as a result of declining effectiveness of the Permanent Arms Economy as a countervailing tendency) was the reason for the falling rate of profit. Brenner rejects this explanation (see 14–15, note 1), but both he and Harman agree that the latter process is central to the crisis.
54. Al Campbell, "The Birth of Neoliberalism in the United States," in *Neoliberalism: A Critical Reader,* edited by Alfredo Saad-Filho and Deborah Johnson (London: Pluto Press, 2005), 189.
55. T. S. Eliot [1948], *Notes Towards the Definition of Culture* (London: Faber and Faber, 1962), 88–89.
56. Moody, *US Labor in Trouble and Transition,* 43–47.
57. Graham Turner, *The Credit Crunch: Housing Bubbles, Globalization and the Worldwide Economic Crisis* (London: Pluto Press, 2008), 10.
58. Keith Joseph, letter to *Economist* (September 28, 1974).
59. Wolf, *Why Globalization Works,* 132.
60. Andrew Gamble, "Neo-liberalism," *Capital and Class* 75 (Autumn 2001), 133.

61. Wolf, *Why Globalization Works,* 133.
62. See, for example, Chris Harman, "Theorising Neoliberalism," *International Socialism* 2:117 (Winter 2008), 89–92, 100–104.
63. Naomi Klein, "After a Week of Turmoil, Has the World Changed?," interview by Emily Butsellaar, *The Guardian* (September 20, 2008).
64. Klein, *The Shock Doctrine,* 443–66.

Chapter 10: Antonio Gramsci's Reception in Scotland

1. Originally published in *Scottish Labor History* 45 (2010).
2. Gordon Brown, "Introduction: The Socialist Challenge," in *The Red Paper on Scotland,* edited by Gordon Brown (Edinburgh: Edinburgh University Student Publications Board, 1975), 18. Brown was not the only contributor to this volume to subsequently achieve political eminence: one chapter entitled "Glasgow: Area of Need" was written by one Vincent Cable, then working for the Foreign Office, now an ornament of the Conservative-Liberal Democrat coalition government. It does not refer to Gramsci.
3. Angus Calder, "Worker's Culture–Popular Culture–Defining our Terms," in *Revolving Culture: Notes from the Scottish Republic* (London: I. B. Tauris, 1994), 238. For similar claims, by an American scholar now based in Scotland, see Jonathan Hearn, *Claiming Scotland: National Identity and Liberal Culture* (Edinburgh: Polygon, 2000), 21.
4. Tom Nairn, "Culture and Nationalism: An Open Letter from Tom Nairn," *Scottish International* (April 1973), 8.
5. Hamish Henderson, "Introduction," to Antonio Gramsci, *Prison Letters* (London: Pluto Press, 1996), 1–2.
6. Henderson to *The Scotsman,* July 28, 1988, in *The Armstrong Nose: Selected Letters of Hamish Henderson,* edited by Alec Finlay (Edinburgh: Polygon, 1996), 277.
7. Ibid.; Henderson, "Introduction," 14–15. For the full text of the letter from Gramsci that Henderson quotes in part, see Gramsci to Teresina, March 23, 1927, in *Prison Letters,* 47.
8. "Antonio Gramsci: A Letter," *Calgacus* 2 (Summer 1975), 3.
9. James D. Young, "Nationalism, 'Marxism' and Scottish History," *Journal of Contemporary History* 20, no. 2 (April 1985), 352–53.
10. Christopher Harvie, *Scotland and Nationalism: Scottish Society and Politics, 1707–1977* (London: Allen and Unwin, 1977), 17.
11. Antonio Gramsci, "Vita politica internazionale," *L'Ordine nuovo* (May 15, 1919).
12. The first of several references by Lenin to Maclean describes him as "the Scottish school-master whom the English bourgeoisie sentenced to hard labor for supporting the workers' class struggle," which does rather absolve the Scottish bourgeoisie of responsibility for his treatment in jail. See Vladimir I. Lenin, "An Open Letter to Boris Souvarine," in *Collected Works,* vol. 23 (Moscow: Progress Publishers, 1964), 201.
13. Editorial note to Antonio Gramsci, "Notes on Italian History," in *Selections from the Prison Notebooks,* edited by Quintin Hoare and Geoffrey Nowell Smith (London: Lawrence and Wishart, 1971), 103, note 94.
14. Timothy Neat, *Hamish Henderson: A Biography,* vol. 1, *The Making of the Poet (1919–1953)* (Edinburgh: Polygon, 2007), 263.

15. Henderson to MacDiarmid, May 2, 1950, in *The Armstrong Nose,* 43; Sraffa to Henderson, June 17, 1950, ibid., 43–44; Henderson to *The Scotsman,* March 9, 1968, ibid., 169–70.

16. Neat, *Hamish Henderson,* vol. 1, 245–46.

17. Ibid., chapter 14.

18. Hamish Henderson, "Flower and Iron of the Truth: A Survey of Contemporary Scottish Writing," *Our Time* 10 (September 1948), 305.

19. Compare Antonio Gramsci, "The Study of Philosophy," in *Selections from the Prison Notebooks,* 372, Q4§37 and Karl Marx, "Preface to *A Contribution to the Critique of Political Economy,*" in *Early Writings* (Harmondsworth: Penguin/New Left Review, 1975), 425–426. See also the discussion in Peter D. Thomas, *The Gramscian Moment: Philosophy, Hegemony and Marxism* (Leiden: E. J. Brill, 2009), 95–102.

20. Henderson to Grieve, May 2, 1950, in "Selected Letters," *Chapman* 82 (1995), 53. The context suggests that Henderson did not expect MacDiarmid to know that Gramsci was "certainly the most important Marxist outside Russia in the period 1920–1935."

21. Hugh MacDiarmid, *In Memoriam James Joyce, from a Vision of World Language* (Glasgow: W. Maclellan, 1955), 27.

22. Henderson, "Introduction," 14.

23. Hamish Henderson, "'It Was in You That It A' Began': Some Thoughts on the Folk Conference," in *The People's Past,* edited by Edward J. Cowan (Edinburgh: Polygon, 1980), 13–14.

24. Hamish Henderson, *The Edinburgh People's Festival, 1951–54* (Edinburgh People's Festival: Edinburgh, 2008), [3]. http://www.edinburghpeoplesfestival.org.uk/background/hamish.html.

25. Neat, *Hamish Henderson,* vol. 1, 301.

26. Henderson, *The Edinburgh People's Festival;* Ailie Munro, *The Folk Song Revival in Scotland* (London: Kahn & Averill, 1983), 50–53.

27. Ibid., 359–60; Sam Aaronovitch et al., *The American Threat to British Culture,* special issue of *Arena* 2, no. 8 (June/July 1951).

28. Antonio Gramsci, "Intellectuals: Notes on English Culture [i]," in *Selections from the Cultural Writings,* edited by David Forgacs and Geoffrey Nowell-Smith (London: Lawrence and Wishart, 1985), 284, Q4§93.

29. See, for example, Antonio Gramsci, "Marinetti the Revolutionary," in *Selections from the Cultural Writings,* 49–51.

30. Munro, *The Folk Song Revival in Scotland,* 235.

31. Gramsci, "Problems of Marxism," 419–425, Q11§13; "Observations on Folklore: Giovanni Crocioni," in *Selections from the Cultural Writings,* 188–191, Q27§1.

32. Gramsci, "The Study of Philosophy," 332, Q11§12.

33. Timothy Neat, *Hamish Henderson: A Biography,* vol. 2, *Poetry Becomes People (1952–2002)* (Edinburgh: Polygon, 2009), 106.

34. Giuseppe Vacca, *Togliatti sconosciuto* (Rome: L'Unita editrice, 1994), 144–45.

35. Antonio Gramsci, *The Modern Prince and Other Writings,* translated and introduced by Louis Marks (New York: International Publishers, 1957); Carl Marzani, *The Open Marxism of Antonio Gramsci* (New York: Monthly Review Press, 1957); "Gramsci on the Jews," translated by Hamish Henderson, *The New*

Reasoner 9 (Summer 1959), 141–44; Peter Worsley, "Further Letters from Gramsci," translated by Hamish Henderson, *The New Reasoner* 10 (Autumn 1959), 123–27; Antonio Gramsci, "In Search of the Educational Principle," *New Left Review* I/32 (July/August 1965), 53–62.

36. H. Stuart Hughes [1958], *Consciousness and Society: The Reorientation of European Social Thought, 1890–1930* (London: Paladin, 1974), 96–104.

37. Gwyn A Williams, "The Concept of 'Egomania' in the Thought of Antonio Gramsci: Some Notes on Interpretation," *Journal of the History of Ideas* 21, no. 4 (October/December 1960), 586–599. For his retraction, see Gwyn A. Williams, "The Making and Unmaking of Antonio Gramsci," *New Edinburgh Review* 27, Special Gramsci Issue 3 (1975), 12.

38. Edward P. Thompson, "The Peculiarities of the English," *The Socialist Register 1965,* 345–346; Perry Anderson, "Socialism and Pseudo-Empiricism," *New Left Review* I/35 (January/February 1966), 27–28.

39. Tom Nairn, "La nemesi borghese," *Il Contemporaneo* 6, nos. 63–64 (1963).

40. David Forgacs, "Gramsci and Marxism in Britain," *New Left Review* I/176 (July/August 1989), 75–77; Willie Thompson, "Tom Nairn and the Crisis of the British State," *Contemporary Record* 6, no. 2 (Autumn 1992), 307–311.

41. Nairn, "La nemesi borghese," 161.

42. Perry Anderson, "Origins of the Present Crisis," *New Left Review* I/23 (January/February 1964), 39–50. Gramsci is name-checked on the first page.

43. Tom Nairn, "The Nature of the Labor Party–1," *New Left Review,* I/27 (September/October 1964), 39.

44. Neat, *Hamish Henderson,* vol. 2, 243–45.

45. Antonio Gramsci, "Soviets in Italy," *New Left Review* I/51 (September/October 1968), 28–58; Antonio Gramsci, *Soviets in Italy* (Nottingham: Institute for Workers' Control, 1969).

46. John M. Cammett, *Antonio Gramsci and the Origins of Italian Communism* (Stanford: Stanford University Press, 1967); Eugene D. Genovese, "On Antonio Gramsci" (review of Cammett), *Studies on the Left* 7 (March/April 1967), 83–108; Chris Harman, "Gramsci" (review of Cammett), *International Socialism* 1:32 (Spring 1968), 37; Alastair Davidson, *Antonio Gramsci: The Man, His Ideas* (Sydney: Australian Left Review Publications, 1968); John M. Merrington, "Theory and Practice in Gramsci's Marxism," *The Socialist Register 1968,* 145–174; Alberto Pozzolini [1968], *Antonio Gramsci: An Introduction to His Thought* (London: Pluto Press, 1970); Giuseppe Fiori [1965], *Antonio Gramsci: Life of a Revolutionary* (London: New Left Books, 1970); Lucio Colletti [1965], "Antonio Gramsci and the Italian Revolution" (review of Fiori), *New Left Review* I/65 (January/February 1971), 87–94.

47. See, for example, Cliff Slaughter, "What is Revolutionary Leadership?," *Labour Review* 5, no. 3 (October/November 1960), 93, 106 and Chris Harman, "Party and Class," *International Socialism* 1:35 (Winter 1968/9), 27–30.

48. Ray Burnett, "When the Finger Points at the Moon," in *Scotland at the Crossroads: A Socialist Answer,* edited by James D. Young (Glasgow: Clydeside Press, 1990), 98.

49. Ibid., 102.

50. Eamonn McCann [1974], *War and an Irish Town* (New updated edition, London:

Pluto Press, 1981), 62.

51. "Derry: Fighting under the Flag of the Citizens' Army," interview with Eamonn McCann and Ray Burnett, *Socialist Worker* (August 21, 1969).

52. Burnett, "When the Finger Points at the Moon," 99.

53. Ibid., 99–100.

54. Ray Burnett, "Scotland and Antonio Gramsci," *Scottish International* 5, no. 9 (November 1972), 12.

55. Burnett, "When the Finger Points at the Moon," 95, 98–99.

56. The relevant passages are not cited by Burnett, but for the main discussion see Antonio Gramsci, "State and Civil Society," in *Selections from the Prison Notebooks*, 229–239, Q1§134, Q1§133, Q7§16, Q6§138, Q6§117.

57. Burnett, "Scotland and Antonio Gramsci," 14; Ray Burnett, "Socialists and the SNP," in *The Red Paper on Scotland*, 120.

58. Burnett, "Scotland and Antonio Gramsci," 14.

59. Ibid., 15; Antonio Gramsci, "The Modern Prince," in *Selections from the Prison Notebooks*, 201, Q9§63.

60. Burnett, "Scotland and Antonio Gramsci," 15.

61. Neil Williamson, "Ten Years After–The Revolutionary Left in Scotland," *The Scottish Government Yearbook 1979*, 79–70.

62. Neat, *Hamish Henderson*, vol. 2, 183–84.

63. *New Edinburgh Review*, special issues on Antonio Gramsci, no. 25 (1973), 26 (1974), and 27 (1975).

64. Burnett, "When the Finger Points at the Moon," 100; Neat, *Hamish Henderson*, vol. 2, 184; Williamson, "Ten Years After–The Revolutionary Left in Scotland," 74–75.

65. Neil K. Rafeek, *Communist Women in Scotland: Red Clydeside from the Russian Revolution to the End of the Soviet Union* (London: I. B. Tauris, 2008), 188.

66. David G. Whitfield, "Antonio Gramsci: Signposts to Scottish Action," *Scottish International* (1974), 9.

67. Nairn, "Culture and Nationalism," 8.

68. Ibid., 94–99, 101–05.

69. Tom Nairn, "Old Nationalism and New Nationalism," in *The Red Paper on Scotland*, 25. In his own contribution to *The Red Paper on Scotland*, Burnett still invoked the need for the Modern Prince and rejected the idea that SNP could play the role of consolidating counter-hegemony among the working class. See Burnett, "Socialists and the SNP," 120.

70. Gramsci, "State and Civil Society," 258–60, Q8§179.

71. Nairn, "Old Nationalism and New Nationalism," 26, 27–28, 31.

72. I discuss these comparisons in "Scotland: Birthplace of Passive Revolution?," *Approaching Passive Revolution*, special issue of *Capital and Class*, vol. 34, no. 3 (Autumn 2010). See also *The Origins of Scottish Nationhood*, 78; *Discovering the Scottish Revolution, 1692–1746*, 272–73; and "The Scottish Path to Capitalist Agriculture 3: The Enlightenment as the Theory and Practice of Improvement," *Journal of Agrarian Change* 5, no. 1 (January 2005), 39–40.

73. Tom Nairn, "Dr Jekyll's Case: Model or Warning?," *Bulletin of Scottish Politics* 1, no. 1 (Autumn 1980), 138.

74. Nairn, "Old Nationalism and New Nationalism," 39.

75. Ibid., 35.
76. Gramsci, "State and Civil Society," 223–26, Q3§42.
77. See, for example, Sigmund Freud, "Totem and Taboo," in *The Freud Reader*, edited by Peter Gay (New York: W. W. Norton, 1989), 511.
78. Nairn, "Old and New Nationalism," 47, 49.
79. Gramsci, "Problems of Marxism," 438, Q7§32.
80. Nairn, "Old and New Nationalism," 24.
81. Perry Anderson, "Foreword," in *English Questions* (London: Verso, 1992), 5.
82. See, for example, Craig Beveridge and Ronald Turnbull, "Scottish Nationalist, British Marxist: The Strange Case of Tom Nairn," in *The Eclipse of Scottish Culture* (Edinburgh: Polygon, 1989), 59, 60.
83. See, above all, "Old and New Nationalism," 39.
84. Nairn, "The Modern Janus," *New Left Review* I/94 (November/December 1975), 22.
85. See, for example, Louis Althusser [1964], "Marxism and Humanism," in *For Marx* (London: New Left Books, 1969), 235.
86. Gramsci, "The Study of Philosophy," 332–33, Q11§12.
87. Michael Hechter, *Internal Colonialism: The Celtic Fringe in British National Development, 1536–1966* (London: Routledge and Kegan Paul, 1975), 8–9, 239.
88. Ibid., 342–43; Michael Hechter, "Internal Colonialism Revisited," *Cencrastus* 10 (Autumn 1982), 9.
89. Christopher Harvie, "Beyond Bairn's Play: A New Agenda for Scottish Politics," *Cencrastus* 10 (Autumn 1982), 11.
90. Harvie, *Scotland and Nationalism*, 232.
91. "Notes on Contributors," in *The Red Paper on Scotland*, 5–6.
92. See chapter 8 in this volume.
93. Harvie, *Scotland and Nationalism*, 17.
94. Christopher Harvie, "Nationalism, Journalism and Cultural Politics," in *Nationalism in the Nineties*, edited by Tom Gallagher (Edinburgh: Polygon, 1991), 33.
95. Thomas, *The Gramscian Moment*, 417 and 414–21 more generally. See also Adam David Morton, *Unravelling Gramsci: Hegemony and Passive Revolution in the Global Economy* (London: Pluto Press, 2007), 90–92.
96. Harvie, *Scotland and Nationalism*, 125.
97. Ibid. See also 274.
98. Harvie, "Nationalism, Journalism and Cultural Politics," 33, 45.
99. Whitfield treated socialist intellectuals as a third category, rather than as the organic intellectuals of the working class. See "Antonio Gramsci," 8.
100. Antonio Gramsci, "The Intellectuals," in *Selections from the Prison Notebooks*, 9–10, Q12§3.
101. James D. Young, *The Rousing of the Scottish Working Class* (London: Croom Helm, 1979), 47. One wonders whether Young thinks that alcoholism is a virtuous habit.
102. Ibid., 11. See also 14–15 for his further reliance on Hechter.
103. Ibid., 168; Gramsci, "Notes on Italian History," 80, Q1§48. Young uses a different translation.
104. Young, *The Rousing of the Scottish Working Class*, 168.
105. Williamson, "Ten Years After–The Revolutionary Left in Scotland," 76.

106. Lindsay Paterson, *The Autonomy of Modern Scotland* (Edinburgh: Edinburgh University Press, 1994), 8.

107. Perry Anderson, "The Antinomies of Antonio Gramsci," *New Left Review,* I/100 (November 1976/January 1977), 69–70, 75–76.

108. As Thomas has definitively demonstrated, this is a misreading of Gramsci's dialectic of coercion and consent. See *The Gramscian Moment,* 161–67.

109. Keith Burgess et al., "Scotland and the First British Empire, 1707–1770s," in *Scottish Capitalism: Class, State and Nation from Before the Union to the Present,* edited by Tony Dickson (London: Lawrence and Wishart, 1980), 124.

110. Rafeek, *Communist Women in Scotland,* 205.

111. For a comprehensive statement, see Stuart Hall, "Gramsci and Us," *Marxism Today* (June 1987), 16–21.

112. Henderson, "Introduction," 11.

113. Pat Kane, "Scotland by Starlight," in *Tinsel Show: Pop, Politics, Scotland* (Edinburgh: Polygon, 1992), 184.

114. Keith Hartley, *The Vigorous Imagination: New Scottish Art* (Edinburgh: National Galleries of Scotland, 1987).

115. Henderson, "Introduction," 1.

116. Angus Calder, "Art for a New Scotland?" in *Revolving Culture,* 253.

117. Paul Wood, "The Dotage of Authenticity: Realism(s) and National Culture(s)," *Edinburgh Review* 80/81 (1988), 53.

118. Hoare and Nowell-Smith, editorial note to "Problems of Marxism," 421, note 65.

119. Paul Tritschler, "Gramsci," *Radical Scotland* 20 (April/May 1986), 31.

120. S. Hosie and S. Robison, *A Left Nationalist Response to the CPB Critique of Scottish Nationalism* (Glasgow: National Popular Publications, 1991), 2.

121. Gramsci, "State and Civil Society," 240, Q14§68.

122. Antonio Gramsci and Palmiro Togliatti, "The Italian Situation and the Tasks of the PCI ('Lyons Thesis')," in *Selections from the Political Writings,* 340.

123. Cammett, *Antonio Gramsci and the Origins of Italian Communism,* 9–13; Davidson, *Antonio Gramsci,* 48–50, 57–65; Fiori, *Antonio Gramsci,* 93–94; Morton, *Unravelling Gramsci,* 80–81.

124. Gramsci to Tania, October 12, 1931, in *Prison Letters,* 175.

125. Antonio Gramsci, "Julien Benda," in *Selections from the Cultural Writings,* 260, Q3§2.

126. Robert Q. Gray, *The Labor Aristocracy in Victorian Edinburgh* (Oxford: Oxford University Press, 1976), 5–6, 185–86; John Holford, *Reshaping Labor: Organisation, Work and Politics–Edinburgh in the Great War and After* (London: Croom Helm, 1988), 5–6, 235, 240. The key passages are in Gramsci, "The Study of Philosophy," 323–43, Q11§12.

127. Sean Damer, *From Moorepark to "Wine Alley": The Rise and Fall of a Glasgow Housing Scheme* (Edinburgh: Edinburgh University Press, 1989), 23–24, 150–51; Grant Jarvie, "Culture, Social Development and the Scottish Highland Gatherings," in *The Making of Scotland: Nation, Culture and Social Change,* edited by David McCrone, Stephen Kendrick and Pat Straw (Edinburgh: Edinburgh University Press, 1989), 191–92; David McCrone, *Understanding Scotland: The Sociology of a Stateless Nation* (London: Routledge, 1992), 27.

128. Colin McArthur, *Brigadoon, Braveheart and the Scots: Distortions of Scotland in Hol-*

lywood Cinema (London: I. B. Tauris, 2003), 112, 113.

129. Davidson, "The Scottish Path to Capitalist Agriculture 3," 37–38; Neil Davidson, "Neoliberal Politics in a Devolved Scotland," in *Neoliberal Scotland: Class and Society in a Stateless Nation,* edited by Neil Davidson, Patricia McCafferty, and David Miller (Newcastle: Cambridge Scholars Press, 2010), 367–69. See also Hearn, *Claiming Scotland,* 88.

130. Tom Nairn, "From Civil Society to Civic Nationalism," in *Faces of Nationalism: Janus Revisited* (London: Verso, 1998), 81–82.

131. Allan Harkness, "The Popular Imagination: An Interview with Ken Currie," *Cencrastus* 27 (Autumn 1987), 31. In fact, the repressive power of the state in Western liberal democracies is actually greater than that of the East. In this regard, at least, the formulations of Gramsci's opponent within the PCI, Amadeo Bordiga, may have been superior to his own. See Anderson, "The Antinomies of Antonio Gramsci," 49–55.

132. Paterson, *The Autonomy of Modern Scotland,* 17.

133. Nairn, "From Civil Society to Civic Nationalism," 82. For the significance of this reassessment of Gramsci in the context of Nairn's wider rejection of Marxism, see chapter 1 in this volume.

134. Nairn, "From Civil Society to Civic Nationalism," 82. The quote by Neil Harding is from "Intellectuals, Socialism and Proletariat," in *Intellectuals and Politics: From the Dreyfus Affair to Salman Rushdie,* edited by Jeremy Jennings and Anthony Kemp-Walsh (London: Routledge, 1997), 211.

135. Hughes, *Consciousness and Society,* 101–02.

136. Neat, *Hamish Henderson,* vol. 2, 364–65.

Chapter II: Women and the Lost World of Scottish Communism

1. Originally published in *Critique* 39, no. 2 (May 2011) as a review of Neil C. Rafeek, *Communist Women in Scotland: Red Clydeside from the Russian Revolution to the End of the Soviet Union* (London: Tauris Academic Studies, 2008).

2. Steven Fielding, "Review of Noreen Branson, *History of the Communist Party of Great Britain, 1941–1951,*" *Socialist History* 14 (1999), 80. Similar if less extreme judgments have been made by former members of the party such as Willie Thompson: "The Communist Party of Great Britain (CPGB) throughout the seven decades of its effective existence was never of more than marginal significance in British political life." See *The Good Old Cause: British Communism, 1920–1991* (London: Pluto Press, 1992), 1.

3. Thompson, *The Good Old Cause,* 218.

4. "Former members" in the sense that, since the original CPGB dissolved itself in November 1992, *everyone* who held a party card prior to that date is now a former member: many of Rafeek's interviewees make clear that they would have remained members had the party continued to exist.

5. Rafeek, *Communist Women in Scotland,* 3. See also 15.

6. Timothy Neat, *Hamish Henderson: A Biography,* vol. 2, *Poetry Becomes People (1952–2002)* (Edinburgh: Birlinn, 2009), 108.

7. Rafeek, *Communist Women in Scotland,* 112–16.

8. Ibid., 232.

9. William McIlvanney, "The Shallowing of Scotland," in *Surviving the Shipwreck*

(Edinburgh: Mainstream, 1991), 120.

10. Not all the similarities are positive, of course. Rafeek quotes Ouaine Bain on "the tyranny of the Contribution" and adds his own gloss: "The political committee would hand down a political statement and then committee members would make their own rehearsed offerings while the meeting was strongly controlled by the chair." Rafeek, *Communist Women in Scotland*, 196. Needless to say the problem of tyrannical contributions has not been restricted to the CPGB.

11. Ibid., 68.

12. Ibid., 99.

13. Some of the cultural differences with today, particularly in male-female relations, are striking. Jenny Richardson recalls one woman on the CPGB Scottish Women's Advisory Committee speaking at a meeting at Clydebank: "Peter Kerrigan was the main speaker and Sarah turned up with her nail varnish on her fingers and on her *toes* and Peter got rather annoyed. . . . She was being '*frivolous*' in front of the workmen." Ibid., 95.

14. Ibid., 13–15.

15. Ibid., 91, 104.

16. Jackie Kay, "Non-Stop Party," in *Children of the Revolution: Communist Childhood in Cold War Britain,* edited by Phil Cohen (London: Lawrence and Wishart, 1997), 38.

17. For an early but characteristic statement of the CPGB"s position, see John Gollan, *Scottish Prospect: An Economic, Administrative and Social Survey* (Glasgow: Caledonian Books, 1948), chapter 16, "Self-Government for Scotland."

18. Rafeek, *Communist Women in Scotland,* 171–75.

19. Neil Davidson, "Neoliberal Politics in a Devolved Scotland," in *Neoliberal Scotland: Class and Nation in a Stateless Nation,* edited by Neil Davidson, Patricia McCafferty, and David Miller (Newcastle: Cambridge Scholars Press, 2010), 373–75. See also chapter 1 in this volume.

20. Rafeek, *Communist Women in Scotland,* 215 and 211–216 more generally.

21. Ibid., 207.

22. Ibid., 223.

23. Tom Nairn, "Old and New Nationalism," in *The Red Paper on Scotland,* edited by Gordon Brown (Edinburgh: Edinburgh University Special Publications Board, 1975), 34.

24. Rafeek, *Communist Women in Scotland,* 55.

25. Ibid., 85.

26. Ibid., 69.

27. Ibid., 93.

28. Ibid., 120.

29. Ibid., 187.

30. Ibid., 7.

31. Ibid.

32. Which is not to pretend that all members were exemplary in all aspects of their behavior: Rafeek's interviewees are critical of some party members who regarded themselves as superior to others, particularly when this was in no way justified by their theory or practice. The late Jimmy Reid was thought by some

interviewees to have displayed "complacency and arrogance" during his 1974 General Election campaign in Clydebank, despite having, as Rafeek puts it, a "history of organizational incompetence." See ibid., 175–76.

33. Ibid., 126, 139–44.
34. Franz Borkenau [1939], *World Communism: A History of the Communist International* (Ann Arbor: University of Michigan Press, 1962), 413–19.
35. Rafeek, *Communist Women in Scotland,* 89, 90.
36. Peter Bain, "'Is You Is or Is You Ain't My Baby': Women's Pay and the Clydeside Strikes of 1943," *Scottish Labour History* 30 (1995), 52.
37. Ibid, 54.
38. Rafeek, *Communist Women in Scotland,* 151.
39. Ibid., 143.
40. Ibid., 166.
41. Ibid., 177.
42. See, for example, "Christine Buchan," in *Dutiful Daughters: Women Talk about Their Lives,* edited by Jean McCrindle and Sheila Rowbotham (Harmondsworth: Penguin Books, 1979), 326–29. McCrindle was herself interviewed by Rafeek for *Communist Women in Scotland.*
43. Rafeek, *Communist Women in Scotland,* 144.
44. Tommy Sheridan with Joan McAlpine, *A Time to Rage* (Edinburgh: Polygon, 1994), 50, 51, 52.
45. Kay, "Non-Stop Party," 42.
46. For the most important, based partly on interviews with former members in and around Manchester, see Kevin Morgan, Gidon Cohen, and Andrew Flinn, *Communists and British Society, 1920–91: People of a Special Mould* (London: Rivers Oram, 2005).

Chapter 12: Eric Hobsbawm's Unanswered Question

1. Originally published in *Economic and Political Weekly* 47, no. 38 (September 22, 2012) as a review of Eric J. Hobsbawm, *How to Change the World: Tales of Marx and Marxism* (London: Little, Brown, 2011).
2. Of these historians, only Manning and Ste. Croix were never members of the Communist Party of Great Britain, although the former was involved with its Historians Group through the journal *Past and Present.*
3. He announced that he would no longer be appearing in public at the launch of this book for the Socialist History Society at Bishopsgate Library, London, on February 25, 2011. For an example of a recent appearance in the British media see Andrew Whitehead, "Eric Hobsbawm on the Arab Spring: 'It Reminds Me of 1848 . . . ,'" *BBC News Magazine* (December 23, 2011), www.bbc.co.uk/news/magazine-16217726.
4. Eric J. Hobsbawm, *Interesting Times: A Twentieth-Century Life* (London: Allen Lane, 2002), 96.
5. Ibid., 200, footnote; Eric J. Hobsbawm, "Preface," in *On History* (London: Weidenfeld and Nicolson, 1997), ix.
6. Eric J. Hobsbawm, "The Historians Group of the Communist Party," in *Rebels and Their Causes: Essays in Honour of A. L. Morton,* edited by Maurice Cornforth (London: Lawrence and Wishart, 1978), 31–32.

7. Hobsbawm, *Interesting Times,* 291.

8. For a discussion of right-wing attempts to appropriate Thompson's work in support of social neoliberalism, see Anthony Iles and Tom Roberts, *All Knees and Elbows of Susceptibility and Refusal: Reading History from Below* (London: Strickland Distribution, Transmission, and Mute Books, 2012), 247–65.

9. See, for example, Harvey J. Kaye, *The British Marxist Historians: An Introductory Analysis* (Cambridge: Polity Press, 1984), 132, 153–56.

10. See, for example, Eric J. Hobsbawm [1984], "Marx and History," in *On History,* 160–65.

11. See, for example, Eric J. Hobsbawm [1972], "From Social History to the History of Society," in *On History,* 79–83.

12. Eric J. Hobsbawm [1954], "The Crisis of the Seventeenth Century," in *Crisis in Europe, 1560–1660: Essays from Past and Present,* edited by Trevor Ashton (London: Routledge and Kegan Paul, 1965), 5–6.

13. Edward P. Thompson [1963], *The Making of the English Working Class* (Second edition, Harmondsworth: Penguin Books, 1980), 12.

14. Thomas Gray [1751], "Elegy Written in a Country Churchyard," in *The Faber Book of Political Verse,* edited by Tom Paulin (London: Faber and Faber, 1986), 195.

15. Eric J. Hobsbawm [1959], *Primitive Rebels: Studies in Archaic Forms of Social Movement in the 19th and 20th Centuries* (Manchester: Manchester University Press, 1971); *Bandits* (London: Weidenfeld and Nicolson, 1969).

16. Eric J. Hobsbawm, "Foreword," in *How to Change the World,* vii.

17. Eric J. Hobsbawm [1964], "Marx on Pre-Capitalist Formations," in *How to Change the World,* 134, 135. For a similar position by a Marxist nominally operating within the discipline of geography, see David Harvey [1978], "On Countering the Marxian Myth—Chicago Style," in *Spaces of Capital: Towards a Critical Geography* (Edinburgh: Edinburgh University Press, 2001), 75, 78. For a more polemical statement of the same position by a writer unclassifiable in disciplinary terms see John Berger, "Where Are We?," in *Hold Everything Dear: Dispatches on Survival and Resistance* (London: Verso, 2007), 38.

18. Eric J. Hobsbawm [1982], "The Influence of Marxism, 1945–83," in *How to Change the World,* 364–66.

19. Hobsbawm, "Marx on Pre-Capitalist Formations," 152 and 147–52 more generally.

20. Ibid., 143–44.

21. Eric J. Hobsbawm [1998], "On the *Communist Manifesto*" [1998], in *How to Change the World,* 109–10.

22. Eric J. Hobsbawm [1982], "Gramsci," in *How to Change the World,* 326–27.

23. Ibid., 87.

24. Eric J. Hobsbawm [1982], "Marx, Engels and Politics," in *How to Change the World,* 61–62.

25. Eric J. Hobsbawm [2006], "Marx Today," in *How to Change the World,* 13.

26. Karl Marx and Friedrich Engels [1848], "Manifesto of the Communist Party," in *Political Writings,* vol. 1, *The Revolutions of 1848,* edited by David Fernbach, (Harmondsworth: Penguin Books/New Left Review, 1973), 86–87.

27. Hal Draper, "The Death of the State in Marx and Engels," *The Socialist Register 1970,* edited by Ralph Miliband and John Saville (London: Merlin Press, 1970),

286 and 285–89 more generally.

28. Karl Marx [1871], "The Civil War in France," in *Political Writings*, vol. 3, *The First International and After*, edited by David Fernbach (Harmondsworth: Penguin Books/New Left Review, 1973), 212.

29. Friedrich Engels [1872], "Preface to the German Edition of 1872," in Karl Marx and Friedrich Engels, *The Communist Manifesto* (Harmondsworth: Penguin Books, 2002), 194.

30. Hobsbawm, "Marx, Engels and Politics," 56–57. Compare the discussion in Hal Draper, *Karl Marx's Theory of Revolution*, vol. 3, *The "Dictatorship of the Proletariat"* (New York: Monthly Review Press, 1986), 269–74, 315–17.

31. Vladimir I. Lenin [1917], "The State and Revolution: The Marxist Theory of the State and the Tasks of the Proletariat in the Revolution," in *Collected Works*, vol. 25, *June-September 1917* (Moscow: Progress Publishers, 1964), 418–37.

32. Hobsbawm, "Marx, Engels and Politics," 57.

33. Hobsbawm, "Gramsci," 332.

34. Louis Althusser [1962], "Contradiction and Overdetermination: Notes for an Investigation," in *For Marx* (London: Verso, 2005), 115–16.

35. See, for example, Eric J. Hobsbawm [1995], "The Reception of Gramsci," in *How to Change the World*, 339: "Who now expects another vogue for Althusser, any more than for Spengler?" Hobsbawm's skepticism about Althusser reaches all the way back to the French publication of *For Marx* and *Reading Capital*. See Eric J. Hobsbawm [1966], "The Structure of Capital," in *Revolutionaries: Contemporary Essays* (London: Quartet Books, 1977), 145–52.

36. Antonio Gramsci, "The Nature and History of Economic Science: 4. Brief Notes on Economics [1]. The Concept of 'Homo oeconomicus,'" in *Further Selections from the Prison Notebooks*, edited by David Boothman (Minneapolis: University of Minnesota Press, 1995), 167, Q10II§15.

37. Eric J. Hobsbawm, "Waking from History's Great Dream," interview by Paul Barker, *Independent on Sunday* (February 4, 1990).

38. "Marx Today," 9.

39. Ibid., 316.

40. See, for example, Eric J. Hobsbawm [1985], "The Retreat into Extremism," in *Politics for a Rational Left: Political Writings, 1977–1988* (London: Verso, 1989), 92–94. For his own assessment of the influence of the Popular Front on his politics, see *Interesting Times*, esp. chapter 8, "Against Fascism and War," and 322–24.

41. Eric J. Hobsbawm, *Age of Extremes: The Short Twentieth Century, 1914–1991* (London: Michael Joseph, 1994), chapter 4, "Against the Common Enemy."

42. Eric J. Hobsbawm [1982], "In the Era of Anti-Fascism, 1929–45," in *How to Change the World*, 273–74, 308.

43. Ibid., 307–11.

44. Leon D. Trotsky [1939], "One Again on the Causes of the Defeat in Spain," in *The Spanish Revolution (1931–39)*, edited by Naomi Allen and George Breitman (New York: Pathfinder Press, 1973), 339.

45. Hobsbawm, "In the Era of Anti-Fascism," 310, note 72 (text on 448).

46. Fernando Claudin, *The Communist Movement: From Comintern to Cominform* (Harmondsworth: Penguin, 1975), 242 and 210–42 more generally.

47. Niall Ferguson, "What a Swell Party It Was . . . for Him," *Daily Telegraph* (September 22, 2002).

48. Eric J. Hobsbawm [2000–2010], "Marx and Labor: The Long Century," in *How to Change the World*, 418–19.

49. Tony Judt [2006], "Goodbye to All That? Leszek Kolakowski and the Marxist Legacy," in *Reappraisals: Reflections on the Forgotten Twentieth Century* (London: William Heinemann, 2008), 142–43.

50. Eric J. Hobsbawm, "After the Cold War," *London Review of Books* 34, no. 8 (April 26, 2012), 14.

51. Originally published as the foreword to a reprint of the above review in *International Socialist Review* 86 (November/December 2012).

52. Now published as *Fractured Times: Culture and Society in the Twentieth Century* (London: Little, Brown, 2013).

53. Michael Burleigh, "Eric Hobsbawm: A Believer in the Red Utopia to the Very End," *Telegraph* (October 1, 2012), www.telegraph.co.uk/news/politics/9579092 /Eric-Hobsbawm-A-believer-in-the-Red-utopia-to-the-very-end.html.

54. Niall Ferguson, "A Truly Great Historian," *The Guardian* (October 1, 2012), www.guardian.co.uk/commentisfree/2012/oct/01/eric-hobsbawm-historian.

Chapter 13: The Posthumous Adventures of Adam Smith

1. Originally published in *Scottish Review of Books* 9, no. 1 (March 23, 2013) as "The Battle for Adam Smith."

2. Richard Cockett, *Thinking the Unthinkable: Think-Tanks and the Economic Counter-Revolution, 1931–1983* (London: Fontana Press, 1995), 280–85; Daniel Stedman Jones, *Masters of the Universe: Hayek, Friedman, and the Birth of Neoliberal Politics* (Princeton: Princeton University Press, 2012), 165–67.

3. Federal Reserve Bank of Minneapolis website, www.minneapolisfed.org /publications_papers/pub_display.cfm?id=3708.

4. Adam Smith Institute website, www.adamsmith.org/about-us/frequently -asked-questions.

5. Jacob Viner, "Adam Smith and Laissez Faire," *Journal of Political Economy* 35, no. 2 (April, 1927), 207.

6. Emma Rothschild, *Economic Sentiments: Adam Smith, Condorcet, and the Enlightenment* (Cambridge, Massachusetts: Harvard University Press, 2001), 52.

7. Anthony Waterman, "Reappraisal of 'Malthus the Economist,' 1933–1997," *History of Political Economy* 45, no. 1 (February 1998), 295.

8. Richard E. Teichgraeber III, "'Less Abused Than I Had Reason to Expect': The Reception of The Wealth of Nations in Britain, 1776–1790," *Historical Journal* 30, no. 2 (June 1987), 366.

9. Rothschild, *Economic Sentiments*, 53.

10. See, for example, Dugald Stewart [1792], *Elements of the Philosophy of the Human Mind,* in *Collected Works*, vol. 2, edited by W. Hamilton (Edinburgh: Thomas Constable, 1854), 228.

11. John Saville, *The Consolidation of the Capitalist State, 1800–1850* (London: Pluto Press, 1994), 36.

12. Unlike his predecessors, Smith regarded acts of self-interest as virtuous in themselves, not merely as the cause of unintended virtuous consequences. As Lucio

Colletti writes: "For Mandeville, the selfish activity of man is a *vice:* a vice he certainly rejoices in, as against the hypocrisy and bigotry of priests and puritans, yet still a vice, at least in the sense that the individuals–being in competition with each other–seem to him to be intent on deceiving and swindling each other. For Smith, on the other hand, the selfish activity of the individual (in the face of which, he shows, it would be useless to appeal to 'good will' and 'humanity') tends to appear as a positive factor, almost a 'virtue.' This is because he takes it for granted that, in pursuing his *private* interests, the individual is collaborating in the promotion of the *general* interest. In the first case, *negative* factors produce a positive result; in the second case, the positive result arises from the sum of the partial factors which in themselves are already *positive*." See "Mandeville, Rousseau and Smith," in *From Rousseau to Lenin: Studies in Ideology and Society* (London: New Left Books, 1972), 213 and 208–16 more generally.

13. The most comprehensive account of the "problem" and, in my opinion, the most plausible attempt to resolve it is Dogan Göçmen, *The Adam Smith Problem: Human Nature and Society in* The Theory of Moral Sentiments *and* The Wealth of Nations (London: Taurus Academic Studies, 2007). But see also Richard Teichgraeber III, "Rethinking *Das Adam Smith Problem*," in *New Perspectives on the Politics and Culture of Early Modern Scotland*, edited by John Dwyer, Roger A. Mason, and Alexander Murdoch (Edinburgh: John Donald Publishers, 1982).

14. Ruth Scurr, "Inequality and Political Stability from the Ancien Regime to Revolution: The Reception of Adam Smith's *Theory of Moral Sentiments* in France," *History of European Ideas* 35, no. 4 (December 2009), 413–17.

15. Teichgraeber III, "'Less Abused Than I Had Reason to Expect,'" 339, 340.

16. Horner to Thompson, August 15, 1803, in *Memoirs and Correspondence of Francis Horner, M.P.,* edited by Leonard Horner (London: John Murray, 1843), vol. 1, 229.

17. Robert Burns [1790], "On the Late Death of Dr Adam Smith," in *The Canongate Burns*, edited by Andrew Noble and Patrick Scott Hogg (Edinburgh: Canongate, 2001), 445.

18. Thomas Paine [1791–2], *Rights of Man*, edited by Henry Collins (Harmondsworth: Penguin Books, 1969), 97.

19. Edward P. Thompson [1963], *The Making of the English Working Class* (Second edition, Harmondsworth: Penguin Books, 1980), 104–05.

20. Adam Smith [1759], *The Theory of Moral Sentiments*, edited by David D. Raphael and Alexander L. Macfie (Oxford: Clarendon Press, 1976), 158–59.

21. See, for example, Iain McLean, *Adam Smith: Radical and Egalitarian* (Edinburgh: Edinburgh University Press, 2006), vi–vii, 54–55.

22. Robert Burns [1786], "To a Louse: On Seeing One on a Lady's Bonnet at Church," in *The Canongate Burns,* 132. For the contrast between Smith and Burns, see Gavin Kennedy, *Adam Smith: A Moral Philosopher and His Political Economy* (Houndmills: Palgrave Macmillan, 2008), 48–50.

23. David McNally, *Against the Market: Political Economy, Market Socialism and the Marxist Critique* (London: Verso, 1993), 43.

24. *Edinburgh Review or Critical Journal* 14 (April/July 1809), 50–51.

25. See, for example, William Lovett's comments in *Northern Star,* March 31, 1839.

26. A Traveller Underground [John R. Leifchild], *Our Coal and Coal Pits, the People in Them, and the Scenes around Them* (London: Thomas Nelson, 1856), 223–24.

27. Alan B. Campbell, *The Lanarkshire Miners: A Social History of Their Trade Unions, 1775–1874* (Edinburgh: John Donald Publishers, 1979), 254–55.

28. Karl Marx [1862–3], *Theories of Surplus Value,* part 1, edited by S. Ryazanskaya (Moscow: Progress Publishers, 1963), 288, 300.

29. Karl Marx [1862–3], *Theories of Surplus Value,* part 2, edited by S. Ryazanskaya (Moscow: Progress Publishers, 1969), 165, 169.

30. Marx, *Theories of Surplus Value,* part 1, 81.

31. Ibid., 97.

32. Adam Smith [1776], *An Inquiry into the Nature and Causes of the Wealth of Nations,* edited by Edwin Cannan (Chicago: University of Chicago Press, 1976), Book II, Introduction, 291–92; Karl Marx [1867], *Capital: A Critique of Political Economy,* vol. 1 (Harmondsworth: Penguin/New Left Review, 1976), 873–74.

33. James Steuart [1767], *An Inquiry into the Principles of Political Economy,* vol. 1, edited by Andrew. S. Skinner (Edinburgh: Oliver and Boyd for the Scottish Economic Society, 1966), 171, 176.

34. Marx, *Theories of Surplus Value,* vol. 1, 43.

35. McLean, *Adam Smith,* 69, 82, note 1, and chapter 4 more generally.

36. Michael Perelman, *The Invention of Capitalism: Classical Political Economy and the Secret History of Primitive Accumulation* (Durham, North Carolina: Duke University Press, 2000), 166, 170.

37. Milonakis and Fine, *From Political Economy to Economics,* 12, 93.

38. Murray Milgate and Shannon C. Stimson, *After Adam Smith: A Century of Transformation in Politics and Political Economy* (Princeton: Princeton University Press, 2009), 32.

39. Dimitris Milonakis and Ben Fine, *From Political Economy to Economics: Method, the Social and the Historical in the Evolution of Economic Theory* (Abingdon: Routledge, 2009), 94–95, 102–03.

40. Rothschild, *Economic Sentiments,* 65 and 64–66 more generally.

41. Frederick von Hayek, "The Complexity of Problems of Human Interaction," in *The Fatal Conceit: The Errors of Socialism,* edited by W. W. Bartley III (London: Routledge, 1988), 148.

42. See, for example, Kennedy, *Adam Smith,* chapter 12 or Milgate and Stimson, *After Adam Smith,* 89–94.

43. Jonathan Rose, *The Intellectual Life of the British Working Classes* (New Haven: Yale University Press, 2001), 300. To a large extent interest in Smith went in parallel with how sectarian institutions of working-class education were. "Henry Heslop, the Durham miner-novelist, attended the CLC [Central Labour College] in 1925–26 and found the curriculum dismally propagandistic. 'They insisted that there was no viable reasoning on economics before Marx, and none whatever since,' so the students learned nothing of Adam Smith, David Ricardo, or John Stuart Mill." Ibid., 303.

44. James Buchan, *Adam Smith and the Pursuit of Perfect Liberty* (London: Profile Books, 2006), 5.

45. Milton Friedman, *The Relevance of Adam Smith for 1976,* University of Chicago Graduate School of Business, *Selected Papers* no. 50 (1976), 1, 3.

46. Stedman Jones, *Masters of the Universe,* 104–07.

47. Margaret Thatcher, *The Downing Street Years* (London: HarperCollins, 1993),

618. See also David Torrance, *"We in Scotland": Thatcherism in a Cold Climate* (Edinburgh: Birlinn, 2009), 25, 57, 161 and 165.

48. Dennis MacLeod and Michael Russell, *Grasping the Thistle: How Scotland Must React to the Three Key Challenges of the Twenty First Century* (Glendaruel: Argyll Publishing, 2006), 95–96.

49. Milonakis and Fine, *From Political Economy to Economics,* 48.

50. Elmar Altvater, "The Roots of Neoliberalism," *The Socialist Register 2008: Global Flashpoints. Reactions to Imperialism and Neoliberalism,* edited by Leo Panitch and Colin Leys (London: Merlin Press, 2007), 346.

51. James D. Young, letter in *The Herald* (March 21, 2007).

52. Michael Perelman, *The Invisible Handcuffs of Capitalism: How Market Tyranny Stifles the Economy by Stunting Workers* (New York: Monthly Review Press, 2011), 174–175 and 160–76 more generally. A subsequent chapter is entitled "The Dark Side of Adam Smith"–somewhat redundantly since for Perelman Smith's work, like the moon in Pink Floyd's 1973 album, is all dark. For his entire discussion, see ibid., 149–99. See also Perelman, *The Invention of Capitalism,* 171–228.

53. In this respect there is a major difference between the reception of Smith and that of David Ricardo, aspects of whose work were consciously used by economists hostile to neoclassicism (the "neo-Ricardians") but unconvinced by the labor theory of value in its Marxist form, which they saw as being unable to determine producer prices. The main source for the revival of Ricardo's thought was Piero Sraffa, *Production of Commodities by Means of Commodities: Prelude to a Critique of Economic Theory* (Cambridge: Cambridge University Press, 1960). For the classic statement of the neo-Ricardian position, which is by no means identical with Sraffa's, see Ian Steedman, *Marx after Sraffa* (London: New Left Books, 1977). Smith has rarely been used to "correct" Marx in this way; his influence has either been unconscious or deliberately posed as an alternative to Marxism, not a supplement to it.

54. Robert Brenner, "The Origins of Capitalist Development: A Critique of Neo-Smithian Marxism," *New Left Review* I/104 (July/August 1977), 27–41; "Property and Progress: Where Adam Smith Went Wrong," *Marxist History Writing for the Twenty-First Century,* edited by Chris Wickham (Oxford: Oxford University Press for The British Academy, 2007), 49–50, 82–89. Perelman makes an interesting argument for seeing Lenin as a Smithian Marxist in relation to the development of capitalism in Russia. See *The Invention of Capitalism,* 352–365.

55. Immanuel Wallerstein, "From Feudalism to Capitalism: Transition or Transitions?," *Social Forces* 55, no. 2 (December 1976), 273, 280.

56. Smith, *The Wealth of Nations,* book I, chapter 2, 17.

57. See, for example, Stephen Miller, "French Absolutism and Agricultural Capitalism: A Comment on Henry Heller's Essays," *Historical Materialism* 20, no. 4 (2012), 144.

58. David Graeber, *Debt: The First 5,000 Years* (New York: Melville House, 2011), chapter 2.

59. "Capitalists" seems to have been used from the late 1780s, "capitalism" from the 1850s; Marx's first use of the latter term occurs as late as 1870. See Neil Davidson, *How Revolutionary Were the Bourgeois Revolutions?* (Chicago: Haymarket Books, 2012), 73, 131–32.

60. Smith, *The Wealth of Nations*, book I, chapter 2, 17.
61. Göçmen, *The Adam Smith Problem*, 159.
62. Giovanni Arrighi: *Adam Smith in Beijing: Lineages of the Twenty-First Century* (London:Verso, 2007), 39 and 13–68 more generally.
63. John McMurty, *The Cancer Stage of Capitalism* (London: Pluto Press, 1999), 45 and 41–45 more generally.
64. David C. Korten, *When Corporations Rule the World* (London: Kumerian Press, 1995), 78.
65. Ibid., 80, 88.
66. Eric J. Hobsbawm, *Age of Extremes: The Short Twentieth Century, 1914–1991*(London: Michael Joseph, 1994), 225–400.
67. Neil Davidson,"What Was Neoliberalism?," in *Neoliberal Scotland: Class and Society in a Stateless Nation*, edited by Neil Davidson, Patricia McCafferty, and David Miller (Newcastle: Cambridge Scholars Press, 2010), 10–21.
68. Ashley Lavelle, *The Death of Social Democracy: Political Consequences in the 21st Century* (Aldershot:Ashgate, 2008), 11–16.
69. Gordon Brown,"Foreword," in McLean, *Adam Smith*, viii.
70. McLean, *Adam Smith*, 139. See also Craig Smith,"Adam Smith: Left or Right?," *Political Studies* (2012), onlinelibrary.wiley.com/doi/10.1111/j.1467–9248.2012 .00985.x/full.
71. See the classic discussion in Leszek Kolakowski [1957], "The Concept of the Left," in *Marxism and Beyond: On Historical Understanding and Individual Responsibility* (London: Paladin, 1971).
72. McLean, *Adam Smith*, 147.
73. Brown, "Foreword," ix. See McLean, chapter 5 for an attempt to substantiate this claim.
74. Timothy Garton Ash, "The US Democratic-Capitalist Model Is on Trial. No Schadenfreude, Please," *The Guardian* (October 2, 2008).
75. Göçmen, *The Adam Smith Problem*, 162.
76. P. J. O'Rourke, *On The Wealth of Nations* (London:Atlantic Books, 2007), 51.
77. Bank of England website, www.bankofengland.co.uk/banknotes/Pages/current /smith.aspx.
78. Ryan Patrick Hanley, *Adam Smith and the Character of Virtue* (Cambridge: Cambridge University Press, 2009), 211.
79. Smith, *The Wealth of Nations*, book II, chapter 1, 405.
80. Ibid., Book III, chapter 4, 437, 440.
81. Adam Smith [1762–63, 1766], *Lectures on Jurisprudence*, edited by Ronald L. Meek, David D. Raphael, and Peter G. Stein (Oxford: Oxford University Press, 1978), 264.
82. Henri de Saint-Simon [1818],"On the Political History of Industry," in *Selected Writings on Science, Industry and Social Organization*, edited by Keith Taylor (London: Croom Helm, 1975), 178.
83. Smith, *The Wealth of Nations*, Book I, chapter 1, 8–9.
84. Smith, *Lectures on Jurisprudence*, 340–341.
85. Smith, *The Wealth of Nations*, Book 5, chapter 1, 302–03.
86. Ibid., book 5, chapter 1, 303.
87. See, for example, Adam Ferguson [1767], *An Essay on the History of Civil Society,*

edited by Duncan Forbes (Edinburgh: Edinburgh University Press, 1966), 181. The connections are explored in Buchan, *Adam Smith and the Pursuit of Perfect Liberty,* 5–7, 9; Neil Davidson, "The Scottish Path to Capitalist Agriculture 3: The Enlightenment as the Theory and Practice of Improvement," *Journal of Agrarian Change* 5, no. 1 (2005), 47–53, 62–64; Göçmen, *The Adam Smith Problem,* 114–18; and Lisa Hill, "Adam Smith, Adam Ferguson and Karl Marx on the Division of Labor," *Journal of Classical Sociology* 7, no. 3 (2007).

88. Smith, *The Wealth of Nations,* Book V, chapter 1, 305, 306.

89. Kennedy lists twenty-five areas in total, all but three from *The Wealth of Nations.* See Kennedy, *Adam Smith,* 247–48.

90. Smith, *The Wealth of Nations,* book 1, chapter 10, 143. See also ibid., book I, chapter 11, 277–78.

91. Ibid., book I, chapter 10, 144.

92. Ibid., book V, chapter 1, 236; book IV, chapter 7, 81.

93. David McNally, *Political Economy and the Rise of Capitalism: A Reinterpretation* (Berkeley: University of California Press, 1988), 256–57. See also Richard Koebner, "Adam Smith and the Industrial Revolution," *Economic History Review* 2:11, no. 3 (April 1959), 389–91.

94. Neil Davidson, "The Scottish Path to Capitalist Agriculture 2: The Capitalist Offensive (1847–1815)," *Journal of Agrarian Change* 4, no. 4 (October 2004), 423–31, 438–43. See also Davidson, "The Scottish Path to Capitalist Agriculture 3," 47–53.

95. Perelman, *The Invisible Handcuffs of Capitalism,* 159.

96. Smith, *The Wealth of Nations,* book IV, chapter 7, 75–158. Smith supported a federal solution that would have allowed colonial representatives to sit in the British parliament, thus removing the basis of the demand for "no taxation without representation" within an overall context of free trade between Britain and the American colonies. See Dalphy I. Fagerstrom, "Scottish Opinion and the American Revolution," *William and Mary Quarterly* 3:11, no. 2 (April 1954), 258–61 and Ned C. Landsman, "The Provinces and Empire: Scotland, the American Development of British Provincial Identity," in *An Imperial State at War: Britain, 1689–1815,* edited by Lawrence Stone (London: Routledge, 1994), 264–67.

97. Michael Merrill, "The Anticapitalist Origins of the United States," *Review* 13, no. 4 (Fall 1990), 477.

98. Franklin to Babcock, January 13, 1772, in *The Papers of Benjamin Franklin,* vol. 19, edited by William B. Willcox (New Haven, CT: Yale University Press, 1975), 7.

99. Perelman, *The Invention of Capitalism,* 256–60.

100. Nicholas Phillipson, *Adam Smith: An Enlightened Life* (London: Allen Lane, 2010), 229–30.

101. Charles Post [2009], "Agrarian Class Structure and Economic Development in Colonial British North America: The Place of the American Revolution in the Origins of Capitalism in the USA," in *The American Road to Capitalism: Studies in Class-Structure, Economic Development and Political Conflict, 1620–1877* (Leiden: E. J. Brill, 2011), 171–73, 180–84. Marx made a similar point about white colonial-settler societies, although tending to describe their economies

as based on small commodity production. See Marx, *Capital,* vol. 1, 931–40 and *Theories of Surplus Value,* part 2, 302.

102. Albert O. Hirschman [1977], *The Passions and the Interests: Political Arguments for Capitalism before Its Triumph* (Twentieth anniversary edition, Princeton, NJ: Princeton University Press, 1997), 69–70.

103. Ibid., 100.

104. John Dwyer, *The Age of the Passions: An Interpretation of Adam Smith and Scottish Enlightenment Culture* (East Linton: Tuckwell Press, 1998), 103.

105. Joseph Cropsey, *Polity and Economy: An Appreciation of the Principles of Adam Smith* (The Hague: Martinus Nijhoff, 1957), x.

Index

About the Author

© Cathy Watkins

Neil Davidson lectures in Sociology with the School of Social and Political Science at the University of Glasgow, Scotland. He is the author of *The Origins of Scottish Nationhood* (2000), *Discovering the Scottish Revolution* (2003), for which he was awarded the Deutscher Memorial Prize, and *How Revolutionary Were the Bourgeois Revolutions?* (2012). Davidson has also co-edited and contributed to *Alasdair MacIntyre's Engagement with Marxism* (2008) and *Neoliberal Scotland* (2010).